TUNE IN TOMORROW

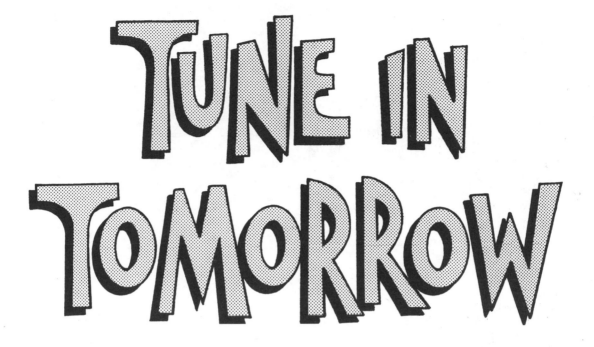

Books by Tom Tomorrow:

Greetings From This Modern World
Tune in Tomorrow

TUNE IN TOMORROW

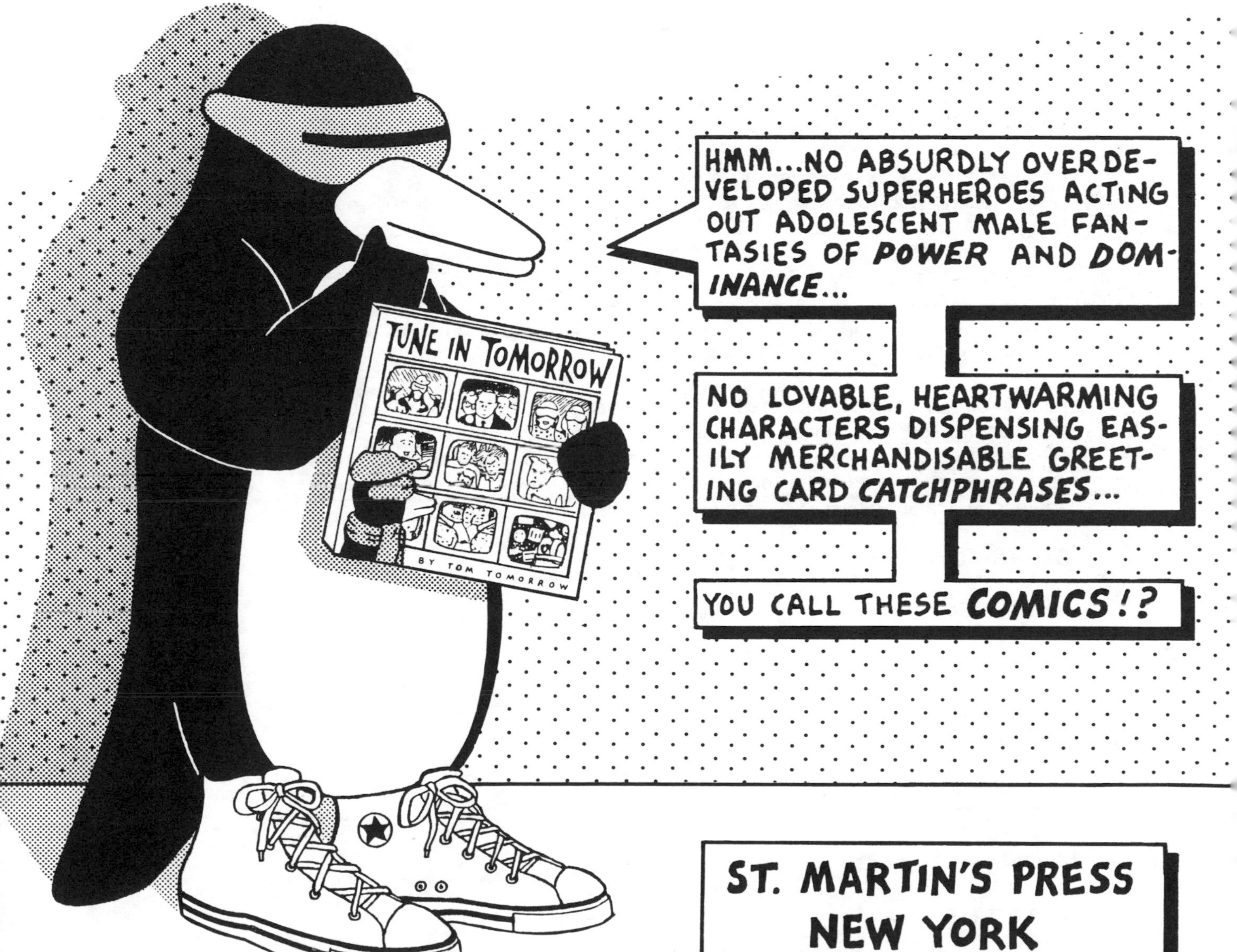

TUNE IN TOMORROW
BY TOM TOMORROW
HMM...NO ABSURDLY OVERDEVELOPED SUPERHEROES ACTING OUT ADOLESCENT MALE FANTASIES OF *POWER* AND *DOMINANCE*...
NO LOVABLE, HEARTWARMING CHARACTERS DISPENSING EASILY MERCHANDISABLE GREETING CARD *CATCHPHRASES*...
YOU CALL THESE *COMICS!?*

ST. MARTIN'S PRESS
NEW YORK

This book is dedicated to my father,
Larry Leighton Perkins

and to the memory of my mother,
Phyllis Ann Hulvey
1938–1993

The cartoon on page 31 originally ran on the op-ed page of *The New York Times* on the morning after the 1992 election. "Sparky Goes to Paris" (pp. 39–46) initially appeared in the *San Francisco Examiner*, as did the cartoon on pp. 96–97. The cartoons on pp. 100–102 were first published in *Spin* magazine under the title "Tune in Tomorrow." Zippy the Pinhead is © copyright Bill Griffith and appears with permission.

The renditions of Sparky gracing the inside covers were drawn by: S. W. Conser (City Lights Sparky); Buck Dawson (Sparky as Einstein); Steven M. deFrance (Ghenghis Penguin); Martin Fuller (Sparky as Bart Simpson); Adele Hunt (Gargoyle Sparky); Mary Kocher (Whistler's Mother, the Scream, Statue of Liberty); A. Koford (George Washington Sparky); Andrew Mutchler (Sparky vs. Sparky); Lori Puster (Easter Island, Mt. Rushmore Sparky); Steve Silberberg (Elroy Jetson Sparky); Andrew Singer (Charles Bukowski Sparky); George Suggs (Sparky LaForge); Stephen Taylor (Dancin' Sparky); and David Wright (Paul Klee Sparky).

Design by Dan Perkins

Library of Congress Cataloging-in-Publication Data

Tomorrow, Tom.
   Tune in Tomorrow / Tom Tomorrow.
       p.   cm.
   ISBN 0-312-11344-7
   I. Title.
   PN6727.T66T86   1994
   741.5'973—dc20
                                        94-18212
                                           CIP

10 9 8 7 6 5 4 3 2

A newspaper . . . must at all times antagonize the selfish interests of that very class which furnishes the larger part of a newspaper's income. . . . The press in this country is now and has always been so thoroughly dominated by the wealthy few of the country that it cannot be depended upon to give the great mass of the people that correct information concerning political, economical, and social subjects which it is necessary that the mass of people shall have in order that they shall vote and in all ways act in the best way to protect themselves from the brutal force and chicanery of the ruling and employing classes. . . . I have only one principle and that is represented by an effort to make it harder for the rich to grow richer and easier for the poor to keep from growing poorer.

—Edward Wyllis Scripps, founder of
the first modern newspaper chain

FOREWORD

In November of 1992, American voters decided to exchange a moderate, pro-business Republican president for a moderate, pro-business Democratic president—an event which inexplicably led many to believe that social change of a magnitude not seen since the days of the French Revolution was at hand. Conservatives were aghast, certain that the election of Bill Clinton presaged the end of civilization as they knew it, and the volume of mail I received from such readers increased exponentially—as if this segment of my audience felt that the only way to check the tidal wave of liberalism headed their way was to quickly send off letters of complaint about a small, weekly cartoon whose political impact might accurately be described as, well, nonexistent. Many on the left/liberal side of the spectrum, meanwhile, were convinced that all of America's problems had been solved in one bold stroke, and that social commentators such as myself might as well start looking for other work. "What are you going to do cartoons about *now?*" I was repeatedly asked by those who had mistaken campaign promises for reality, forgetting that basic law of semiotics—*the map is not the territory.*

As I write these words, it's been a little over a year and a half since that election. There have been about-faces and outright betrayals by Clinton on NAFTA, the environment, Lani Guinier, gays in the military, Haitian refugees, China's MFN status—and on and on. His idea of health care reform has been to propose a hopelessly complex plan of "managed competition," the sole advantage of which seems to be that it would leave major insurance companies firmly in control of the system. To my mind, the only question here is whether Clinton is a weenie who just wasn't *able* to stand up to the nation's entrenched corporate interests, or if he was bought and paid for so long ago that he never had any

intention of standing up to those interests. It will probably come as no surprise to my readers that I tend to suspect the latter.

Despite the nightly Punch-and-Judy sparring matches between Pat Buchanan and Michael Kinsley and their ilk, I believe the real debate in this country has little to do with either of the simplistic extremes represented by, on the one hand, rabid conservatives who despise Clinton despite the fact that he kowtows almost completely to their economic agenda, and, on the other, oblivious liberals who seem utterly disinterested in anything Clinton actually *does* as long as he continues to mouth those vague platitudes about hope and change which leave them feeling all warm and fuzzy inside. Which is not to deny that real and heartfelt differences exist between the two sides, particularly on such hot-button social issues as abortion or gay rights, but rather to argue that such differences often serve to distract attention from the real, underlying debate—which is and always will be between the wealthy and the poor, the haves and the have-nots. It has nothing to do with right or left, conservative or liberal; it has everything to do with up or down, ruling or working class. If you doubt this, consider that it is the official policy of the Federal Reserve—and, therefore, of the United States Government—to maintain an unemployment rate of at least eight million Americans. Let me repeat that: *it is the official policy of the United States Government to maintain an unemployment rate of at least eight million Americans.*

This may be the single most important point necessary to an understanding of the American political system, and it isn't some sort of radical leftist wacko social analysis taken from a xeroxed leaflet handed out at a Save the Whales rally—it's a fact which is discussed quite openly in the business pages of the mainstream media whenever the Fed deems it necessary to raise interest rates. *The New York Times,* for instance, recently explained matter-of-factly that as unemployment falls near the "danger mark" of only eight million jobless, rates are raised "to discourage borrowing and spending . . . (forcing) business activity, and the economy, to slow down. Fewer jobs are created and unemployment rises." In other words, the laws of supply and demand dictate that as unemployment falls, the cost of labor increases, a situation which, according to conventional economic wisdom, leads inexorably to inflation—since, of course, it's a given that corporations must in turn raise their prices in order to maintain their obscene profit margins. They've got to be able to pay those ten gazillion dollar bonuses to their CEOs after all.

And if you agree with me that the system is fucked up, but believe that Clinton's people are doing all they can to change it, let me bring to your attention the manner in which Presidential economic adviser Laura Tyson recently attempted to reassure inflation-wary investors—by noting that "wage growth has been stagnant over the past year," and that "it is likely that wages will begin to drift upward only gradually." Which *has* to strike anyone who accepts the conventional liberal vs. conservative paradigm as a damned peculiar thing for a Democratic administration to be crowing about. But come on . . . how much change did you honestly expect from a President whose cabinet contains more millionaires than that of his Republican predecessor, and whose earliest appointments included such noted radical reformers as Lloyd Bentsen and Ron Brown? Call me cynical if you will, but remember Ambrose Bierce's definition of a cynic: "A blackguard whose faulty vision sees things as they are, not as they ought to be."

And do me one favor if you ever meet me: no matter who's in the White House, please don't ask me what I'm going to do cartoons about *now* . . .

*   *   *

A few notes about this book: the preceding musings notwithstanding, politics are not the sole focus of my work, as I hope the following pages will make clear. Most of these cartoons have been culled from my weekly self-syndicated strip, *This Modern World*, but there are some rarities included here as well, such as the story of our opinionated penguin's trip to Paris (not to mention his breakfast with a certain well-known pinhead . . .)

As always, many thanks are due many people (and a few organizations). They include (in no particular order): Keith Kahla, Bill Griffith, Tom Erikson, J.R. Swanson, Steve Rhodes, Gary Frank, Randy Mills, Kimberly Burns, Dave Eggers, Jello Biafra, the Northern California Independent Booksellers Association, Fairness and Accuracy in Reporting, and Project Censored . . . as well as others I'm sure I'm forgetting. I'd also like to thank the friends who helped out during a year that had some rough patches; and perhaps most importantly, I want to express my sincere and heartfelt gratitude to all the editors who choose to run my cartoons in their newspapers each week. Without them, I would be relegated to the status of a tree falling in an empty forest, and this book would most certainly not exist.

—Dan Perkins
("Tom Tomorrow")
San Francisco
June 1994

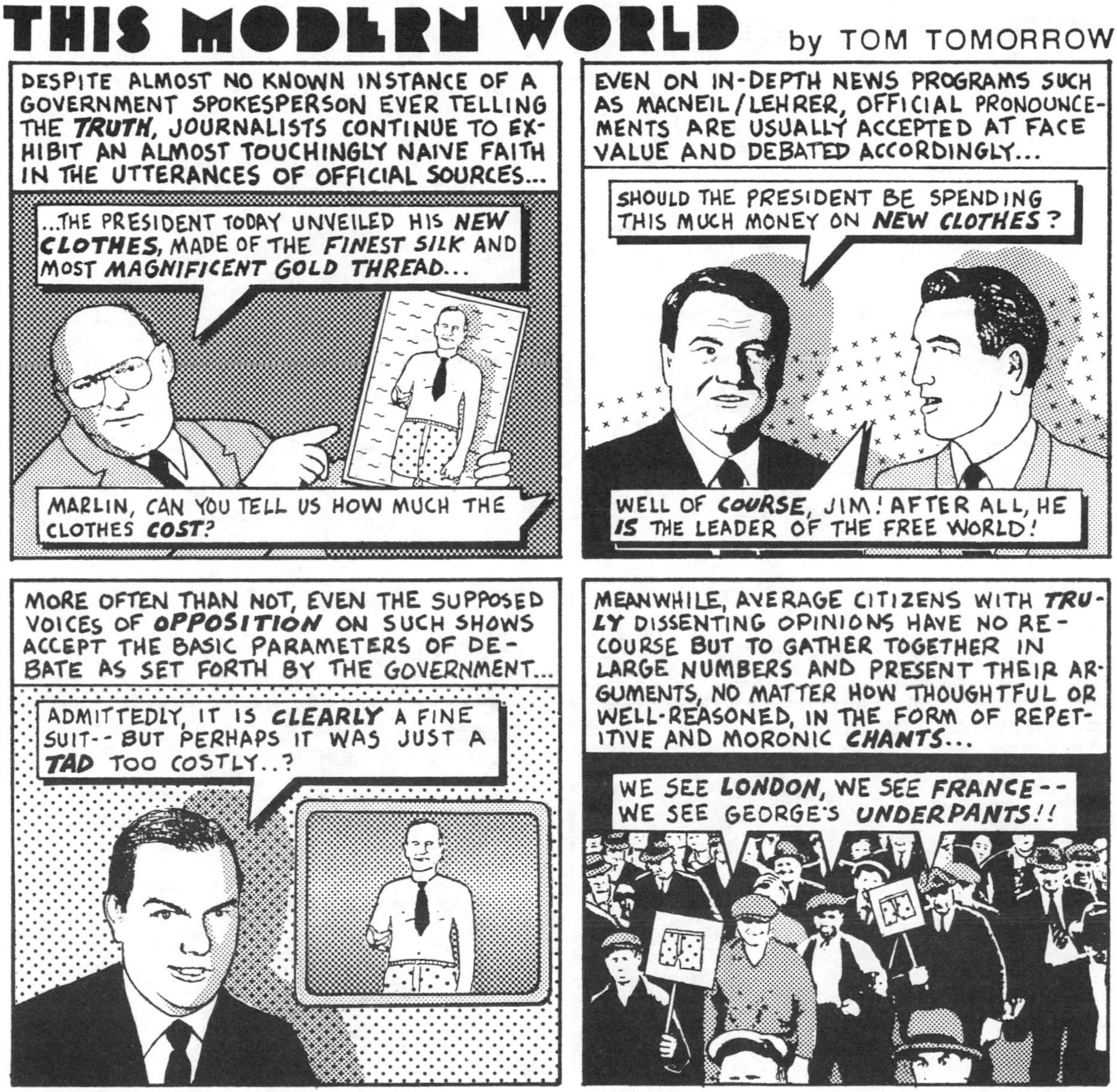
THIS MODERN WORLD
by TOM TOMORROW
DESPITE ALMOST NO KNOWN INSTANCE OF A GOVERNMENT SPOKESPERSON EVER TELLING THE TRUTH, JOURNALISTS CONTINUE TO EXHIBIT AN ALMOST TOUCHINGLY NAIVE FAITH IN THE UTTERANCES OF OFFICIAL SOURCES...
...THE PRESIDENT TODAY UNVEILED HIS NEW CLOTHES, MADE OF THE FINEST SILK AND MOST MAGNIFICENT GOLD THREAD...
MARLIN, CAN YOU TELL US HOW MUCH THE CLOTHES COST?
EVEN ON IN-DEPTH NEWS PROGRAMS SUCH AS MACNEIL/LEHRER, OFFICIAL PRONOUNCEMENTS ARE USUALLY ACCEPTED AT FACE VALUE AND DEBATED ACCORDINGLY...
SHOULD THE PRESIDENT BE SPENDING THIS MUCH MONEY ON NEW CLOTHES?
WELL OF COURSE, JIM! AFTER ALL, HE IS THE LEADER OF THE FREE WORLD!
MORE OFTEN THAN NOT, EVEN THE SUPPOSED VOICES OF OPPOSITION ON SUCH SHOWS ACCEPT THE BASIC PARAMETERS OF DEBATE AS SET FORTH BY THE GOVERNMENT...
ADMITTEDLY, IT IS CLEARLY A FINE SUIT-- BUT PERHAPS IT WAS JUST A TAD TOO COSTLY..?
MEANWHILE, AVERAGE CITIZENS WITH TRULY DISSENTING OPINIONS HAVE NO RECOURSE BUT TO GATHER TOGETHER IN LARGE NUMBERS AND PRESENT THEIR ARGUMENTS, NO MATTER HOW THOUGHTFUL OR WELL-REASONED, IN THE FORM OF REPETITIVE AND MORONIC CHANTS...
WE SEE LONDON, WE SEE FRANCE--
WE SEE GEORGE'S UNDERPANTS!!

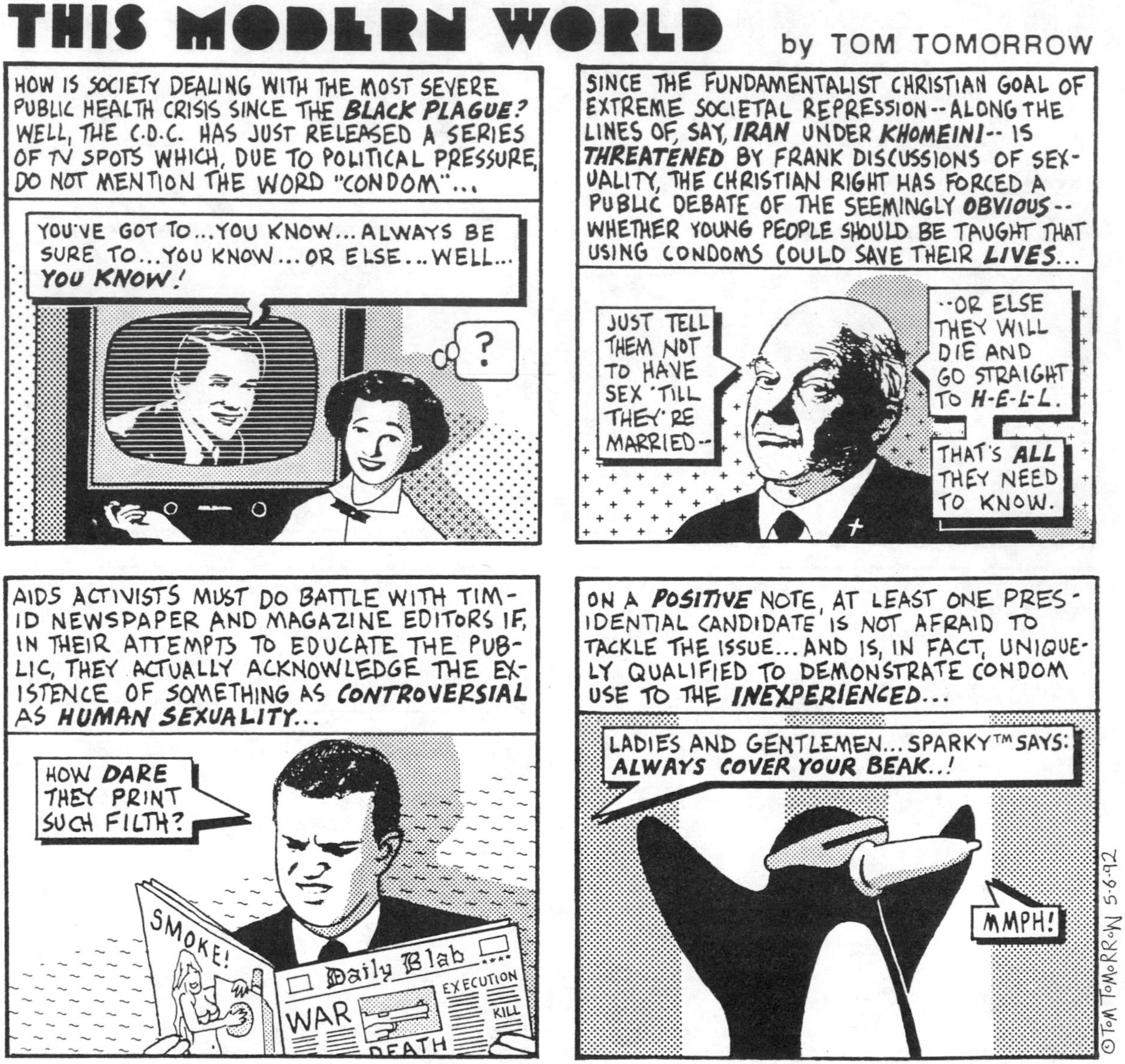
THIS MODERN WORLD
by TOM TOMORROW
HOW IS SOCIETY DEALING WITH THE MOST SEVERE PUBLIC HEALTH CRISIS SINCE THE BLACK PLAGUE? WELL, THE C.D.C. HAS JUST RELEASED A SERIES OF TV SPOTS WHICH, DUE TO POLITICAL PRESSURE, DO NOT MENTION THE WORD "CONDOM"...
YOU'VE GOT TO... YOU KNOW... ALWAYS BE SURE TO... YOU KNOW... OR ELSE... WELL... YOU KNOW!
?
SINCE THE FUNDAMENTALIST CHRISTIAN GOAL OF EXTREME SOCIETAL REPRESSION--ALONG THE LINES OF, SAY, IRAN UNDER KHOMEINI--IS THREATENED BY FRANK DISCUSSIONS OF SEXUALITY, THE CHRISTIAN RIGHT HAS FORCED A PUBLIC DEBATE OF THE SEEMINGLY OBVIOUS--WHETHER YOUNG PEOPLE SHOULD BE TAUGHT THAT USING CONDOMS COULD SAVE THEIR LIVES...
JUST TELL THEM NOT TO HAVE SEX 'TILL THEY'RE MARRIED--
--OR ELSE THEY WILL DIE AND GO STRAIGHT TO H-E-L-L.
THAT'S ALL THEY NEED TO KNOW.
AIDS ACTIVISTS MUST DO BATTLE WITH TIMID NEWSPAPER AND MAGAZINE EDITORS IF, IN THEIR ATTEMPTS TO EDUCATE THE PUBLIC, THEY ACTUALLY ACKNOWLEDGE THE EXISTENCE OF SOMETHING AS CONTROVERSIAL AS HUMAN SEXUALITY...
HOW DARE THEY PRINT SUCH FILTH?
SMOKE!
Daily Blab
EXECUTION
WAR
KILL
DEATH
ON A POSITIVE NOTE, AT LEAST ONE PRESIDENTIAL CANDIDATE IS NOT AFRAID TO TACKLE THE ISSUE... AND IS, IN FACT, UNIQUELY QUALIFIED TO DEMONSTRATE CONDOM USE TO THE INEXPERIENCED...
LADIES AND GENTLEMEN... SPARKY™ SAYS: ALWAYS COVER YOUR BEAK..!
MMPH!
©TOM TOMORROW 5-6-92

THIS MODERN WORLD by TOM TOMORROW

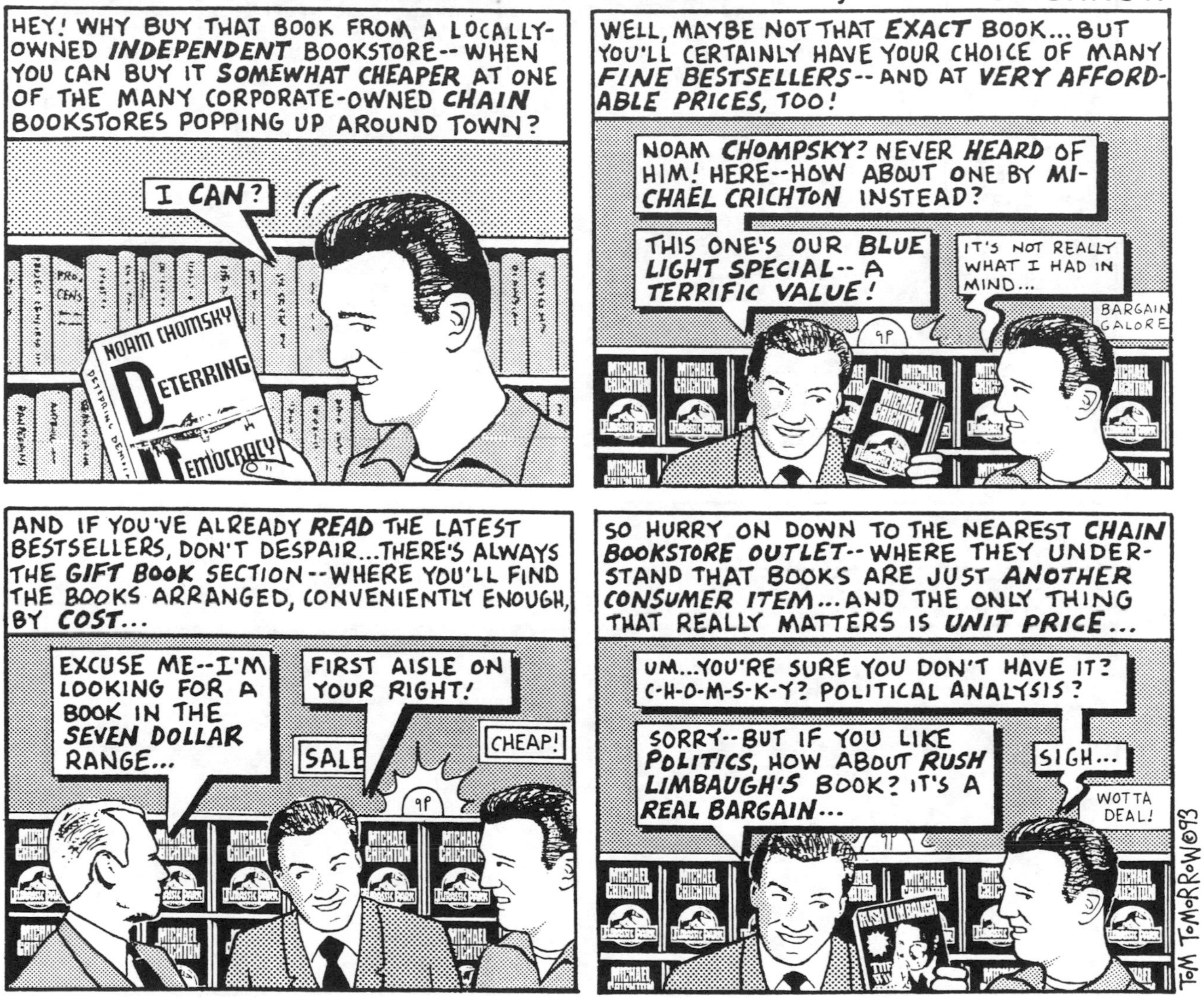

HEY! WHY BUY THAT BOOK FROM A LOCALLY-OWNED INDEPENDENT BOOKSTORE-- WHEN YOU CAN BUY IT SOMEWHAT CHEAPER AT ONE OF THE MANY CORPORATE-OWNED CHAIN BOOKSTORES POPPING UP AROUND TOWN?
I CAN?
NOAM CHOMSKY
DETERRING DEMOCRACY
WELL, MAYBE NOT THAT EXACT BOOK... BUT YOU'LL CERTAINLY HAVE YOUR CHOICE OF MANY FINE BESTSELLERS-- AND AT VERY AFFORDABLE PRICES, TOO!
NOAM CHOMPSKY? NEVER HEARD OF HIM! HERE--HOW ABOUT ONE BY MICHAEL CRICHTON INSTEAD?
THIS ONE'S OUR BLUE LIGHT SPECIAL-- A TERRIFIC VALUE!
IT'S NOT REALLY WHAT I HAD IN MIND...
BARGAIN GALORE
MICHAEL CRICHTON
JURASSIC PARK
AND IF YOU'VE ALREADY READ THE LATEST BESTSELLERS, DON'T DESPAIR...THERE'S ALWAYS THE GIFT BOOK SECTION--WHERE YOU'LL FIND THE BOOKS ARRANGED, CONVENIENTLY ENOUGH, BY COST...
EXCUSE ME--I'M LOOKING FOR A BOOK IN THE SEVEN DOLLAR RANGE...
FIRST AISLE ON YOUR RIGHT!
SALE
CHEAP!
SO HURRY ON DOWN TO THE NEAREST CHAIN BOOKSTORE OUTLET-- WHERE THEY UNDERSTAND THAT BOOKS ARE JUST ANOTHER CONSUMER ITEM... AND THE ONLY THING THAT REALLY MATTERS IS UNIT PRICE...
UM...YOU'RE SURE YOU DON'T HAVE IT? C-H-O-M-S-K-Y? POLITICAL ANALYSIS?
SORRY--BUT IF YOU LIKE POLITICS, HOW ABOUT RUSH LIMBAUGH'S BOOK? IT'S A REAL BARGAIN...
SIGH...
WOTTA DEAL!
RUSH LIMBAUGH
TOM TOMORROW©93

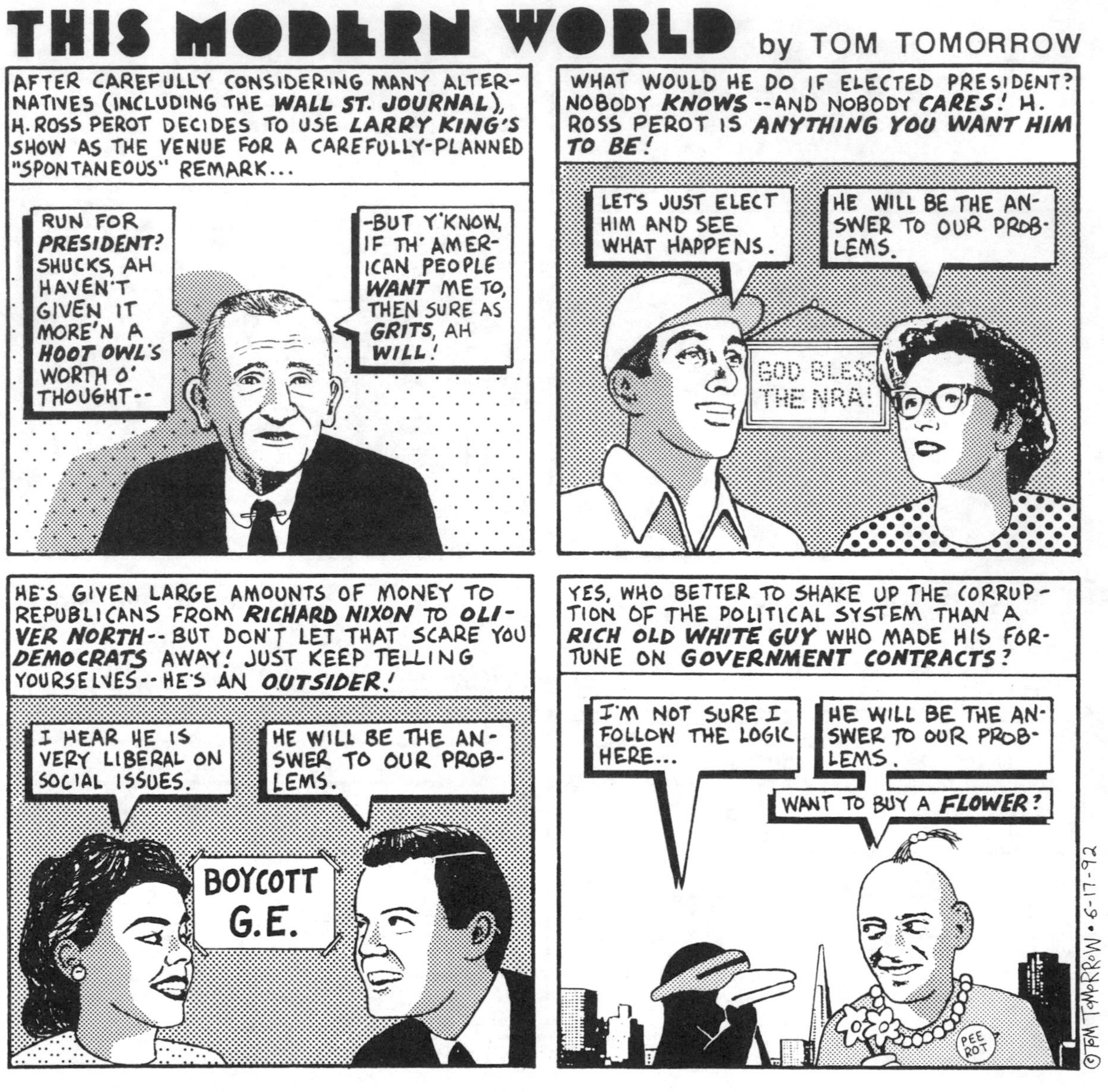
THIS MODERN WORLD by TOM TOMORROW
AFTER CAREFULLY CONSIDERING MANY ALTERNATIVES (INCLUDING THE WALL ST. JOURNAL), H. ROSS PEROT DECIDES TO USE LARRY KING'S SHOW AS THE VENUE FOR A CAREFULLY-PLANNED "SPONTANEOUS" REMARK...
RUN FOR PRESIDENT? SHUCKS, AH HAVEN'T GIVEN IT MORE'N A HOOT OWL'S WORTH O' THOUGHT--
-BUT Y'KNOW, IF TH' AMERICAN PEOPLE WANT ME TO, THEN SURE AS GRITS, AH WILL!
WHAT WOULD HE DO IF ELECTED PRESIDENT? NOBODY KNOWS--AND NOBODY CARES! H. ROSS PEROT IS ANYTHING YOU WANT HIM TO BE!
LET'S JUST ELECT HIM AND SEE WHAT HAPPENS.
HE WILL BE THE ANSWER TO OUR PROBLEMS.
GOD BLESS THE NRA!
HE'S GIVEN LARGE AMOUNTS OF MONEY TO REPUBLICANS FROM RICHARD NIXON TO OLIVER NORTH-- BUT DON'T LET THAT SCARE YOU DEMOCRATS AWAY! JUST KEEP TELLING YOURSELVES-- HE'S AN OUTSIDER!
I HEAR HE IS VERY LIBERAL ON SOCIAL ISSUES.
HE WILL BE THE ANSWER TO OUR PROBLEMS.
BOYCOTT G.E.
YES, WHO BETTER TO SHAKE UP THE CORRUPTION OF THE POLITICAL SYSTEM THAN A RICH OLD WHITE GUY WHO MADE HIS FORTUNE ON GOVERNMENT CONTRACTS?
I'M NOT SURE I FOLLOW THE LOGIC HERE...
HE WILL BE THE ANSWER TO OUR PROBLEMS.
WANT TO BUY A FLOWER?
PEE ROT
© TOM TOMORROW • 6-17-92

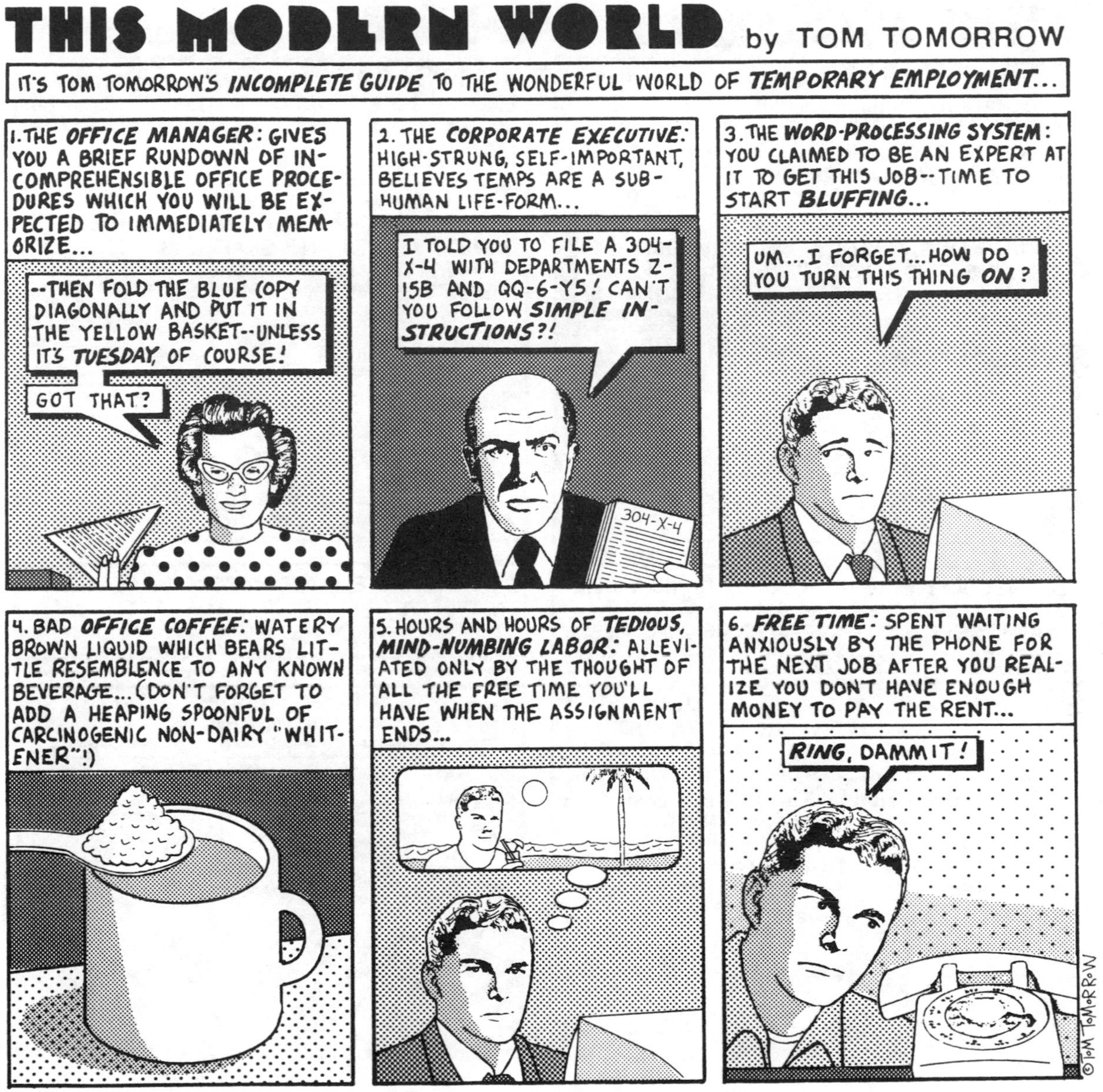
THIS MODERN WORLD by TOM TOMORROW
IT'S TOM TOMORROW'S INCOMPLETE GUIDE TO THE WONDERFUL WORLD OF TEMPORARY EMPLOYMENT...
1. THE OFFICE MANAGER: GIVES YOU A BRIEF RUNDOWN OF INCOMPREHENSIBLE OFFICE PROCEDURES WHICH YOU WILL BE EXPECTED TO IMMEDIATELY MEMORIZE...
--THEN FOLD THE BLUE COPY DIAGONALLY AND PUT IT IN THE YELLOW BASKET--UNLESS IT'S TUESDAY, OF COURSE!
GOT THAT?
2. THE CORPORATE EXECUTIVE: HIGH-STRUNG, SELF-IMPORTANT, BELIEVES TEMPS ARE A SUB-HUMAN LIFE-FORM...
I TOLD YOU TO FILE A 304-X-4 WITH DEPARTMENTS Z-15B AND QQ-6-Y5! CAN'T YOU FOLLOW SIMPLE INSTRUCTIONS?!
304-X-4
3. THE WORD-PROCESSING SYSTEM: YOU CLAIMED TO BE AN EXPERT AT IT TO GET THIS JOB--TIME TO START BLUFFING...
UM...I FORGET...HOW DO YOU TURN THIS THING ON?
4. BAD OFFICE COFFEE: WATERY BROWN LIQUID WHICH BEARS LITTLE RESEMBLENCE TO ANY KNOWN BEVERAGE...(DON'T FORGET TO ADD A HEAPING SPOONFUL OF CARCINOGENIC NON-DAIRY "WHITENER"!)
5. HOURS AND HOURS OF TEDIOUS, MIND-NUMBING LABOR: ALLEVIATED ONLY BY THE THOUGHT OF ALL THE FREE TIME YOU'LL HAVE WHEN THE ASSIGNMENT ENDS...
6. FREE TIME: SPENT WAITING ANXIOUSLY BY THE PHONE FOR THE NEXT JOB AFTER YOU REALIZE YOU DON'T HAVE ENOUGH MONEY TO PAY THE RENT...
RING, DAMMIT!
© TOM TOMORROW

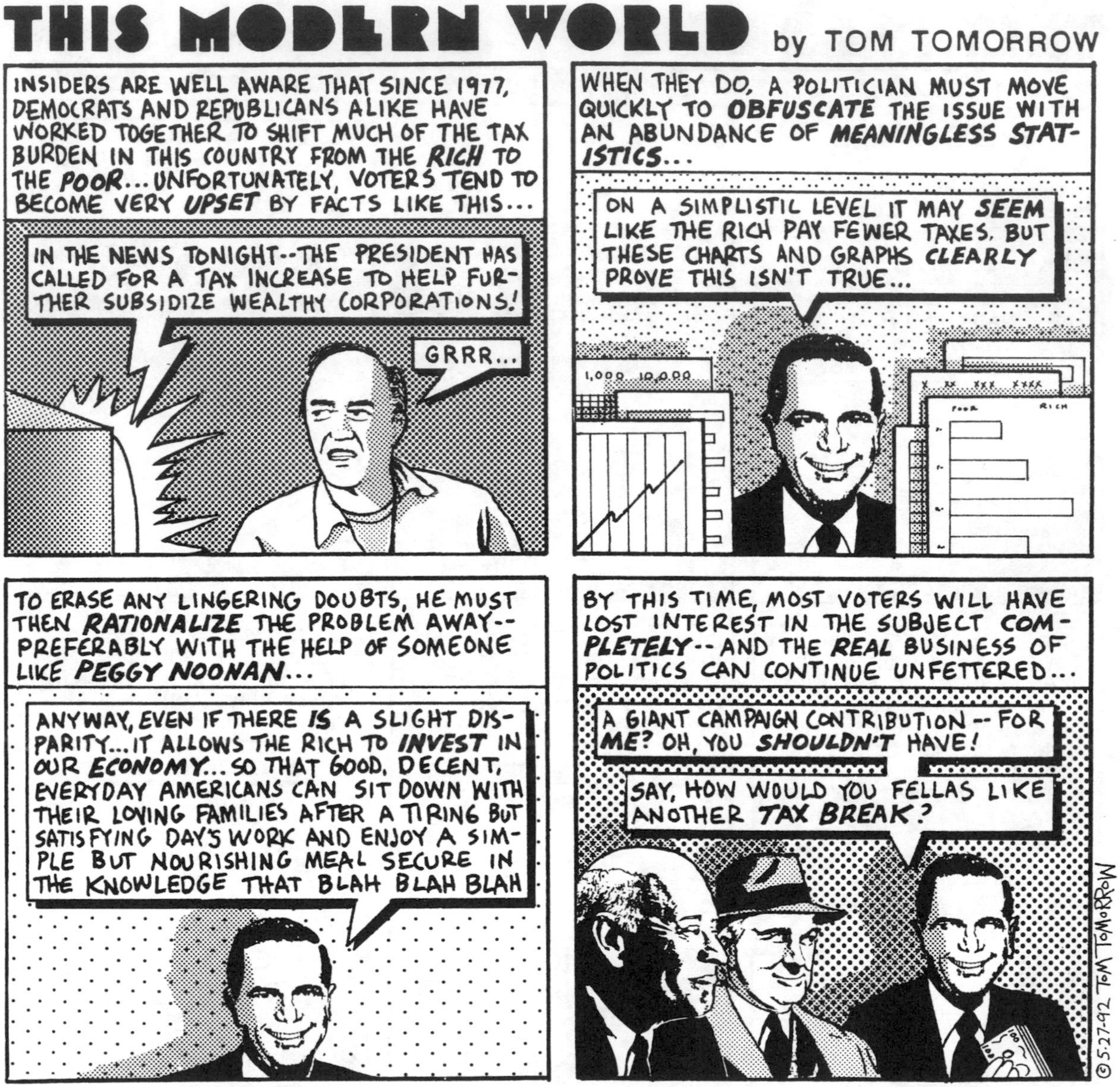
THIS MODERN WORLD by TOM TOMORROW
INSIDERS ARE WELL AWARE THAT SINCE 1977, DEMOCRATS AND REPUBLICANS ALIKE HAVE WORKED TOGETHER TO SHIFT MUCH OF THE TAX BURDEN IN THIS COUNTRY FROM THE *RICH* TO THE *POOR*... UNFORTUNATELY, VOTERS TEND TO BECOME VERY *UPSET* BY FACTS LIKE THIS...
IN THE NEWS TONIGHT--THE PRESIDENT HAS CALLED FOR A TAX INCREASE TO HELP FURTHER SUBSIDIZE WEALTHY CORPORATIONS!
GRRR...
WHEN THEY DO, A POLITICIAN MUST MOVE QUICKLY TO *OBFUSCATE* THE ISSUE WITH AN ABUNDANCE OF *MEANINGLESS STATISTICS*...
ON A SIMPLISTIC LEVEL IT MAY *SEEM* LIKE THE RICH PAY FEWER TAXES, BUT THESE CHARTS AND GRAPHS *CLEARLY* PROVE THIS ISN'T TRUE...
1,000 10,000
POOR RICH
TO ERASE ANY LINGERING DOUBTS, HE MUST THEN *RATIONALIZE* THE PROBLEM AWAY--PREFERABLY WITH THE HELP OF SOMEONE LIKE *PEGGY NOONAN*...
ANYWAY, EVEN IF THERE *IS* A SLIGHT DISPARITY... IT ALLOWS THE RICH TO *INVEST* IN OUR *ECONOMY*... SO THAT GOOD, DECENT, EVERYDAY AMERICANS CAN SIT DOWN WITH THEIR LOVING FAMILIES AFTER A TIRING BUT SATISFYING DAY'S WORK AND ENJOY A SIMPLE BUT NOURISHING MEAL SECURE IN THE KNOWLEDGE THAT BLAH BLAH BLAH
BY THIS TIME, MOST VOTERS WILL HAVE LOST INTEREST IN THE SUBJECT *COMPLETELY*--AND THE *REAL* BUSINESS OF POLITICS CAN CONTINUE UNFETTERED...
A GIANT CAMPAIGN CONTRIBUTION--FOR *ME*? OH, YOU *SHOULDN'T* HAVE!
SAY, HOW WOULD YOU FELLAS LIKE ANOTHER *TAX BREAK*?
©5-27-92 TOM TOMORROW

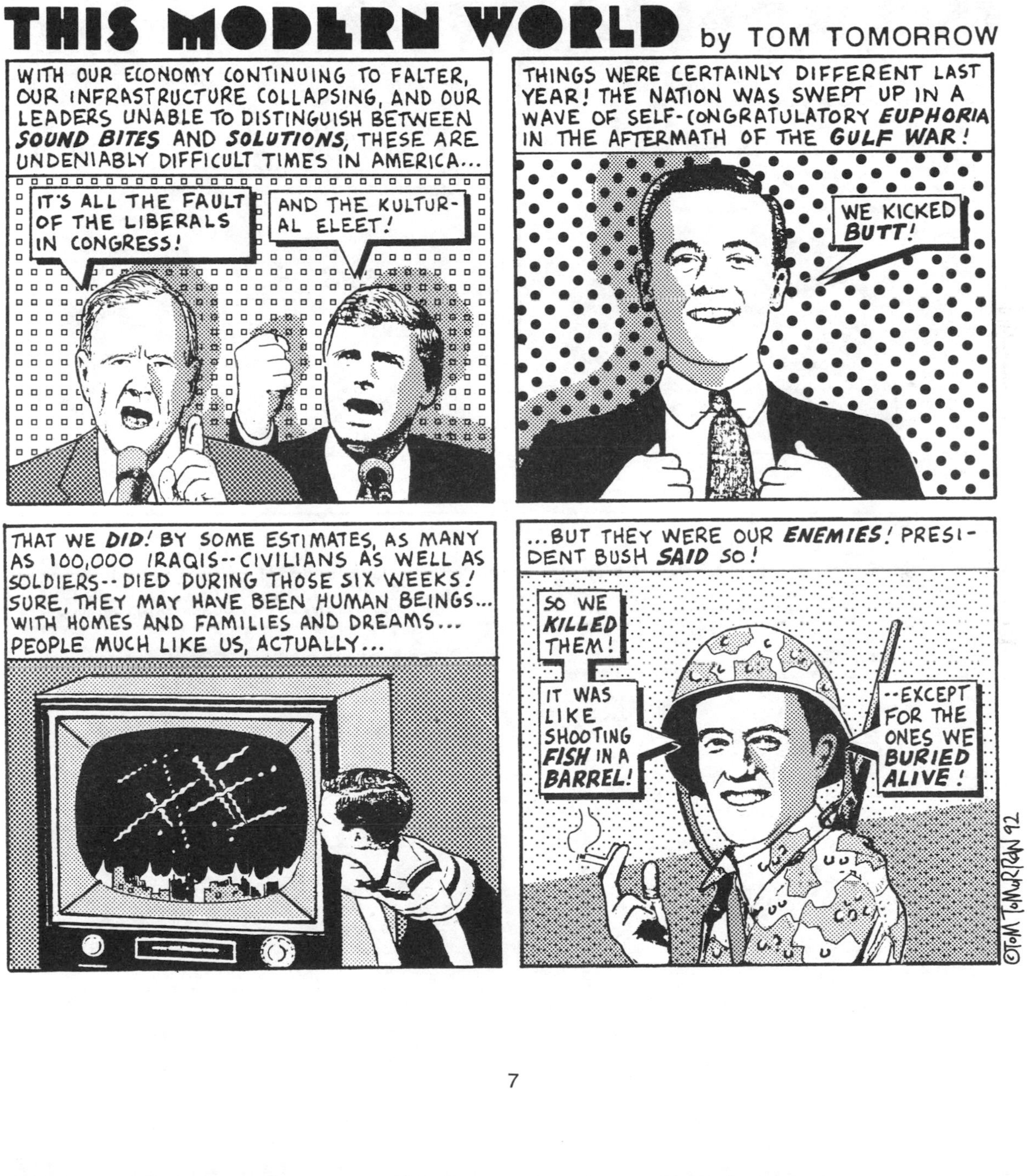
THIS MODERN WORLD by TOM TOMORROW
WITH OUR ECONOMY CONTINUING TO FALTER, OUR INFRASTRUCTURE COLLAPSING, AND OUR LEADERS UNABLE TO DISTINGUISH BETWEEN SOUND BITES AND SOLUTIONS, THESE ARE UNDENIABLY DIFFICULT TIMES IN AMERICA...
IT'S ALL THE FAULT OF THE LIBERALS IN CONGRESS!
AND THE KULTURAL ELEET!
THINGS WERE CERTAINLY DIFFERENT LAST YEAR! THE NATION WAS SWEPT UP IN A WAVE OF SELF-CONGRATULATORY EUPHORIA IN THE AFTERMATH OF THE GULF WAR!
WE KICKED BUTT!
THAT WE DID! BY SOME ESTIMATES, AS MANY AS 100,000 IRAQIS--CIVILIANS AS WELL AS SOLDIERS--DIED DURING THOSE SIX WEEKS! SURE, THEY MAY HAVE BEEN HUMAN BEINGS... WITH HOMES AND FAMILIES AND DREAMS... PEOPLE MUCH LIKE US, ACTUALLY...
...BUT THEY WERE OUR ENEMIES! PRESIDENT BUSH SAID SO!
SO WE KILLED THEM!
IT WAS LIKE SHOOTING FISH IN A BARREL!
--EXCEPT FOR THE ONES WE BURIED ALIVE!
©TOM TOMORROW '92

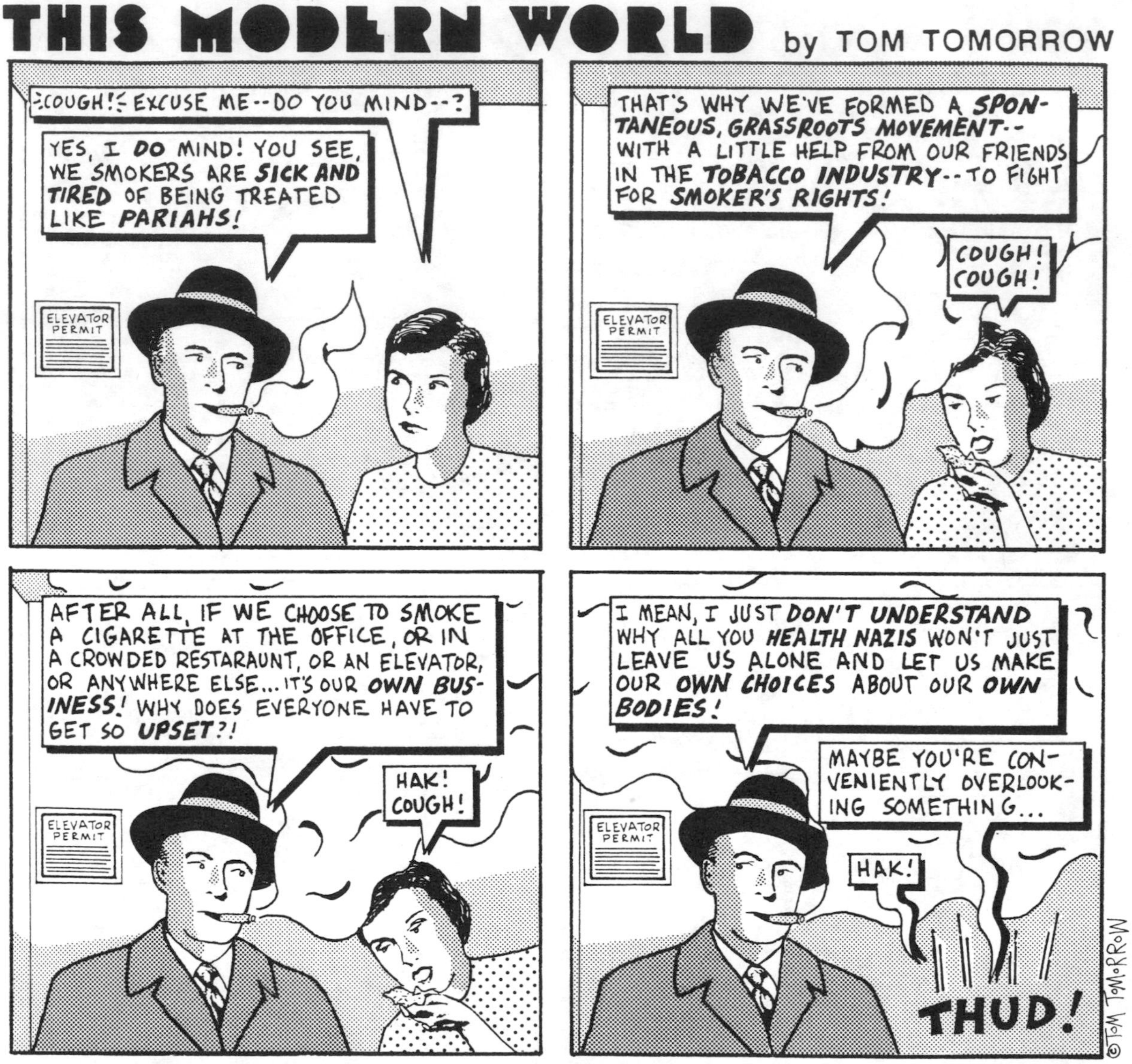
THIS MODERN WORLD by TOM TOMORROW
:COUGH!: EXCUSE ME--DO YOU MIND--?
YES, I DO MIND! YOU SEE, WE SMOKERS ARE SICK AND TIRED OF BEING TREATED LIKE PARIAHS!
ELEVATOR PERMIT
THAT'S WHY WE'VE FORMED A SPONTANEOUS, GRASSROOTS MOVEMENT--WITH A LITTLE HELP FROM OUR FRIENDS IN THE TOBACCO INDUSTRY--TO FIGHT FOR SMOKER'S RIGHTS!
COUGH! COUGH!
ELEVATOR PERMIT
AFTER ALL, IF WE CHOOSE TO SMOKE A CIGARETTE AT THE OFFICE, OR IN A CROWDED RESTARAUNT, OR AN ELEVATOR, OR ANYWHERE ELSE... IT'S OUR OWN BUSINESS! WHY DOES EVERYONE HAVE TO GET SO UPSET?!
HAK! COUGH!
ELEVATOR PERMIT
I MEAN, I JUST DON'T UNDERSTAND WHY ALL YOU HEALTH NAZIS WON'T JUST LEAVE US ALONE AND LET US MAKE OUR OWN CHOICES ABOUT OUR OWN BODIES!
MAYBE YOU'RE CONVENIENTLY OVERLOOKING SOMETHING...
HAK!
ELEVATOR PERMIT
THUD!
©TOM TOMORROW

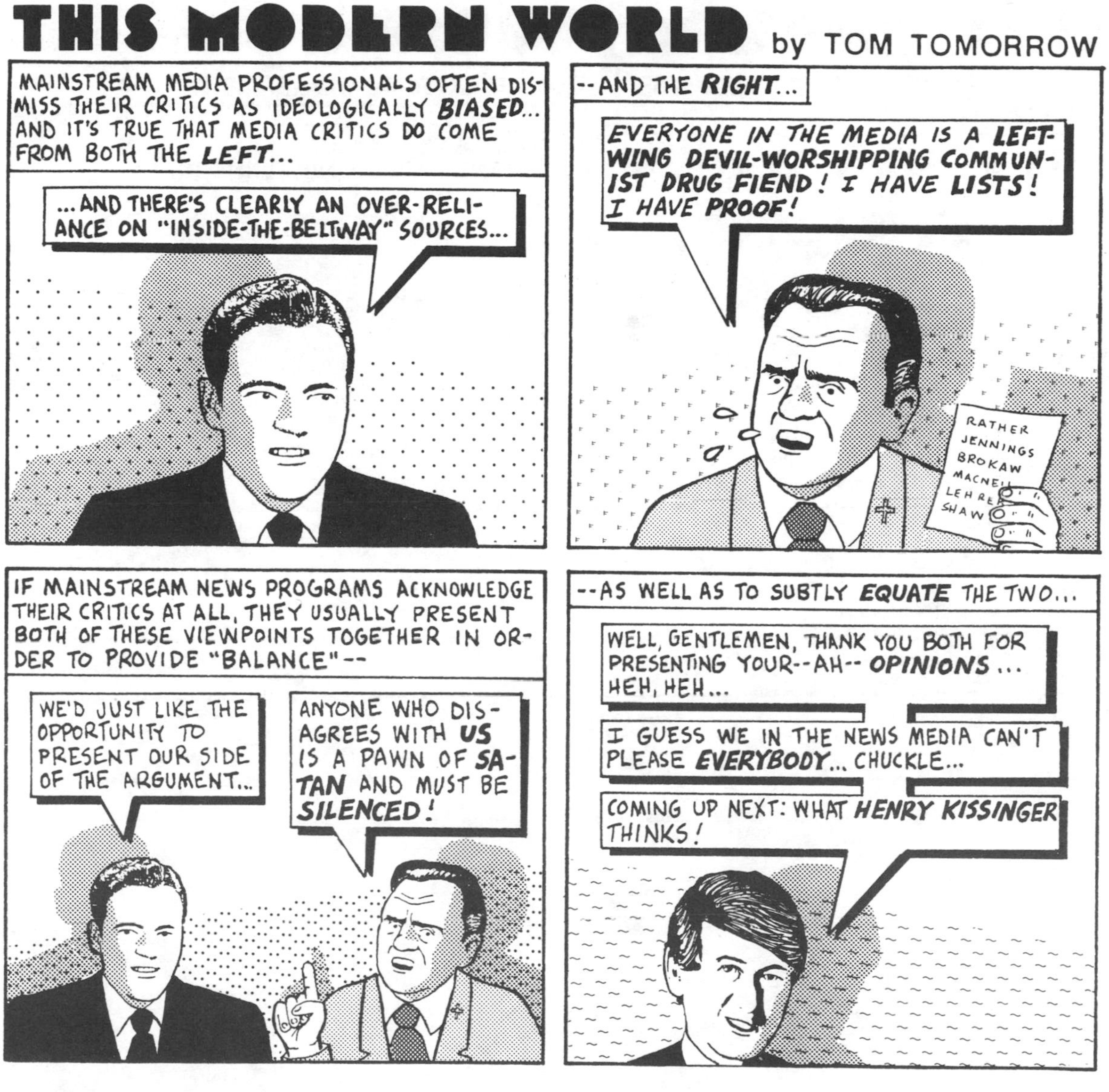
THIS MODERN WORLD by TOM TOMORROW
MAINSTREAM MEDIA PROFESSIONALS OFTEN DISMISS THEIR CRITICS AS IDEOLOGICALLY BIASED... AND IT'S TRUE THAT MEDIA CRITICS DO COME FROM BOTH THE LEFT...
...AND THERE'S CLEARLY AN OVER-RELIANCE ON "INSIDE-THE-BELTWAY" SOURCES...
--AND THE RIGHT...
EVERYONE IN THE MEDIA IS A LEFT-WING DEVIL-WORSHIPPING COMMUNIST DRUG FIEND! I HAVE LISTS! I HAVE PROOF!
RATHER
JENNINGS
BROKAW
IF MAINSTREAM NEWS PROGRAMS ACKNOWLEDGE THEIR CRITICS AT ALL, THEY USUALLY PRESENT BOTH OF THESE VIEWPOINTS TOGETHER IN ORDER TO PROVIDE "BALANCE"--
WE'D JUST LIKE THE OPPORTUNITY TO PRESENT OUR SIDE OF THE ARGUMENT...
ANYONE WHO DISAGREES WITH US IS A PAWN OF SATAN AND MUST BE SILENCED!
--AS WELL AS TO SUBTLY EQUATE THE TWO...
WELL, GENTLEMEN, THANK YOU BOTH FOR PRESENTING YOUR--AH-- OPINIONS... HEH, HEH...
I GUESS WE IN THE NEWS MEDIA CAN'T PLEASE EVERYBODY... CHUCKLE...
COMING UP NEXT: WHAT HENRY KISSINGER THINKS!

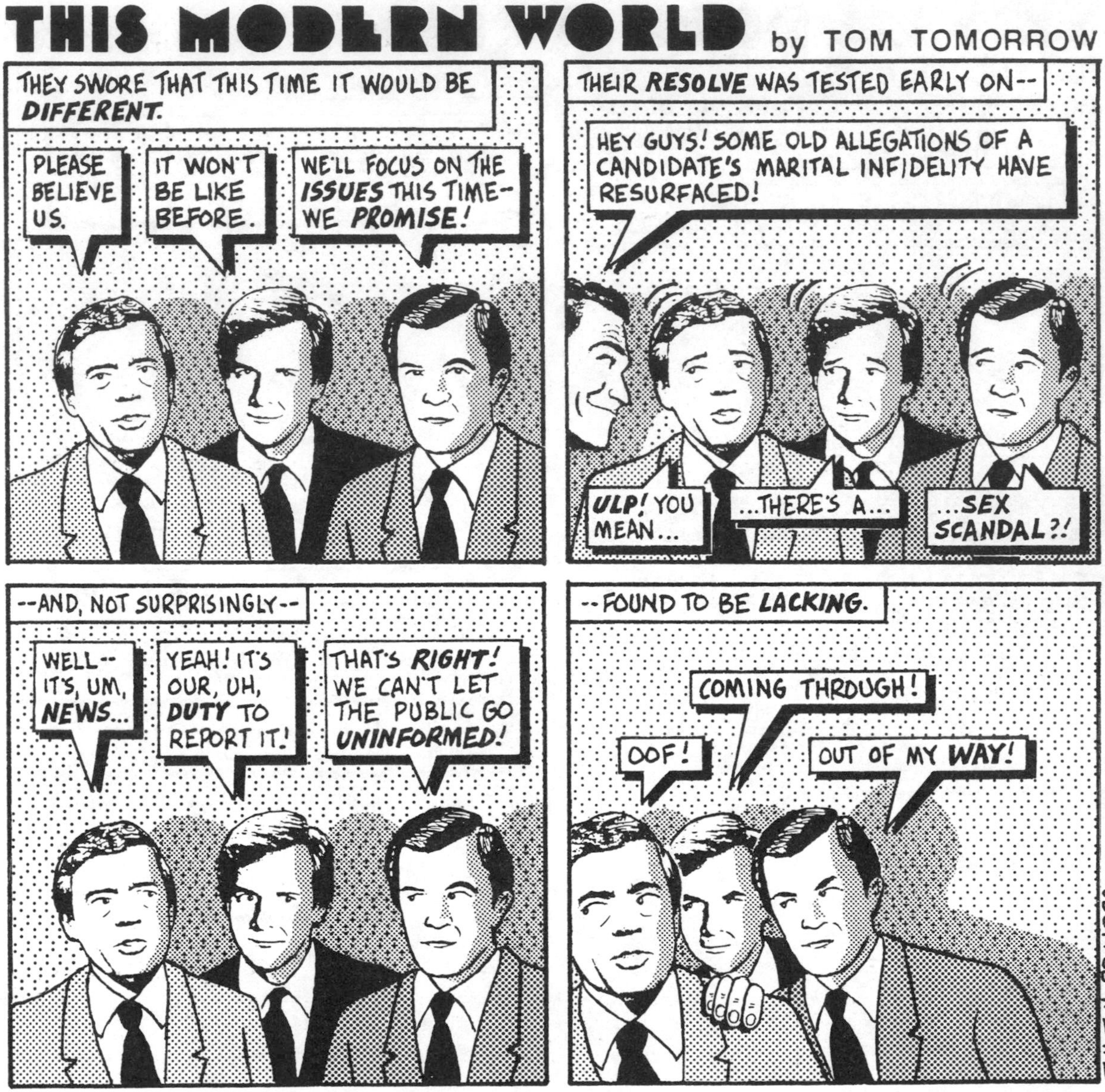
THIS MODERN WORLD by TOM TOMORROW
THEY SWORE THAT THIS TIME IT WOULD BE DIFFERENT.
PLEASE BELIEVE US.
IT WON'T BE LIKE BEFORE.
WE'LL FOCUS ON THE ISSUES THIS TIME-- WE PROMISE!
THEIR RESOLVE WAS TESTED EARLY ON--
HEY GUYS! SOME OLD ALLEGATIONS OF A CANDIDATE'S MARITAL INFIDELITY HAVE RESURFACED!
ULP! YOU MEAN...
...THERE'S A...
...SEX SCANDAL?!
--AND, NOT SURPRISINGLY--
WELL-- IT'S, UM, NEWS...
YEAH! IT'S OUR, UH, DUTY TO REPORT IT!
THAT'S RIGHT! WE CAN'T LET THE PUBLIC GO UNINFORMED!
--FOUND TO BE LACKING.
COMING THROUGH!
OOF!
OUT OF MY WAY!
TOM TOMORROW©92

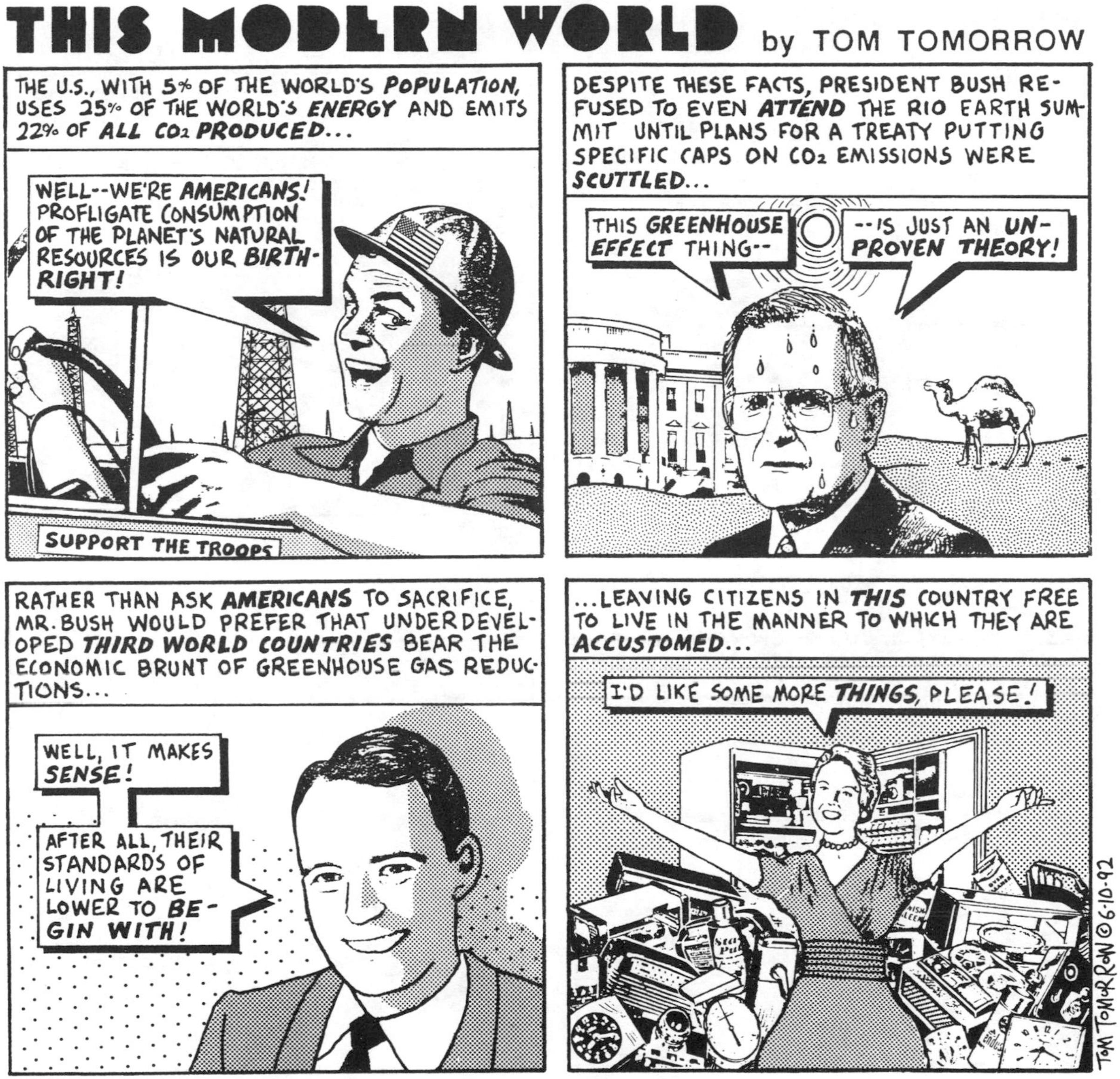
THIS MODERN WORLD by TOM TOMORROW
THE U.S., WITH 5% OF THE WORLD'S POPULATION, USES 25% OF THE WORLD'S ENERGY AND EMITS 22% OF ALL CO_2 PRODUCED...
WELL--WE'RE AMERICANS! PROFLIGATE CONSUMPTION OF THE PLANET'S NATURAL RESOURCES IS OUR BIRTH-RIGHT!
SUPPORT THE TROOPS
DESPITE THESE FACTS, PRESIDENT BUSH REFUSED TO EVEN ATTEND THE RIO EARTH SUMMIT UNTIL PLANS FOR A TREATY PUTTING SPECIFIC CAPS ON CO_2 EMISSIONS WERE SCUTTLED...
THIS GREENHOUSE EFFECT THING--
--IS JUST AN UNPROVEN THEORY!
RATHER THAN ASK AMERICANS TO SACRIFICE, MR. BUSH WOULD PREFER THAT UNDERDEVELOPED THIRD WORLD COUNTRIES BEAR THE ECONOMIC BRUNT OF GREENHOUSE GAS REDUCTIONS...
WELL, IT MAKES SENSE!
AFTER ALL, THEIR STANDARDS OF LIVING ARE LOWER TO BEGIN WITH!
...LEAVING CITIZENS IN THIS COUNTRY FREE TO LIVE IN THE MANNER TO WHICH THEY ARE ACCUSTOMED...
I'D LIKE SOME MORE THINGS, PLEASE!
TOM TOMORROW ©6-10-92

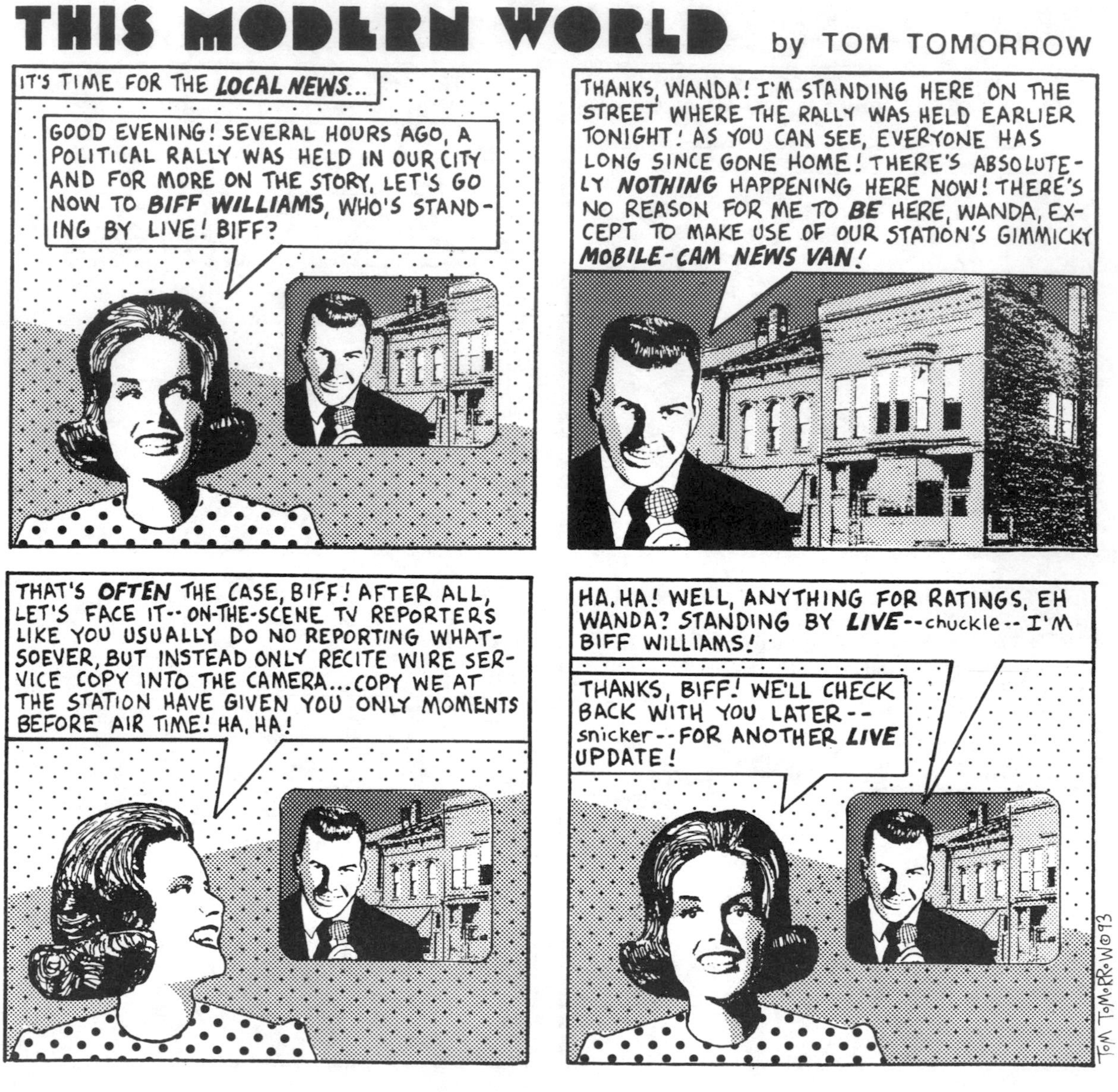
THIS MODERN WORLD by TOM TOMORROW
IT'S TIME FOR THE LOCAL NEWS...
GOOD EVENING! SEVERAL HOURS AGO, A POLITICAL RALLY WAS HELD IN OUR CITY AND FOR MORE ON THE STORY, LET'S GO NOW TO BIFF WILLIAMS, WHO'S STANDING BY LIVE! BIFF?
THANKS, WANDA! I'M STANDING HERE ON THE STREET WHERE THE RALLY WAS HELD EARLIER TONIGHT! AS YOU CAN SEE, EVERYONE HAS LONG SINCE GONE HOME! THERE'S ABSOLUTELY NOTHING HAPPENING HERE NOW! THERE'S NO REASON FOR ME TO BE HERE, WANDA, EXCEPT TO MAKE USE OF OUR STATION'S GIMMICKY MOBILE-CAM NEWS VAN!
THAT'S OFTEN THE CASE, BIFF! AFTER ALL, LET'S FACE IT-- ON-THE-SCENE TV REPORTERS LIKE YOU USUALLY DO NO REPORTING WHATSOEVER, BUT INSTEAD ONLY RECITE WIRE SERVICE COPY INTO THE CAMERA... COPY WE AT THE STATION HAVE GIVEN YOU ONLY MOMENTS BEFORE AIR TIME! HA, HA!
HA, HA! WELL, ANYTHING FOR RATINGS, EH WANDA? STANDING BY LIVE--chuckle-- I'M BIFF WILLIAMS!
THANKS, BIFF! WE'LL CHECK BACK WITH YOU LATER --snicker-- FOR ANOTHER LIVE UPDATE!
TOM TOMORROW©93

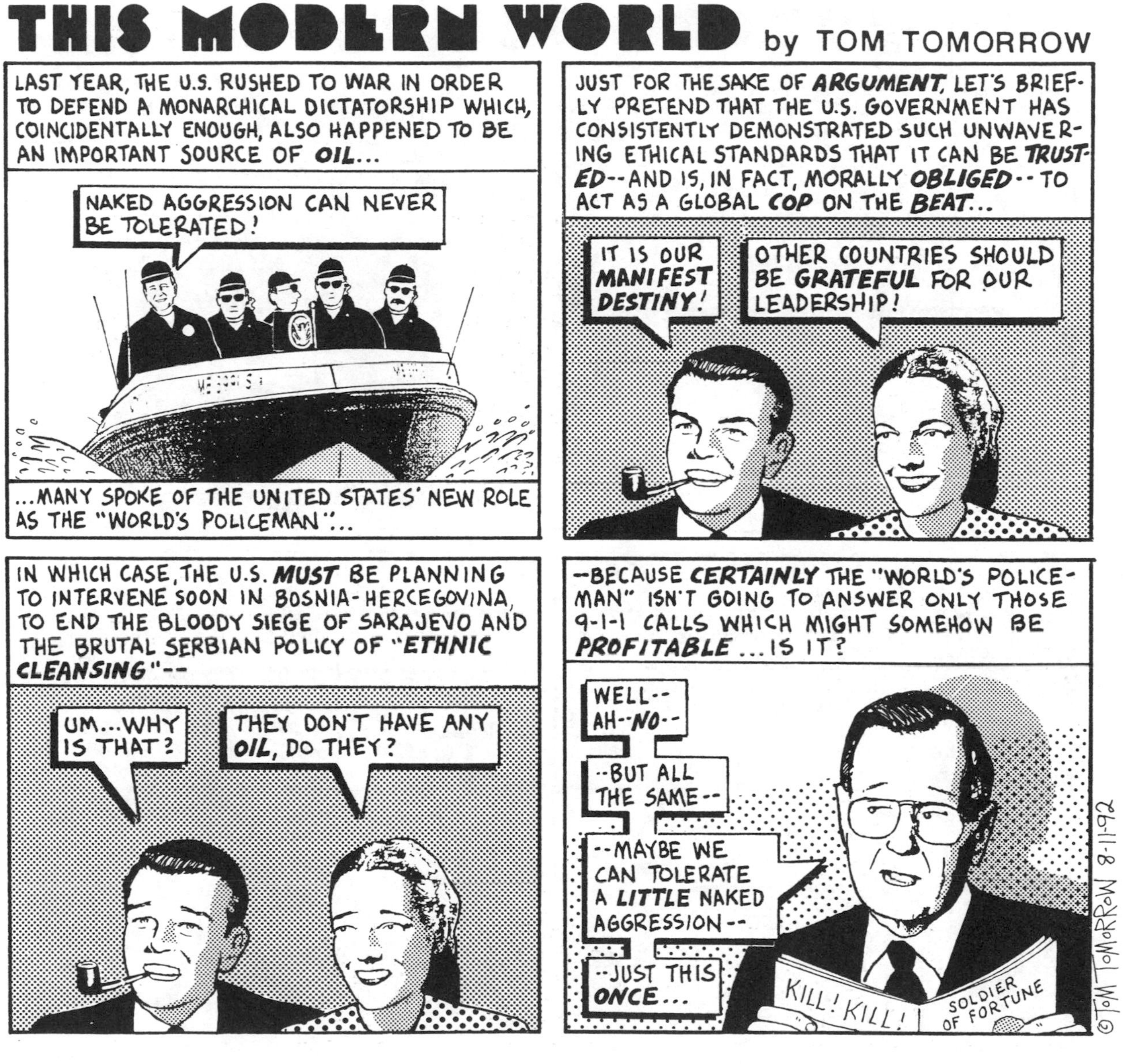
THIS MODERN WORLD by TOM TOMORROW
LAST YEAR, THE U.S. RUSHED TO WAR IN ORDER TO DEFEND A MONARCHICAL DICTATORSHIP WHICH, COINCIDENTALLY ENOUGH, ALSO HAPPENED TO BE AN IMPORTANT SOURCE OF OIL...
NAKED AGGRESSION CAN NEVER BE TOLERATED!
...MANY SPOKE OF THE UNITED STATES' NEW ROLE AS THE "WORLD'S POLICEMAN"...
JUST FOR THE SAKE OF ARGUMENT, LET'S BRIEFLY PRETEND THAT THE U.S. GOVERNMENT HAS CONSISTENTLY DEMONSTRATED SUCH UNWAVERING ETHICAL STANDARDS THAT IT CAN BE TRUSTED--AND IS, IN FACT, MORALLY OBLIGED--TO ACT AS A GLOBAL COP ON THE BEAT...
IT IS OUR MANIFEST DESTINY!
OTHER COUNTRIES SHOULD BE GRATEFUL FOR OUR LEADERSHIP!
IN WHICH CASE, THE U.S. MUST BE PLANNING TO INTERVENE SOON IN BOSNIA-HERCEGOVINA, TO END THE BLOODY SIEGE OF SARAJEVO AND THE BRUTAL SERBIAN POLICY OF "ETHNIC CLEANSING"--
UM...WHY IS THAT?
THEY DON'T HAVE ANY OIL, DO THEY?
--BECAUSE CERTAINLY THE "WORLD'S POLICEMAN" ISN'T GOING TO ANSWER ONLY THOSE 9-1-1 CALLS WHICH MIGHT SOMEHOW BE PROFITABLE...IS IT?
WELL--AH--NO--
--BUT ALL THE SAME--
--MAYBE WE CAN TOLERATE A LITTLE NAKED AGGRESSION--
--JUST THIS ONCE...
KILL! KILL!
SOLDIER OF FORTUNE
©TOM TOMORROW 8-11-92

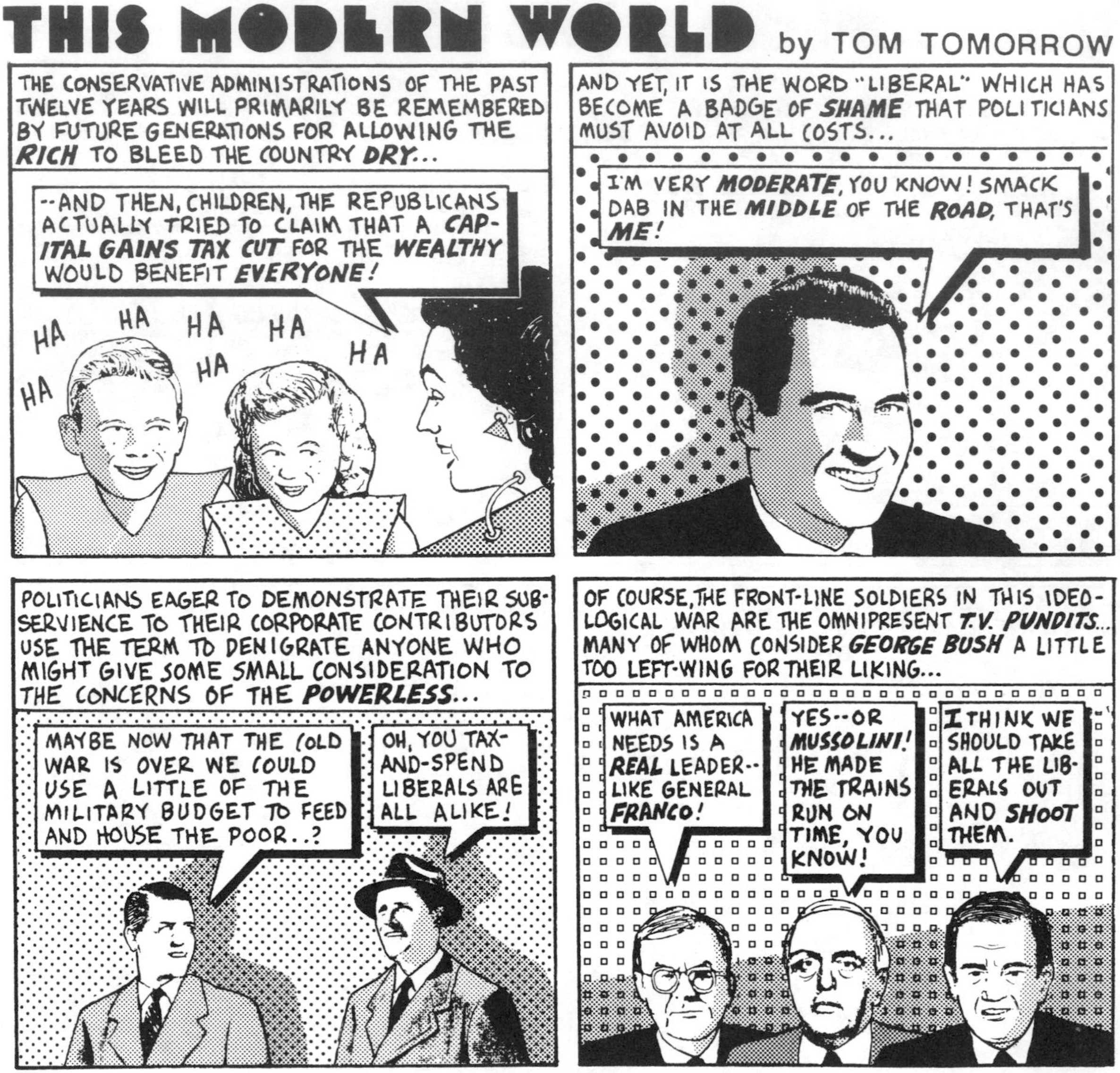
THIS MODERN WORLD by TOM TOMORROW
THE CONSERVATIVE ADMINISTRATIONS OF THE PAST TWELVE YEARS WILL PRIMARILY BE REMEMBERED BY FUTURE GENERATIONS FOR ALLOWING THE RICH TO BLEED THE COUNTRY DRY...
--AND THEN, CHILDREN, THE REPUBLICANS ACTUALLY TRIED TO CLAIM THAT A CAPITAL GAINS TAX CUT FOR THE WEALTHY WOULD BENEFIT EVERYONE!
HA HA HA HA HA HA HA
AND YET, IT IS THE WORD "LIBERAL" WHICH HAS BECOME A BADGE OF SHAME THAT POLITICIANS MUST AVOID AT ALL COSTS...
I'M VERY MODERATE, YOU KNOW! SMACK DAB IN THE MIDDLE OF THE ROAD, THAT'S ME!
POLITICIANS EAGER TO DEMONSTRATE THEIR SUBSERVIENCE TO THEIR CORPORATE CONTRIBUTORS USE THE TERM TO DENIGRATE ANYONE WHO MIGHT GIVE SOME SMALL CONSIDERATION TO THE CONCERNS OF THE POWERLESS...
MAYBE NOW THAT THE COLD WAR IS OVER WE COULD USE A LITTLE OF THE MILITARY BUDGET TO FEED AND HOUSE THE POOR..?
OH, YOU TAX-AND-SPEND LIBERALS ARE ALL ALIKE!
OF COURSE, THE FRONT-LINE SOLDIERS IN THIS IDEOLOGICAL WAR ARE THE OMNIPRESENT T.V. PUNDITS... MANY OF WHOM CONSIDER GEORGE BUSH A LITTLE TOO LEFT-WING FOR THEIR LIKING...
WHAT AMERICA NEEDS IS A REAL LEADER--LIKE GENERAL FRANCO!
YES--OR MUSSOLINI! HE MADE THE TRAINS RUN ON TIME, YOU KNOW!
I THINK WE SHOULD TAKE ALL THE LIBERALS OUT AND SHOOT THEM.

THIS MODERN WORLD by TOM TOMORROW

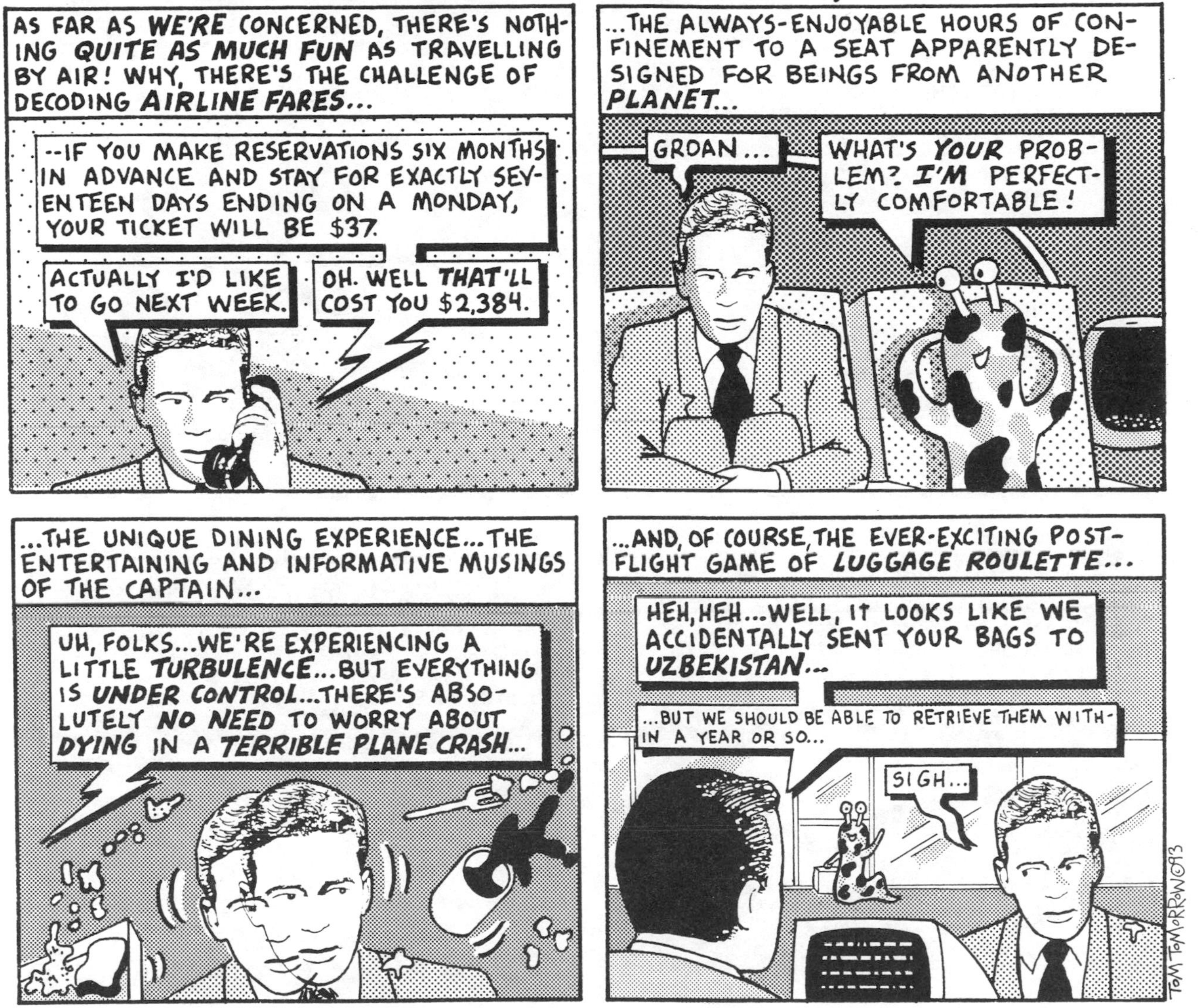

AS FAR AS WE'RE CONCERNED, THERE'S NOTHING QUITE AS MUCH FUN AS TRAVELLING BY AIR! WHY, THERE'S THE CHALLENGE OF DECODING AIRLINE FARES...
--IF YOU MAKE RESERVATIONS SIX MONTHS IN ADVANCE AND STAY FOR EXACTLY SEVENTEEN DAYS ENDING ON A MONDAY, YOUR TICKET WILL BE $37.
ACTUALLY I'D LIKE TO GO NEXT WEEK.
OH. WELL THAT'LL COST YOU $2,384.
...THE ALWAYS-ENJOYABLE HOURS OF CONFINEMENT TO A SEAT APPARENTLY DESIGNED FOR BEINGS FROM ANOTHER PLANET...
GROAN...
WHAT'S YOUR PROBLEM? I'M PERFECTLY COMFORTABLE!
...THE UNIQUE DINING EXPERIENCE...THE ENTERTAINING AND INFORMATIVE MUSINGS OF THE CAPTAIN...
UH, FOLKS...WE'RE EXPERIENCING A LITTLE TURBULENCE...BUT EVERYTHING IS UNDER CONTROL...THERE'S ABSOLUTELY NO NEED TO WORRY ABOUT DYING IN A TERRIBLE PLANE CRASH...
...AND, OF COURSE, THE EVER-EXCITING POST-FLIGHT GAME OF LUGGAGE ROULETTE...
HEH, HEH...WELL, IT LOOKS LIKE WE ACCIDENTALLY SENT YOUR BAGS TO UZBEKISTAN...
...BUT WE SHOULD BE ABLE TO RETRIEVE THEM WITHIN A YEAR OR SO...
SIGH...
TOM TOMORROW©93

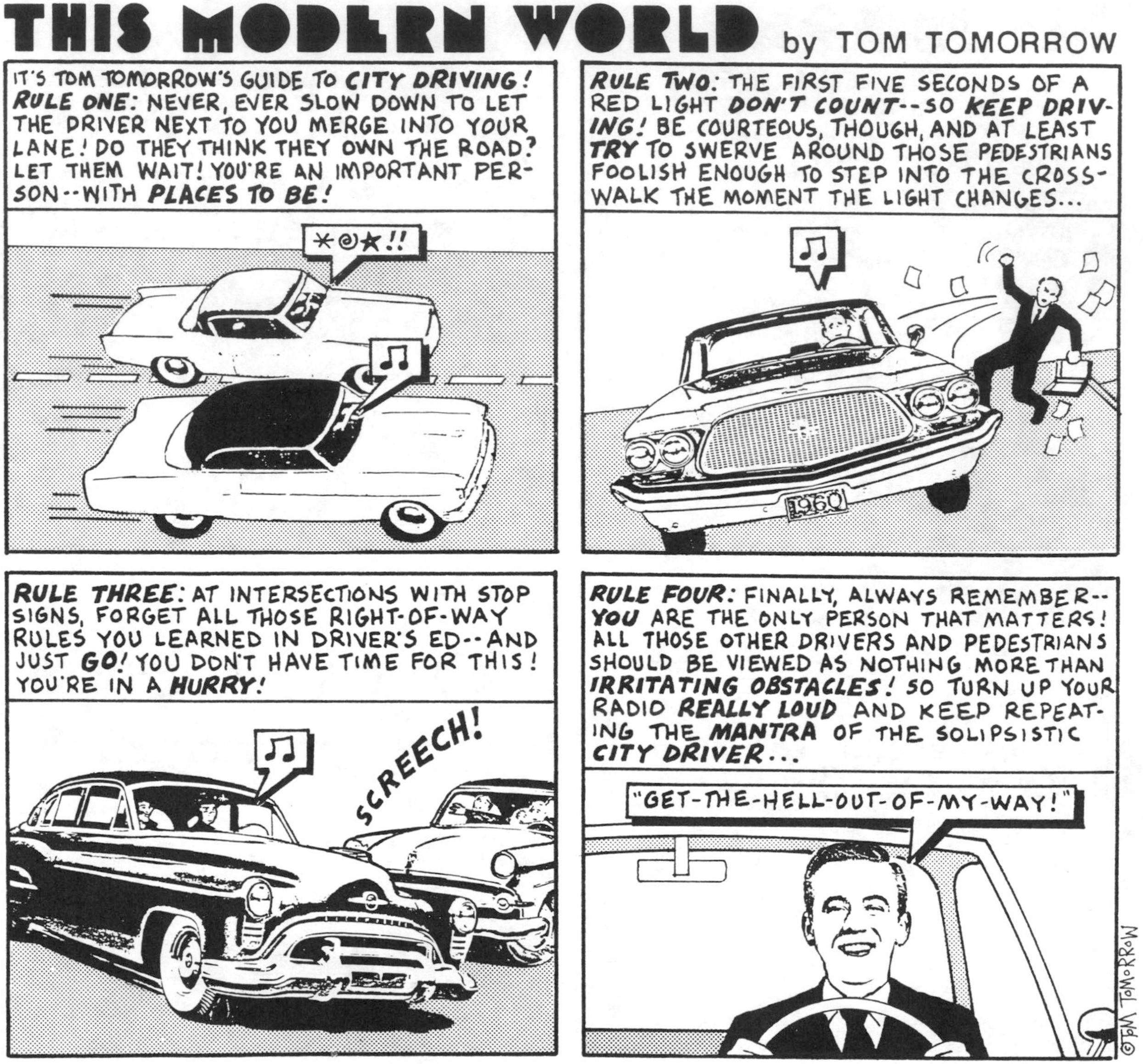
THIS MODERN WORLD by TOM TOMORROW
IT'S TOM TOMORROW'S GUIDE TO CITY DRIVING! RULE ONE: NEVER, EVER SLOW DOWN TO LET THE DRIVER NEXT TO YOU MERGE INTO YOUR LANE! DO THEY THINK THEY OWN THE ROAD? LET THEM WAIT! YOU'RE AN IMPORTANT PERSON--WITH PLACES TO BE!
*@★!!
♫
RULE TWO: THE FIRST FIVE SECONDS OF A RED LIGHT DON'T COUNT--SO KEEP DRIVING! BE COURTEOUS, THOUGH, AND AT LEAST TRY TO SWERVE AROUND THOSE PEDESTRIANS FOOLISH ENOUGH TO STEP INTO THE CROSSWALK THE MOMENT THE LIGHT CHANGES...
♫
1960
RULE THREE: AT INTERSECTIONS WITH STOP SIGNS, FORGET ALL THOSE RIGHT-OF-WAY RULES YOU LEARNED IN DRIVER'S ED--AND JUST GO! YOU DON'T HAVE TIME FOR THIS! YOU'RE IN A HURRY!
♫
SCREECH!
RULE FOUR: FINALLY, ALWAYS REMEMBER--YOU ARE THE ONLY PERSON THAT MATTERS! ALL THOSE OTHER DRIVERS AND PEDESTRIANS SHOULD BE VIEWED AS NOTHING MORE THAN IRRITATING OBSTACLES! SO TURN UP YOUR RADIO REALLY LOUD AND KEEP REPEATING THE MANTRA OF THE SOLIPSISTIC CITY DRIVER...
"GET-THE-HELL-OUT-OF-MY-WAY!"
©TOM TOMORROW

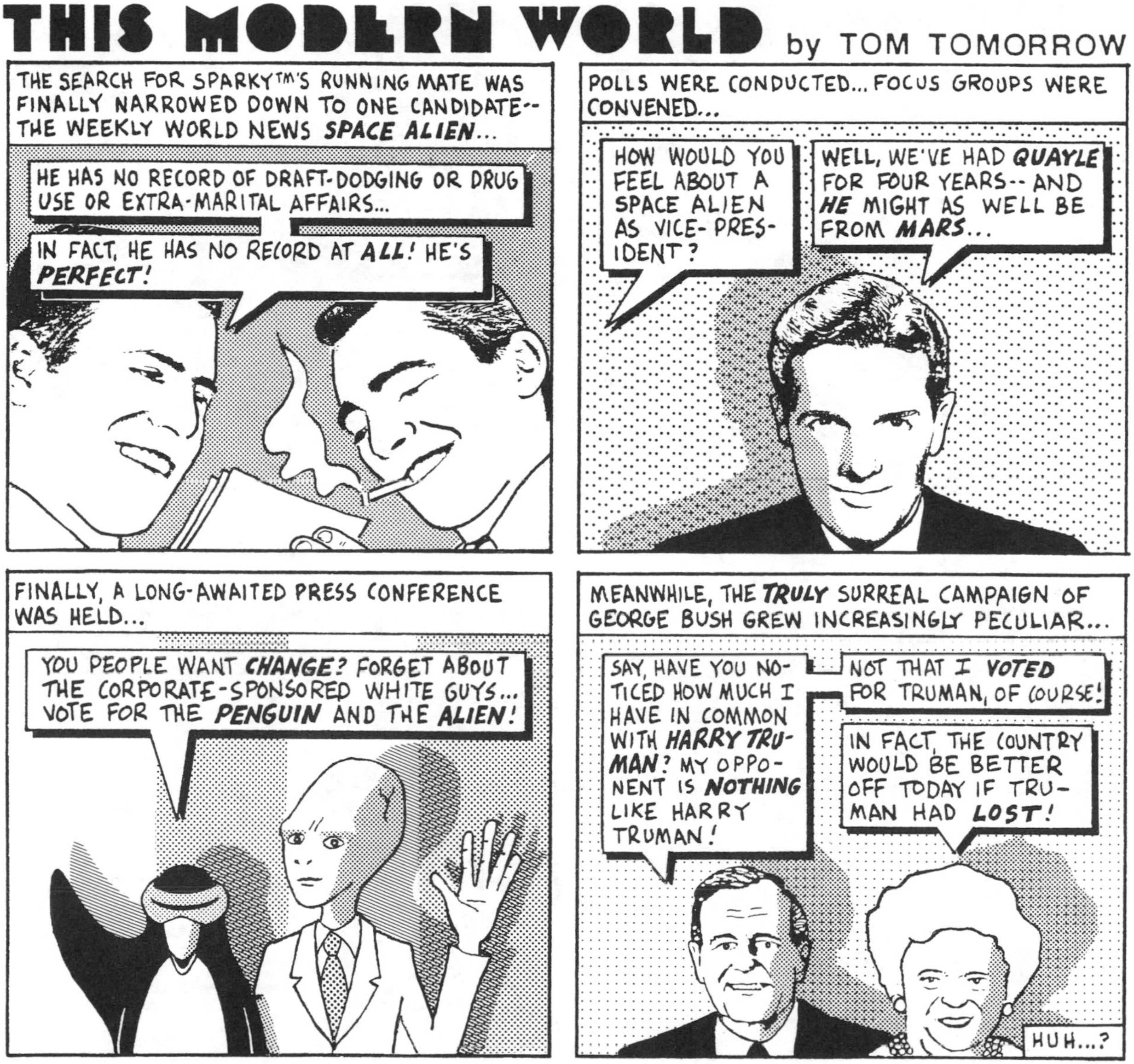
THIS MODERN WORLD by TOM TOMORROW
THE SEARCH FOR SPARKY™'S RUNNING MATE WAS FINALLY NARROWED DOWN TO ONE CANDIDATE-- THE WEEKLY WORLD NEWS SPACE ALIEN...
HE HAS NO RECORD OF DRAFT-DODGING OR DRUG USE OR EXTRA-MARITAL AFFAIRS...
IN FACT, HE HAS NO RECORD AT ALL! HE'S PERFECT!
POLLS WERE CONDUCTED... FOCUS GROUPS WERE CONVENED...
HOW WOULD YOU FEEL ABOUT A SPACE ALIEN AS VICE-PRESIDENT?
WELL, WE'VE HAD QUAYLE FOR FOUR YEARS-- AND HE MIGHT AS WELL BE FROM MARS...
FINALLY, A LONG-AWAITED PRESS CONFERENCE WAS HELD...
YOU PEOPLE WANT CHANGE? FORGET ABOUT THE CORPORATE-SPONSORED WHITE GUYS... VOTE FOR THE PENGUIN AND THE ALIEN!
MEANWHILE, THE TRULY SURREAL CAMPAIGN OF GEORGE BUSH GREW INCREASINGLY PECULIAR...
SAY, HAVE YOU NOTICED HOW MUCH I HAVE IN COMMON WITH HARRY TRUMAN? MY OPPONENT IS NOTHING LIKE HARRY TRUMAN!
NOT THAT I VOTED FOR TRUMAN, OF COURSE!
IN FACT, THE COUNTRY WOULD BE BETTER OFF TODAY IF TRUMAN HAD LOST!
HUH...?

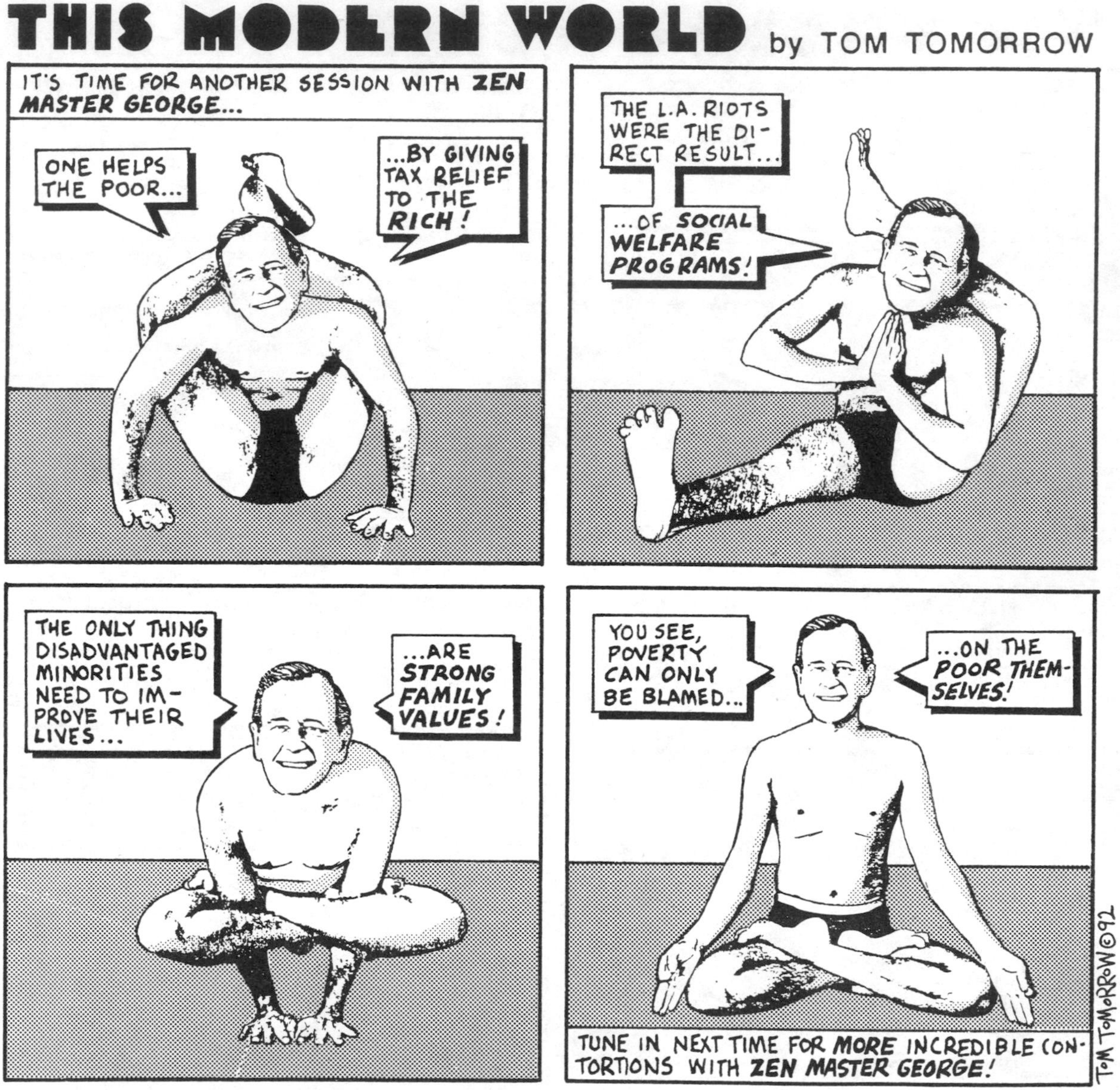
THIS MODERN WORLD by TOM TOMORROW
IT'S TIME FOR ANOTHER SESSION WITH ZEN MASTER GEORGE...
ONE HELPS THE POOR...
...BY GIVING TAX RELIEF TO THE RICH!
THE L.A. RIOTS WERE THE DIRECT RESULT...
...OF SOCIAL WELFARE PROGRAMS!
THE ONLY THING DISADVANTAGED MINORITIES NEED TO IMPROVE THEIR LIVES...
...ARE STRONG FAMILY VALUES!
YOU SEE, POVERTY CAN ONLY BE BLAMED...
...ON THE POOR THEMSELVES!
TUNE IN NEXT TIME FOR MORE INCREDIBLE CONTORTIONS WITH ZEN MASTER GEORGE!
TOM TOMORROW©92

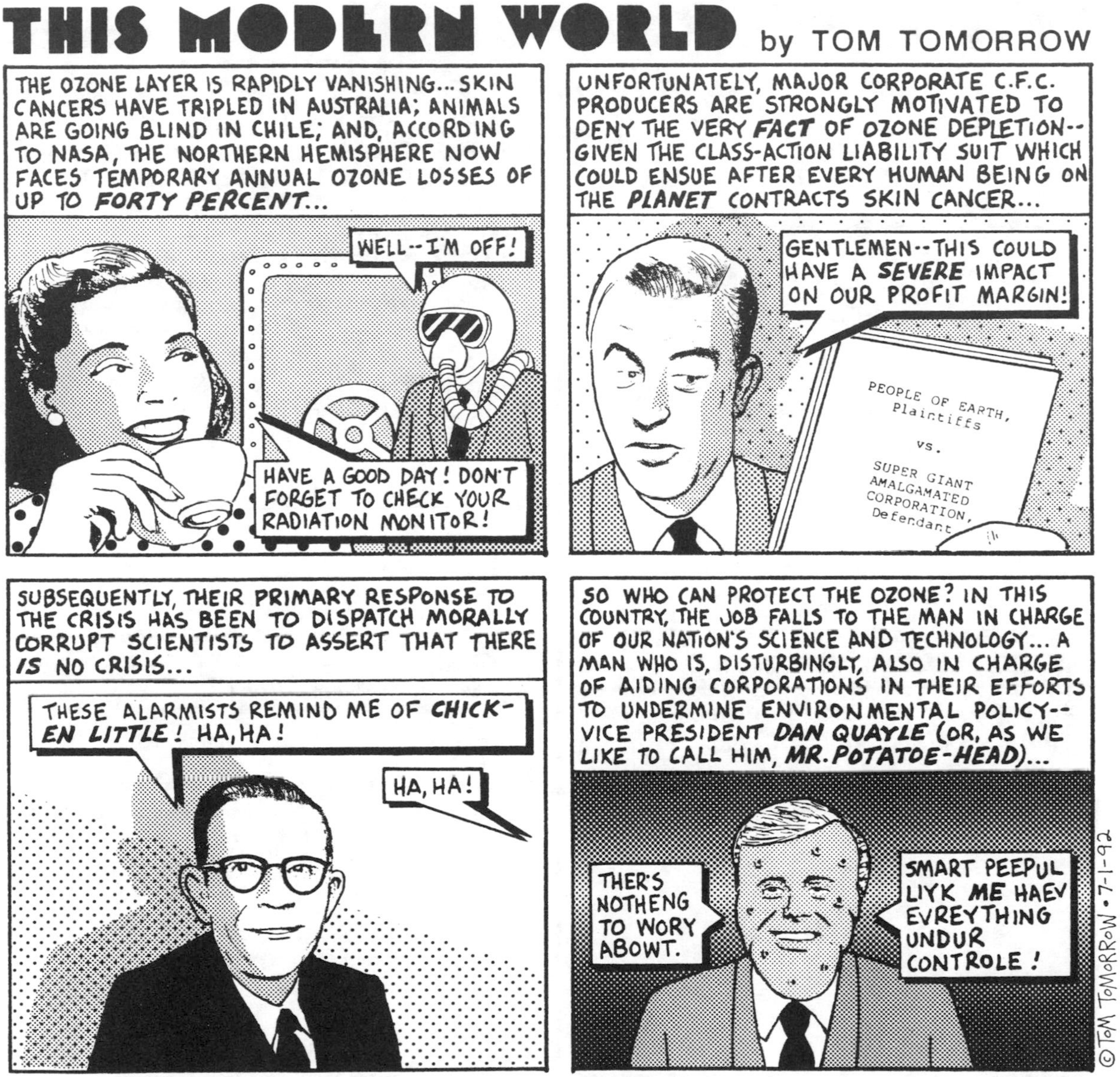
THIS MODERN WORLD by TOM TOMORROW
THE OZONE LAYER IS RAPIDLY VANISHING... SKIN CANCERS HAVE TRIPLED IN AUSTRALIA; ANIMALS ARE GOING BLIND IN CHILE; AND, ACCORDING TO NASA, THE NORTHERN HEMISPHERE NOW FACES TEMPORARY ANNUAL OZONE LOSSES OF UP TO FORTY PERCENT...
WELL--I'M OFF!
HAVE A GOOD DAY! DON'T FORGET TO CHECK YOUR RADIATION MONITOR!
UNFORTUNATELY, MAJOR CORPORATE C.F.C. PRODUCERS ARE STRONGLY MOTIVATED TO DENY THE VERY FACT OF OZONE DEPLETION--GIVEN THE CLASS-ACTION LIABILITY SUIT WHICH COULD ENSUE AFTER EVERY HUMAN BEING ON THE PLANET CONTRACTS SKIN CANCER...
GENTLEMEN--THIS COULD HAVE A SEVERE IMPACT ON OUR PROFIT MARGIN!
PEOPLE OF EARTH, Plaintiffs vs. SUPER GIANT AMALGAMATED CORPORATION, Defendant
SUBSEQUENTLY, THEIR PRIMARY RESPONSE TO THE CRISIS HAS BEEN TO DISPATCH MORALLY CORRUPT SCIENTISTS TO ASSERT THAT THERE IS NO CRISIS...
THESE ALARMISTS REMIND ME OF CHICKEN LITTLE! HA, HA!
HA, HA!
SO WHO CAN PROTECT THE OZONE? IN THIS COUNTRY, THE JOB FALLS TO THE MAN IN CHARGE OF OUR NATION'S SCIENCE AND TECHNOLOGY... A MAN WHO IS, DISTURBINGLY, ALSO IN CHARGE OF AIDING CORPORATIONS IN THEIR EFFORTS TO UNDERMINE ENVIRONMENTAL POLICY--VICE PRESIDENT DAN QUAYLE (OR, AS WE LIKE TO CALL HIM, MR. POTATOE-HEAD)...
THER'S NOTHENG TO WORY ABOWT.
SMART PEEPUL LIYK ME HAEV EVREYTHING UNDUR CONTROLE!
©TOM TOMORROW • 7-1-92

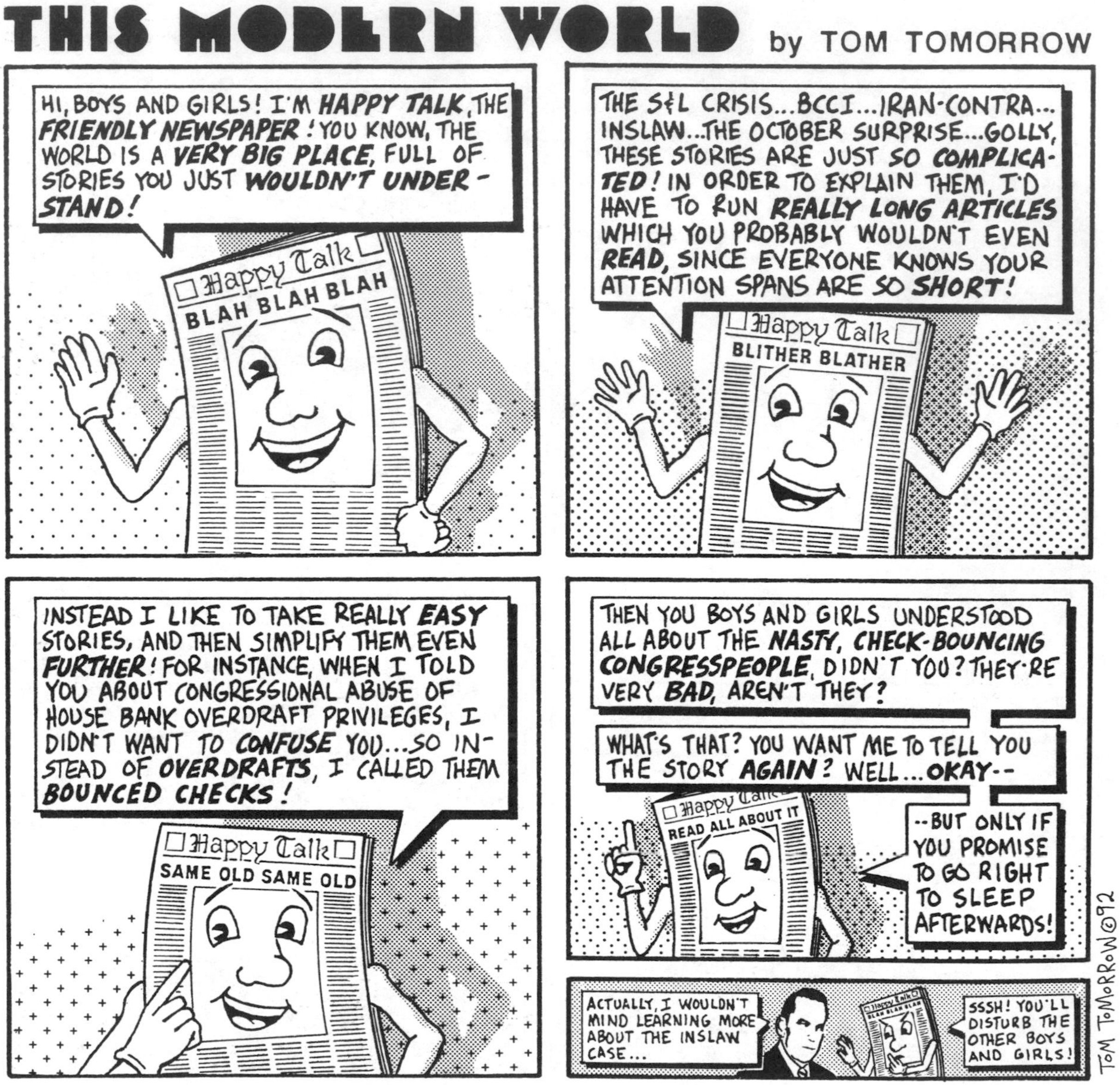
THIS MODERN WORLD by TOM TOMORROW
HI, BOYS AND GIRLS! I'M HAPPY TALK, THE FRIENDLY NEWSPAPER! YOU KNOW, THE WORLD IS A VERY BIG PLACE, FULL OF STORIES YOU JUST WOULDN'T UNDER-STAND!
Happy Talk
BLAH BLAH BLAH
THE S&L CRISIS...BCCI...IRAN-CONTRA...INSLAW...THE OCTOBER SURPRISE...GOLLY, THESE STORIES ARE JUST SO COMPLICA-TED! IN ORDER TO EXPLAIN THEM, I'D HAVE TO RUN REALLY LONG ARTICLES WHICH YOU PROBABLY WOULDN'T EVEN READ, SINCE EVERYONE KNOWS YOUR ATTENTION SPANS ARE SO SHORT!
Happy Talk
BLITHER BLATHER
INSTEAD I LIKE TO TAKE REALLY EASY STORIES, AND THEN SIMPLIFY THEM EVEN FURTHER! FOR INSTANCE, WHEN I TOLD YOU ABOUT CONGRESSIONAL ABUSE OF HOUSE BANK OVERDRAFT PRIVILEGES, I DIDN'T WANT TO CONFUSE YOU...SO IN-STEAD OF OVERDRAFTS, I CALLED THEM BOUNCED CHECKS!
Happy Talk
SAME OLD SAME OLD
THEN YOU BOYS AND GIRLS UNDERSTOOD ALL ABOUT THE NASTY, CHECK-BOUNCING CONGRESSPEOPLE, DIDN'T YOU? THEY'RE VERY BAD, AREN'T THEY?
WHAT'S THAT? YOU WANT ME TO TELL YOU THE STORY AGAIN? WELL...OKAY--
READ ALL ABOUT IT
--BUT ONLY IF YOU PROMISE TO GO RIGHT TO SLEEP AFTERWARDS!
ACTUALLY, I WOULDN'T MIND LEARNING MORE ABOUT THE INSLAW CASE...
SSSH! YOU'LL DISTURB THE OTHER BOYS AND GIRLS!
TOM TOMORROW ©92

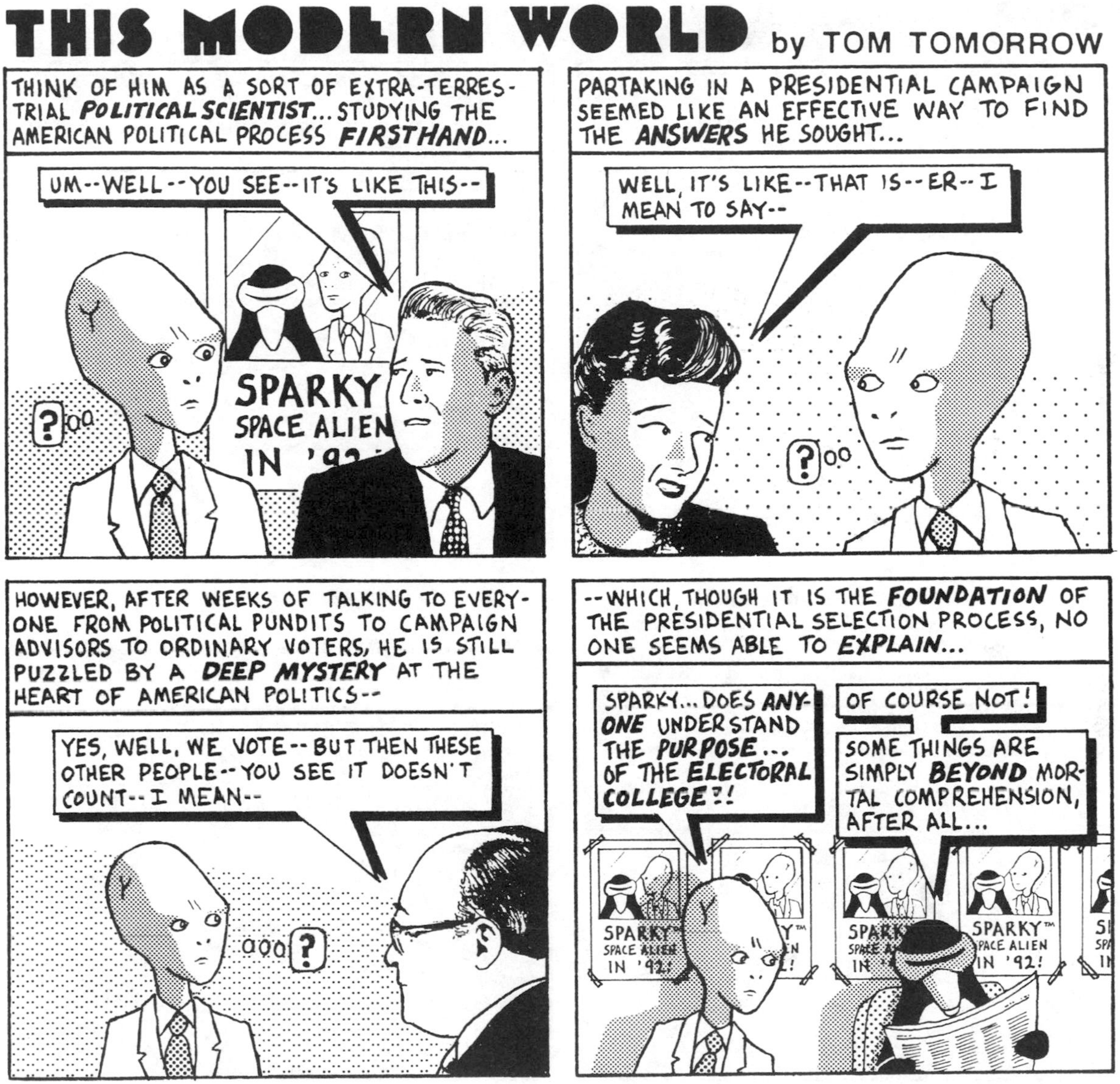
THIS MODERN WORLD by TOM TOMORROW
THINK OF HIM AS A SORT OF EXTRA-TERRESTRIAL *POLITICAL SCIENTIST*... STUDYING THE AMERICAN POLITICAL PROCESS *FIRSTHAND*...
UM--WELL--YOU SEE--IT'S LIKE THIS--
SPARKY
SPACE ALIEN
PARTAKING IN A PRESIDENTIAL CAMPAIGN SEEMED LIKE AN EFFECTIVE WAY TO FIND THE *ANSWERS* HE SOUGHT...
WELL, IT'S LIKE--THAT IS--ER--I MEAN TO SAY--
HOWEVER, AFTER WEEKS OF TALKING TO EVERYONE FROM POLITICAL PUNDITS TO CAMPAIGN ADVISORS TO ORDINARY VOTERS, HE IS STILL PUZZLED BY A *DEEP MYSTERY* AT THE HEART OF AMERICAN POLITICS--
YES, WELL, WE VOTE--BUT THEN THESE OTHER PEOPLE--YOU SEE IT DOESN'T COUNT--I MEAN--
--WHICH, THOUGH IT IS THE *FOUNDATION* OF THE PRESIDENTIAL SELECTION PROCESS, NO ONE SEEMS ABLE TO *EXPLAIN*...
SPARKY... DOES *ANYONE* UNDERSTAND THE *PURPOSE*... OF THE *ELECTORAL COLLEGE*?!
OF COURSE NOT!
SOME THINGS ARE SIMPLY *BEYOND* MORTAL COMPREHENSION, AFTER ALL...
SPARKY™ SPACE ALIEN IN '92!

THIS MODERN WORLD by TOM TOMORROW

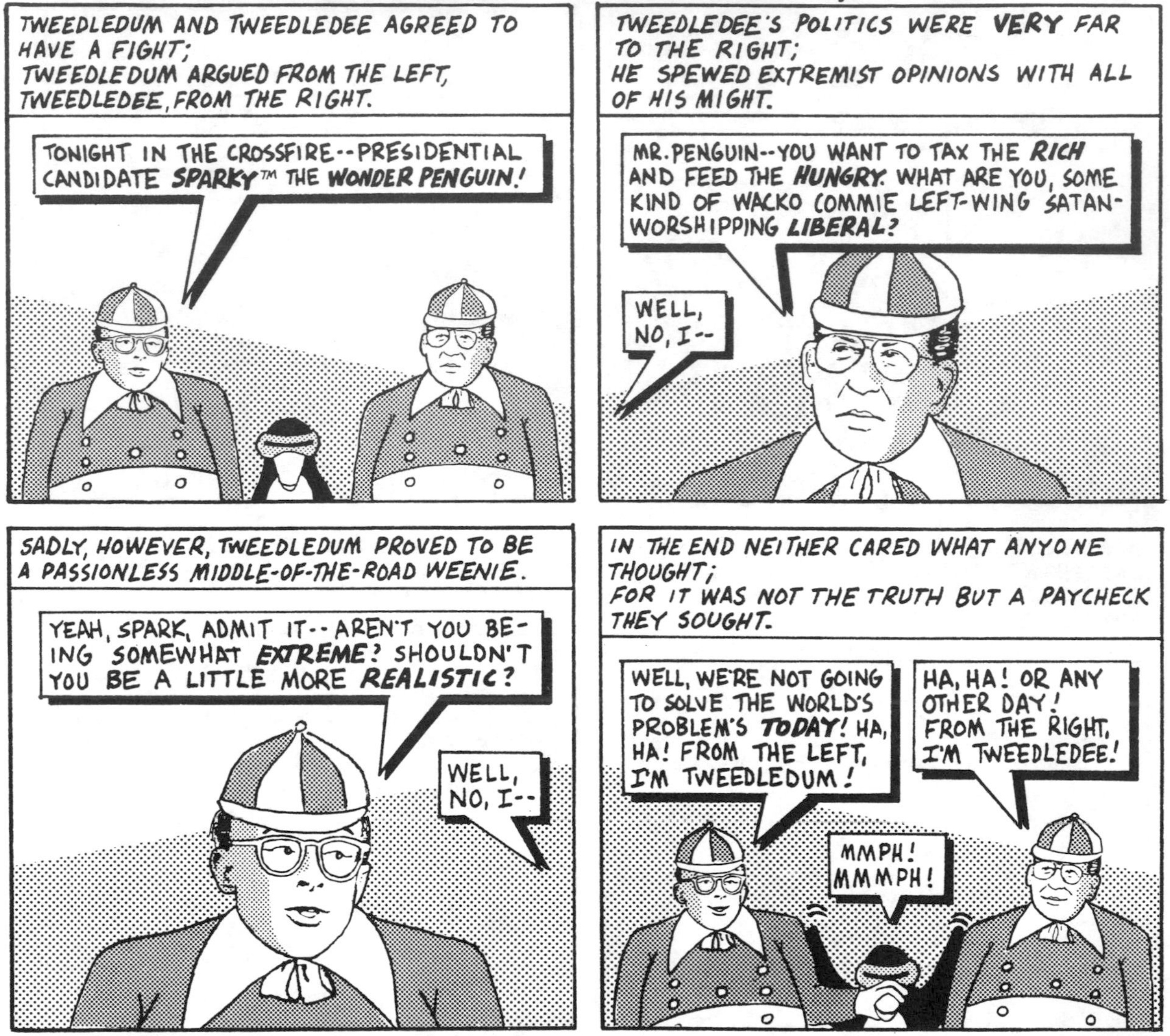
TWEEDLEDUM AND TWEEDLEDEE AGREED TO HAVE A FIGHT; TWEEDLEDUM ARGUED FROM THE LEFT, TWEEDLEDEE, FROM THE RIGHT.
TONIGHT IN THE CROSSFIRE--PRESIDENTIAL CANDIDATE SPARKY™ THE WONDER PENGUIN!
TWEEDLEDEE'S POLITICS WERE VERY FAR TO THE RIGHT; HE SPEWED EXTREMIST OPINIONS WITH ALL OF HIS MIGHT.
MR. PENGUIN--YOU WANT TO TAX THE RICH AND FEED THE HUNGRY. WHAT ARE YOU, SOME KIND OF WACKO COMMIE LEFT-WING SATAN-WORSHIPPING LIBERAL?
WELL, NO, I--
SADLY, HOWEVER, TWEEDLEDUM PROVED TO BE A PASSIONLESS MIDDLE-OF-THE-ROAD WEENIE.
YEAH, SPARK, ADMIT IT--AREN'T YOU BE-ING SOMEWHAT EXTREME? SHOULDN'T YOU BE A LITTLE MORE REALISTIC?
WELL, NO, I--
IN THE END NEITHER CARED WHAT ANYONE THOUGHT; FOR IT WAS NOT THE TRUTH BUT A PAYCHECK THEY SOUGHT.
WELL, WE'RE NOT GOING TO SOLVE THE WORLD'S PROBLEM'S TODAY! HA, HA! FROM THE LEFT, I'M TWEEDLEDUM!
HA, HA! OR ANY OTHER DAY! FROM THE RIGHT, I'M TWEEDLEDEE!
MMPH! MMMPH!

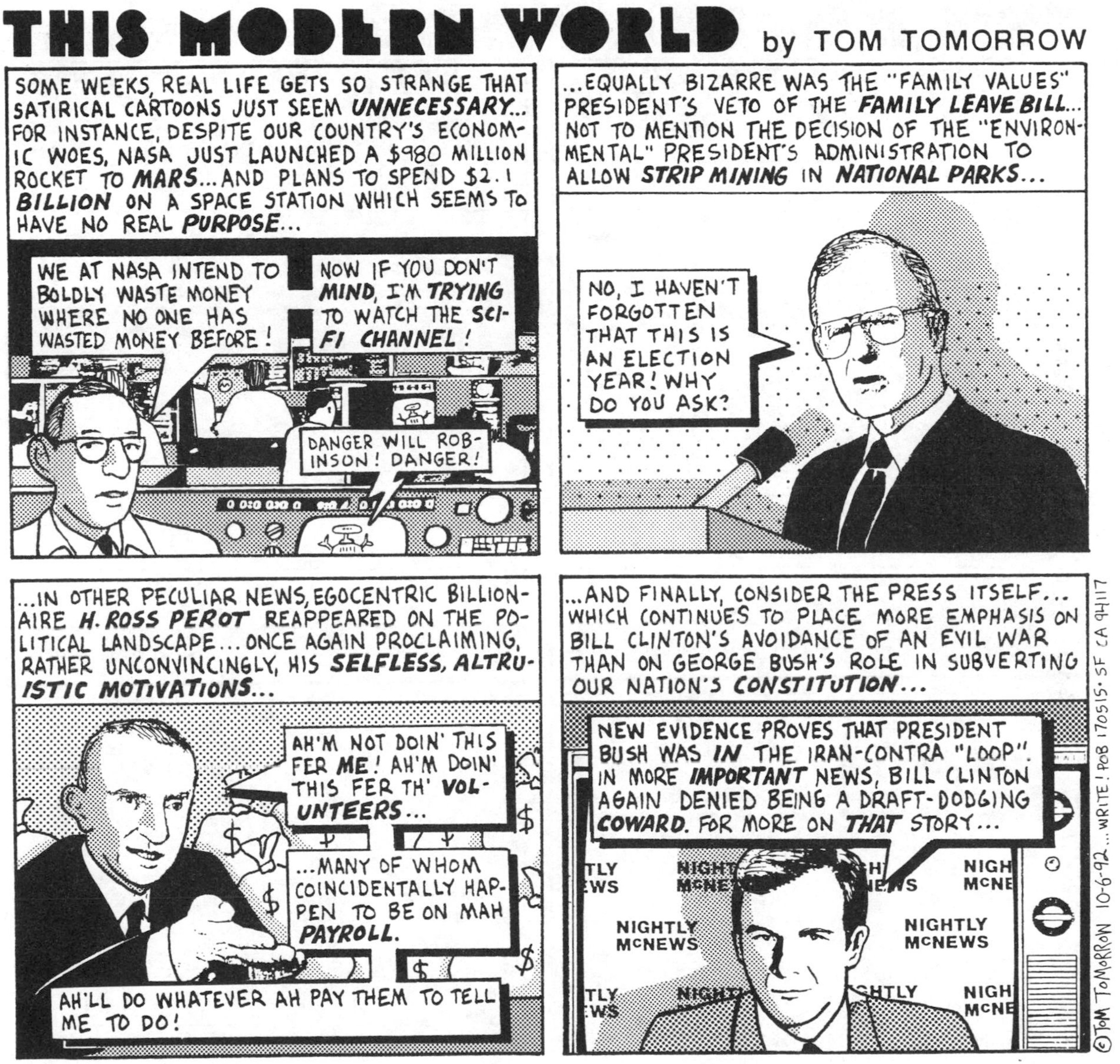
THIS MODERN WORLD by TOM TOMORROW
SOME WEEKS, REAL LIFE GETS SO STRANGE THAT SATIRICAL CARTOONS JUST SEEM UNNECESSARY... FOR INSTANCE, DESPITE OUR COUNTRY'S ECONOMIC WOES, NASA JUST LAUNCHED A $980 MILLION ROCKET TO MARS... AND PLANS TO SPEND $2.1 BILLION ON A SPACE STATION WHICH SEEMS TO HAVE NO REAL PURPOSE...
WE AT NASA INTEND TO BOLDLY WASTE MONEY WHERE NO ONE HAS WASTED MONEY BEFORE!
NOW IF YOU DON'T MIND, I'M TRYING TO WATCH THE SCI-FI CHANNEL!
DANGER WILL ROBINSON! DANGER!
...EQUALLY BIZARRE WAS THE "FAMILY VALUES" PRESIDENT'S VETO OF THE FAMILY LEAVE BILL... NOT TO MENTION THE DECISION OF THE "ENVIRONMENTAL" PRESIDENT'S ADMINISTRATION TO ALLOW STRIP MINING IN NATIONAL PARKS...
NO, I HAVEN'T FORGOTTEN THAT THIS IS AN ELECTION YEAR! WHY DO YOU ASK?
...IN OTHER PECULIAR NEWS, EGOCENTRIC BILLIONAIRE H. ROSS PEROT REAPPEARED ON THE POLITICAL LANDSCAPE... ONCE AGAIN PROCLAIMING, RATHER UNCONVINCINGLY, HIS SELFLESS, ALTRUISTIC MOTIVATIONS...
AH'M NOT DOIN' THIS FER ME! AH'M DOIN' THIS FER TH' VOLUNTEERS...
...MANY OF WHOM COINCIDENTALLY HAPPEN TO BE ON MAH PAYROLL.
AH'LL DO WHATEVER AH PAY THEM TO TELL ME TO DO!
...AND FINALLY, CONSIDER THE PRESS ITSELF... WHICH CONTINUES TO PLACE MORE EMPHASIS ON BILL CLINTON'S AVOIDANCE OF AN EVIL WAR THAN ON GEORGE BUSH'S ROLE IN SUBVERTING OUR NATION'S CONSTITUTION...
NEW EVIDENCE PROVES THAT PRESIDENT BUSH WAS IN THE IRAN-CONTRA "LOOP". IN MORE IMPORTANT NEWS, BILL CLINTON AGAIN DENIED BEING A DRAFT-DODGING COWARD. FOR MORE ON THAT STORY...
NIGHTLY McNEWS
NIGHTLY McNEWS
©TOM TOMORROW 10-6-92... WRITE! POB 170515 · SF CA 94117

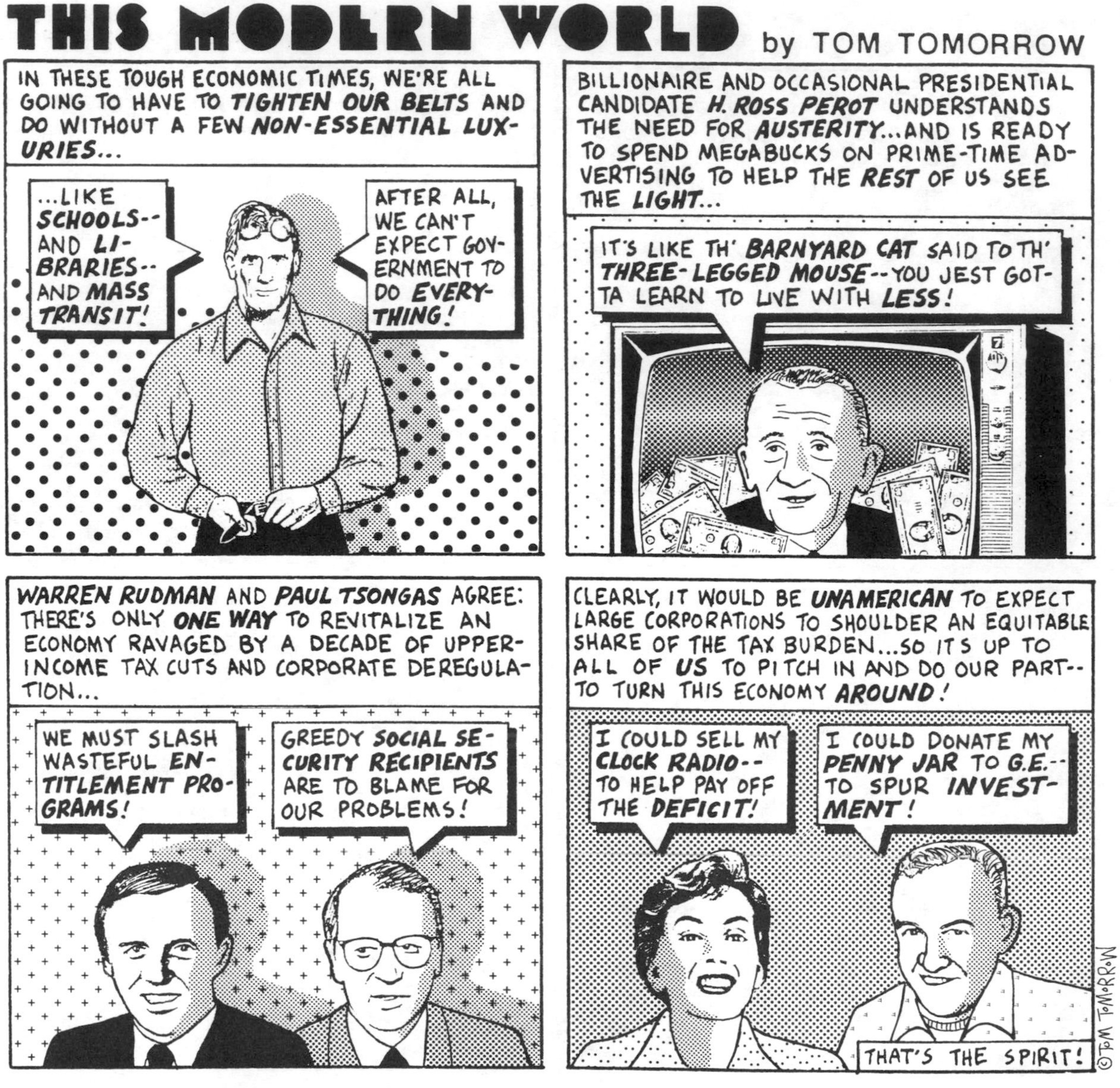
THIS MODERN WORLD by TOM TOMORROW
IN THESE TOUGH ECONOMIC TIMES, WE'RE ALL GOING TO HAVE TO TIGHTEN OUR BELTS AND DO WITHOUT A FEW NON-ESSENTIAL LUXURIES...
...LIKE SCHOOLS-- AND LIBRARIES-- AND MASS TRANSIT!
AFTER ALL, WE CAN'T EXPECT GOVERNMENT TO DO EVERYTHING!
BILLIONAIRE AND OCCASIONAL PRESIDENTIAL CANDIDATE H. ROSS PEROT UNDERSTANDS THE NEED FOR AUSTERITY...AND IS READY TO SPEND MEGABUCKS ON PRIME-TIME ADVERTISING TO HELP THE REST OF US SEE THE LIGHT...
IT'S LIKE TH' BARNYARD CAT SAID TO TH' THREE-LEGGED MOUSE--YOU JEST GOTTA LEARN TO LIVE WITH LESS!
WARREN RUDMAN AND PAUL TSONGAS AGREE: THERE'S ONLY ONE WAY TO REVITALIZE AN ECONOMY RAVAGED BY A DECADE OF UPPER-INCOME TAX CUTS AND CORPORATE DEREGULATION...
WE MUST SLASH WASTEFUL ENTITLEMENT PROGRAMS!
GREEDY SOCIAL SECURITY RECIPIENTS ARE TO BLAME FOR OUR PROBLEMS!
CLEARLY, IT WOULD BE UNAMERICAN TO EXPECT LARGE CORPORATIONS TO SHOULDER AN EQUITABLE SHARE OF THE TAX BURDEN...SO IT'S UP TO ALL OF US TO PITCH IN AND DO OUR PART--TO TURN THIS ECONOMY AROUND!
I COULD SELL MY CLOCK RADIO--TO HELP PAY OFF THE DEFICIT!
I COULD DONATE MY PENNY JAR TO G.E.--TO SPUR INVESTMENT!
THAT'S THE SPIRIT!
©TOM TOMORROW

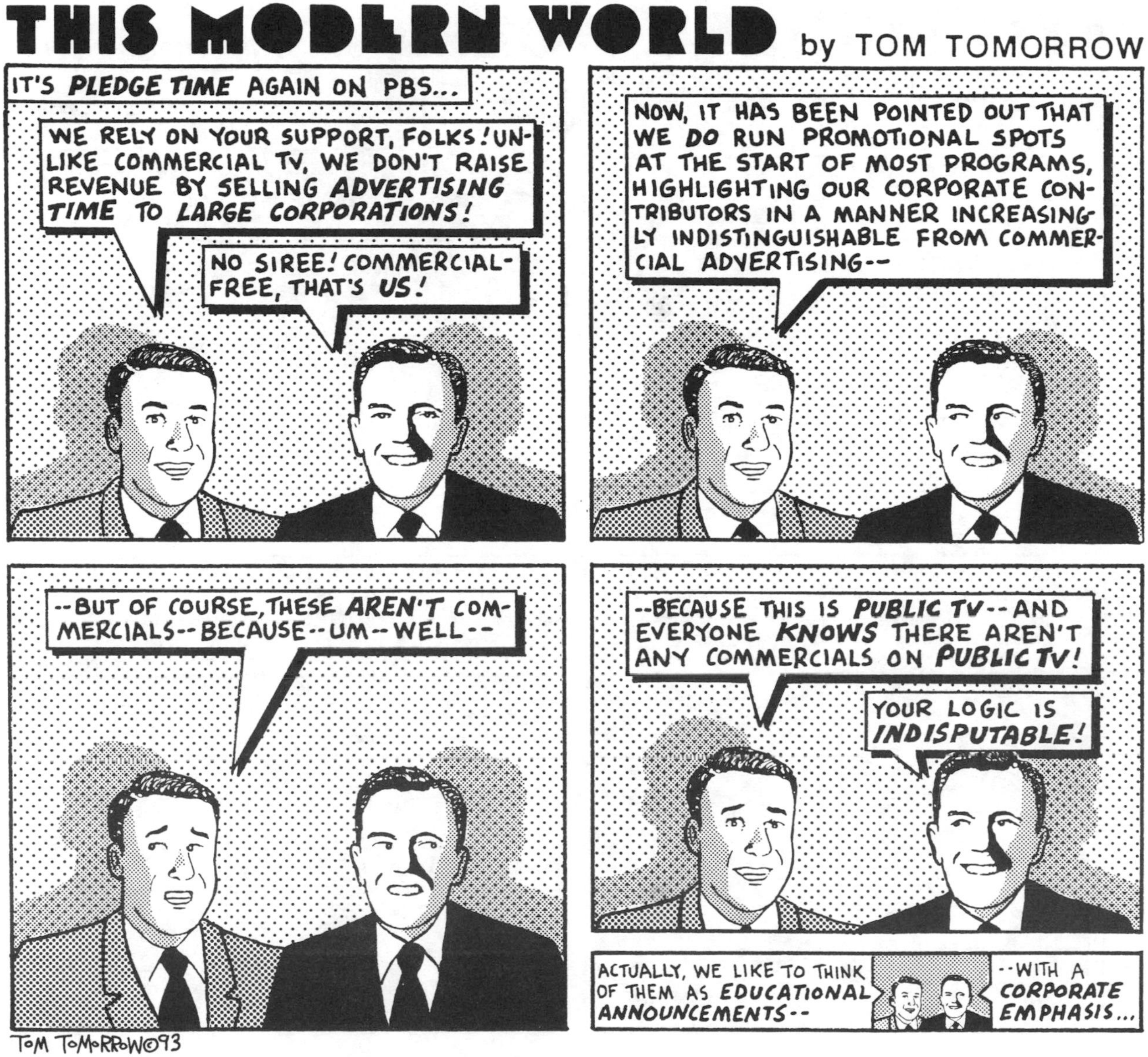
THIS MODERN WORLD by TOM TOMORROW
IT'S PLEDGE TIME AGAIN ON PBS...
WE RELY ON YOUR SUPPORT, FOLKS! UNLIKE COMMERCIAL TV, WE DON'T RAISE REVENUE BY SELLING ADVERTISING TIME TO LARGE CORPORATIONS!
NO SIREE! COMMERCIAL-FREE, THAT'S US!
NOW, IT HAS BEEN POINTED OUT THAT WE DO RUN PROMOTIONAL SPOTS AT THE START OF MOST PROGRAMS, HIGHLIGHTING OUR CORPORATE CONTRIBUTORS IN A MANNER INCREASINGLY INDISTINGUISHABLE FROM COMMERCIAL ADVERTISING--
--BUT OF COURSE, THESE AREN'T COMMERCIALS--BECAUSE--UM--WELL--
--BECAUSE THIS IS PUBLIC TV--AND EVERYONE KNOWS THERE AREN'T ANY COMMERCIALS ON PUBLIC TV!
YOUR LOGIC IS INDISPUTABLE!
ACTUALLY, WE LIKE TO THINK OF THEM AS EDUCATIONAL ANNOUNCEMENTS--
--WITH A CORPORATE EMPHASIS...
TOM TOMORROW©93

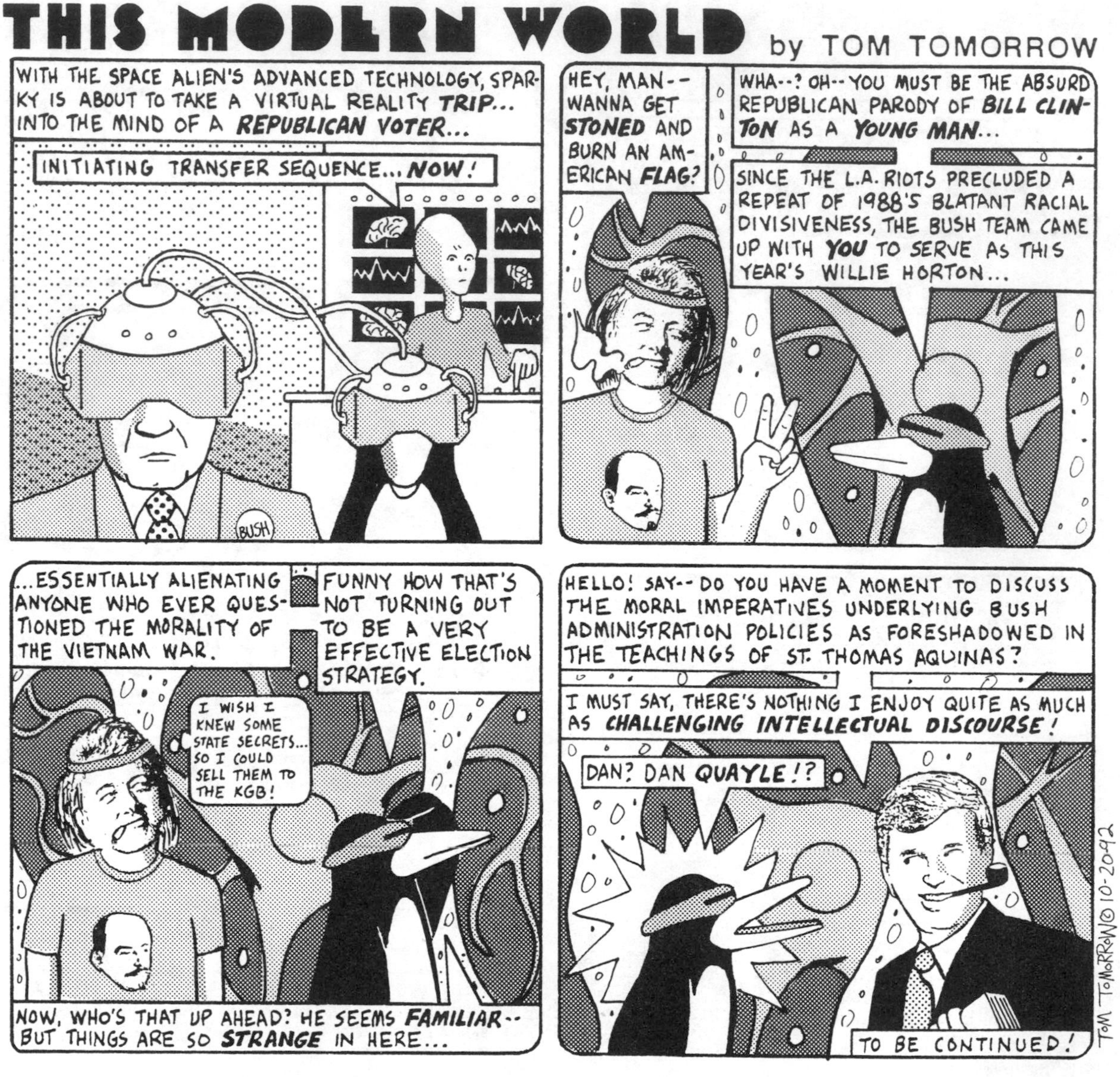
THIS MODERN WORLD by TOM TOMORROW
WITH THE SPACE ALIEN'S ADVANCED TECHNOLOGY, SPARKY IS ABOUT TO TAKE A VIRTUAL REALITY TRIP... INTO THE MIND OF A REPUBLICAN VOTER...
INITIATING TRANSFER SEQUENCE... NOW!
BUSH
HEY, MAN-- WANNA GET STONED AND BURN AN AMERICAN FLAG?
WHA--? OH-- YOU MUST BE THE ABSURD REPUBLICAN PARODY OF BILL CLINTON AS A YOUNG MAN...
SINCE THE L.A. RIOTS PRECLUDED A REPEAT OF 1988'S BLATANT RACIAL DIVISIVENESS, THE BUSH TEAM CAME UP WITH YOU TO SERVE AS THIS YEAR'S WILLIE HORTON...
...ESSENTIALLY ALIENATING ANYONE WHO EVER QUESTIONED THE MORALITY OF THE VIETNAM WAR.
FUNNY HOW THAT'S NOT TURNING OUT TO BE A VERY EFFECTIVE ELECTION STRATEGY.
I WISH I KNEW SOME STATE SECRETS... SO I COULD SELL THEM TO THE KGB!
NOW, WHO'S THAT UP AHEAD? HE SEEMS FAMILIAR-- BUT THINGS ARE SO STRANGE IN HERE...
HELLO! SAY-- DO YOU HAVE A MOMENT TO DISCUSS THE MORAL IMPERATIVES UNDERLYING BUSH ADMINISTRATION POLICIES AS FORESHADOWED IN THE TEACHINGS OF ST. THOMAS AQUINAS?
I MUST SAY, THERE'S NOTHING I ENJOY QUITE AS MUCH AS CHALLENGING INTELLECTUAL DISCOURSE!
DAN? DAN QUAYLE!?
TO BE CONTINUED!
TOM TOMORROW© 10-20-92

THIS MODERN WORLD by TOM TOMORROW

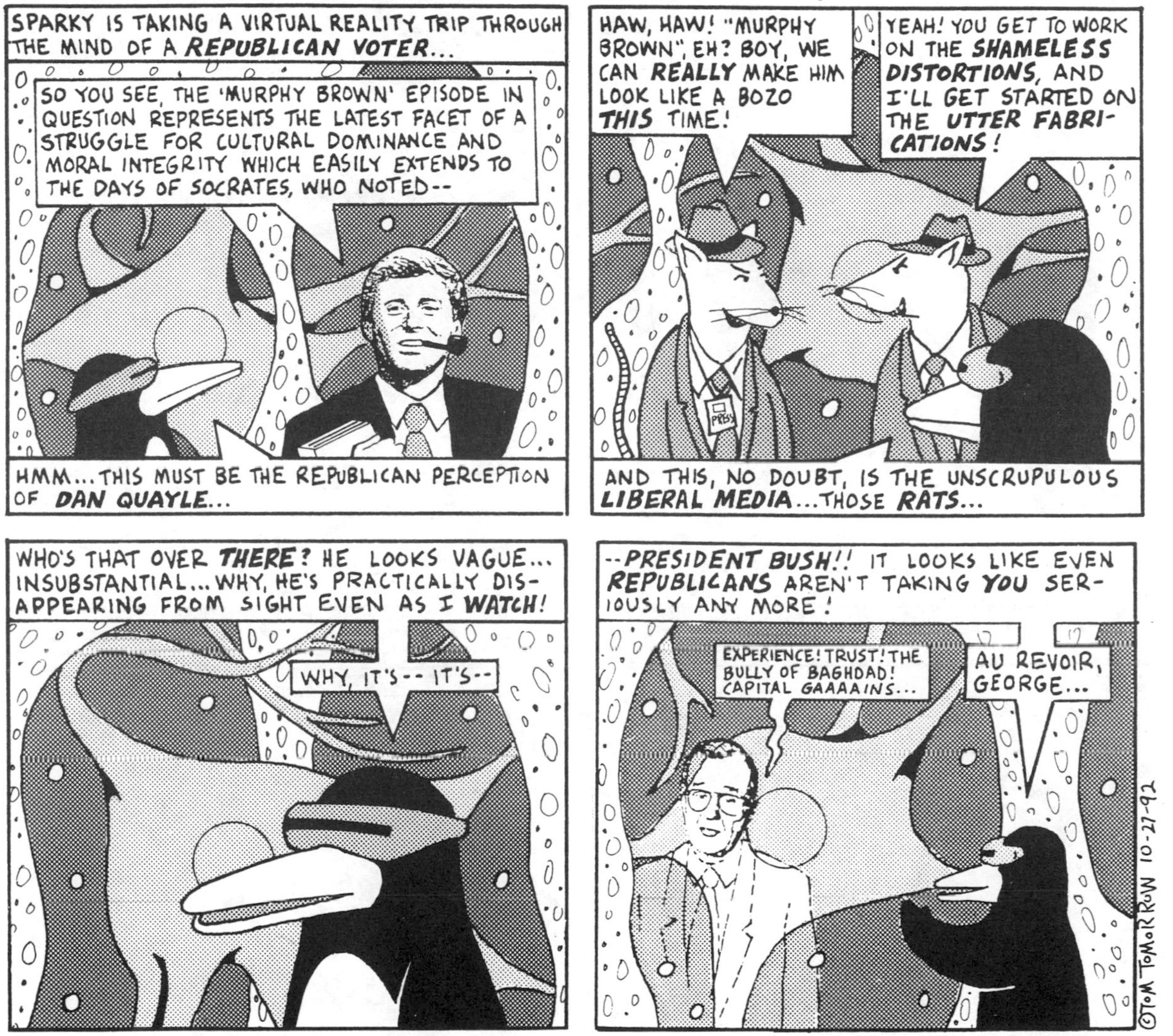
SPARKY IS TAKING A VIRTUAL REALITY TRIP THROUGH THE MIND OF A REPUBLICAN VOTER...
SO YOU SEE, THE 'MURPHY BROWN' EPISODE IN QUESTION REPRESENTS THE LATEST FACET OF A STRUGGLE FOR CULTURAL DOMINANCE AND MORAL INTEGRITY WHICH EASILY EXTENDS TO THE DAYS OF SOCRATES, WHO NOTED--
HMM... THIS MUST BE THE REPUBLICAN PERCEPTION OF DAN QUAYLE...
HAW, HAW! "MURPHY BROWN", EH? BOY, WE CAN REALLY MAKE HIM LOOK LIKE A BOZO THIS TIME!
YEAH! YOU GET TO WORK ON THE SHAMELESS DISTORTIONS, AND I'LL GET STARTED ON THE UTTER FABRICATIONS!
PRESS
AND THIS, NO DOUBT, IS THE UNSCRUPULOUS LIBERAL MEDIA... THOSE RATS...
WHO'S THAT OVER THERE? HE LOOKS VAGUE... INSUBSTANTIAL... WHY, HE'S PRACTICALLY DISAPPEARING FROM SIGHT EVEN AS I WATCH!
WHY, IT'S-- IT'S--
--PRESIDENT BUSH!! IT LOOKS LIKE EVEN REPUBLICANS AREN'T TAKING YOU SERIOUSLY ANY MORE!
EXPERIENCE! TRUST! THE BULLY OF BAGHDAD! CAPITAL GAAAAINS...
AU REVOIR, GEORGE...
©TOM TOMORROW 10-27-92

THIS MODERN WORLD by TOM TOMORROW

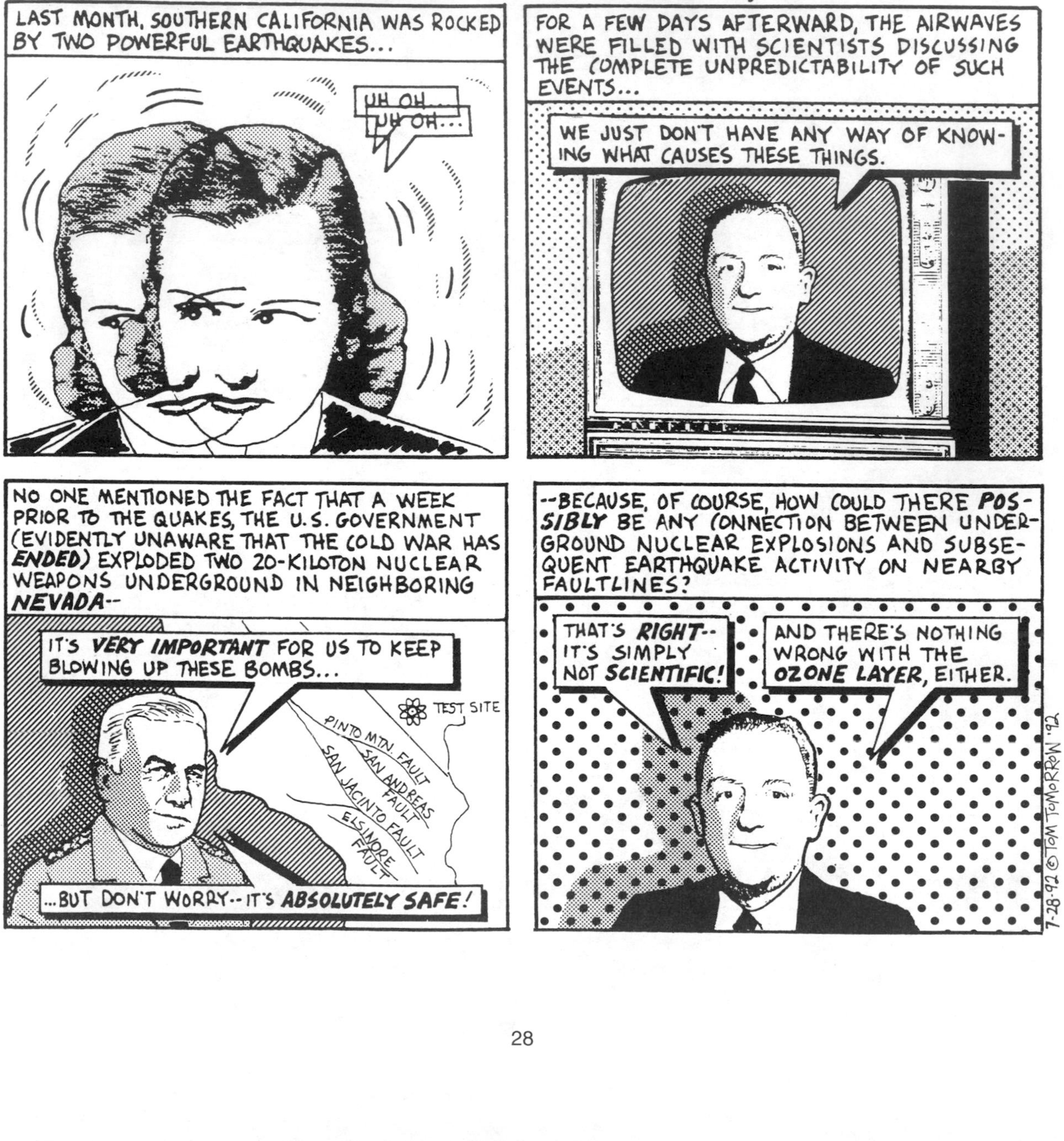
LAST MONTH, SOUTHERN CALIFORNIA WAS ROCKED BY TWO POWERFUL EARTHQUAKES...
UH OH...
UH OH...
FOR A FEW DAYS AFTERWARD, THE AIRWAVES WERE FILLED WITH SCIENTISTS DISCUSSING THE COMPLETE UNPREDICTABILITY OF SUCH EVENTS...
WE JUST DON'T HAVE ANY WAY OF KNOWING WHAT CAUSES THESE THINGS.
NO ONE MENTIONED THE FACT THAT A WEEK PRIOR TO THE QUAKES, THE U.S. GOVERNMENT (EVIDENTLY UNAWARE THAT THE COLD WAR HAS **ENDED**) EXPLODED TWO 20-KILOTON NUCLEAR WEAPONS UNDERGROUND IN NEIGHBORING **NEVADA**--
IT'S **VERY IMPORTANT** FOR US TO KEEP BLOWING UP THESE BOMBS...
TEST SITE
PINTO MTN. FAULT
SAN ANDREAS FAULT
SAN JACINTO FAULT
ELSINORE FAULT
...BUT DON'T WORRY-- IT'S **ABSOLUTELY SAFE**!
--BECAUSE, OF COURSE, HOW COULD THERE **POSSIBLY** BE ANY CONNECTION BETWEEN UNDERGROUND NUCLEAR EXPLOSIONS AND SUBSEQUENT EARTHQUAKE ACTIVITY ON NEARBY FAULTLINES?
THAT'S **RIGHT**-- IT'S SIMPLY NOT **SCIENTIFIC**!
AND THERE'S NOTHING WRONG WITH THE **OZONE LAYER**, EITHER.
7-28-92 © TOM TOMORROW '92

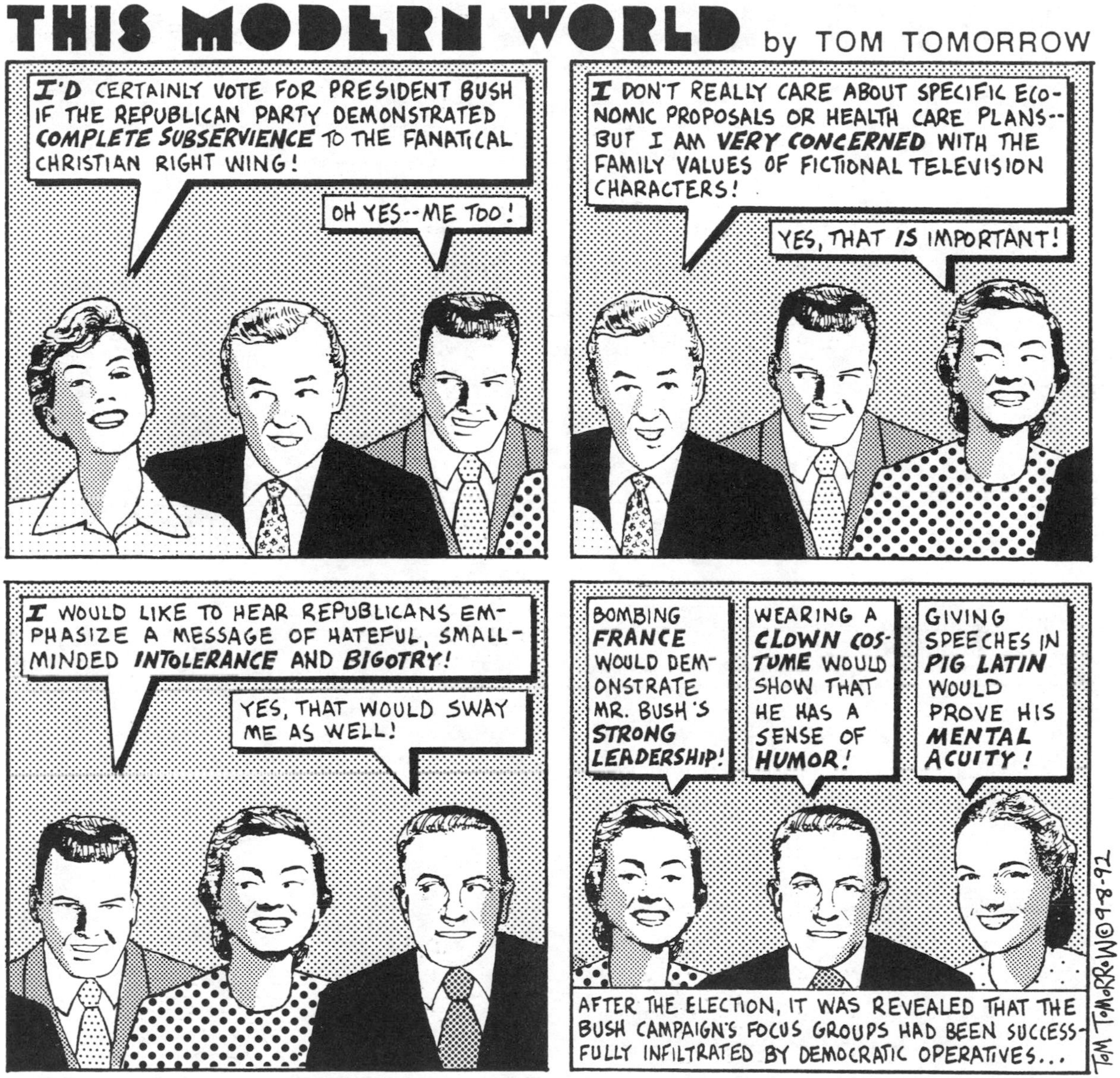
THIS MODERN WORLD by TOM TOMORROW
I'D CERTAINLY VOTE FOR PRESIDENT BUSH IF THE REPUBLICAN PARTY DEMONSTRATED COMPLETE SUBSERVIENCE TO THE FANATICAL CHRISTIAN RIGHT WING!
OH YES--ME TOO!
I DON'T REALLY CARE ABOUT SPECIFIC ECONOMIC PROPOSALS OR HEALTH CARE PLANS-- BUT I AM VERY CONCERNED WITH THE FAMILY VALUES OF FICTIONAL TELEVISION CHARACTERS!
YES, THAT IS IMPORTANT!
I WOULD LIKE TO HEAR REPUBLICANS EMPHASIZE A MESSAGE OF HATEFUL, SMALL-MINDED INTOLERANCE AND BIGOTRY!
YES, THAT WOULD SWAY ME AS WELL!
BOMBING FRANCE WOULD DEMONSTRATE MR. BUSH'S STRONG LEADERSHIP!
WEARING A CLOWN COSTUME WOULD SHOW THAT HE HAS A SENSE OF HUMOR!
GIVING SPEECHES IN PIG LATIN WOULD PROVE HIS MENTAL ACUITY!
AFTER THE ELECTION, IT WAS REVEALED THAT THE BUSH CAMPAIGN'S FOCUS GROUPS HAD BEEN SUCCESSFULLY INFILTRATED BY DEMOCRATIC OPERATIVES...
TOM TOMORROW ©9-8-92

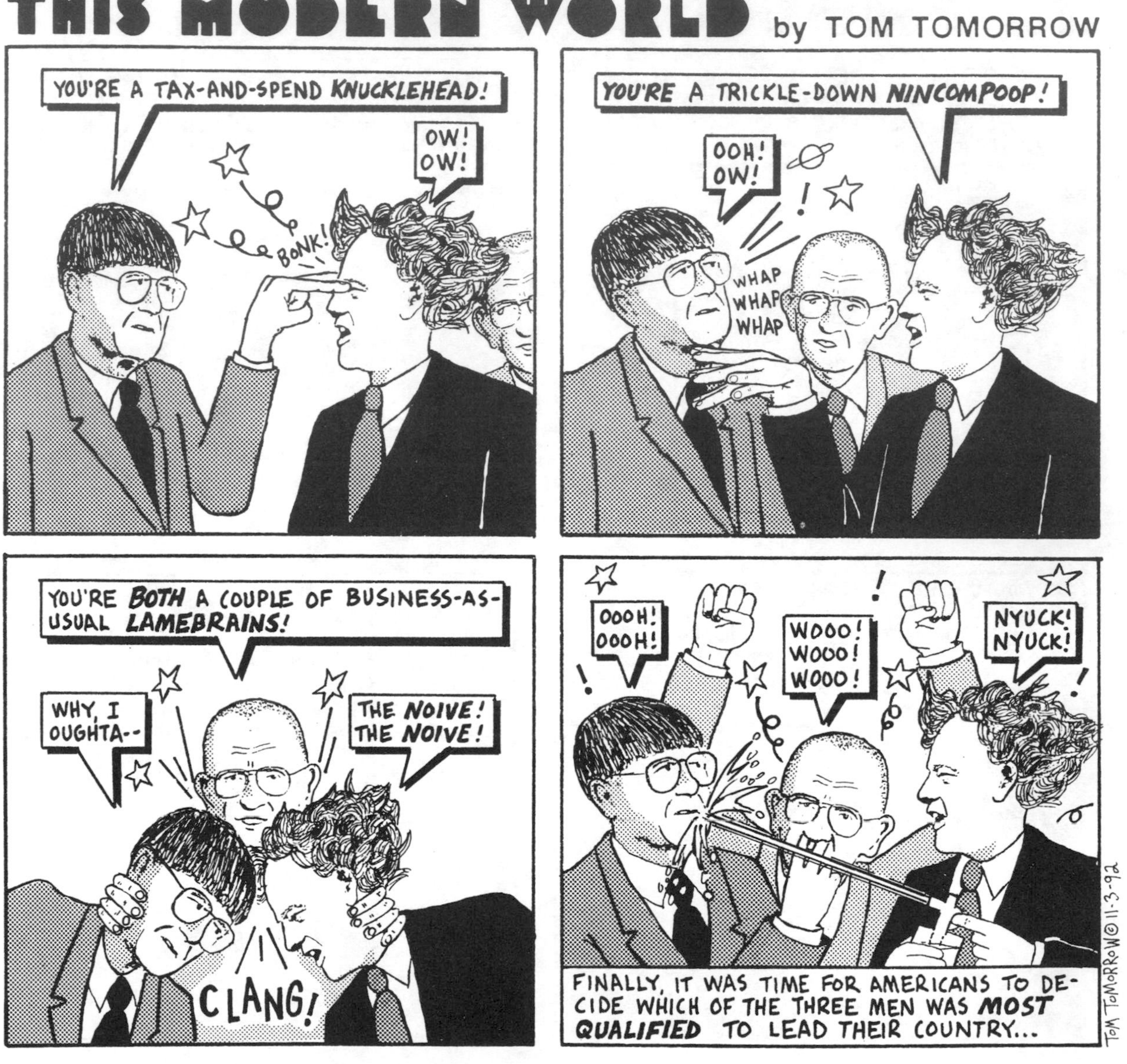
THIS MODERN WORLD by TOM TOMORROW
YOU'RE A TAX-AND-SPEND KNUCKLEHEAD!
OW! OW!
BONK!
YOU'RE A TRICKLE-DOWN NINCOMPOOP!
OOH! OW!
WHAP WHAP WHAP
YOU'RE BOTH A COUPLE OF BUSINESS-AS-USUAL LAMEBRAINS!
WHY, I OUGHTA--
THE NOIVE! THE NOIVE!
CLANG!
OOOH! OOOH!
WOOO! WOOO! WOOO!
NYUCK! NYUCK!
FINALLY, IT WAS TIME FOR AMERICANS TO DECIDE WHICH OF THE THREE MEN WAS MOST QUALIFIED TO LEAD THEIR COUNTRY...
TOM TOMORROW © 11-3-92

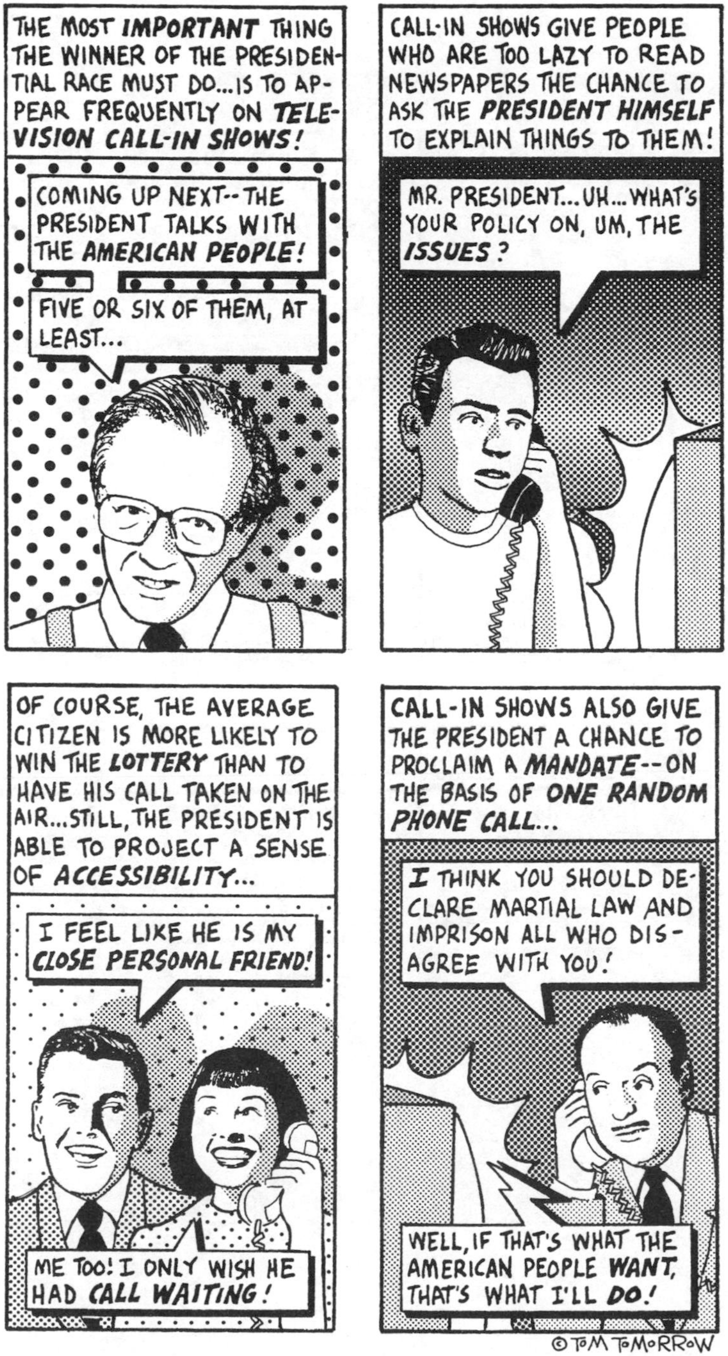
THE MOST IMPORTANT THING THE WINNER OF THE PRESIDENTIAL RACE MUST DO...IS TO APPEAR FREQUENTLY ON TELEVISION CALL-IN SHOWS!
COMING UP NEXT--THE PRESIDENT TALKS WITH THE AMERICAN PEOPLE!
FIVE OR SIX OF THEM, AT LEAST...
CALL-IN SHOWS GIVE PEOPLE WHO ARE TOO LAZY TO READ NEWSPAPERS THE CHANCE TO ASK THE PRESIDENT HIMSELF TO EXPLAIN THINGS TO THEM!
MR. PRESIDENT...UH...WHAT'S YOUR POLICY ON, UM, THE ISSUES?
OF COURSE, THE AVERAGE CITIZEN IS MORE LIKELY TO WIN THE LOTTERY THAN TO HAVE HIS CALL TAKEN ON THE AIR...STILL, THE PRESIDENT IS ABLE TO PROJECT A SENSE OF ACCESSIBILITY...
I FEEL LIKE HE IS MY CLOSE PERSONAL FRIEND!
ME TOO! I ONLY WISH HE HAD CALL WAITING!
CALL-IN SHOWS ALSO GIVE THE PRESIDENT A CHANCE TO PROCLAIM A MANDATE--ON THE BASIS OF ONE RANDOM PHONE CALL...
I THINK YOU SHOULD DECLARE MARTIAL LAW AND IMPRISON ALL WHO DISAGREE WITH YOU!
WELL, IF THAT'S WHAT THE AMERICAN PEOPLE WANT, THAT'S WHAT I'LL DO!
© TOM TOMORROW

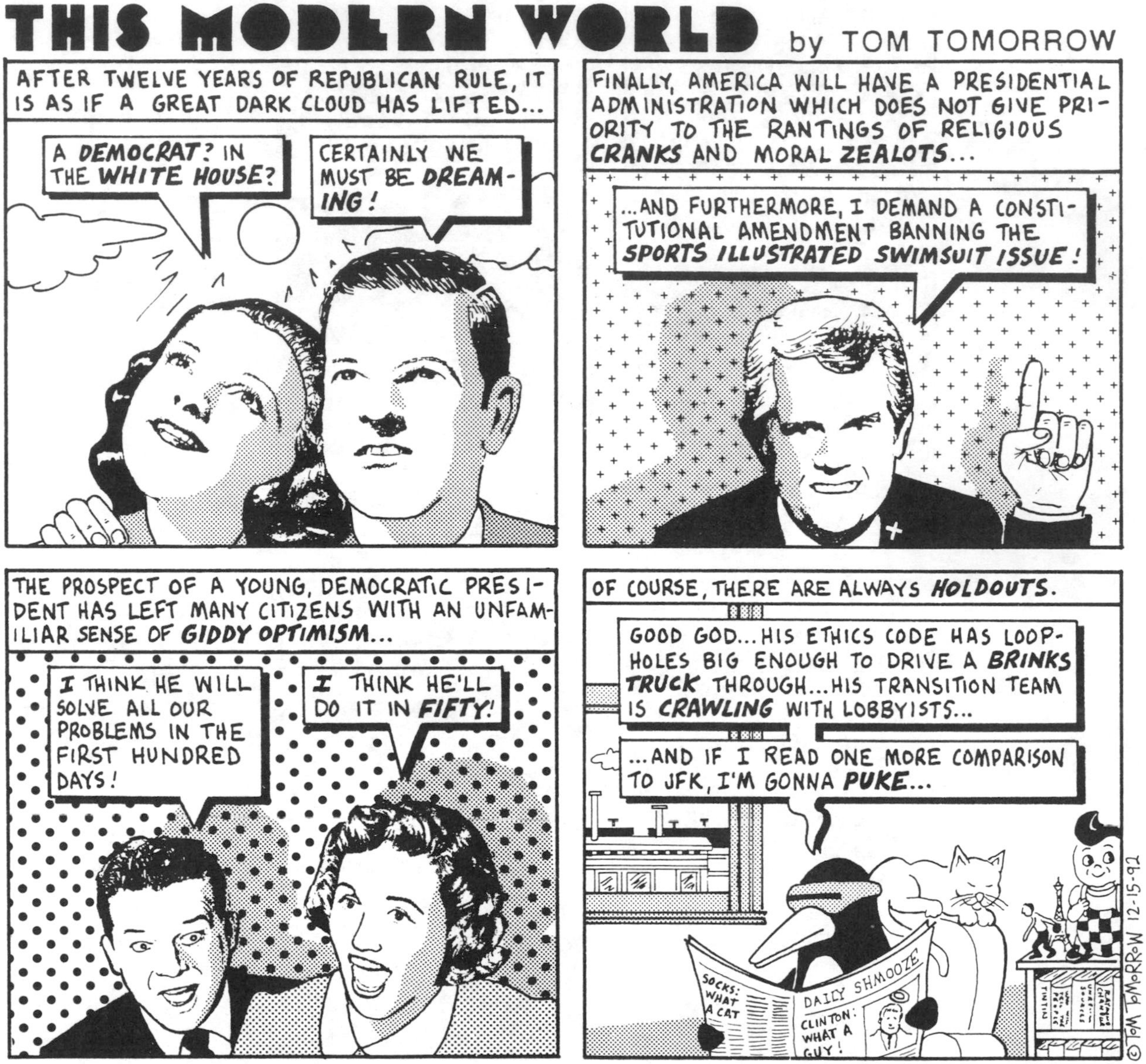
THIS MODERN WORLD by TOM TOMORROW
AFTER TWELVE YEARS OF REPUBLICAN RULE, IT IS AS IF A GREAT DARK CLOUD HAS LIFTED...
A DEMOCRAT? IN THE WHITE HOUSE?
CERTAINLY WE MUST BE DREAMING!
FINALLY, AMERICA WILL HAVE A PRESIDENTIAL ADMINISTRATION WHICH DOES NOT GIVE PRIORITY TO THE RANTINGS OF RELIGIOUS CRANKS AND MORAL ZEALOTS...
...AND FURTHERMORE, I DEMAND A CONSTITUTIONAL AMENDMENT BANNING THE SPORTS ILLUSTRATED SWIMSUIT ISSUE!
THE PROSPECT OF A YOUNG, DEMOCRATIC PRESIDENT HAS LEFT MANY CITIZENS WITH AN UNFAMILIAR SENSE OF GIDDY OPTIMISM...
I THINK HE WILL SOLVE ALL OUR PROBLEMS IN THE FIRST HUNDRED DAYS!
I THINK HE'LL DO IT IN FIFTY!
OF COURSE, THERE ARE ALWAYS HOLDOUTS.
GOOD GOD... HIS ETHICS CODE HAS LOOPHOLES BIG ENOUGH TO DRIVE A BRINKS TRUCK THROUGH... HIS TRANSITION TEAM IS CRAWLING WITH LOBBYISTS...
...AND IF I READ ONE MORE COMPARISON TO JFK, I'M GONNA PUKE...
SOCKS: WHAT A CAT
DAILY SHMOOZE
CLINTON: WHAT A GUY!
© TOM TOMORROW 12-15-92

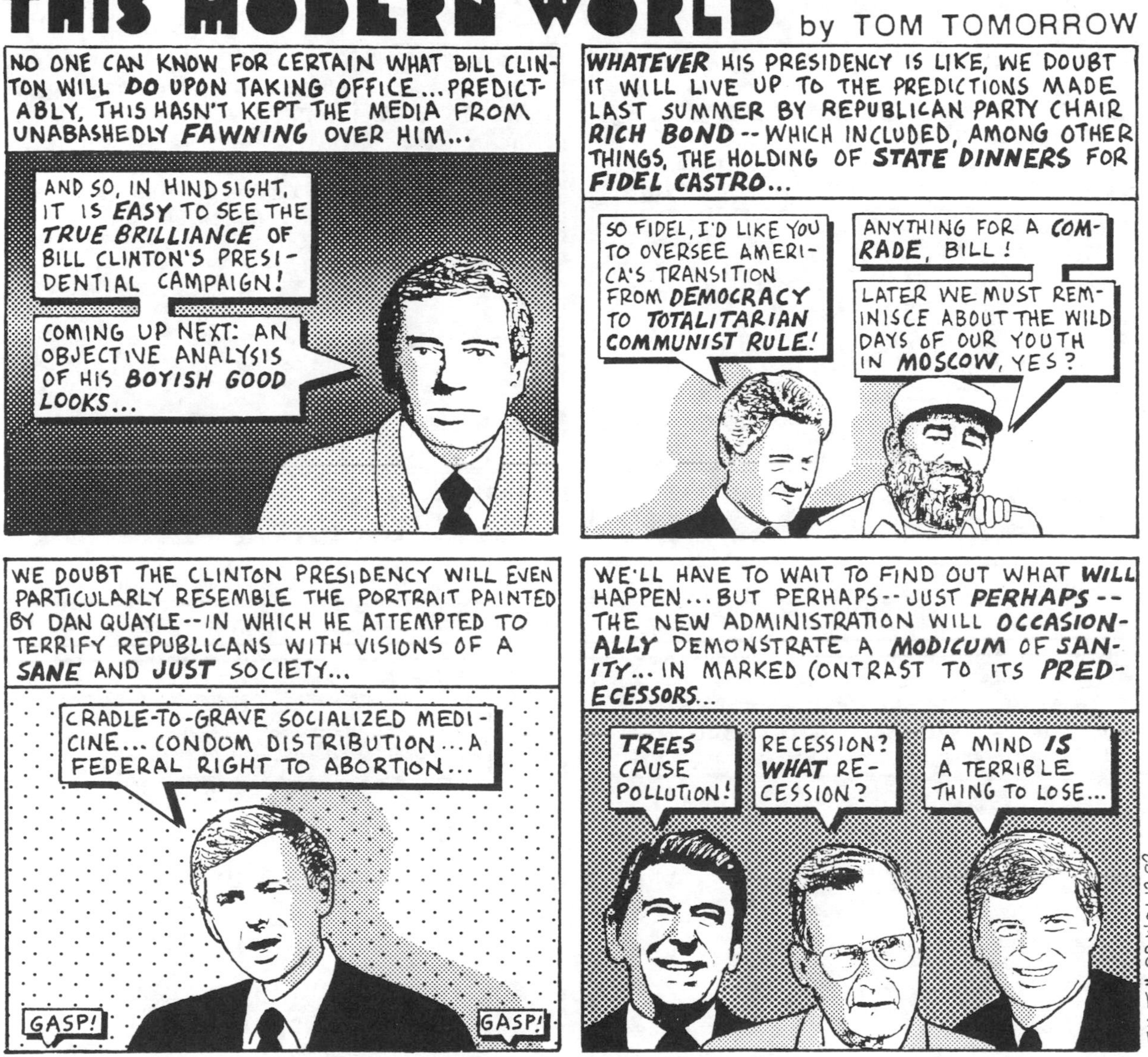
THIS MODERN WORLD by TOM TOMORROW
NO ONE CAN KNOW FOR CERTAIN WHAT BILL CLINTON WILL DO UPON TAKING OFFICE... PREDICTABLY, THIS HASN'T KEPT THE MEDIA FROM UNABASHEDLY FAWNING OVER HIM...
AND SO, IN HINDSIGHT, IT IS EASY TO SEE THE TRUE BRILLIANCE OF BILL CLINTON'S PRESIDENTIAL CAMPAIGN!
COMING UP NEXT: AN OBJECTIVE ANALYSIS OF HIS BOYISH GOOD LOOKS...
WHATEVER HIS PRESIDENCY IS LIKE, WE DOUBT IT WILL LIVE UP TO THE PREDICTIONS MADE LAST SUMMER BY REPUBLICAN PARTY CHAIR RICH BOND -- WHICH INCLUDED, AMONG OTHER THINGS, THE HOLDING OF STATE DINNERS FOR FIDEL CASTRO...
SO FIDEL, I'D LIKE YOU TO OVERSEE AMERICA'S TRANSITION FROM DEMOCRACY TO TOTALITARIAN COMMUNIST RULE!
ANYTHING FOR A COMRADE, BILL!
LATER WE MUST REMINISCE ABOUT THE WILD DAYS OF OUR YOUTH IN MOSCOW, YES?
WE DOUBT THE CLINTON PRESIDENCY WILL EVEN PARTICULARLY RESEMBLE THE PORTRAIT PAINTED BY DAN QUAYLE -- IN WHICH HE ATTEMPTED TO TERRIFY REPUBLICANS WITH VISIONS OF A SANE AND JUST SOCIETY...
CRADLE-TO-GRAVE SOCIALIZED MEDICINE... CONDOM DISTRIBUTION... A FEDERAL RIGHT TO ABORTION...
GASP!
GASP!
WE'LL HAVE TO WAIT TO FIND OUT WHAT WILL HAPPEN... BUT PERHAPS -- JUST PERHAPS -- THE NEW ADMINISTRATION WILL OCCASIONALLY DEMONSTRATE A MODICUM OF SANITY... IN MARKED CONTRAST TO ITS PREDECESSORS...
TREES CAUSE POLLUTION!
RECESSION? WHAT RECESSION?
A MIND IS A TERRIBLE THING TO LOSE...
TOM TOMORROW©1-12-93

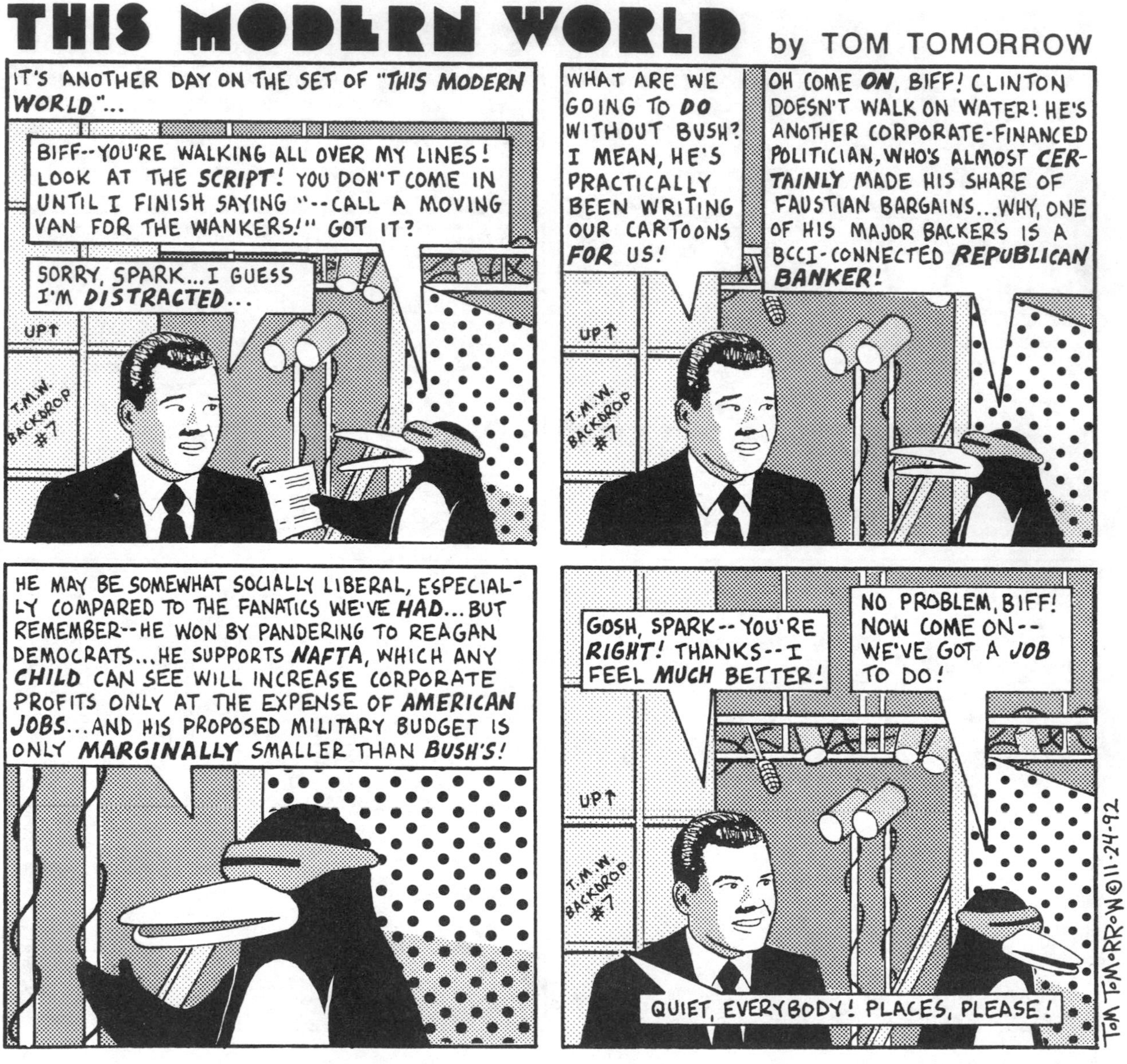
THIS MODERN WORLD by TOM TOMORROW
IT'S ANOTHER DAY ON THE SET OF "THIS MODERN WORLD"...
BIFF--YOU'RE WALKING ALL OVER MY LINES! LOOK AT THE SCRIPT! YOU DON'T COME IN UNTIL I FINISH SAYING "--CALL A MOVING VAN FOR THE WANKERS!" GOT IT?
SORRY, SPARK...I GUESS I'M DISTRACTED...
UP↑
T.M.W. BACKDROP #7
WHAT ARE WE GOING TO DO WITHOUT BUSH? I MEAN, HE'S PRACTICALLY BEEN WRITING OUR CARTOONS FOR US!
OH COME ON, BIFF! CLINTON DOESN'T WALK ON WATER! HE'S ANOTHER CORPORATE-FINANCED POLITICIAN, WHO'S ALMOST CERTAINLY MADE HIS SHARE OF FAUSTIAN BARGAINS...WHY, ONE OF HIS MAJOR BACKERS IS A BCCI-CONNECTED REPUBLICAN BANKER!
UP↑
T.M.W. BACKDROP #7
HE MAY BE SOMEWHAT SOCIALLY LIBERAL, ESPECIALLY COMPARED TO THE FANATICS WE'VE HAD... BUT REMEMBER--HE WON BY PANDERING TO REAGAN DEMOCRATS...HE SUPPORTS NAFTA, WHICH ANY CHILD CAN SEE WILL INCREASE CORPORATE PROFITS ONLY AT THE EXPENSE OF AMERICAN JOBS...AND HIS PROPOSED MILITARY BUDGET IS ONLY MARGINALLY SMALLER THAN BUSH'S!
GOSH, SPARK--YOU'RE RIGHT! THANKS--I FEEL MUCH BETTER!
NO PROBLEM, BIFF! NOW COME ON--WE'VE GOT A JOB TO DO!
UP↑
T.M.W. BACKDROP #7
QUIET, EVERYBODY! PLACES, PLEASE!
TOM TOMORROW©11-24-92

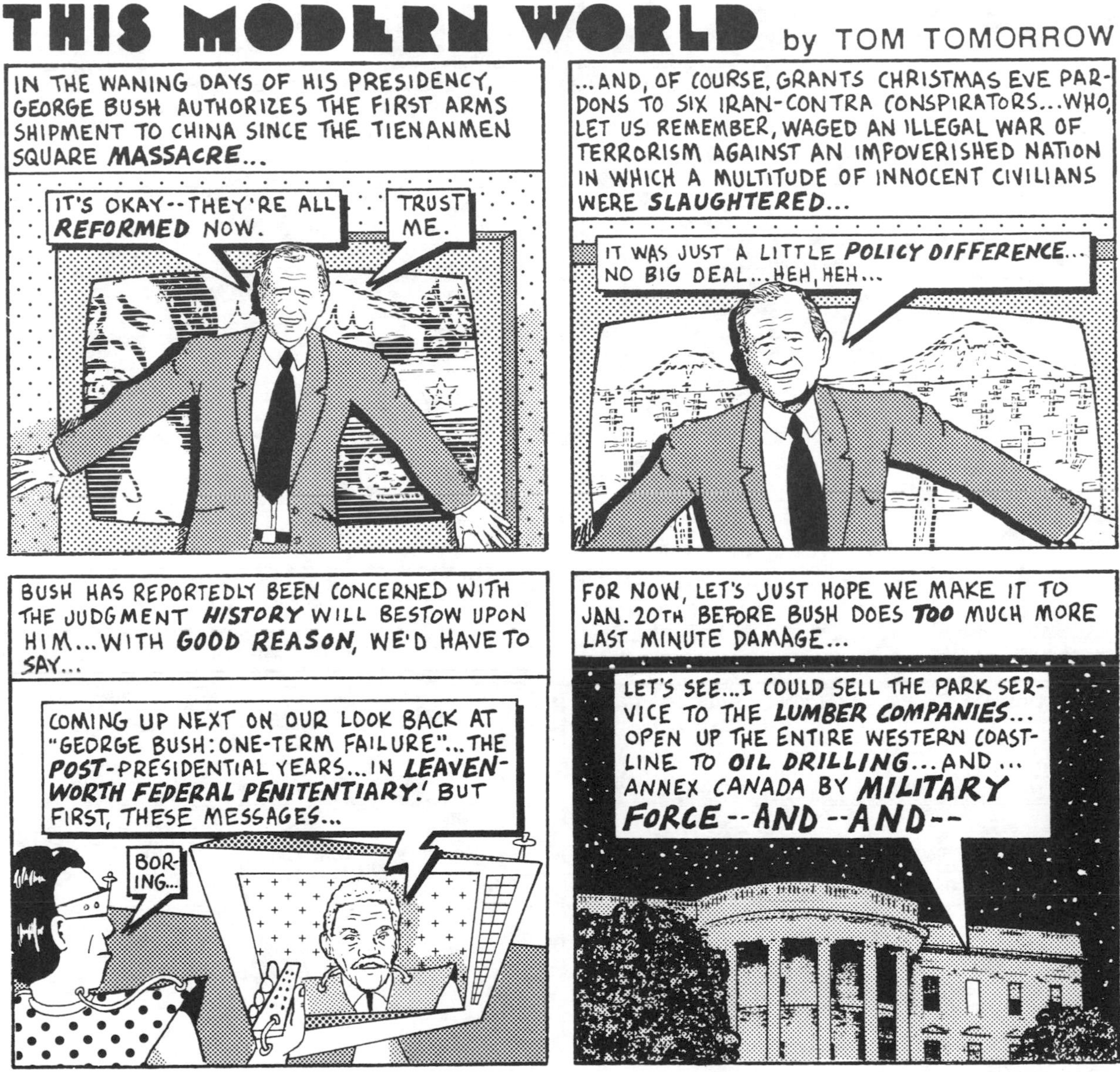
THIS MODERN WORLD by TOM TOMORROW
IN THE WANING DAYS OF HIS PRESIDENCY, GEORGE BUSH AUTHORIZES THE FIRST ARMS SHIPMENT TO CHINA SINCE THE TIENANMEN SQUARE MASSACRE...
IT'S OKAY--THEY'RE ALL REFORMED NOW.
TRUST ME.
...AND, OF COURSE, GRANTS CHRISTMAS EVE PARDONS TO SIX IRAN-CONTRA CONSPIRATORS...WHO, LET US REMEMBER, WAGED AN ILLEGAL WAR OF TERRORISM AGAINST AN IMPOVERISHED NATION IN WHICH A MULTITUDE OF INNOCENT CIVILIANS WERE SLAUGHTERED...
IT WAS JUST A LITTLE POLICY DIFFERENCE... NO BIG DEAL...HEH, HEH...
BUSH HAS REPORTEDLY BEEN CONCERNED WITH THE JUDGMENT HISTORY WILL BESTOW UPON HIM...WITH GOOD REASON, WE'D HAVE TO SAY...
COMING UP NEXT ON OUR LOOK BACK AT "GEORGE BUSH: ONE-TERM FAILURE"... THE POST-PRESIDENTIAL YEARS...IN LEAVENWORTH FEDERAL PENITENTIARY! BUT FIRST, THESE MESSAGES...
BORING...
FOR NOW, LET'S JUST HOPE WE MAKE IT TO JAN. 20TH BEFORE BUSH DOES TOO MUCH MORE LAST MINUTE DAMAGE...
LET'S SEE...I COULD SELL THE PARK SERVICE TO THE LUMBER COMPANIES... OPEN UP THE ENTIRE WESTERN COASTLINE TO OIL DRILLING...AND... ANNEX CANADA BY MILITARY FORCE--AND--AND--
© TOM TOMORROW '92

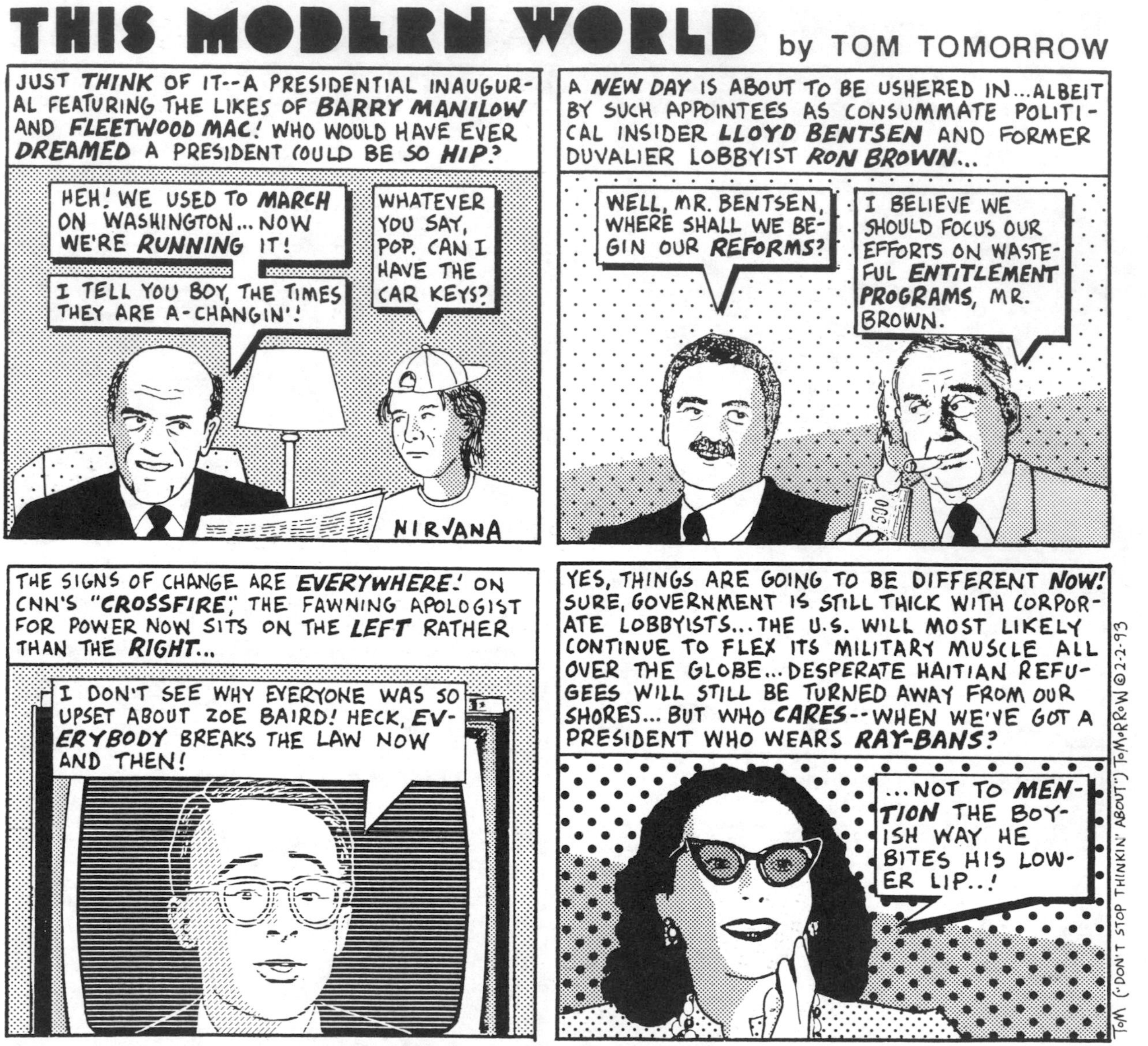
THIS MODERN WORLD by TOM TOMORROW
JUST THINK OF IT--A PRESIDENTIAL INAUGURAL FEATURING THE LIKES OF BARRY MANILOW AND FLEETWOOD MAC! WHO WOULD HAVE EVER DREAMED A PRESIDENT COULD BE SO HIP?
HEH! WE USED TO MARCH ON WASHINGTON... NOW WE'RE RUNNING IT!
I TELL YOU BOY, THE TIMES THEY ARE A-CHANGIN'!
WHATEVER YOU SAY, POP. CAN I HAVE THE CAR KEYS?
NIRVANA
A NEW DAY IS ABOUT TO BE USHERED IN...ALBEIT BY SUCH APPOINTEES AS CONSUMMATE POLITICAL INSIDER LLOYD BENTSEN AND FORMER DUVALIER LOBBYIST RON BROWN...
WELL, MR. BENTSEN, WHERE SHALL WE BEGIN OUR REFORMS?
I BELIEVE WE SHOULD FOCUS OUR EFFORTS ON WASTEFUL ENTITLEMENT PROGRAMS, MR. BROWN.
500
THE SIGNS OF CHANGE ARE EVERYWHERE! ON CNN'S "CROSSFIRE," THE FAWNING APOLOGIST FOR POWER NOW SITS ON THE LEFT RATHER THAN THE RIGHT...
I DON'T SEE WHY EVERYONE WAS SO UPSET ABOUT ZOE BAIRD! HECK, EVERYBODY BREAKS THE LAW NOW AND THEN!
YES, THINGS ARE GOING TO BE DIFFERENT NOW! SURE, GOVERNMENT IS STILL THICK WITH CORPORATE LOBBYISTS... THE U.S. WILL MOST LIKELY CONTINUE TO FLEX ITS MILITARY MUSCLE ALL OVER THE GLOBE... DESPERATE HAITIAN REFUGEES WILL STILL BE TURNED AWAY FROM OUR SHORES... BUT WHO CARES--WHEN WE'VE GOT A PRESIDENT WHO WEARS RAY-BANS?
...NOT TO MENTION THE BOYISH WAY HE BITES HIS LOWER LIP..!
TOM ("DON'T STOP THINKIN' ABOUT") TOMORROW ©2-2-93

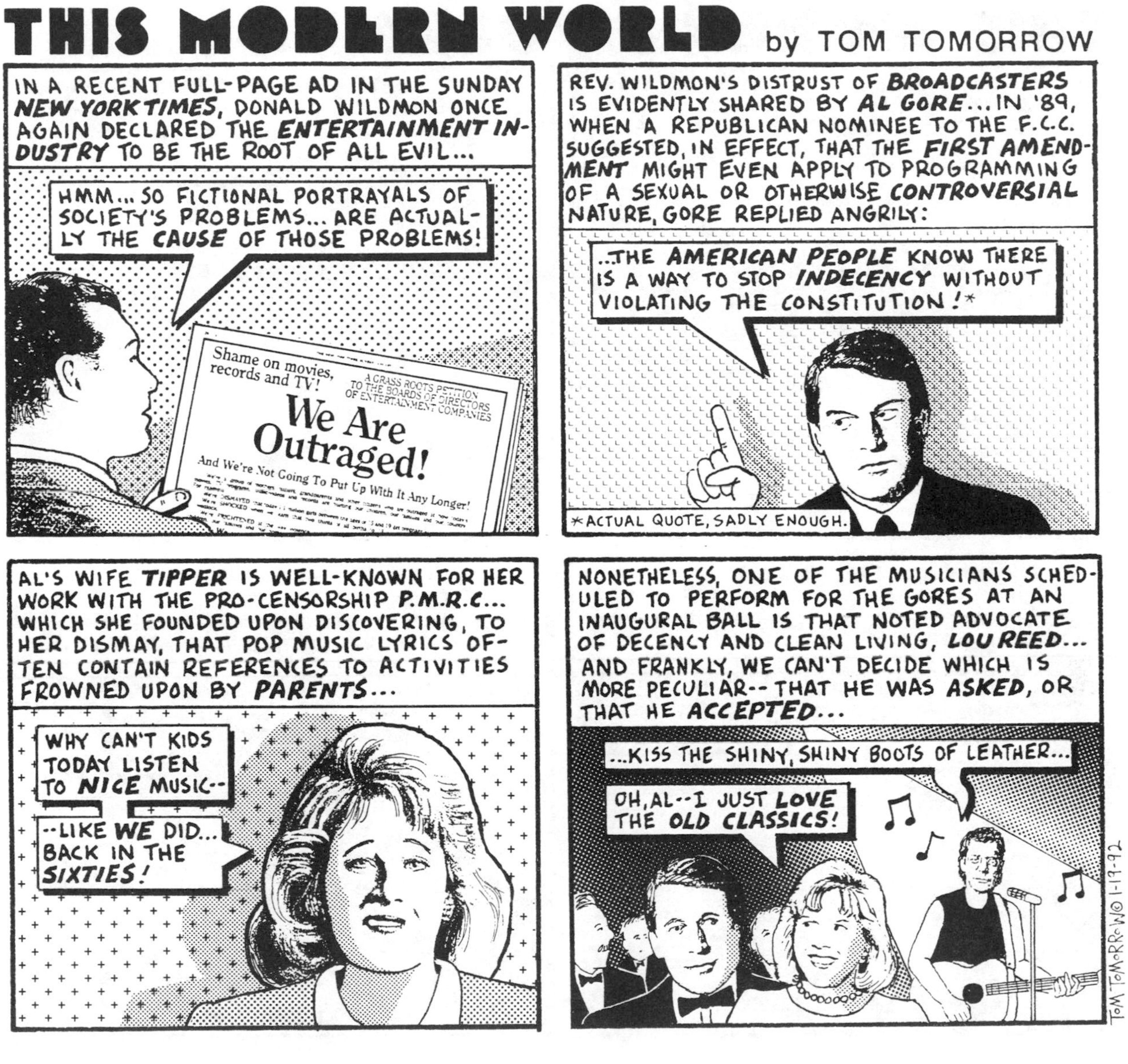
THIS MODERN WORLD by TOM TOMORROW
IN A RECENT FULL-PAGE AD IN THE SUNDAY NEW YORK TIMES, DONALD WILDMON ONCE AGAIN DECLARED THE ENTERTAINMENT INDUSTRY TO BE THE ROOT OF ALL EVIL...
HMM... SO FICTIONAL PORTRAYALS OF SOCIETY'S PROBLEMS... ARE ACTUALLY THE CAUSE OF THOSE PROBLEMS!
Shame on movies, records and TV!
A GRASS ROOTS PETITION TO THE BOARDS OF DIRECTORS OF ENTERTAINMENT COMPANIES
We Are Outraged!
And We're Not Going To Put Up With It Any Longer!
REV. WILDMON'S DISTRUST OF BROADCASTERS IS EVIDENTLY SHARED BY AL GORE... IN '89, WHEN A REPUBLICAN NOMINEE TO THE F.C.C. SUGGESTED, IN EFFECT, THAT THE FIRST AMENDMENT MIGHT EVEN APPLY TO PROGRAMMING OF A SEXUAL OR OTHERWISE CONTROVERSIAL NATURE, GORE REPLIED ANGRILY:
...THE AMERICAN PEOPLE KNOW THERE IS A WAY TO STOP INDECENCY WITHOUT VIOLATING THE CONSTITUTION!*
*ACTUAL QUOTE, SADLY ENOUGH.
AL'S WIFE TIPPER IS WELL-KNOWN FOR HER WORK WITH THE PRO-CENSORSHIP P.M.R.C... WHICH SHE FOUNDED UPON DISCOVERING, TO HER DISMAY, THAT POP MUSIC LYRICS OFTEN CONTAIN REFERENCES TO ACTIVITIES FROWNED UPON BY PARENTS...
WHY CAN'T KIDS TODAY LISTEN TO NICE MUSIC--
--LIKE WE DID... BACK IN THE SIXTIES!
NONETHELESS, ONE OF THE MUSICIANS SCHEDULED TO PERFORM FOR THE GORES AT AN INAUGURAL BALL IS THAT NOTED ADVOCATE OF DECENCY AND CLEAN LIVING, LOU REED... AND FRANKLY, WE CAN'T DECIDE WHICH IS MORE PECULIAR-- THAT HE WAS ASKED, OR THAT HE ACCEPTED...
...KISS THE SHINY, SHINY BOOTS OF LEATHER...
OH, AL--I JUST LOVE THE OLD CLASSICS!
TOM TOMORROW © 1-19-92

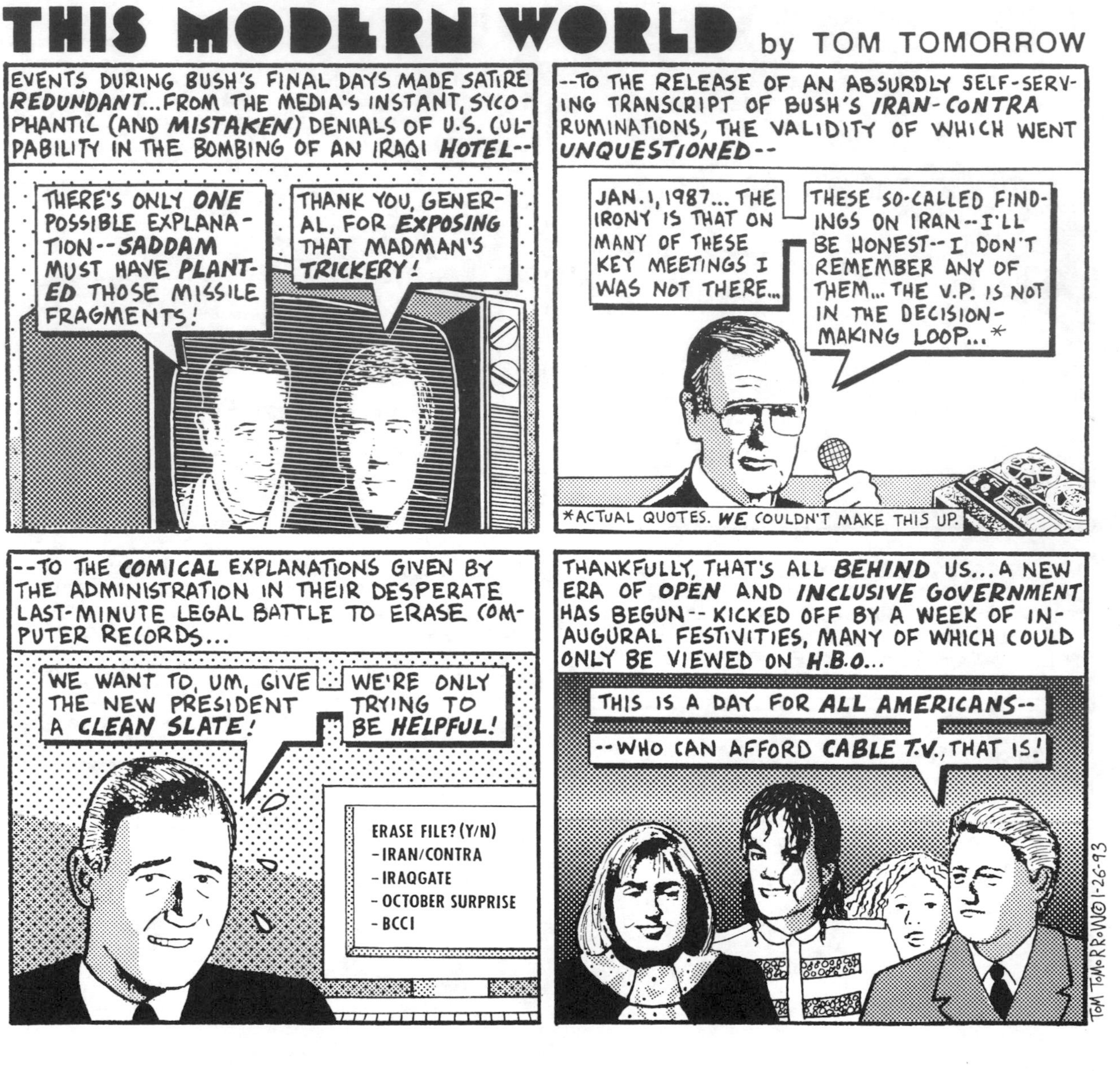
THIS MODERN WORLD by TOM TOMORROW
EVENTS DURING BUSH'S FINAL DAYS MADE SATIRE REDUNDANT... FROM THE MEDIA'S INSTANT, SYCOPHANTIC (AND MISTAKEN) DENIALS OF U.S. CULPABILITY IN THE BOMBING OF AN IRAQI HOTEL--
THERE'S ONLY ONE POSSIBLE EXPLANATION--SADDAM MUST HAVE PLANTED THOSE MISSILE FRAGMENTS!
THANK YOU, GENERAL, FOR EXPOSING THAT MADMAN'S TRICKERY!
--TO THE RELEASE OF AN ABSURDLY SELF-SERVING TRANSCRIPT OF BUSH'S IRAN-CONTRA RUMINATIONS, THE VALIDITY OF WHICH WENT UNQUESTIONED--
JAN. 1, 1987... THE IRONY IS THAT ON MANY OF THESE KEY MEETINGS I WAS NOT THERE...
THESE SO-CALLED FINDINGS ON IRAN--I'LL BE HONEST--I DON'T REMEMBER ANY OF THEM... THE V.P. IS NOT IN THE DECISION-MAKING LOOP...*
*ACTUAL QUOTES. WE COULDN'T MAKE THIS UP.
--TO THE COMICAL EXPLANATIONS GIVEN BY THE ADMINISTRATION IN THEIR DESPERATE LAST-MINUTE LEGAL BATTLE TO ERASE COMPUTER RECORDS...
WE WANT TO, UM, GIVE THE NEW PRESIDENT A CLEAN SLATE!
WE'RE ONLY TRYING TO BE HELPFUL!
ERASE FILE? (Y/N)
-IRAN/CONTRA
-IRAQGATE
-OCTOBER SURPRISE
-BCCI
THANKFULLY, THAT'S ALL BEHIND US... A NEW ERA OF OPEN AND INCLUSIVE GOVERNMENT HAS BEGUN--KICKED OFF BY A WEEK OF INAUGURAL FESTIVITIES, MANY OF WHICH COULD ONLY BE VIEWED ON H.B.O...
THIS IS A DAY FOR ALL AMERICANS--
--WHO CAN AFFORD CABLE T.V., THAT IS!
TOM TOMORROW©1-26-93

DURING THE INAUGURAL *HOOPLA*, A CERTAIN CYNICAL PENGUIN DECIDES THE ONLY WAY TO AVOID LISTENING TO "DON'T STOP THINKIN' ABOUT TOMORROW" FOR A SOLID *WEEK* IS TO LEAVE THE *COUNTRY*... SO, WHILE AMERICANS *FAWN* OVER THEIR NEW PRESIDENT--

SPARKY goes to PARIS

A MOSTLY-TRUE CARTOON TRAVELOGUE BY **TOM TOMORROW**

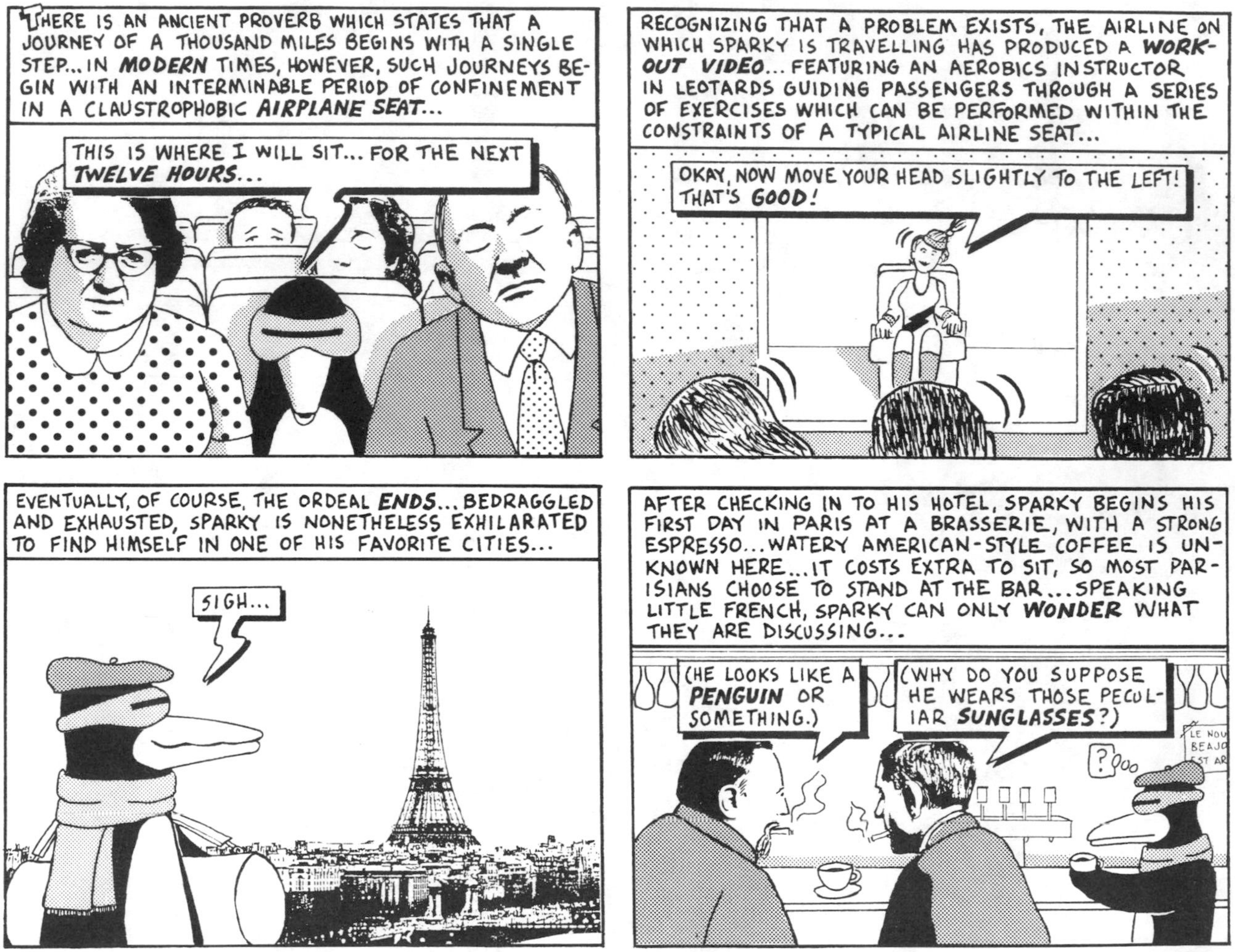
THERE IS AN ANCIENT PROVERB WHICH STATES THAT A JOURNEY OF A THOUSAND MILES BEGINS WITH A SINGLE STEP... IN MODERN TIMES, HOWEVER, SUCH JOURNEYS BEGIN WITH AN INTERMINABLE PERIOD OF CONFINEMENT IN A CLAUSTROPHOBIC AIRPLANE SEAT...
THIS IS WHERE I WILL SIT... FOR THE NEXT TWELVE HOURS...
RECOGNIZING THAT A PROBLEM EXISTS, THE AIRLINE ON WHICH SPARKY IS TRAVELLING HAS PRODUCED A WORK-OUT VIDEO... FEATURING AN AEROBICS INSTRUCTOR IN LEOTARDS GUIDING PASSENGERS THROUGH A SERIES OF EXERCISES WHICH CAN BE PERFORMED WITHIN THE CONSTRAINTS OF A TYPICAL AIRLINE SEAT...
OKAY, NOW MOVE YOUR HEAD SLIGHTLY TO THE LEFT! THAT'S GOOD!
EVENTUALLY, OF COURSE, THE ORDEAL ENDS... BEDRAGGLED AND EXHAUSTED, SPARKY IS NONETHELESS EXHILARATED TO FIND HIMSELF IN ONE OF HIS FAVORITE CITIES...
SIGH...
AFTER CHECKING IN TO HIS HOTEL, SPARKY BEGINS HIS FIRST DAY IN PARIS AT A BRASSERIE, WITH A STRONG ESPRESSO... WATERY AMERICAN-STYLE COFFEE IS UNKNOWN HERE... IT COSTS EXTRA TO SIT, SO MOST PARISIANS CHOOSE TO STAND AT THE BAR... SPEAKING LITTLE FRENCH, SPARKY CAN ONLY WONDER WHAT THEY ARE DISCUSSING...
(HE LOOKS LIKE A PENGUIN OR SOMETHING.)
(WHY DO YOU SUPPOSE HE WEARS THOSE PECULIAR SUNGLASSES?)
?

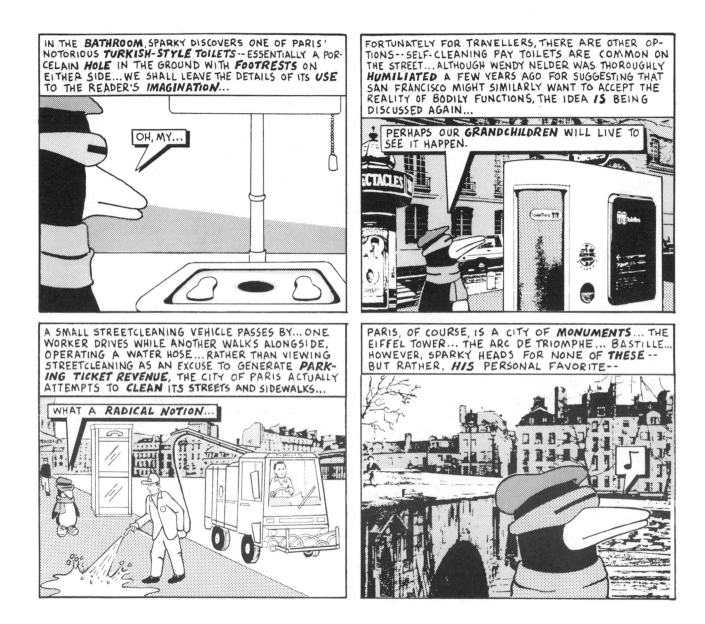

IN THE **BATHROOM**, SPARKY DISCOVERS ONE OF PARIS' NOTORIOUS **TURKISH-STYLE TOILETS** -- ESSENTIALLY A PORCELAIN **HOLE** IN THE GROUND WITH **FOOTRESTS** ON EITHER SIDE... WE SHALL LEAVE THE DETAILS OF ITS **USE** TO THE READER'S **IMAGINATION**...

OH, MY...

FORTUNATELY FOR TRAVELLERS, THERE ARE OTHER OPTIONS -- SELF-CLEANING PAY TOILETS ARE COMMON ON THE STREET... ALTHOUGH WENDY NELDER WAS THOROUGHLY **HUMILIATED** A FEW YEARS AGO FOR SUGGESTING THAT SAN FRANCISCO MIGHT SIMILARLY WANT TO ACCEPT THE REALITY OF BODILY FUNCTIONS, THE IDEA **IS** BEING DISCUSSED AGAIN...

PERHAPS OUR **GRANDCHILDREN** WILL LIVE TO SEE IT HAPPEN.

A SMALL STREETCLEANING VEHICLE PASSES BY... ONE WORKER DRIVES WHILE ANOTHER WALKS ALONGSIDE, OPERATING A WATER HOSE... RATHER THAN VIEWING STREETCLEANING AS AN EXCUSE TO GENERATE **PARKING TICKET REVENUE**, THE CITY OF PARIS ACTUALLY ATTEMPTS TO **CLEAN** ITS STREETS AND SIDEWALKS...

WHAT A **RADICAL NOTION**...

PARIS, OF COURSE, IS A CITY OF **MONUMENTS**... THE EIFFEL TOWER... THE ARC DE TRIOMPHE... BASTILLE... HOWEVER, SPARKY HEADS FOR NONE OF **THESE** -- BUT RATHER, **HIS** PERSONAL FAVORITE --

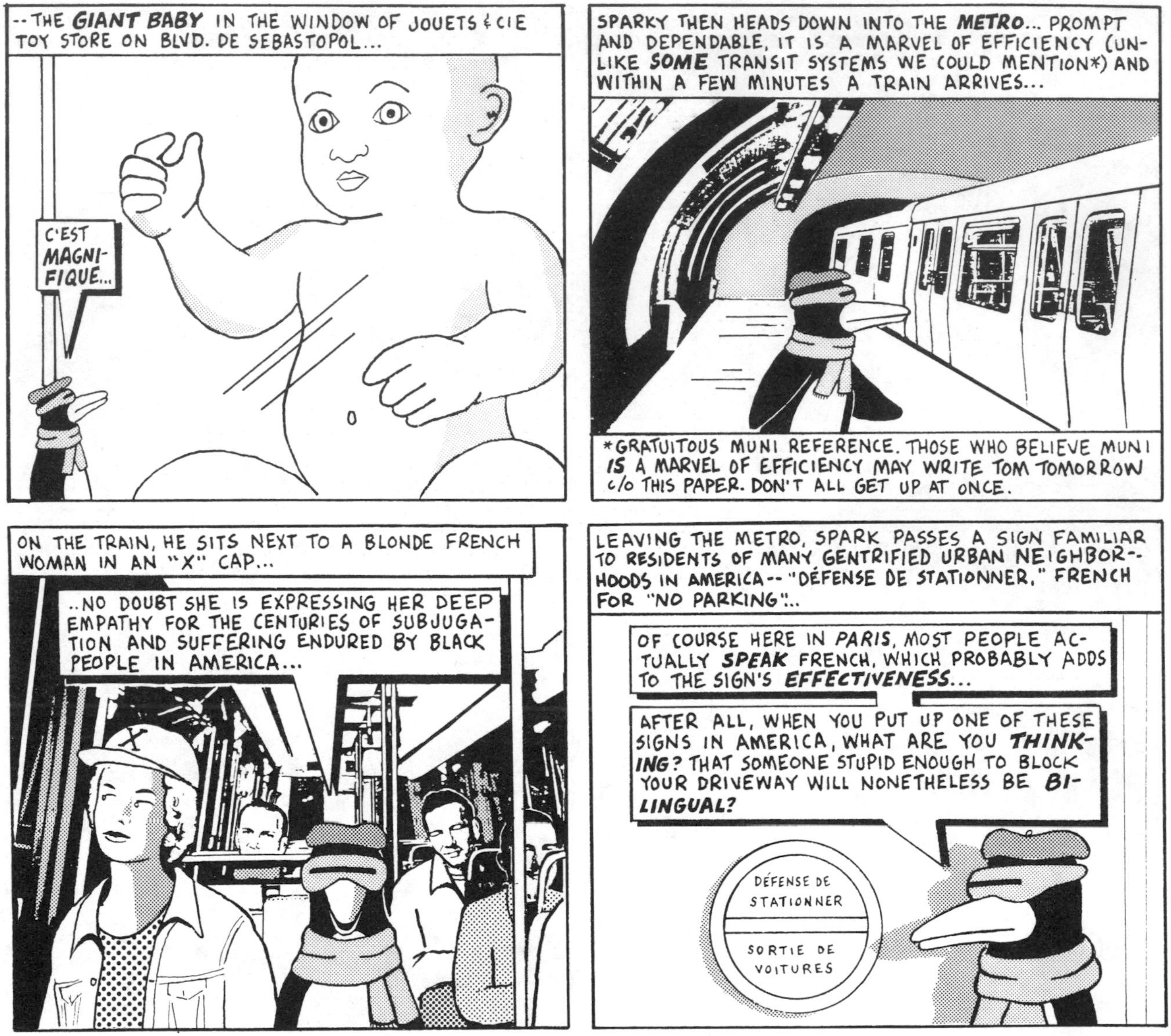
--THE GIANT BABY IN THE WINDOW OF JOUETS & CIE TOY STORE ON BLVD. DE SEBASTOPOL...
C'EST MAGNIFIQUE...
SPARKY THEN HEADS DOWN INTO THE METRO... PROMPT AND DEPENDABLE, IT IS A MARVEL OF EFFICIENCY (UNLIKE SOME TRANSIT SYSTEMS WE COULD MENTION*) AND WITHIN A FEW MINUTES A TRAIN ARRIVES...
*GRATUITOUS MUNI REFERENCE. THOSE WHO BELIEVE MUNI IS A MARVEL OF EFFICIENCY MAY WRITE TOM TOMORROW c/o THIS PAPER. DON'T ALL GET UP AT ONCE.
ON THE TRAIN, HE SITS NEXT TO A BLONDE FRENCH WOMAN IN AN "X" CAP...
..NO DOUBT SHE IS EXPRESSING HER DEEP EMPATHY FOR THE CENTURIES OF SUBJUGATION AND SUFFERING ENDURED BY BLACK PEOPLE IN AMERICA...
X
LEAVING THE METRO, SPARK PASSES A SIGN FAMILIAR TO RESIDENTS OF MANY GENTRIFIED URBAN NEIGHBOR-HOODS IN AMERICA-- "DÉFENSE DE STATIONNER," FRENCH FOR "NO PARKING"..
OF COURSE HERE IN PARIS, MOST PEOPLE ACTUALLY SPEAK FRENCH, WHICH PROBABLY ADDS TO THE SIGN'S EFFECTIVENESS...
AFTER ALL, WHEN YOU PUT UP ONE OF THESE SIGNS IN AMERICA, WHAT ARE YOU THINKING? THAT SOMEONE STUPID ENOUGH TO BLOCK YOUR DRIVEWAY WILL NONETHELESS BE BILINGUAL?
DÉFENSE DE STATIONNER
SORTIE DE VOITURES

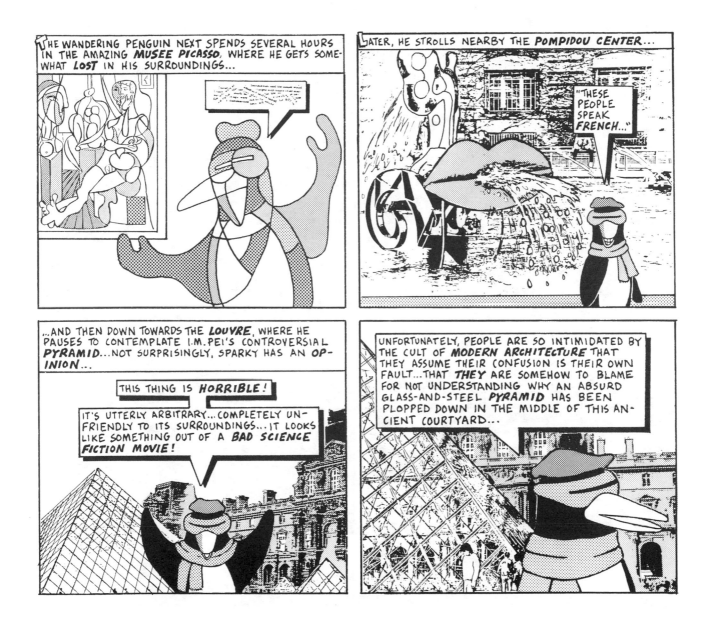

THE WANDERING PENGUIN NEXT SPENDS SEVERAL HOURS IN THE AMAZING *MUSEE PICASSO*, WHERE HE GETS SOMEWHAT *LOST* IN HIS SURROUNDINGS...

LATER, HE STROLLS NEARBY THE POMPIDOU CENTER...

"THESE PEOPLE SPEAK *FRENCH*..."

...AND THEN DOWN TOWARDS THE *LOUVRE*, WHERE HE PAUSES TO CONTEMPLATE I.M.PEI'S CONTROVERSIAL *PYRAMID*...NOT SURPRISINGLY, SPARKY HAS AN OPINION...

THIS THING IS *HORRIBLE!*

IT'S UTTERLY ARBITRARY...COMPLETELY UNFRIENDLY TO ITS SURROUNDINGS...IT LOOKS LIKE SOMETHING OUT OF A *BAD SCIENCE FICTION MOVIE!*

UNFORTUNATELY, PEOPLE ARE SO INTIMIDATED BY THE CULT OF *MODERN ARCHITECTURE* THAT THEY ASSUME THEIR CONFUSION IS THEIR OWN FAULT...THAT *THEY* ARE SOMEHOW TO BLAME FOR NOT UNDERSTANDING WHY AN ABSURD GLASS-AND-STEEL *PYRAMID* HAS BEEN PLOPPED DOWN IN THE MIDDLE OF THIS ANCIENT COURTYARD...

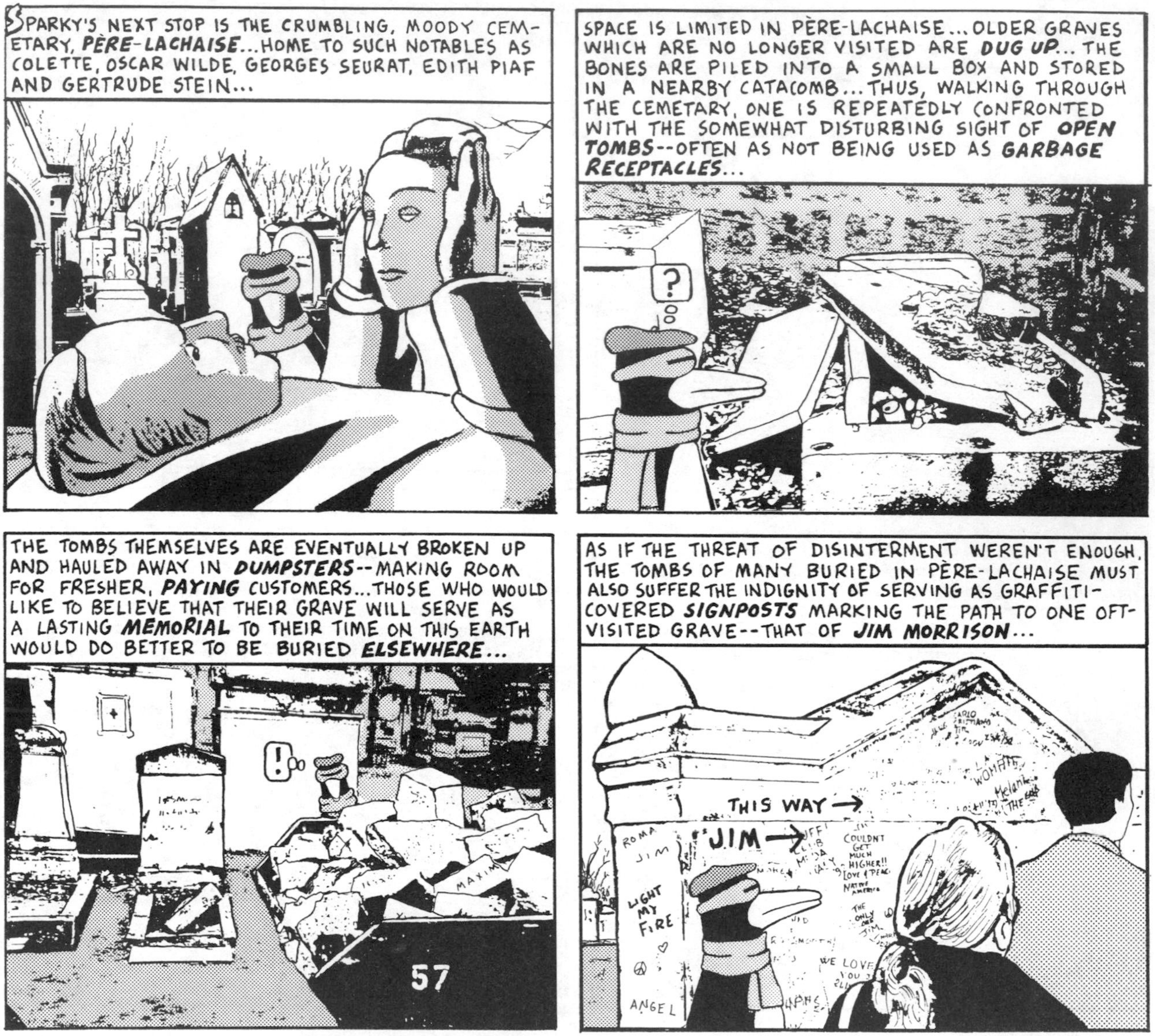
SPARKY'S NEXT STOP IS THE CRUMBLING, MOODY CEMETARY, PÈRE-LACHAISE...HOME TO SUCH NOTABLES AS COLETTE, OSCAR WILDE, GEORGES SEURAT, EDITH PIAF AND GERTRUDE STEIN...
SPACE IS LIMITED IN PÈRE-LACHAISE...OLDER GRAVES WHICH ARE NO LONGER VISITED ARE DUG UP...THE BONES ARE PILED INTO A SMALL BOX AND STORED IN A NEARBY CATACOMB...THUS, WALKING THROUGH THE CEMETARY, ONE IS REPEATEDLY CONFRONTED WITH THE SOMEWHAT DISTURBING SIGHT OF OPEN TOMBS--OFTEN AS NOT BEING USED AS GARBAGE RECEPTACLES...
?
THE TOMBS THEMSELVES ARE EVENTUALLY BROKEN UP AND HAULED AWAY IN DUMPSTERS--MAKING ROOM FOR FRESHER, PAYING CUSTOMERS...THOSE WHO WOULD LIKE TO BELIEVE THAT THEIR GRAVE WILL SERVE AS A LASTING MEMORIAL TO THEIR TIME ON THIS EARTH WOULD DO BETTER TO BE BURIED ELSEWHERE...
!
MAXIM
57
AS IF THE THREAT OF DISINTERMENT WEREN'T ENOUGH, THE TOMBS OF MANY BURIED IN PÈRE-LACHAISE MUST ALSO SUFFER THE INDIGNITY OF SERVING AS GRAFFITI-COVERED SIGNPOSTS MARKING THE PATH TO ONE OFT-VISITED GRAVE--THAT OF JIM MORRISON...
THIS WAY →
JIM →
ROMA
JIM
LIGHT MY FIRE
COULDNT GET MUCH HIGHER!!
WE LOVE YOU
ANGEL

HEADSTONES IN THE IMMEDIATE VICINITY ARE COVERED WITH THE SOPHOMORIC NIHILISM OF DOORS LYRICS... "MOURNERS" SIT ON ADJACENT TOMBS, SMOKING GRASS AND DRINKING BEER... TAPE DECKS BLAST OUT DOORS SONGS AT FULL VOLUME... ON THE 20TH ANNIVERSARY OF MORRISON'S DEATH, OVERZEALOUS FANS HAD TO BE CONTAINED BY *RIOT POLICE*...

AT THE CIMETIÈRE PÈRE-LACHAISE, THE PARTY NEVER *ENDS*...

MES MORRISON
1943-1971

THE END

THE NEXT DAY SPARKY PAUSES IN A SMALL PARK AT THE EDGE OF LES INVALIDES... UPON LEAVING, HE DISCOVERS IT IS DEDICATED TO ANTOINE DE SAINT-EXUPERY--A FRENCH WAR HERO BEST KNOWN AS AUTHOR OF *THE LITTLE PRINCE*...

"THE THING THAT IS IMPORTANT IS THE THING THAT IS NOT SEEN..."

"...IF YOU LOVE A FLOWER THAT LIVES ON A STAR, IT IS SWEET TO LOOK AT THE SKY AT NIGHT..."

"...ALL THE STARS ARE A-BLOOM WITH FLOW- ERS..."

ANTOINE
SAINT-EXUPERY

NEAR INVALIDES, SPARKY DISCOVERS A LARGE GATH- ERING OF ANGRY FRENCH FARMERS PROTESTING AM- ERICAN G.A.T.T. TREATY DEMANDS... FIRECRACKERS ARE EXPLODING... AN IMPASSIONED SPEAKER IS INCIT- ING THE CROWD... AND SPARK HAS A STRONG FEELING THAT IT WOULD BE WISE NOT TO WAVE HIS PASSPORT IN THE AIR...

LES AMÉRICAINS... SONT *COCHONS*! ILS SONT *IMBÉCILES*!

KA-POUW!

AH... LES AMÉRI- CAINS SONT, UM... *WANQUERS*... N'EST-CE PAS?

HEH, HEH...

45

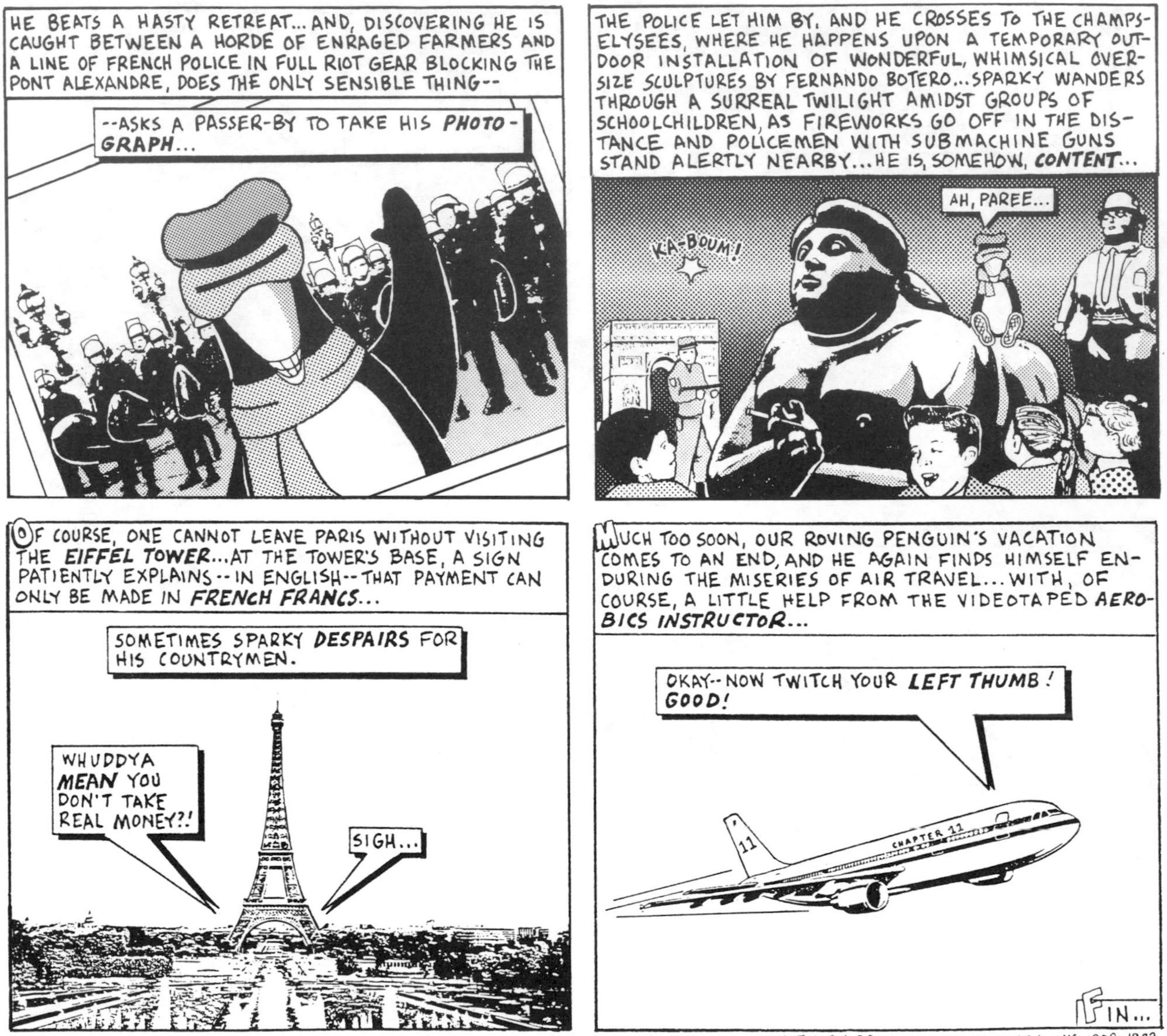
HE BEATS A HASTY RETREAT... AND, DISCOVERING HE IS CAUGHT BETWEEN A HORDE OF ENRAGED FARMERS AND A LINE OF FRENCH POLICE IN FULL RIOT GEAR BLOCKING THE PONT ALEXANDRE, DOES THE ONLY SENSIBLE THING--
--ASKS A PASSER-BY TO TAKE HIS **PHOTOGRAPH**...
THE POLICE LET HIM BY, AND HE CROSSES TO THE CHAMPS-ELYSEES, WHERE HE HAPPENS UPON A TEMPORARY OUTDOOR INSTALLATION OF WONDERFUL, WHIMSICAL OVERSIZE SCULPTURES BY FERNANDO BOTERO... SPARKY WANDERS THROUGH A SURREAL TWILIGHT AMIDST GROUPS OF SCHOOLCHILDREN, AS FIREWORKS GO OFF IN THE DISTANCE AND POLICEMEN WITH SUBMACHINE GUNS STAND ALERTLY NEARBY... HE IS, SOMEHOW, **CONTENT**...
AH, PAREE...
KA-BOUM!
OF COURSE, ONE CANNOT LEAVE PARIS WITHOUT VISITING THE **EIFFEL TOWER**... AT THE TOWER'S BASE, A SIGN PATIENTLY EXPLAINS -- IN ENGLISH -- THAT PAYMENT CAN ONLY BE MADE IN **FRENCH FRANCS**...
SOMETIMES SPARKY **DESPAIRS** FOR HIS COUNTRYMEN.
WHUDDYA **MEAN** YOU DON'T TAKE REAL MONEY?!
SIGH...
MUCH TOO SOON, OUR ROVING PENGUIN'S VACATION COMES TO AN END, AND HE AGAIN FINDS HIMSELF ENDURING THE MISERIES OF AIR TRAVEL... WITH, OF COURSE, A LITTLE HELP FROM THE VIDEOTAPED **AEROBICS INSTRUCTOR**...
OKAY-- NOW TWITCH YOUR **LEFT THUMB**! **GOOD**!
11
CHAPTER 11
FIN...

THIS MODERN WORLD by TOM TOMORROW

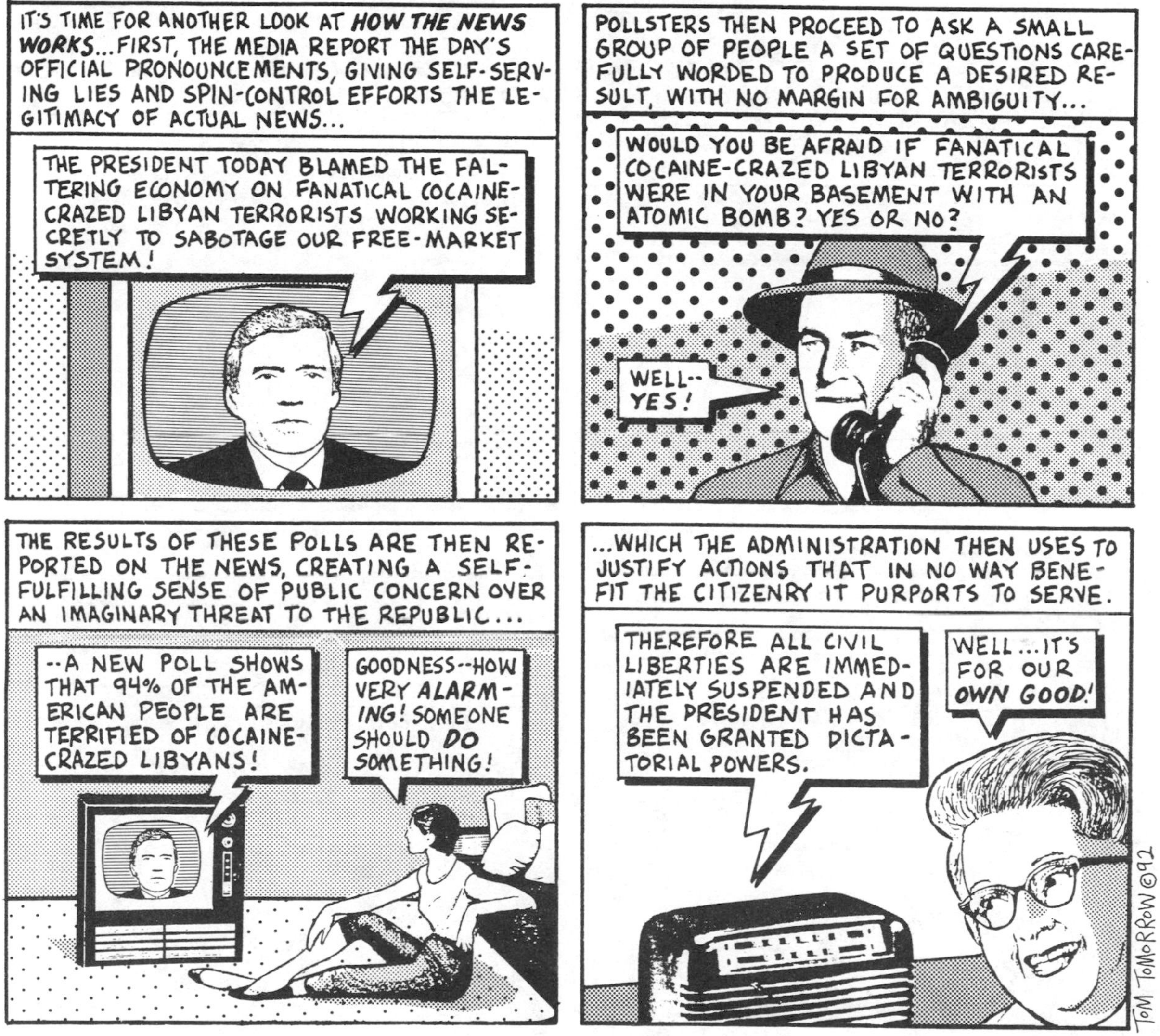
IT'S TIME FOR ANOTHER LOOK AT HOW THE NEWS WORKS... FIRST, THE MEDIA REPORT THE DAY'S OFFICIAL PRONOUNCEMENTS, GIVING SELF-SERVING LIES AND SPIN-CONTROL EFFORTS THE LEGITIMACY OF ACTUAL NEWS...
THE PRESIDENT TODAY BLAMED THE FALTERING ECONOMY ON FANATICAL COCAINE-CRAZED LIBYAN TERRORISTS WORKING SECRETLY TO SABOTAGE OUR FREE-MARKET SYSTEM!
POLLSTERS THEN PROCEED TO ASK A SMALL GROUP OF PEOPLE A SET OF QUESTIONS CAREFULLY WORDED TO PRODUCE A DESIRED RESULT, WITH NO MARGIN FOR AMBIGUITY...
WOULD YOU BE AFRAID IF FANATICAL COCAINE-CRAZED LIBYAN TERRORISTS WERE IN YOUR BASEMENT WITH AN ATOMIC BOMB? YES OR NO?
WELL-- YES!
THE RESULTS OF THESE POLLS ARE THEN REPORTED ON THE NEWS, CREATING A SELF-FULFILLING SENSE OF PUBLIC CONCERN OVER AN IMAGINARY THREAT TO THE REPUBLIC...
--A NEW POLL SHOWS THAT 94% OF THE AMERICAN PEOPLE ARE TERRIFIED OF COCAINE-CRAZED LIBYANS!
GOODNESS--HOW VERY ALARMING! SOMEONE SHOULD DO SOMETHING!
...WHICH THE ADMINISTRATION THEN USES TO JUSTIFY ACTIONS THAT IN NO WAY BENEFIT THE CITIZENRY IT PURPORTS TO SERVE.
THEREFORE ALL CIVIL LIBERTIES ARE IMMEDIATELY SUSPENDED AND THE PRESIDENT HAS BEEN GRANTED DICTATORIAL POWERS.
WELL...IT'S FOR OUR OWN GOOD!
TOM TOMORROW ©92

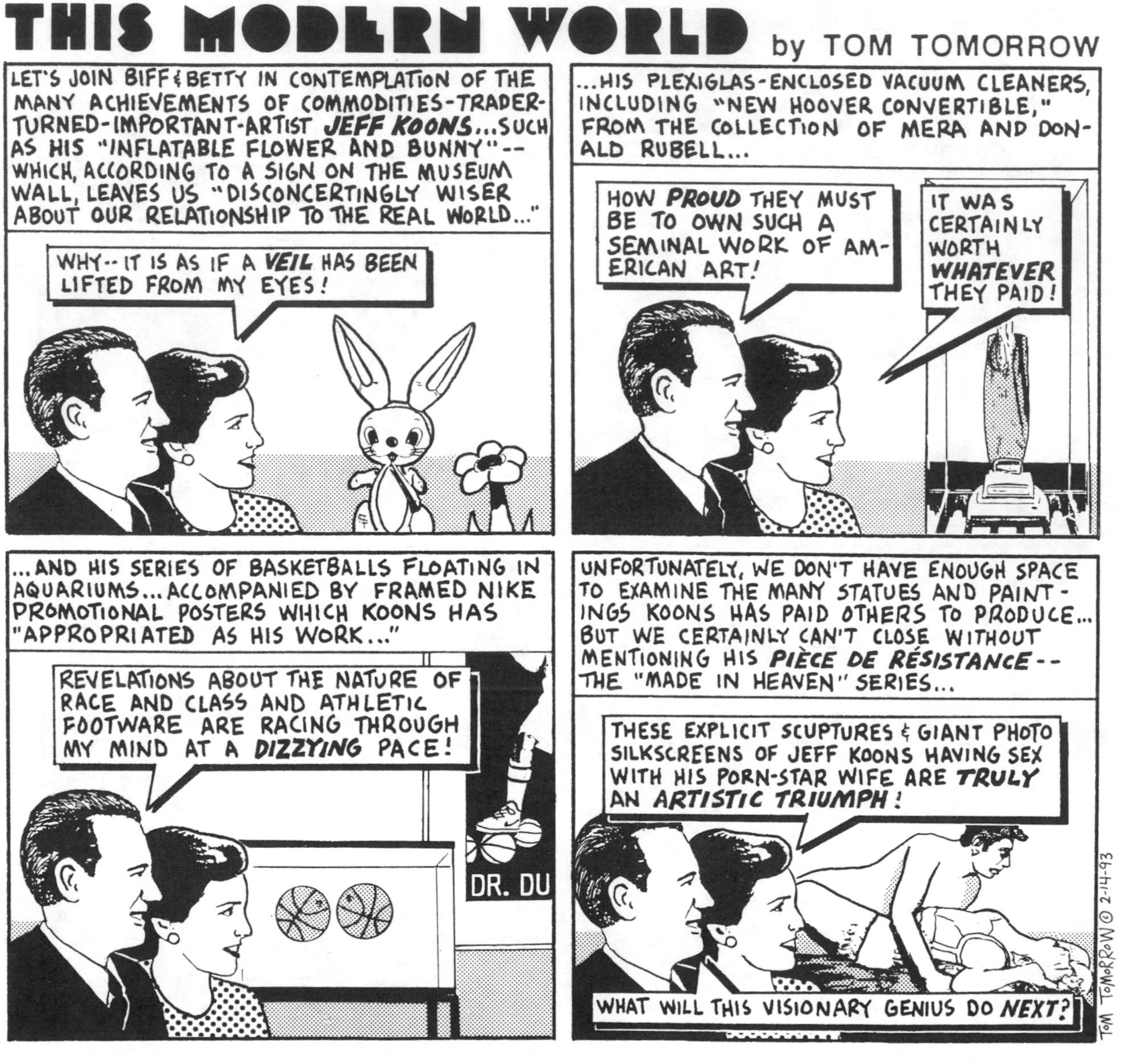
THIS MODERN WORLD by TOM TOMORROW
LET'S JOIN BIFF & BETTY IN CONTEMPLATION OF THE MANY ACHIEVEMENTS OF COMMODITIES-TRADER-TURNED-IMPORTANT-ARTIST JEFF KOONS...SUCH AS HIS "INFLATABLE FLOWER AND BUNNY"-- WHICH, ACCORDING TO A SIGN ON THE MUSEUM WALL, LEAVES US "DISCONCERTINGLY WISER ABOUT OUR RELATIONSHIP TO THE REAL WORLD..."
WHY-- IT IS AS IF A VEIL HAS BEEN LIFTED FROM MY EYES!
...HIS PLEXIGLAS-ENCLOSED VACUUM CLEANERS, INCLUDING "NEW HOOVER CONVERTIBLE," FROM THE COLLECTION OF MERA AND DONALD RUBELL...
HOW PROUD THEY MUST BE TO OWN SUCH A SEMINAL WORK OF AMERICAN ART!
IT WAS CERTAINLY WORTH WHATEVER THEY PAID!
...AND HIS SERIES OF BASKETBALLS FLOATING IN AQUARIUMS...ACCOMPANIED BY FRAMED NIKE PROMOTIONAL POSTERS WHICH KOONS HAS "APPROPRIATED AS HIS WORK..."
REVELATIONS ABOUT THE NATURE OF RACE AND CLASS AND ATHLETIC FOOTWARE ARE RACING THROUGH MY MIND AT A DIZZYING PACE!
DR. DU
UNFORTUNATELY, WE DON'T HAVE ENOUGH SPACE TO EXAMINE THE MANY STATUES AND PAINTINGS KOONS HAS PAID OTHERS TO PRODUCE... BUT WE CERTAINLY CAN'T CLOSE WITHOUT MENTIONING HIS PIÈCE DE RÉSISTANCE-- THE "MADE IN HEAVEN" SERIES...
THESE EXPLICIT SCUPTURES & GIANT PHOTO SILKSCREENS OF JEFF KOONS HAVING SEX WITH HIS PORN-STAR WIFE ARE TRULY AN ARTISTIC TRIUMPH!
WHAT WILL THIS VISIONARY GENIUS DO NEXT?
TOM TOMORROW © 2-14-93

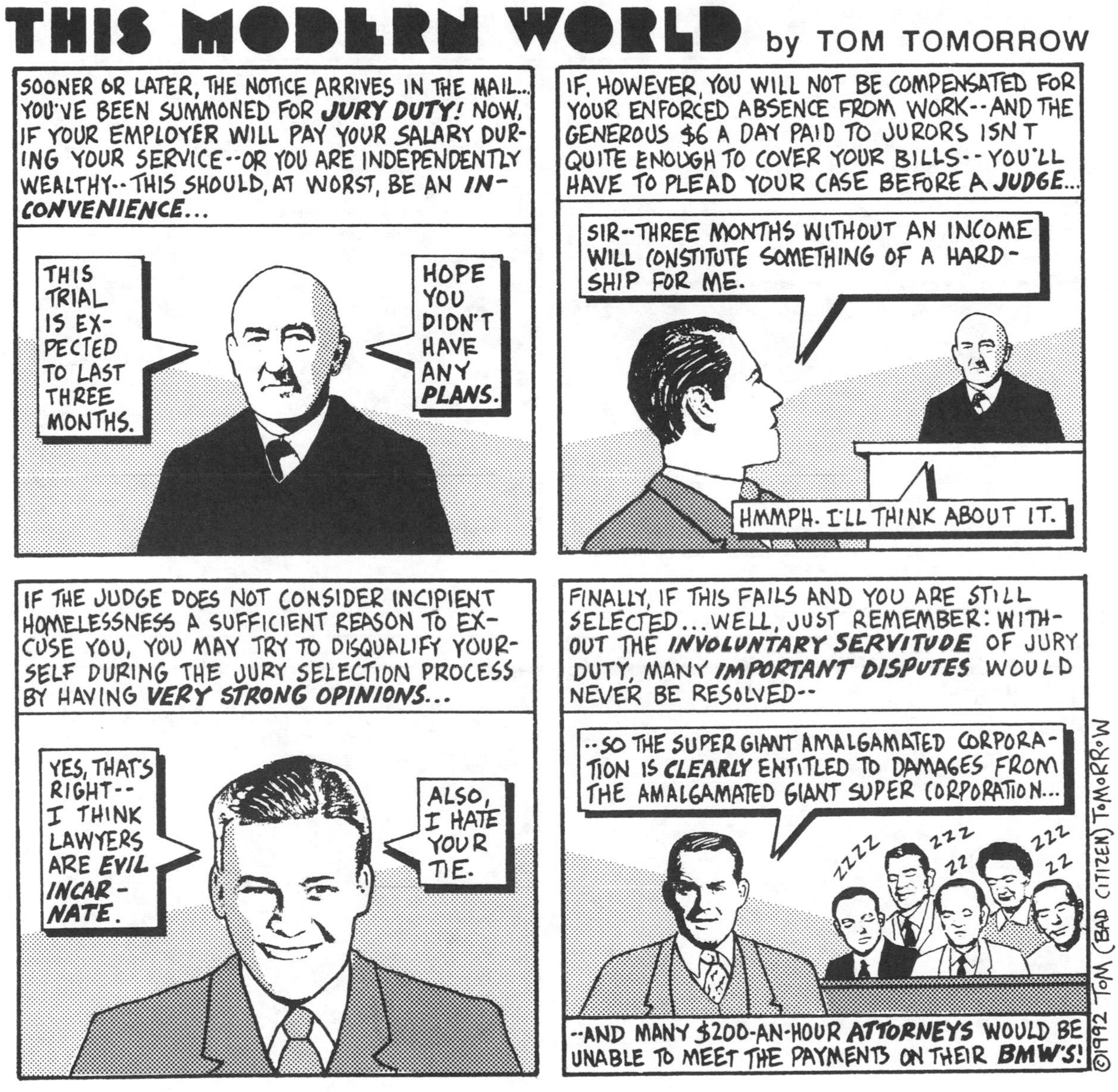
THIS MODERN WORLD by TOM TOMORROW
SOONER OR LATER, THE NOTICE ARRIVES IN THE MAIL... YOU'VE BEEN SUMMONED FOR JURY DUTY! NOW, IF YOUR EMPLOYER WILL PAY YOUR SALARY DURING YOUR SERVICE--OR YOU ARE INDEPENDENTLY WEALTHY--THIS SHOULD, AT WORST, BE AN INCONVENIENCE...
THIS TRIAL IS EXPECTED TO LAST THREE MONTHS.
HOPE YOU DIDN'T HAVE ANY PLANS.
IF, HOWEVER, YOU WILL NOT BE COMPENSATED FOR YOUR ENFORCED ABSENCE FROM WORK--AND THE GENEROUS $6 A DAY PAID TO JURORS ISN'T QUITE ENOUGH TO COVER YOUR BILLS--YOU'LL HAVE TO PLEAD YOUR CASE BEFORE A JUDGE...
SIR--THREE MONTHS WITHOUT AN INCOME WILL CONSTITUTE SOMETHING OF A HARDSHIP FOR ME.
HMMPH. I'LL THINK ABOUT IT.
IF THE JUDGE DOES NOT CONSIDER INCIPIENT HOMELESSNESS A SUFFICIENT REASON TO EXCUSE YOU, YOU MAY TRY TO DISQUALIFY YOURSELF DURING THE JURY SELECTION PROCESS BY HAVING VERY STRONG OPINIONS...
YES, THAT'S RIGHT--I THINK LAWYERS ARE EVIL INCARNATE.
ALSO, I HATE YOUR TIE.
FINALLY, IF THIS FAILS AND YOU ARE STILL SELECTED... WELL, JUST REMEMBER: WITHOUT THE INVOLUNTARY SERVITUDE OF JURY DUTY, MANY IMPORTANT DISPUTES WOULD NEVER BE RESOLVED--
..SO THE SUPER GIANT AMALGAMATED CORPORATION IS CLEARLY ENTITLED TO DAMAGES FROM THE AMALGAMATED GIANT SUPER CORPORATION...
ZZZZ
ZZZ
ZZ
ZZZ
ZZ
--AND MANY $200-AN-HOUR ATTORNEYS WOULD BE UNABLE TO MEET THE PAYMENTS ON THEIR BMW'S!
©1992 TOM (BAD CITIZEN) TOMORROW

THIS MODERN WORLD by TOM TOMORROW

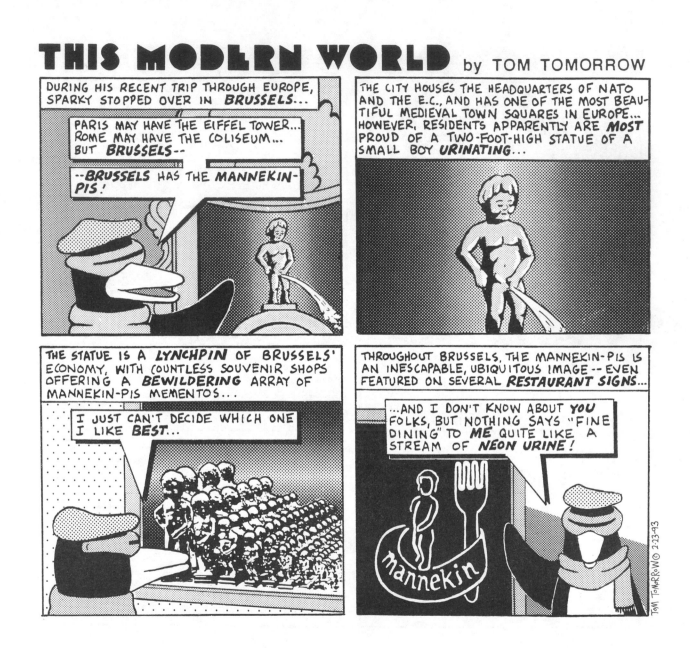

Panel 1:
DURING HIS RECENT TRIP THROUGH EUROPE, SPARKY STOPPED OVER IN *BRUSSELS*...

PARIS MAY HAVE THE EIFFEL TOWER... ROME MAY HAVE THE COLISEUM... BUT *BRUSSELS*--

--*BRUSSELS* HAS THE *MANNEKIN-PIS!*

Panel 2:
THE CITY HOUSES THE HEADQUARTERS OF NATO AND THE E.C., AND HAS ONE OF THE MOST BEAUTIFUL MEDIEVAL TOWN SQUARES IN EUROPE... HOWEVER, RESIDENTS APPARENTLY ARE *MOST* PROUD OF A TWO-FOOT-HIGH STATUE OF A SMALL BOY *URINATING*...

Panel 3:
THE STATUE IS A *LYNCHPIN* OF BRUSSELS' ECONOMY, WITH COUNTLESS SOUVENIR SHOPS OFFERING A *BEWILDERING* ARRAY OF MANNEKIN-PIS MEMENTOS...

I JUST CAN'T DECIDE WHICH ONE I LIKE *BEST*...

Panel 4:
THROUGHOUT BRUSSELS, THE MANNEKIN-PIS IS AN INESCAPABLE, UBIQUITOUS IMAGE -- EVEN FEATURED ON SEVERAL *RESTAURANT SIGNS*...

...AND I DON'T KNOW ABOUT *YOU* FOLKS, BUT NOTHING SAYS "FINE DINING" TO *ME* QUITE LIKE A STREAM OF *NEON URINE!*

mannekin

TOM TOMORROW © 2-23-93

50

THIS MODERN WORLD by TOM TOMORROW

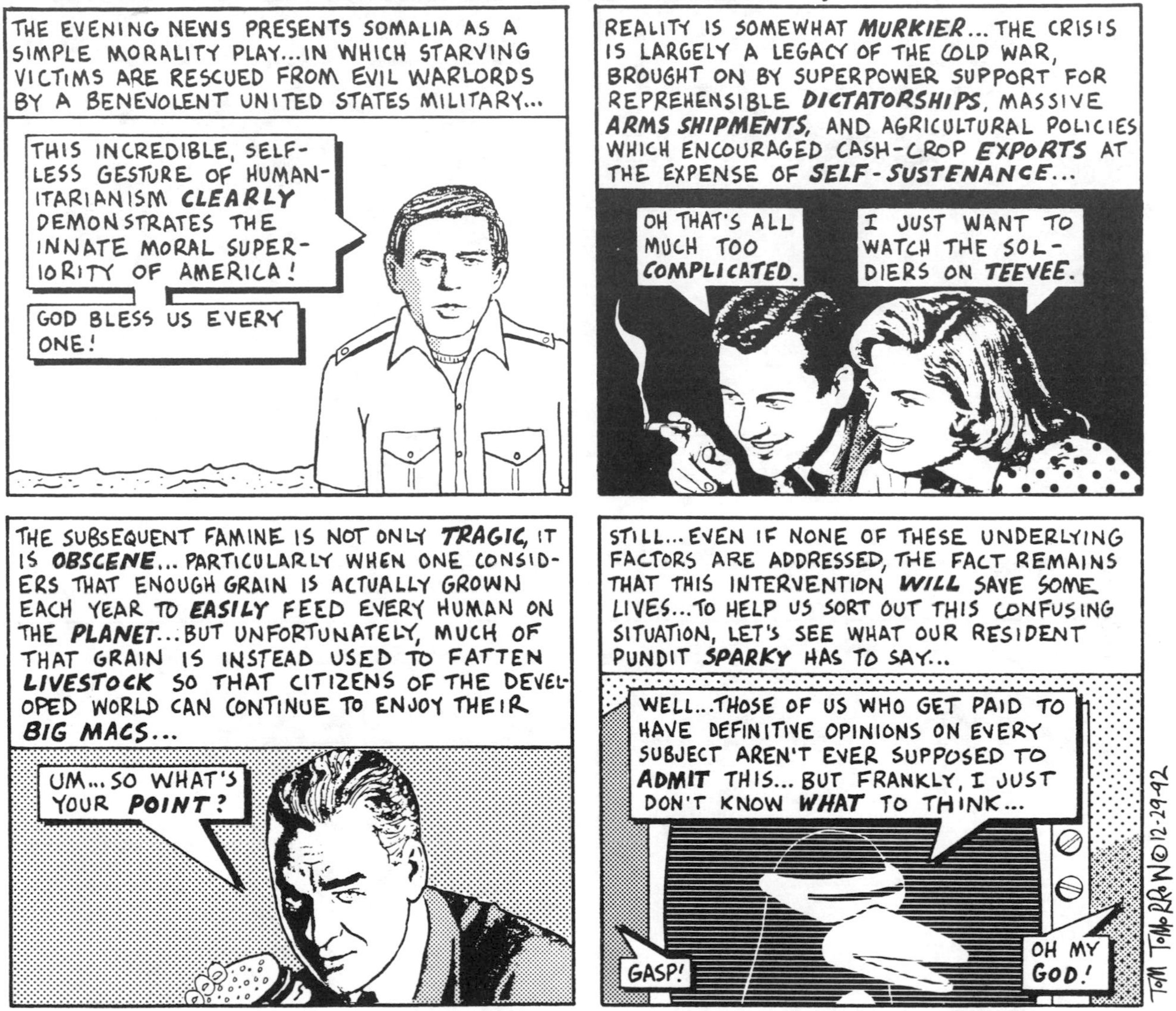

THE EVENING NEWS PRESENTS SOMALIA AS A SIMPLE MORALITY PLAY...IN WHICH STARVING VICTIMS ARE RESCUED FROM EVIL WARLORDS BY A BENEVOLENT UNITED STATES MILITARY...
THIS INCREDIBLE, SELFLESS GESTURE OF HUMANITARIANISM CLEARLY DEMONSTRATES THE INNATE MORAL SUPERIORITY OF AMERICA!
GOD BLESS US EVERY ONE!
REALITY IS SOMEWHAT MURKIER... THE CRISIS IS LARGELY A LEGACY OF THE COLD WAR, BROUGHT ON BY SUPERPOWER SUPPORT FOR REPREHENSIBLE DICTATORSHIPS, MASSIVE ARMS SHIPMENTS, AND AGRICULTURAL POLICIES WHICH ENCOURAGED CASH-CROP EXPORTS AT THE EXPENSE OF SELF-SUSTENANCE...
OH THAT'S ALL MUCH TOO COMPLICATED.
I JUST WANT TO WATCH THE SOLDIERS ON TEEVEE.
THE SUBSEQUENT FAMINE IS NOT ONLY TRAGIC, IT IS OBSCENE... PARTICULARLY WHEN ONE CONSIDERS THAT ENOUGH GRAIN IS ACTUALLY GROWN EACH YEAR TO EASILY FEED EVERY HUMAN ON THE PLANET...BUT UNFORTUNATELY, MUCH OF THAT GRAIN IS INSTEAD USED TO FATTEN LIVESTOCK SO THAT CITIZENS OF THE DEVELOPED WORLD CAN CONTINUE TO ENJOY THEIR BIG MACS...
UM...SO WHAT'S YOUR POINT?
STILL...EVEN IF NONE OF THESE UNDERLYING FACTORS ARE ADDRESSED, THE FACT REMAINS THAT THIS INTERVENTION WILL SAVE SOME LIVES...TO HELP US SORT OUT THIS CONFUSING SITUATION, LET'S SEE WHAT OUR RESIDENT PUNDIT SPARKY HAS TO SAY...
WELL...THOSE OF US WHO GET PAID TO HAVE DEFINITIVE OPINIONS ON EVERY SUBJECT AREN'T EVER SUPPOSED TO ADMIT THIS... BUT FRANKLY, I JUST DON'T KNOW WHAT TO THINK...
GASP!
OH MY GOD!
TOM TOMORROW ©12-29-92

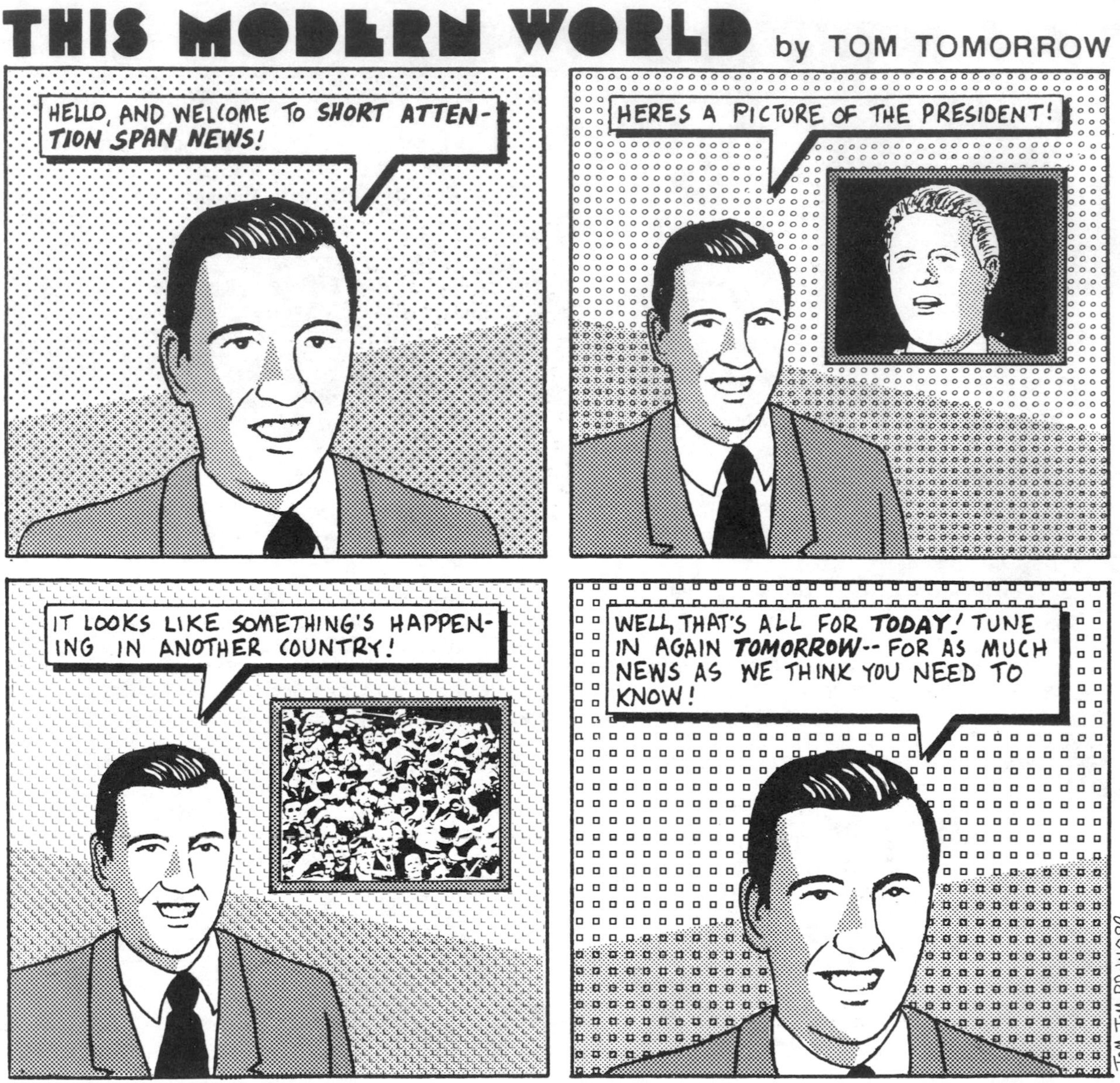
THIS MODERN WORLD by TOM TOMORROW
HELLO, AND WELCOME TO SHORT ATTENTION SPAN NEWS!
HERES A PICTURE OF THE PRESIDENT!
IT LOOKS LIKE SOMETHING'S HAPPENING IN ANOTHER COUNTRY!
WELL, THAT'S ALL FOR TODAY! TUNE IN AGAIN TOMORROW-- FOR AS MUCH NEWS AS WE THINK YOU NEED TO KNOW!
TOM TOMORROW©93

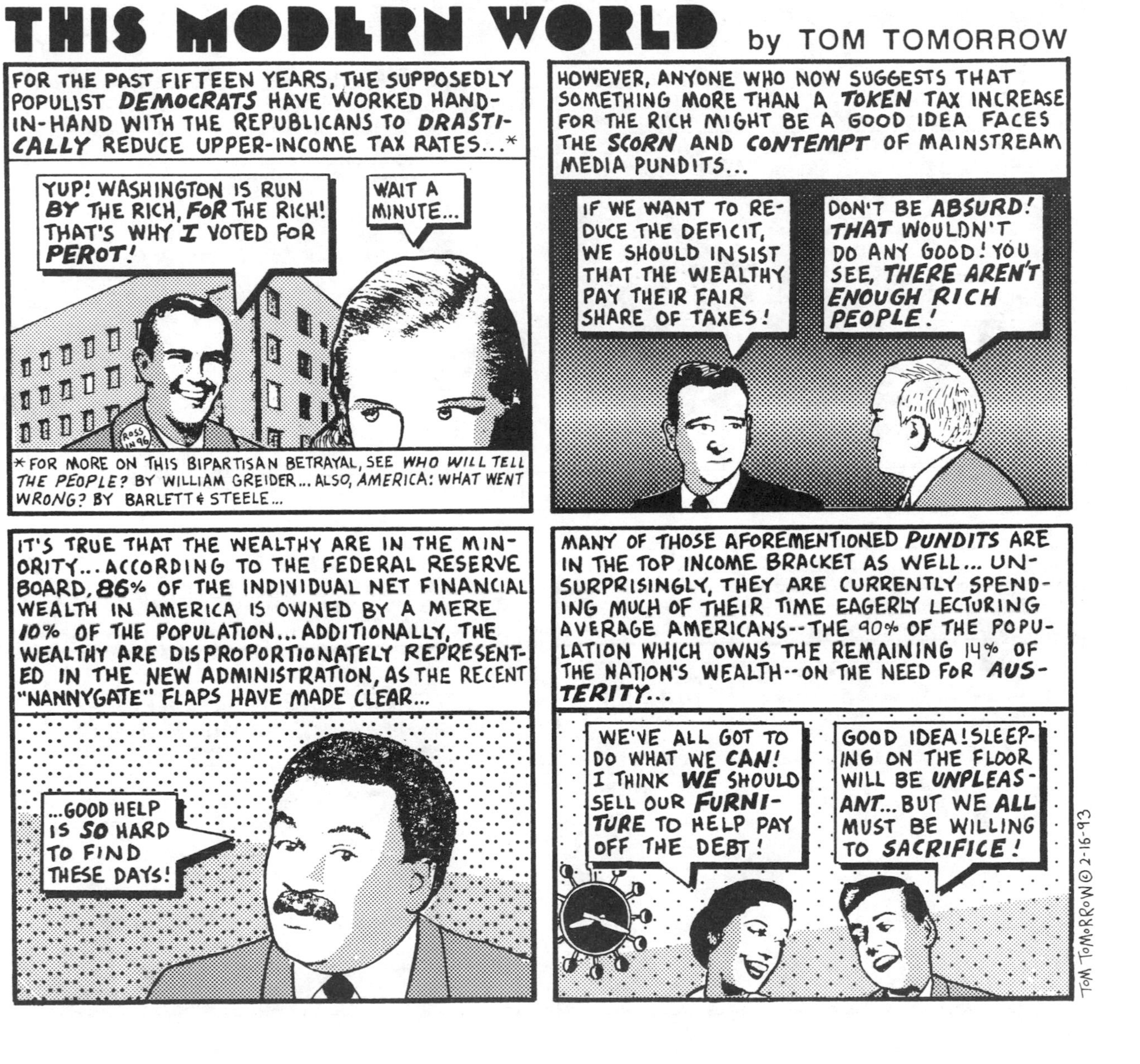
THIS MODERN WORLD by TOM TOMORROW
FOR THE PAST FIFTEEN YEARS, THE SUPPOSEDLY POPULIST DEMOCRATS HAVE WORKED HAND-IN-HAND WITH THE REPUBLICANS TO DRASTICALLY REDUCE UPPER-INCOME TAX RATES...*
YUP! WASHINGTON IS RUN BY THE RICH, FOR THE RICH! THAT'S WHY I VOTED FOR PEROT!
WAIT A MINUTE...
ROSS IN 96
* FOR MORE ON THIS BIPARTISAN BETRAYAL, SEE WHO WILL TELL THE PEOPLE? BY WILLIAM GREIDER... ALSO, AMERICA: WHAT WENT WRONG? BY BARLETT & STEELE...
HOWEVER, ANYONE WHO NOW SUGGESTS THAT SOMETHING MORE THAN A TOKEN TAX INCREASE FOR THE RICH MIGHT BE A GOOD IDEA FACES THE SCORN AND CONTEMPT OF MAINSTREAM MEDIA PUNDITS...
IF WE WANT TO REDUCE THE DEFICIT, WE SHOULD INSIST THAT THE WEALTHY PAY THEIR FAIR SHARE OF TAXES!
DON'T BE ABSURD! THAT WOULDN'T DO ANY GOOD! YOU SEE, THERE AREN'T ENOUGH RICH PEOPLE!
IT'S TRUE THAT THE WEALTHY ARE IN THE MINORITY... ACCORDING TO THE FEDERAL RESERVE BOARD, 86% OF THE INDIVIDUAL NET FINANCIAL WEALTH IN AMERICA IS OWNED BY A MERE 10% OF THE POPULATION... ADDITIONALLY, THE WEALTHY ARE DISPROPORTIONATELY REPRESENTED IN THE NEW ADMINISTRATION, AS THE RECENT "NANNYGATE" FLAPS HAVE MADE CLEAR...
...GOOD HELP IS SO HARD TO FIND THESE DAYS!
MANY OF THOSE AFOREMENTIONED PUNDITS ARE IN THE TOP INCOME BRACKET AS WELL... UNSURPRISINGLY, THEY ARE CURRENTLY SPENDING MUCH OF THEIR TIME EAGERLY LECTURING AVERAGE AMERICANS--THE 90% OF THE POPULATION WHICH OWNS THE REMAINING 14% OF THE NATION'S WEALTH--ON THE NEED FOR AUSTERITY...
WE'VE ALL GOT TO DO WHAT WE CAN! I THINK WE SHOULD SELL OUR FURNITURE TO HELP PAY OFF THE DEBT!
GOOD IDEA! SLEEPING ON THE FLOOR WILL BE UNPLEASANT... BUT WE ALL MUST BE WILLING TO SACRIFICE!
TOM TOMORROW © 2-16-93

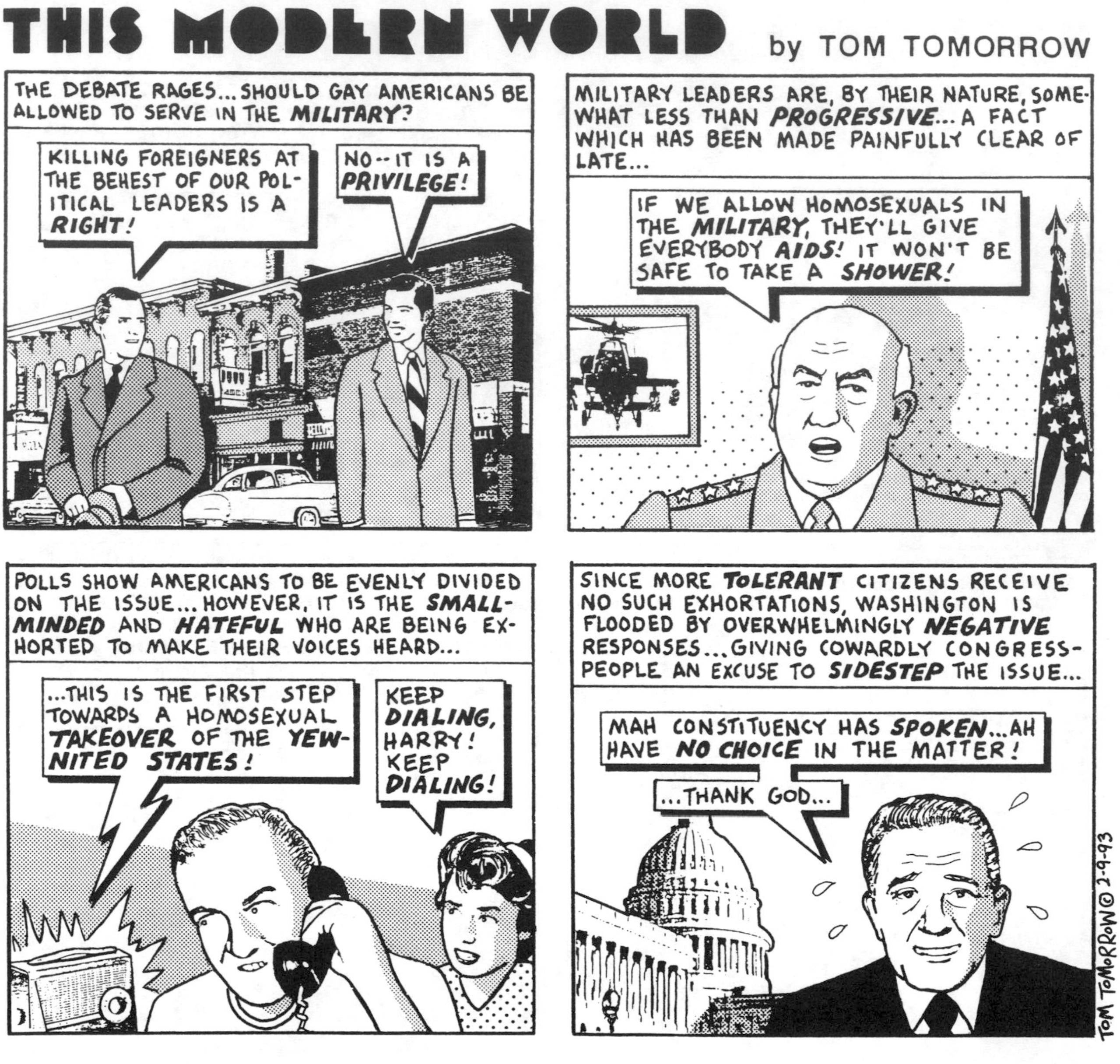
THIS MODERN WORLD
by TOM TOMORROW
THE DEBATE RAGES... SHOULD GAY AMERICANS BE ALLOWED TO SERVE IN THE MILITARY?
KILLING FOREIGNERS AT THE BEHEST OF OUR POLITICAL LEADERS IS A RIGHT!
NO -- IT IS A PRIVILEGE!
MILITARY LEADERS ARE, BY THEIR NATURE, SOMEWHAT LESS THAN PROGRESSIVE... A FACT WHICH HAS BEEN MADE PAINFULLY CLEAR OF LATE...
IF WE ALLOW HOMOSEXUALS IN THE MILITARY, THEY'LL GIVE EVERYBODY AIDS! IT WON'T BE SAFE TO TAKE A SHOWER!
POLLS SHOW AMERICANS TO BE EVENLY DIVIDED ON THE ISSUE... HOWEVER, IT IS THE SMALL-MINDED AND HATEFUL WHO ARE BEING EXHORTED TO MAKE THEIR VOICES HEARD...
...THIS IS THE FIRST STEP TOWARDS A HOMOSEXUAL TAKEOVER OF THE YEW-NITED STATES!
KEEP DIALING, HARRY! KEEP DIALING!
SINCE MORE TOLERANT CITIZENS RECEIVE NO SUCH EXHORTATIONS, WASHINGTON IS FLOODED BY OVERWHELMINGLY NEGATIVE RESPONSES... GIVING COWARDLY CONGRESSPEOPLE AN EXCUSE TO SIDESTEP THE ISSUE...
MAH CONSTITUENCY HAS SPOKEN... AH HAVE NO CHOICE IN THE MATTER!
...THANK GOD...
TOM TOMORROW © 2-9-93

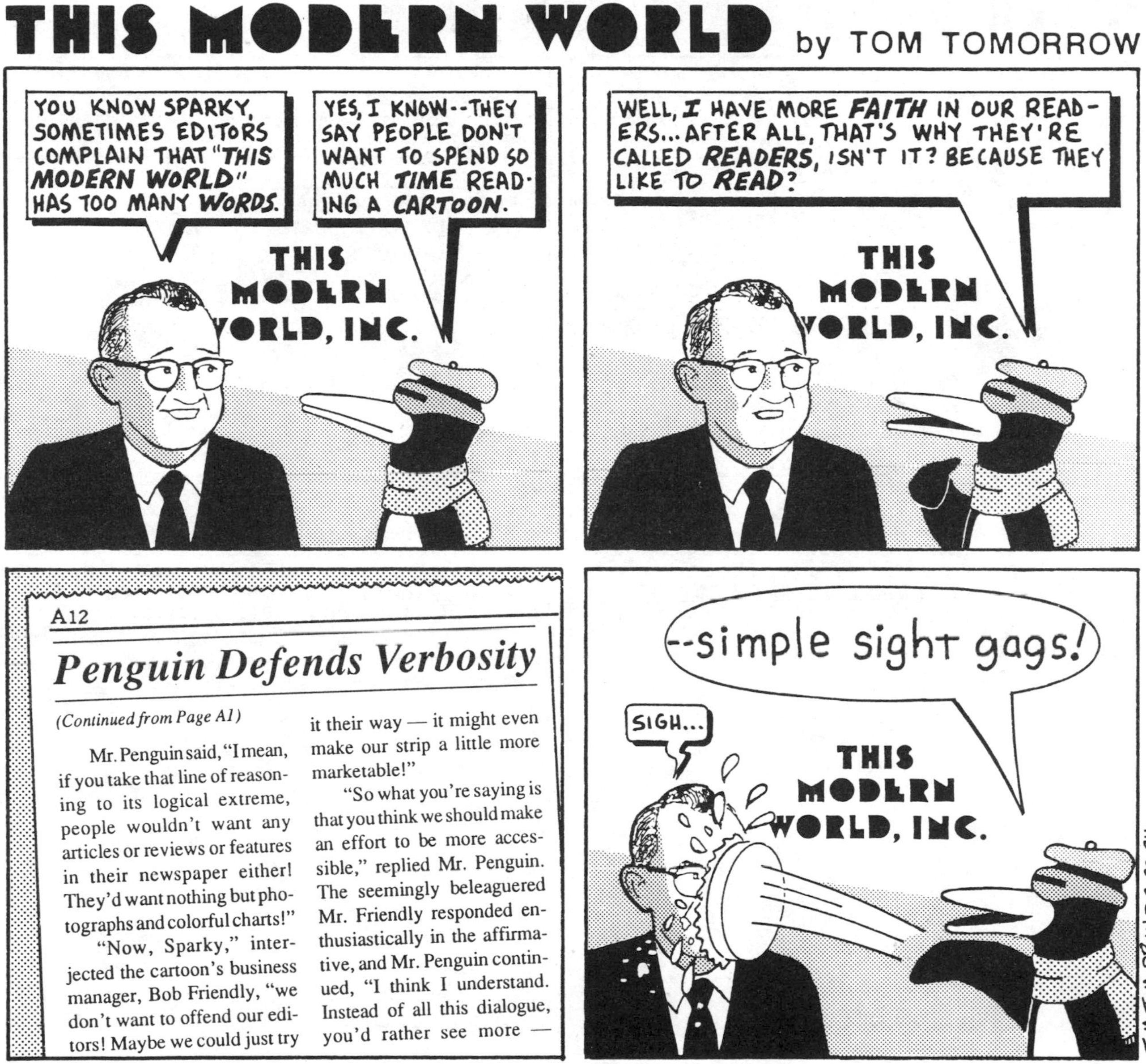
THIS MODERN WORLD by TOM TOMORROW
YOU KNOW SPARKY, SOMETIMES EDITORS COMPLAIN THAT "THIS MODERN WORLD" HAS TOO MANY WORDS.
YES, I KNOW--THEY SAY PEOPLE DON'T WANT TO SPEND SO MUCH TIME READING A CARTOON.
THIS MODERN WORLD, INC.
WELL, I HAVE MORE FAITH IN OUR READERS... AFTER ALL, THAT'S WHY THEY'RE CALLED READERS, ISN'T IT? BECAUSE THEY LIKE TO READ?
THIS MODERN WORLD, INC.
A12
Penguin Defends Verbosity
(Continued from Page A1)
Mr. Penguin said, "I mean, if you take that line of reasoning to its logical extreme, people wouldn't want any articles or reviews or features in their newspaper either! They'd want nothing but photographs and colorful charts!"
"Now, Sparky," interjected the cartoon's business manager, Bob Friendly, "we don't want to offend our editors! Maybe we could just try it their way — it might even make our strip a little more marketable!"
"So what you're saying is that you think we should make an effort to be more accessible," replied Mr. Penguin. The seemingly beleaguered Mr. Friendly responded enthusiastically in the affirmative, and Mr. Penguin continued, "I think I understand. Instead of all this dialogue, you'd rather see more —
--simple sight gags!
SIGH...
THIS MODERN WORLD, INC.
TOM TOMORROW © 2-22-94

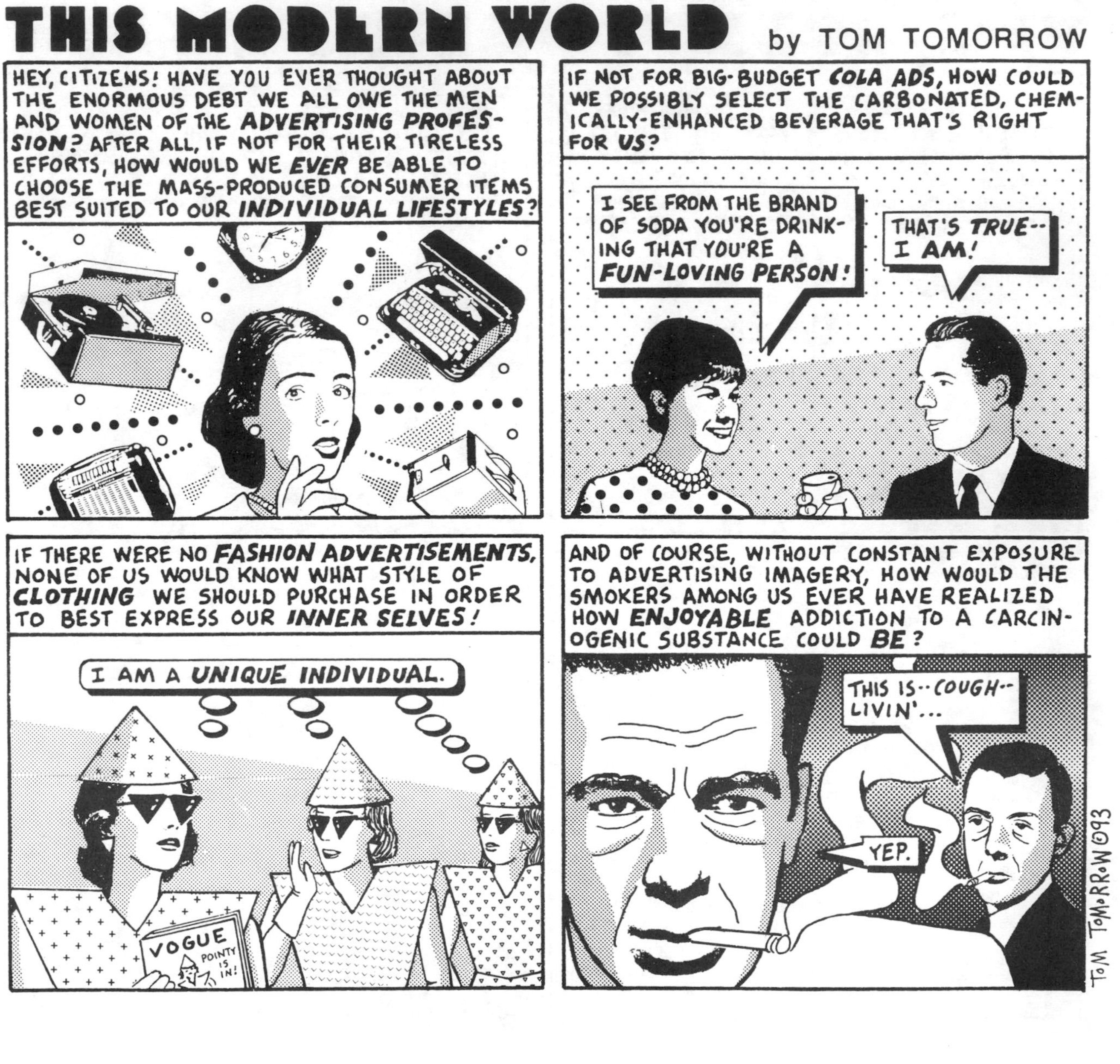
THIS MODERN WORLD by TOM TOMORROW
HEY, CITIZENS! HAVE YOU EVER THOUGHT ABOUT THE ENORMOUS DEBT WE ALL OWE THE MEN AND WOMEN OF THE ADVERTISING PROFESSION? AFTER ALL, IF NOT FOR THEIR TIRELESS EFFORTS, HOW WOULD WE EVER BE ABLE TO CHOOSE THE MASS-PRODUCED CONSUMER ITEMS BEST SUITED TO OUR INDIVIDUAL LIFESTYLES?
IF NOT FOR BIG-BUDGET COLA ADS, HOW COULD WE POSSIBLY SELECT THE CARBONATED, CHEMICALLY-ENHANCED BEVERAGE THAT'S RIGHT FOR US?
I SEE FROM THE BRAND OF SODA YOU'RE DRINKING THAT YOU'RE A FUN-LOVING PERSON!
THAT'S TRUE-- I AM!
IF THERE WERE NO FASHION ADVERTISEMENTS, NONE OF US WOULD KNOW WHAT STYLE OF CLOTHING WE SHOULD PURCHASE IN ORDER TO BEST EXPRESS OUR INNER SELVES!
I AM A UNIQUE INDIVIDUAL.
VOGUE
POINTY IS IN!
AND OF COURSE, WITHOUT CONSTANT EXPOSURE TO ADVERTISING IMAGERY, HOW WOULD THE SMOKERS AMONG US EVER HAVE REALIZED HOW ENJOYABLE ADDICTION TO A CARCINOGENIC SUBSTANCE COULD BE?
THIS IS--COUGH-- LIVIN'...
YEP.
TOM TOMORROW ©93

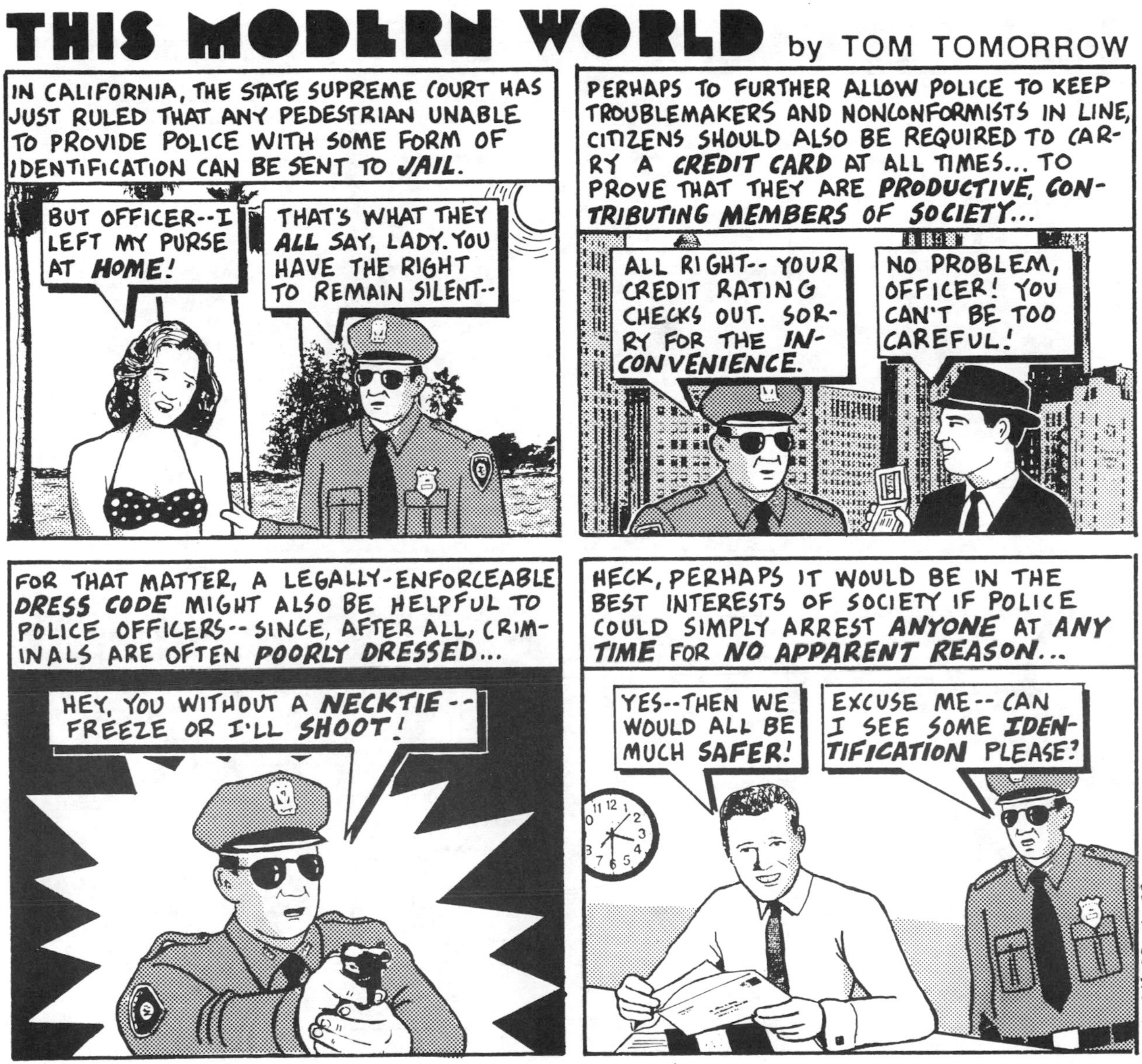
THIS MODERN WORLD by TOM TOMORROW
IN CALIFORNIA, THE STATE SUPREME COURT HAS JUST RULED THAT ANY PEDESTRIAN UNABLE TO PROVIDE POLICE WITH SOME FORM OF IDENTIFICATION CAN BE SENT TO JAIL.
BUT OFFICER--I LEFT MY PURSE AT HOME!
THAT'S WHAT THEY ALL SAY, LADY. YOU HAVE THE RIGHT TO REMAIN SILENT--
PERHAPS TO FURTHER ALLOW POLICE TO KEEP TROUBLEMAKERS AND NONCONFORMISTS IN LINE, CITIZENS SHOULD ALSO BE REQUIRED TO CARRY A CREDIT CARD AT ALL TIMES... TO PROVE THAT THEY ARE PRODUCTIVE, CONTRIBUTING MEMBERS OF SOCIETY...
ALL RIGHT-- YOUR CREDIT RATING CHECKS OUT. SORRY FOR THE INCONVENIENCE.
NO PROBLEM, OFFICER! YOU CAN'T BE TOO CAREFUL!
FOR THAT MATTER, A LEGALLY-ENFORCEABLE DRESS CODE MIGHT ALSO BE HELPFUL TO POLICE OFFICERS--SINCE, AFTER ALL, CRIMINALS ARE OFTEN POORLY DRESSED...
HEY, YOU WITHOUT A NECKTIE--FREEZE OR I'LL SHOOT!
HECK, PERHAPS IT WOULD BE IN THE BEST INTERESTS OF SOCIETY IF POLICE COULD SIMPLY ARREST ANYONE AT ANY TIME FOR NO APPARENT REASON...
YES--THEN WE WOULD ALL BE MUCH SAFER!
EXCUSE ME--CAN I SEE SOME IDENTIFICATION PLEASE?
TOM TOMORROW©93

THIS MODERN WORLD by TOM TOMORROW

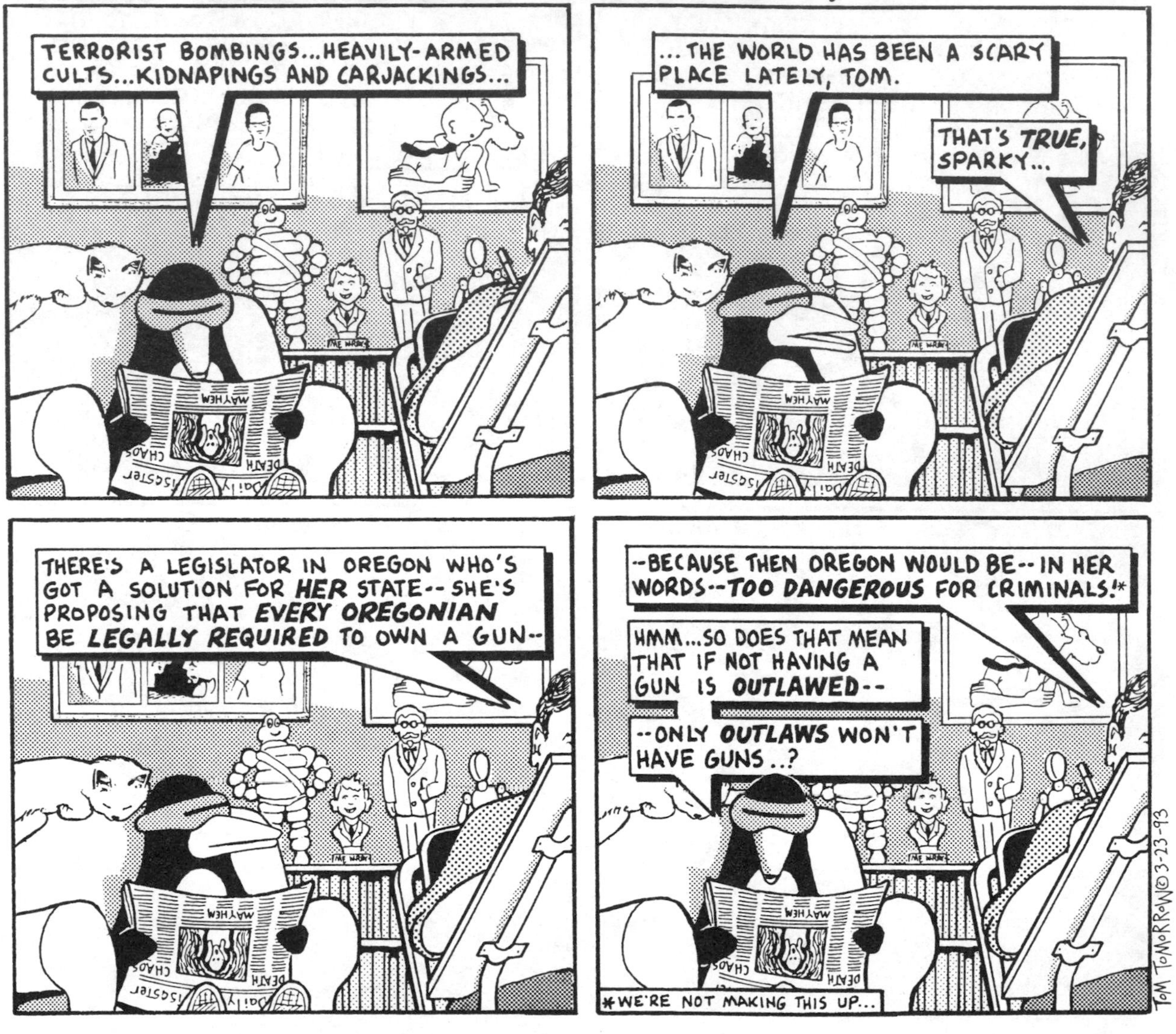

TERRORIST BOMBINGS...HEAVILY-ARMED CULTS...KIDNAPINGS AND CARJACKINGS...
MAYHEM
CHAOS
DEATH
Daily Disaster
...THE WORLD HAS BEEN A SCARY PLACE LATELY, TOM.
THAT'S TRUE, SPARKY...
THERE'S A LEGISLATOR IN OREGON WHO'S GOT A SOLUTION FOR HER STATE-- SHE'S PROPOSING THAT EVERY OREGONIAN BE LEGALLY REQUIRED TO OWN A GUN--
--BECAUSE THEN OREGON WOULD BE-- IN HER WORDS--TOO DANGEROUS FOR CRIMINALS!*
HMM...SO DOES THAT MEAN THAT IF NOT HAVING A GUN IS OUTLAWED--
--ONLY OUTLAWS WON'T HAVE GUNS..?
*WE'RE NOT MAKING THIS UP...
TOM TOMORROW©3-23-93

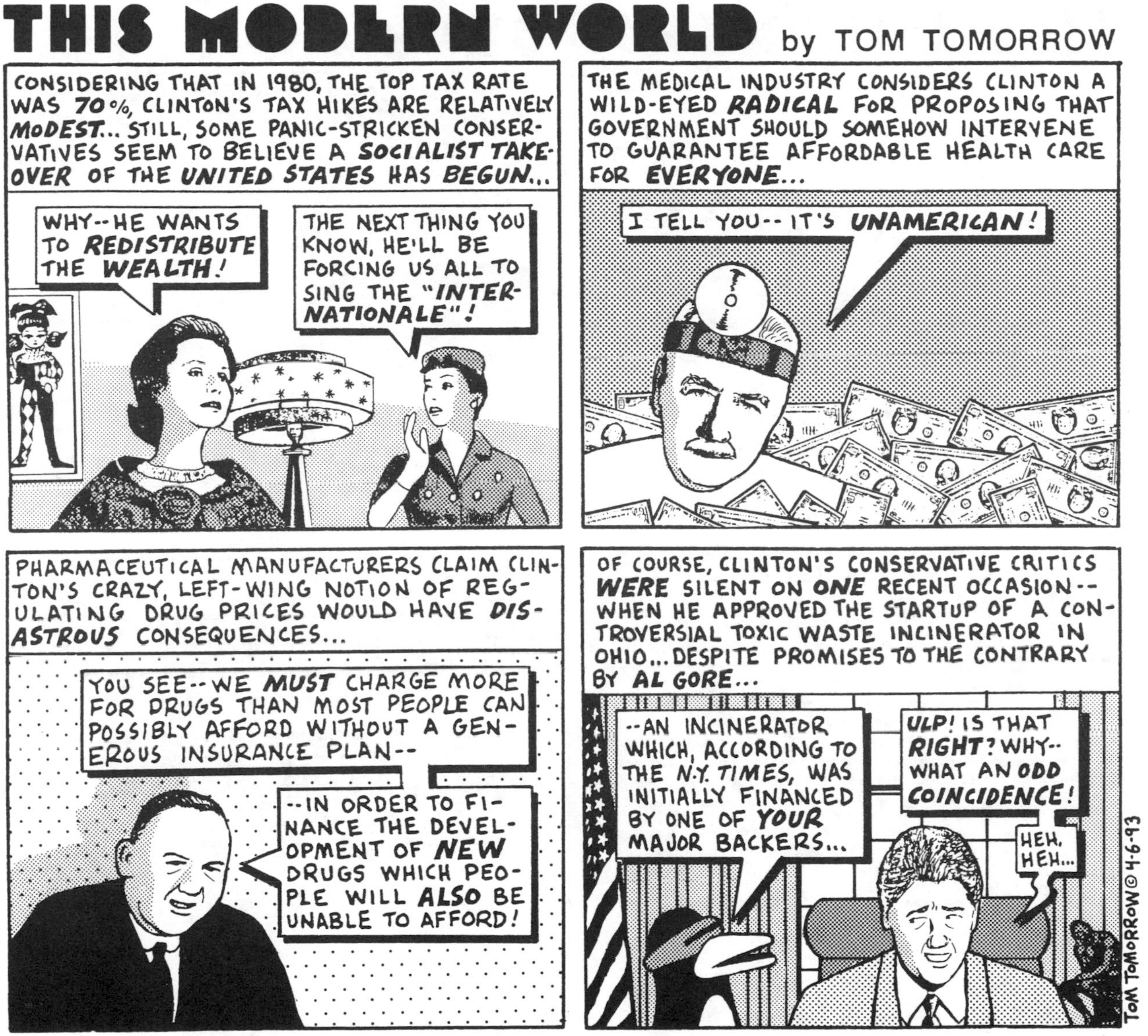
THIS MODERN WORLD by TOM TOMORROW
CONSIDERING THAT IN 1980, THE TOP TAX RATE WAS 70%, CLINTON'S TAX HIKES ARE RELATIVELY MODEST... STILL, SOME PANIC-STRICKEN CONSERVATIVES SEEM TO BELIEVE A SOCIALIST TAKE-OVER OF THE UNITED STATES HAS BEGUN...
WHY--HE WANTS TO REDISTRIBUTE THE WEALTH!
THE NEXT THING YOU KNOW, HE'LL BE FORCING US ALL TO SING THE "INTERNATIONALE"!
THE MEDICAL INDUSTRY CONSIDERS CLINTON A WILD-EYED RADICAL FOR PROPOSING THAT GOVERNMENT SHOULD SOMEHOW INTERVENE TO GUARANTEE AFFORDABLE HEALTH CARE FOR EVERYONE...
I TELL YOU-- IT'S UNAMERICAN!
PHARMACEUTICAL MANUFACTURERS CLAIM CLINTON'S CRAZY, LEFT-WING NOTION OF REGULATING DRUG PRICES WOULD HAVE DISASTROUS CONSEQUENCES...
YOU SEE--WE MUST CHARGE MORE FOR DRUGS THAN MOST PEOPLE CAN POSSIBLY AFFORD WITHOUT A GENEROUS INSURANCE PLAN--
--IN ORDER TO FINANCE THE DEVELOPMENT OF NEW DRUGS WHICH PEOPLE WILL ALSO BE UNABLE TO AFFORD!
OF COURSE, CLINTON'S CONSERVATIVE CRITICS WERE SILENT ON ONE RECENT OCCASION-- WHEN HE APPROVED THE STARTUP OF A CONTROVERSIAL TOXIC WASTE INCINERATOR IN OHIO... DESPITE PROMISES TO THE CONTRARY BY AL GORE...
--AN INCINERATOR WHICH, ACCORDING TO THE N.Y. TIMES, WAS INITIALLY FINANCED BY ONE OF YOUR MAJOR BACKERS...
ULP! IS THAT RIGHT? WHY-- WHAT AN ODD COINCIDENCE!
HEH, HEH...
TOM TOMORROW © 4-6-93

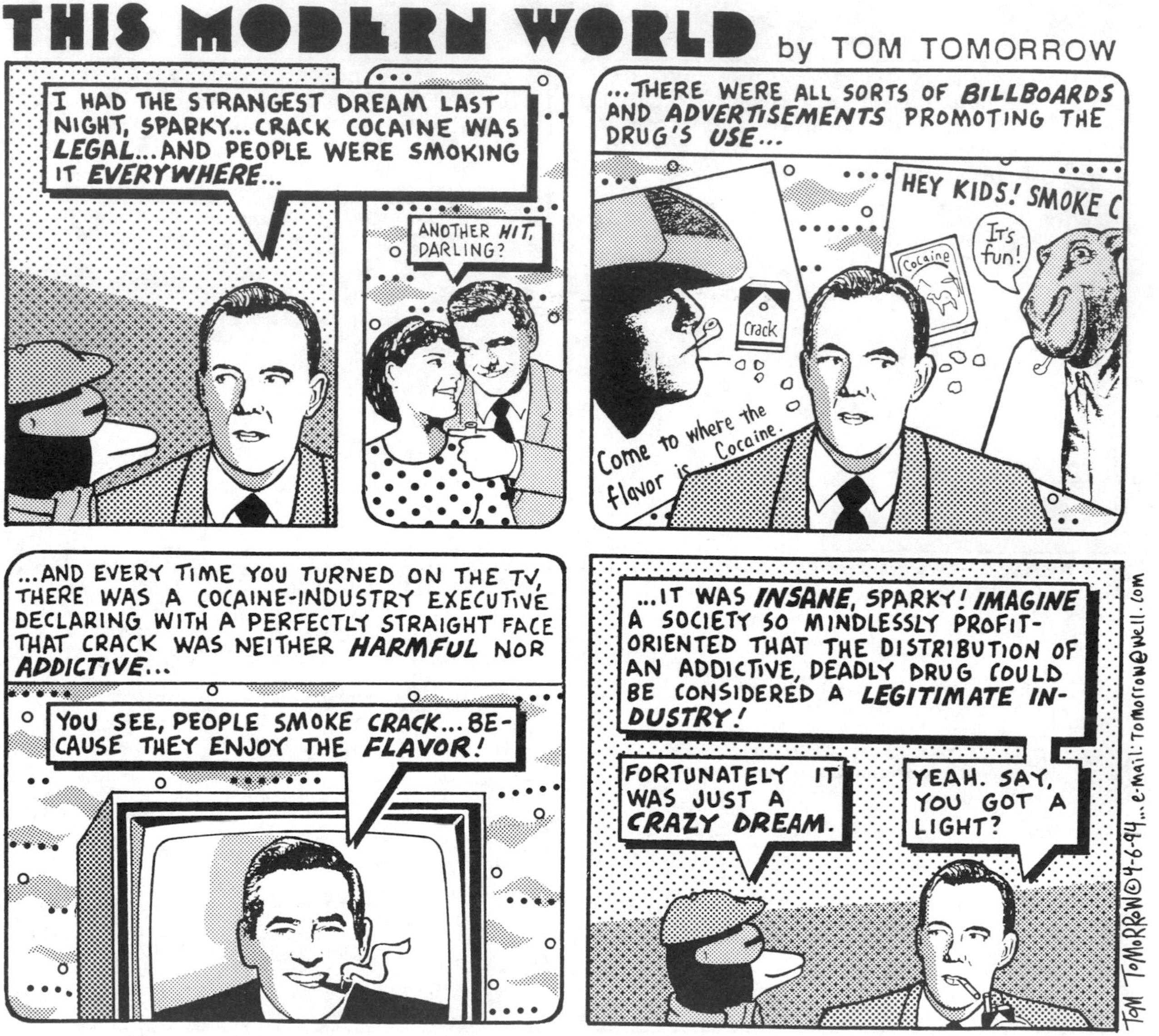
THIS MODERN WORLD by TOM TOMORROW
I HAD THE STRANGEST DREAM LAST NIGHT, SPARKY... CRACK COCAINE WAS LEGAL... AND PEOPLE WERE SMOKING IT EVERYWHERE...
ANOTHER HIT, DARLING?
...THERE WERE ALL SORTS OF BILLBOARDS AND ADVERTISEMENTS PROMOTING THE DRUG'S USE...
Crack
Come to where the flavor is... Cocaine.
HEY KIDS! SMOKE C
It's fun!
Cocaine
...AND EVERY TIME YOU TURNED ON THE TV, THERE WAS A COCAINE-INDUSTRY EXECUTIVE DECLARING WITH A PERFECTLY STRAIGHT FACE THAT CRACK WAS NEITHER HARMFUL NOR ADDICTIVE...
YOU SEE, PEOPLE SMOKE CRACK... BECAUSE THEY ENJOY THE FLAVOR!
...IT WAS INSANE, SPARKY! IMAGINE A SOCIETY SO MINDLESSLY PROFIT-ORIENTED THAT THE DISTRIBUTION OF AN ADDICTIVE, DEADLY DRUG COULD BE CONSIDERED A LEGITIMATE INDUSTRY!
FORTUNATELY IT WAS JUST A CRAZY DREAM.
YEAH. SAY, YOU GOT A LIGHT?
TOM TOMORROW©4-6-94... e-mail: tomorrow@well.com

THIS MODERN WORLD by TOM TOMORROW

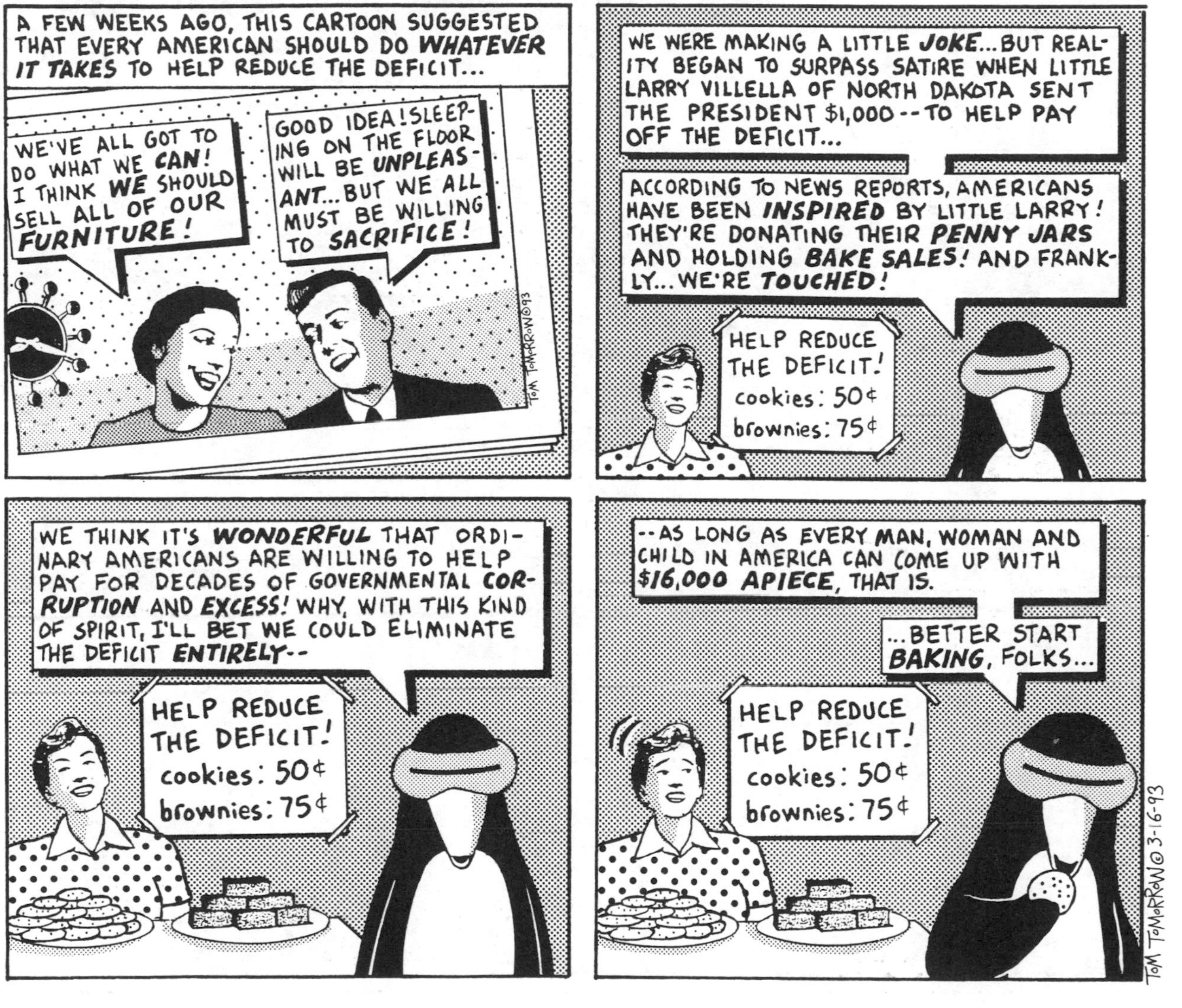

A FEW WEEKS AGO, THIS CARTOON SUGGESTED THAT EVERY AMERICAN SHOULD DO WHATEVER IT TAKES TO HELP REDUCE THE DEFICIT...
WE'VE ALL GOT TO DO WHAT WE CAN! I THINK WE SHOULD SELL ALL OF OUR FURNITURE!
GOOD IDEA! SLEEPING ON THE FLOOR WILL BE UNPLEASANT... BUT WE ALL MUST BE WILLING TO SACRIFICE!
TOM TOMORROW©93
WE WERE MAKING A LITTLE JOKE... BUT REALITY BEGAN TO SURPASS SATIRE WHEN LITTLE LARRY VILLELLA OF NORTH DAKOTA SENT THE PRESIDENT $1,000 -- TO HELP PAY OFF THE DEFICIT...
ACCORDING TO NEWS REPORTS, AMERICANS HAVE BEEN INSPIRED BY LITTLE LARRY! THEY'RE DONATING THEIR PENNY JARS AND HOLDING BAKE SALES! AND FRANKLY... WE'RE TOUCHED!
HELP REDUCE THE DEFICIT! cookies: 50¢ brownies: 75¢
WE THINK IT'S WONDERFUL THAT ORDINARY AMERICANS ARE WILLING TO HELP PAY FOR DECADES OF GOVERNMENTAL CORRUPTION AND EXCESS! WHY, WITH THIS KIND OF SPIRIT, I'LL BET WE COULD ELIMINATE THE DEFICIT ENTIRELY--
HELP REDUCE THE DEFICIT! cookies: 50¢ brownies: 75¢
--AS LONG AS EVERY MAN, WOMAN AND CHILD IN AMERICA CAN COME UP WITH $16,000 APIECE, THAT IS.
...BETTER START BAKING, FOLKS...
HELP REDUCE THE DEFICIT! cookies: 50¢ brownies: 75¢
TOM TOMORROW© 3-16-93

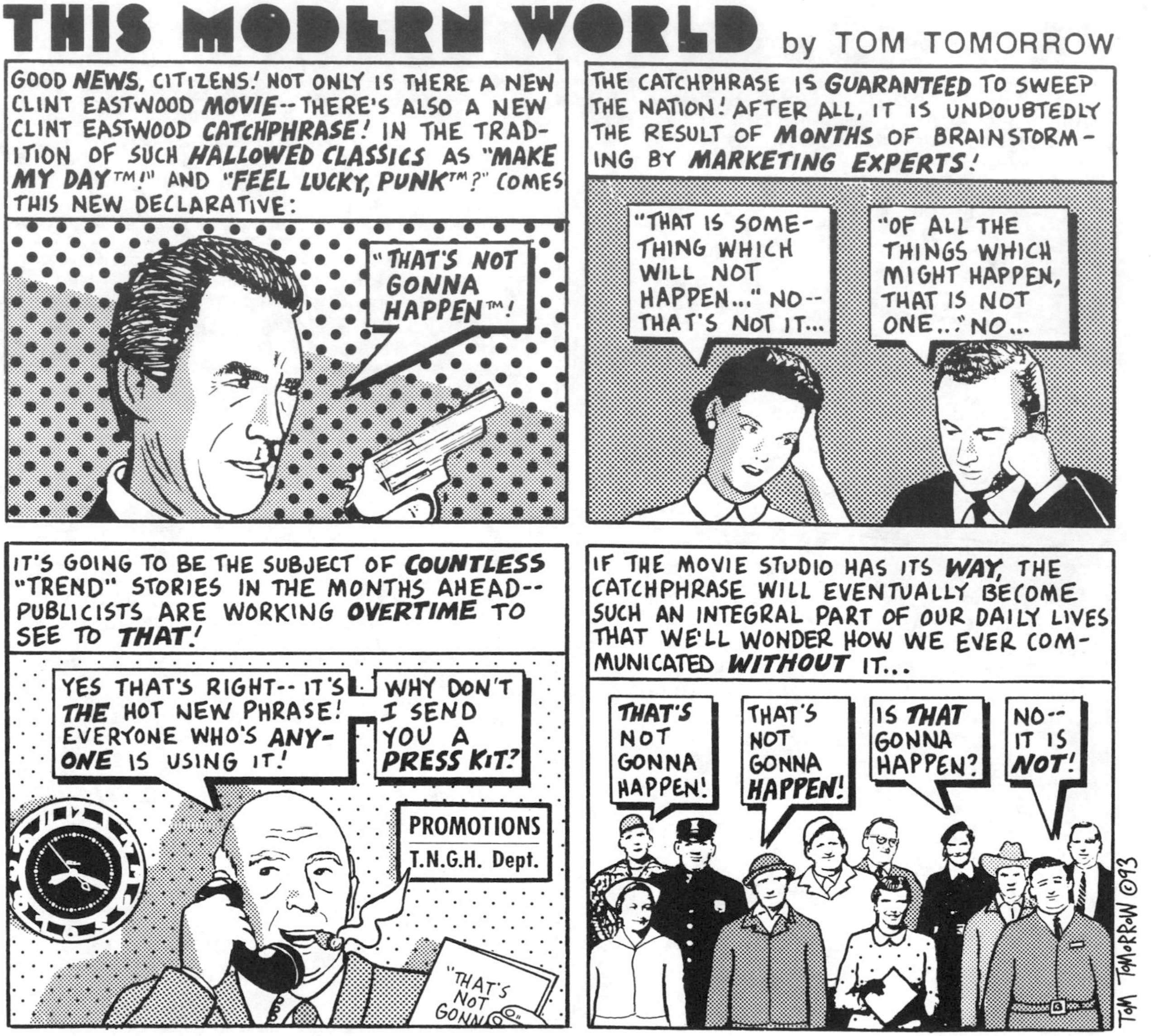
THIS MODERN WORLD by TOM TOMORROW
GOOD NEWS, CITIZENS! NOT ONLY IS THERE A NEW CLINT EASTWOOD MOVIE--THERE'S ALSO A NEW CLINT EASTWOOD CATCHPHRASE! IN THE TRADITION OF SUCH HALLOWED CLASSICS AS "MAKE MY DAY™!" AND "FEEL LUCKY, PUNK™?" COMES THIS NEW DECLARATIVE:
"THAT'S NOT GONNA HAPPEN™!
THE CATCHPHRASE IS GUARANTEED TO SWEEP THE NATION! AFTER ALL, IT IS UNDOUBTEDLY THE RESULT OF MONTHS OF BRAINSTORMING BY MARKETING EXPERTS!
"THAT IS SOMETHING WHICH WILL NOT HAPPEN..." NO-- THAT'S NOT IT...
"OF ALL THE THINGS WHICH MIGHT HAPPEN, THAT IS NOT ONE..." NO...
IT'S GOING TO BE THE SUBJECT OF COUNTLESS "TREND" STORIES IN THE MONTHS AHEAD-- PUBLICISTS ARE WORKING OVERTIME TO SEE TO THAT!
YES THAT'S RIGHT-- IT'S THE HOT NEW PHRASE! EVERYONE WHO'S ANYONE IS USING IT!
WHY DON'T I SEND YOU A PRESS KIT?
PROMOTIONS
T.N.G.H. Dept.
"THAT'S NOT GONN
IF THE MOVIE STUDIO HAS ITS WAY, THE CATCHPHRASE WILL EVENTUALLY BECOME SUCH AN INTEGRAL PART OF OUR DAILY LIVES THAT WE'LL WONDER HOW WE EVER COMMUNICATED WITHOUT IT...
THAT'S NOT GONNA HAPPEN!
THAT'S NOT GONNA HAPPEN!
IS THAT GONNA HAPPEN?
NO-- IT IS NOT!
TOM TOMORROW ©93

THIS MODERN WORLD by TOM TOMORROW

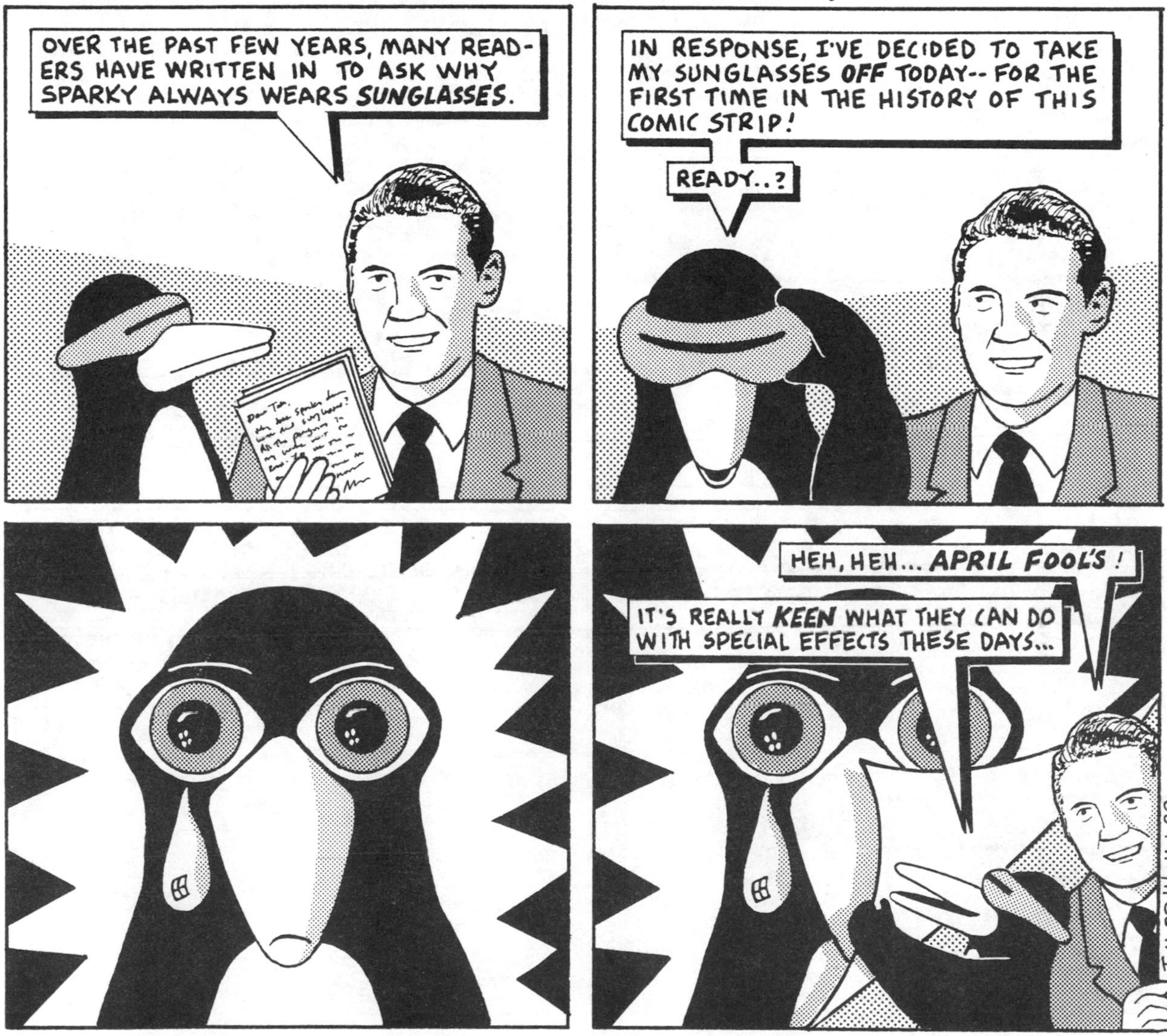
OVER THE PAST FEW YEARS, MANY READERS HAVE WRITTEN IN TO ASK WHY SPARKY ALWAYS WEARS SUNGLASSES.
IN RESPONSE, I'VE DECIDED TO TAKE MY SUNGLASSES OFF TODAY-- FOR THE FIRST TIME IN THE HISTORY OF THIS COMIC STRIP!
READY..?
HEH, HEH... APRIL FOOL'S!
IT'S REALLY KEEN WHAT THEY CAN DO WITH SPECIAL EFFECTS THESE DAYS...
TOM TOMORROW©4-1-93

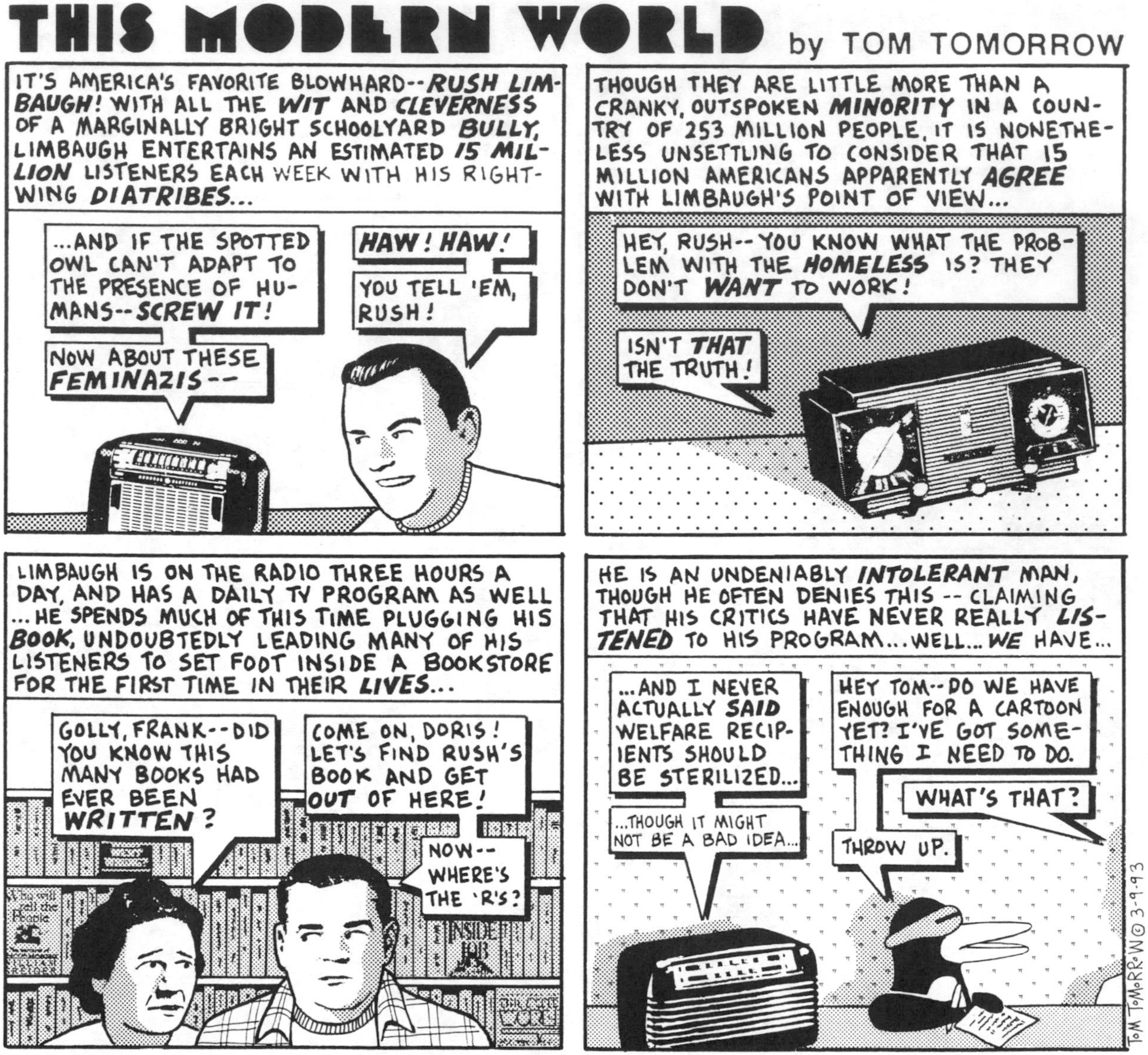
THIS MODERN WORLD by TOM TOMORROW
IT'S AMERICA'S FAVORITE BLOWHARD--RUSH LIMBAUGH! WITH ALL THE WIT AND CLEVERNESS OF A MARGINALLY BRIGHT SCHOOLYARD BULLY, LIMBAUGH ENTERTAINS AN ESTIMATED 15 MILLION LISTENERS EACH WEEK WITH HIS RIGHT-WING DIATRIBES...
...AND IF THE SPOTTED OWL CAN'T ADAPT TO THE PRESENCE OF HUMANS--SCREW IT!
NOW ABOUT THESE FEMINAZIS--
HAW! HAW!
YOU TELL 'EM, RUSH!
THOUGH THEY ARE LITTLE MORE THAN A CRANKY, OUTSPOKEN MINORITY IN A COUNTRY OF 253 MILLION PEOPLE, IT IS NONETHELESS UNSETTLING TO CONSIDER THAT 15 MILLION AMERICANS APPARENTLY AGREE WITH LIMBAUGH'S POINT OF VIEW...
HEY, RUSH--YOU KNOW WHAT THE PROBLEM WITH THE HOMELESS IS? THEY DON'T WANT TO WORK!
ISN'T THAT THE TRUTH!
LIMBAUGH IS ON THE RADIO THREE HOURS A DAY, AND HAS A DAILY TV PROGRAM AS WELL ...HE SPENDS MUCH OF THIS TIME PLUGGING HIS BOOK, UNDOUBTEDLY LEADING MANY OF HIS LISTENERS TO SET FOOT INSIDE A BOOKSTORE FOR THE FIRST TIME IN THEIR LIVES...
GOLLY, FRANK--DID YOU KNOW THIS MANY BOOKS HAD EVER BEEN WRITTEN?
COME ON, DORIS! LET'S FIND RUSH'S BOOK AND GET OUT OF HERE!
NOW--WHERE'S THE 'R'S?
INSIDE JOB
HE IS AN UNDENIABLY INTOLERANT MAN, THOUGH HE OFTEN DENIES THIS -- CLAIMING THAT HIS CRITICS HAVE NEVER REALLY LISTENED TO HIS PROGRAM...WELL...WE HAVE...
...AND I NEVER ACTUALLY SAID WELFARE RECIPIENTS SHOULD BE STERILIZED...
...THOUGH IT MIGHT NOT BE A BAD IDEA...
HEY TOM--DO WE HAVE ENOUGH FOR A CARTOON YET? I'VE GOT SOMETHING I NEED TO DO.
WHAT'S THAT?
THROW UP.
TOM TOMORROW © 3-9-93

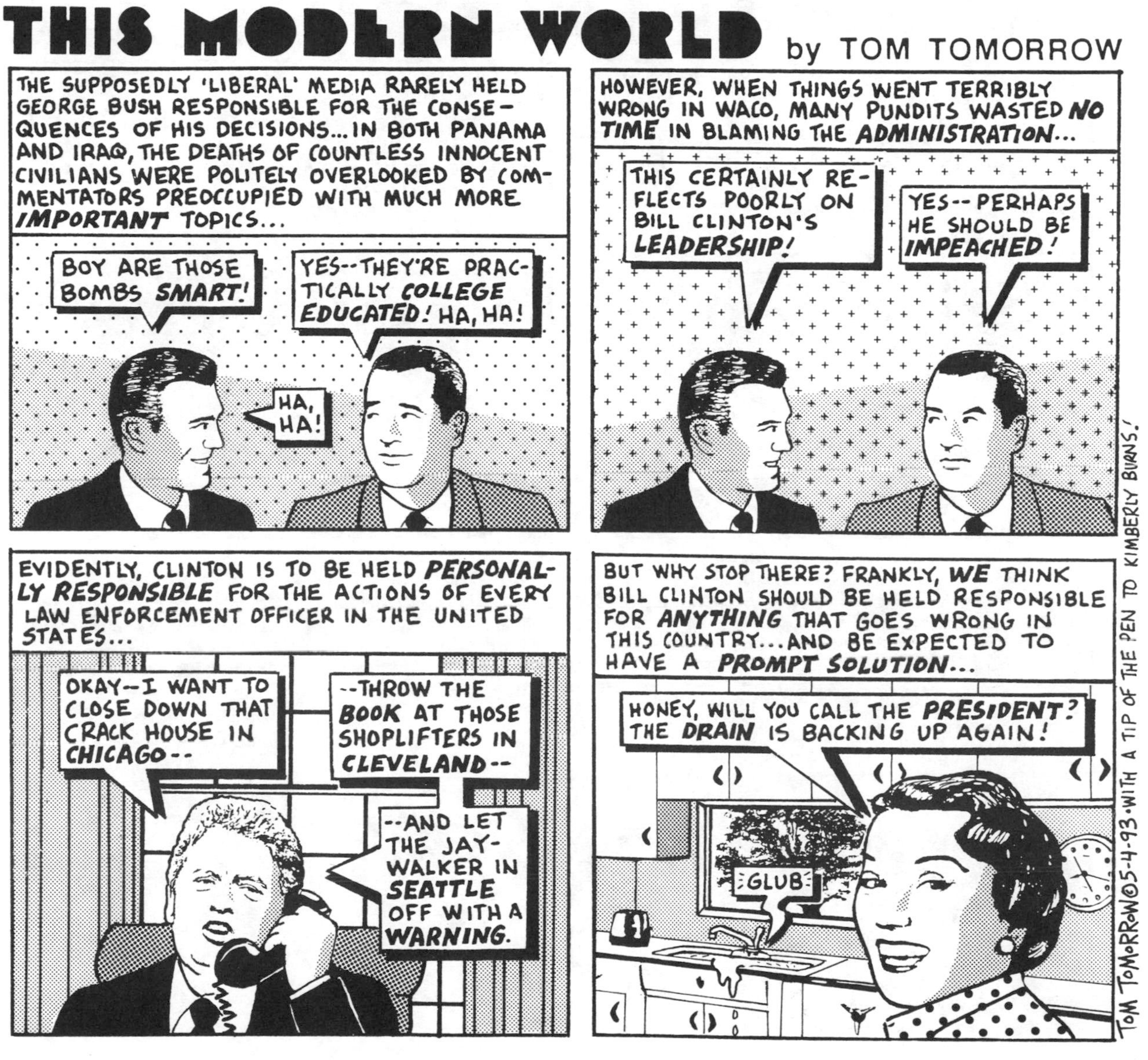
THIS MODERN WORLD by TOM TOMORROW
THE SUPPOSEDLY 'LIBERAL' MEDIA RARELY HELD GEORGE BUSH RESPONSIBLE FOR THE CONSEQUENCES OF HIS DECISIONS... IN BOTH PANAMA AND IRAQ, THE DEATHS OF COUNTLESS INNOCENT CIVILIANS WERE POLITELY OVERLOOKED BY COMMENTATORS PREOCCUPIED WITH MUCH MORE IMPORTANT TOPICS...
BOY ARE THOSE BOMBS SMART!
YES--THEY'RE PRACTICALLY COLLEGE EDUCATED! HA, HA!
HA, HA!
HOWEVER, WHEN THINGS WENT TERRIBLY WRONG IN WACO, MANY PUNDITS WASTED NO TIME IN BLAMING THE ADMINISTRATION...
THIS CERTAINLY REFLECTS POORLY ON BILL CLINTON'S LEADERSHIP!
YES--PERHAPS HE SHOULD BE IMPEACHED!
EVIDENTLY, CLINTON IS TO BE HELD PERSONALLY RESPONSIBLE FOR THE ACTIONS OF EVERY LAW ENFORCEMENT OFFICER IN THE UNITED STATES...
OKAY--I WANT TO CLOSE DOWN THAT CRACK HOUSE IN CHICAGO--
--THROW THE BOOK AT THOSE SHOPLIFTERS IN CLEVELAND--
--AND LET THE JAY-WALKER IN SEATTLE OFF WITH A WARNING.
BUT WHY STOP THERE? FRANKLY, WE THINK BILL CLINTON SHOULD BE HELD RESPONSIBLE FOR ANYTHING THAT GOES WRONG IN THIS COUNTRY... AND BE EXPECTED TO HAVE A PROMPT SOLUTION...
HONEY, WILL YOU CALL THE PRESIDENT? THE DRAIN IS BACKING UP AGAIN!
GLUB
TOM TOMORROW©5-4-93 • WITH A TIP OF THE PEN TO KIMBERLY BURNS!

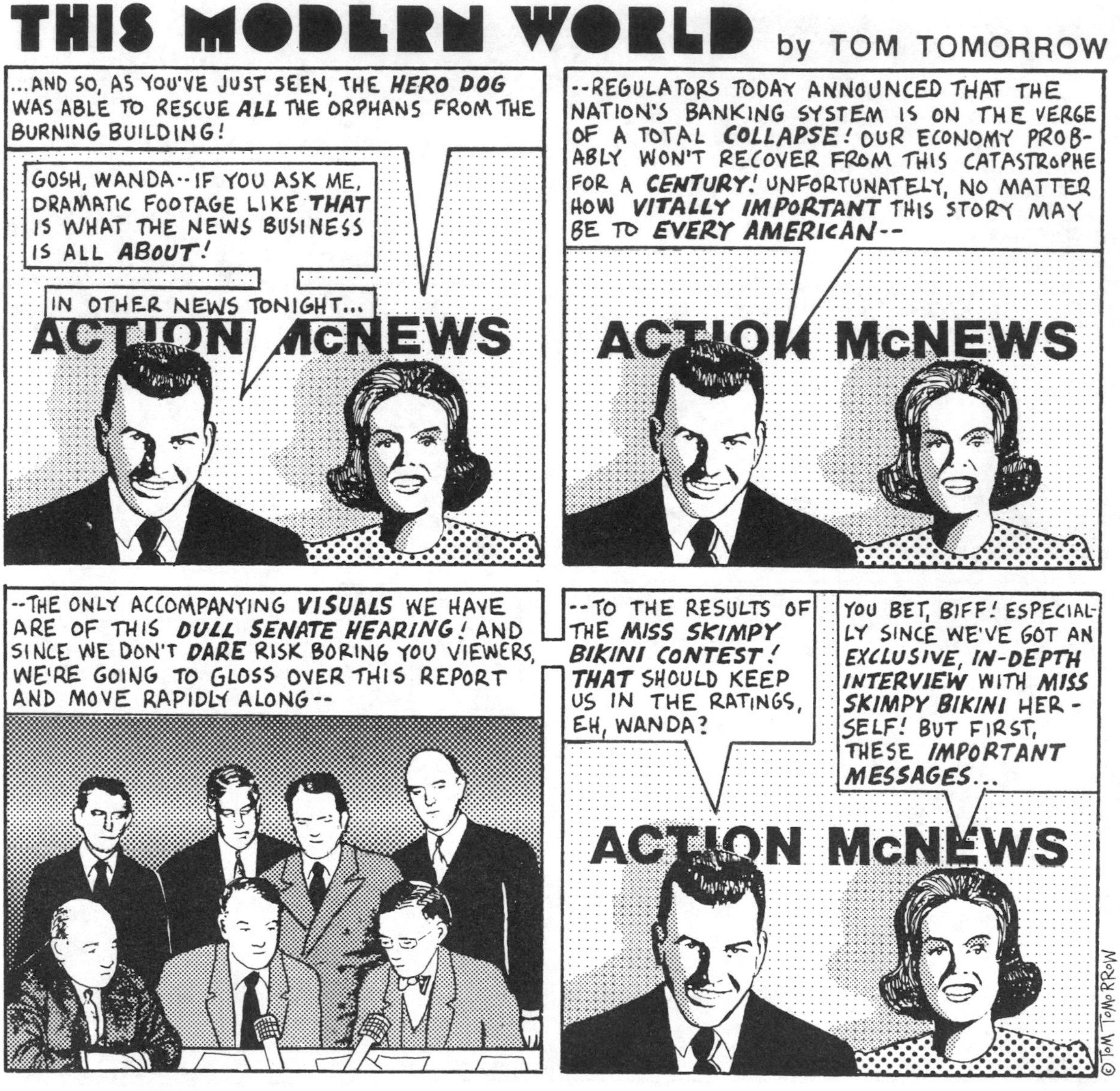
THIS MODERN WORLD by TOM TOMORROW
...AND SO, AS YOU'VE JUST SEEN, THE HERO DOG WAS ABLE TO RESCUE ALL THE ORPHANS FROM THE BURNING BUILDING!
GOSH, WANDA--IF YOU ASK ME, DRAMATIC FOOTAGE LIKE THAT IS WHAT THE NEWS BUSINESS IS ALL ABOUT!
IN OTHER NEWS TONIGHT...
ACTION McNEWS
--REGULATORS TODAY ANNOUNCED THAT THE NATION'S BANKING SYSTEM IS ON THE VERGE OF A TOTAL COLLAPSE! OUR ECONOMY PROBABLY WON'T RECOVER FROM THIS CATASTROPHE FOR A CENTURY! UNFORTUNATELY, NO MATTER HOW VITALLY IMPORTANT THIS STORY MAY BE TO EVERY AMERICAN--
ACTION McNEWS
--THE ONLY ACCOMPANYING VISUALS WE HAVE ARE OF THIS DULL SENATE HEARING! AND SINCE WE DON'T DARE RISK BORING YOU VIEWERS, WE'RE GOING TO GLOSS OVER THIS REPORT AND MOVE RAPIDLY ALONG--
--TO THE RESULTS OF THE MISS SKIMPY BIKINI CONTEST! THAT SHOULD KEEP US IN THE RATINGS, EH, WANDA?
YOU BET, BIFF! ESPECIALLY SINCE WE'VE GOT AN EXCLUSIVE, IN-DEPTH INTERVIEW WITH MISS SKIMPY BIKINI HERSELF! BUT FIRST, THESE IMPORTANT MESSAGES...
ACTION McNEWS
© TOM TOMORROW

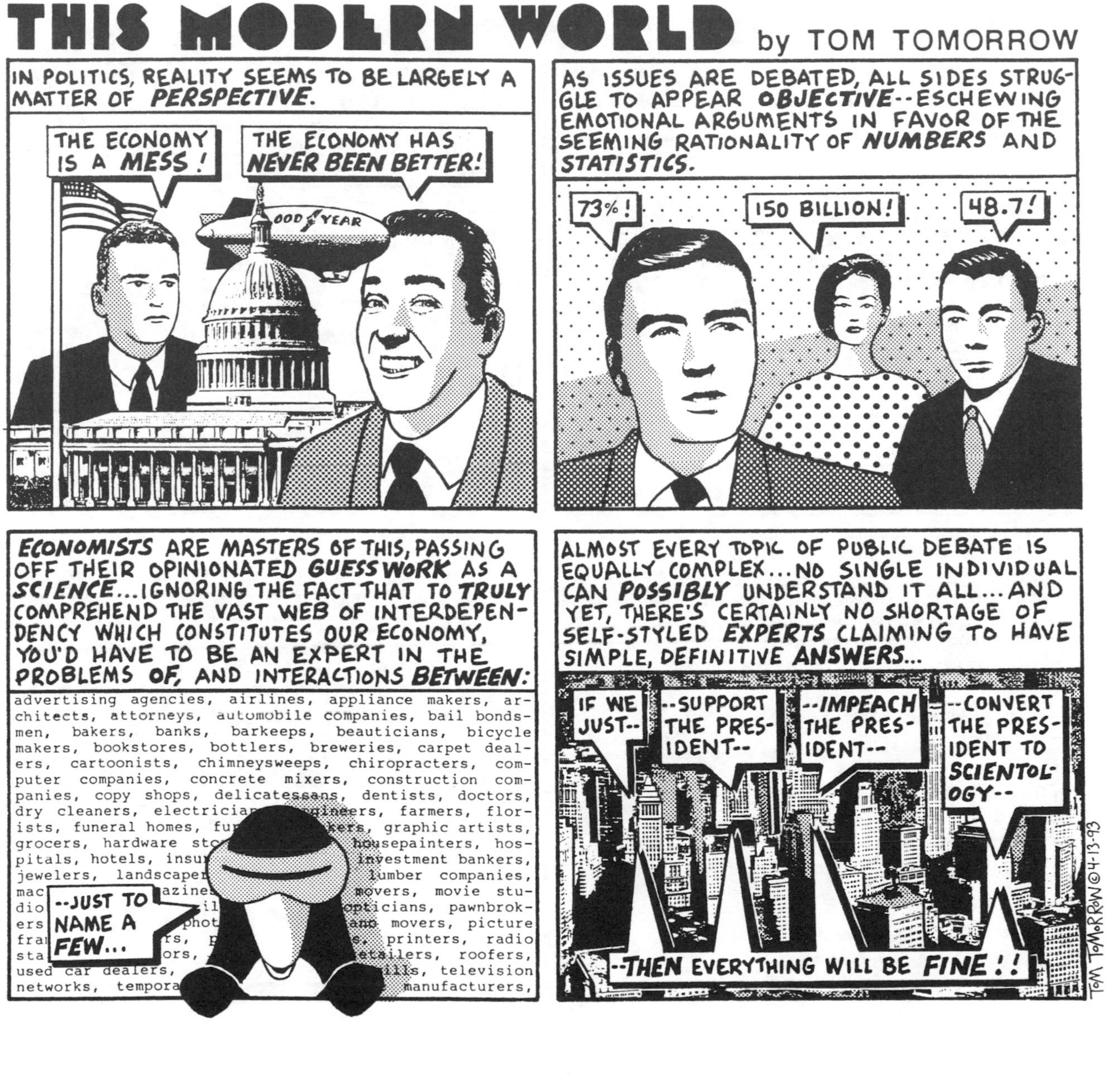
THIS MODERN WORLD by TOM TOMORROW
IN POLITICS, REALITY SEEMS TO BE LARGELY A MATTER OF PERSPECTIVE.
THE ECONOMY IS A MESS!
THE ECONOMY HAS NEVER BEEN BETTER!
OOD YEAR
AS ISSUES ARE DEBATED, ALL SIDES STRUGGLE TO APPEAR OBJECTIVE--ESCHEWING EMOTIONAL ARGUMENTS IN FAVOR OF THE SEEMING RATIONALITY OF NUMBERS AND STATISTICS.
73%!
150 BILLION!
48.7!
ECONOMISTS ARE MASTERS OF THIS, PASSING OFF THEIR OPINIONATED GUESSWORK AS A SCIENCE...IGNORING THE FACT THAT TO TRULY COMPREHEND THE VAST WEB OF INTERDEPENDENCY WHICH CONSTITUTES OUR ECONOMY, YOU'D HAVE TO BE AN EXPERT IN THE PROBLEMS OF, AND INTERACTIONS BETWEEN:
advertising agencies, airlines, appliance makers, architects, attorneys, automobile companies, bail bondsmen, bakers, banks, barkeeps, beauticians, bicycle makers, bookstores, bottlers, breweries, carpet dealers, cartoonists, chimneysweeps, chiropracters, computer companies, concrete mixers, construction companies, copy shops, delicatessans, dentists, doctors,
dry cleaners, electricia ers, farmers, flor-
ists, funeral homes, fu kers, graphic artists,
grocers, hardware st housepainters, hospitals, hotels, insu investment bankers,
jewelers, landscape lumber companies,
mac azines movers, movie studio il opticians, pawnbrok-
ers phot movers, picture
fra rs, printers, radio
sta ors, etailers, roofers,
used car dealers, ills, television
networks, tempora manufacturers,
--JUST TO NAME A FEW...
ALMOST EVERY TOPIC OF PUBLIC DEBATE IS EQUALLY COMPLEX...NO SINGLE INDIVIDUAL CAN POSSIBLY UNDERSTAND IT ALL...AND YET, THERE'S CERTAINLY NO SHORTAGE OF SELF-STYLED EXPERTS CLAIMING TO HAVE SIMPLE, DEFINITIVE ANSWERS...
IF WE JUST--
--SUPPORT THE PRESIDENT--
--IMPEACH THE PRESIDENT--
--CONVERT THE PRESIDENT TO SCIENTOLOGY--
--THEN EVERYTHING WILL BE FINE!!
TOM TOMORROW©4-13-93

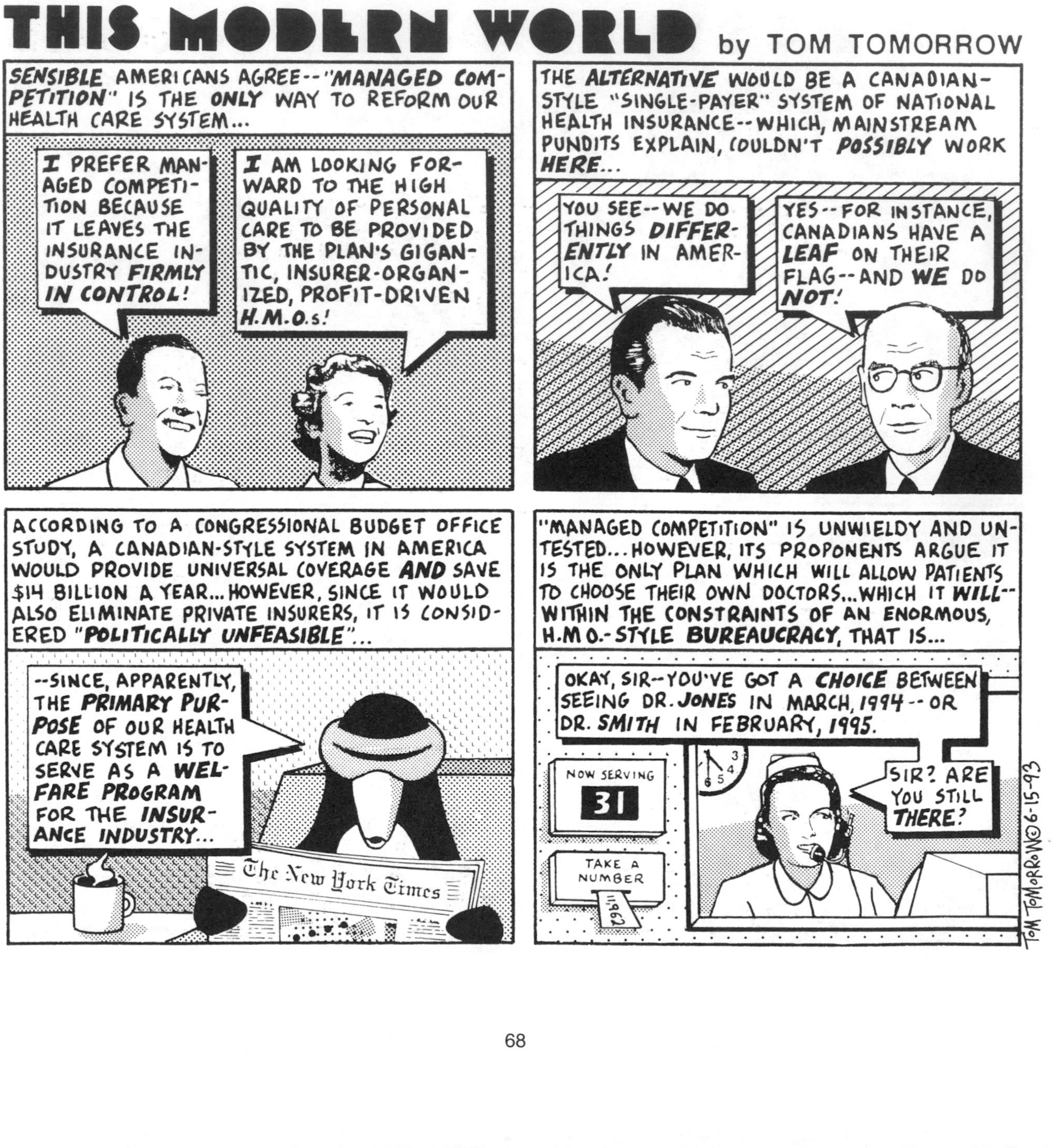
THIS MODERN WORLD
by TOM TOMORROW
SENSIBLE AMERICANS AGREE--"MANAGED COMPETITION" IS THE ONLY WAY TO REFORM OUR HEALTH CARE SYSTEM...
I PREFER MANAGED COMPETITION BECAUSE IT LEAVES THE INSURANCE INDUSTRY FIRMLY IN CONTROL!
I AM LOOKING FORWARD TO THE HIGH QUALITY OF PERSONAL CARE TO BE PROVIDED BY THE PLAN'S GIGANTIC, INSURER-ORGANIZED, PROFIT-DRIVEN H.M.O.s!
THE ALTERNATIVE WOULD BE A CANADIAN-STYLE "SINGLE-PAYER" SYSTEM OF NATIONAL HEALTH INSURANCE--WHICH, MAINSTREAM PUNDITS EXPLAIN, COULDN'T POSSIBLY WORK HERE...
YOU SEE--WE DO THINGS DIFFERENTLY IN AMERICA!
YES--FOR INSTANCE, CANADIANS HAVE A LEAF ON THEIR FLAG--AND WE DO NOT!
ACCORDING TO A CONGRESSIONAL BUDGET OFFICE STUDY, A CANADIAN-STYLE SYSTEM IN AMERICA WOULD PROVIDE UNIVERSAL COVERAGE AND SAVE $14 BILLION A YEAR... HOWEVER, SINCE IT WOULD ALSO ELIMINATE PRIVATE INSURERS, IT IS CONSIDERED "POLITICALLY UNFEASIBLE"...
--SINCE, APPARENTLY, THE PRIMARY PURPOSE OF OUR HEALTH CARE SYSTEM IS TO SERVE AS A WELFARE PROGRAM FOR THE INSURANCE INDUSTRY...
The New York Times
"MANAGED COMPETITION" IS UNWIELDY AND UNTESTED... HOWEVER, ITS PROPONENTS ARGUE IT IS THE ONLY PLAN WHICH WILL ALLOW PATIENTS TO CHOOSE THEIR OWN DOCTORS... WHICH IT WILL--WITHIN THE CONSTRAINTS OF AN ENORMOUS, H.M.O.-STYLE BUREAUCRACY, THAT IS...
OKAY, SIR--YOU'VE GOT A CHOICE BETWEEN SEEING DR. JONES IN MARCH, 1994--OR DR. SMITH IN FEBRUARY, 1995.
NOW SERVING
31
TAKE A NUMBER
SIR? ARE YOU STILL THERE?
TOM TOMORROW©6-15-93

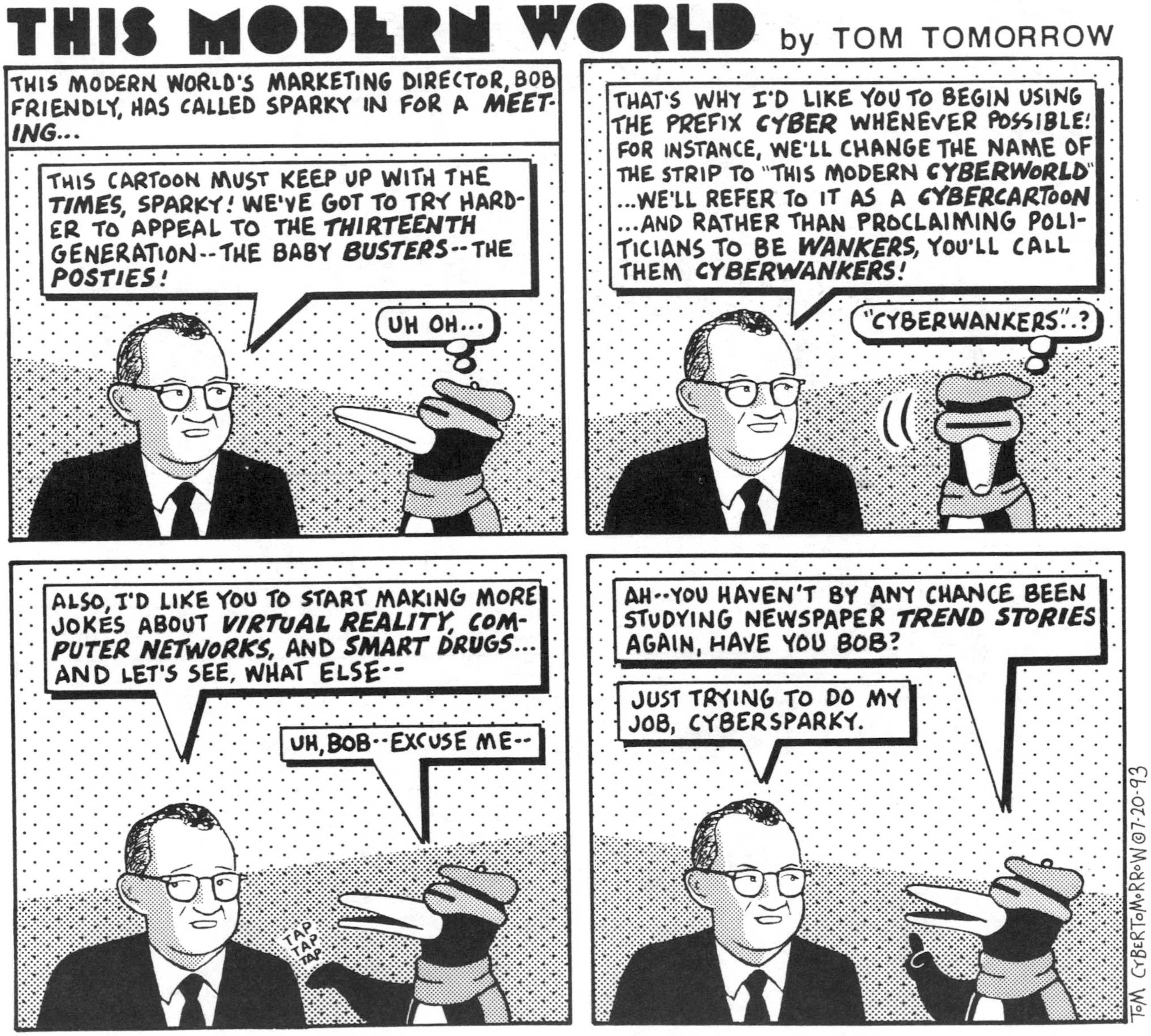
THIS MODERN WORLD by TOM TOMORROW
THIS MODERN WORLD'S MARKETING DIRECTOR, BOB FRIENDLY, HAS CALLED SPARKY IN FOR A MEETING...
THIS CARTOON MUST KEEP UP WITH THE TIMES, SPARKY! WE'VE GOT TO TRY HARDER TO APPEAL TO THE THIRTEENTH GENERATION--THE BABY BUSTERS--THE POSTIES!
UH OH...
THAT'S WHY I'D LIKE YOU TO BEGIN USING THE PREFIX CYBER WHENEVER POSSIBLE! FOR INSTANCE, WE'LL CHANGE THE NAME OF THE STRIP TO "THIS MODERN CYBERWORLD" ...WE'LL REFER TO IT AS A CYBERCARTOON ...AND RATHER THAN PROCLAIMING POLITICIANS TO BE WANKERS, YOU'LL CALL THEM CYBERWANKERS!
"CYBERWANKERS"..?
ALSO, I'D LIKE YOU TO START MAKING MORE JOKES ABOUT VIRTUAL REALITY, COMPUTER NETWORKS, AND SMART DRUGS... AND LET'S SEE, WHAT ELSE--
UH, BOB--EXCUSE ME--
TAP TAP TAP
AH--YOU HAVEN'T BY ANY CHANCE BEEN STUDYING NEWSPAPER TREND STORIES AGAIN, HAVE YOU BOB?
JUST TRYING TO DO MY JOB, CYBERSPARKY.
TOM CYBERTOMORROW©7-20-93

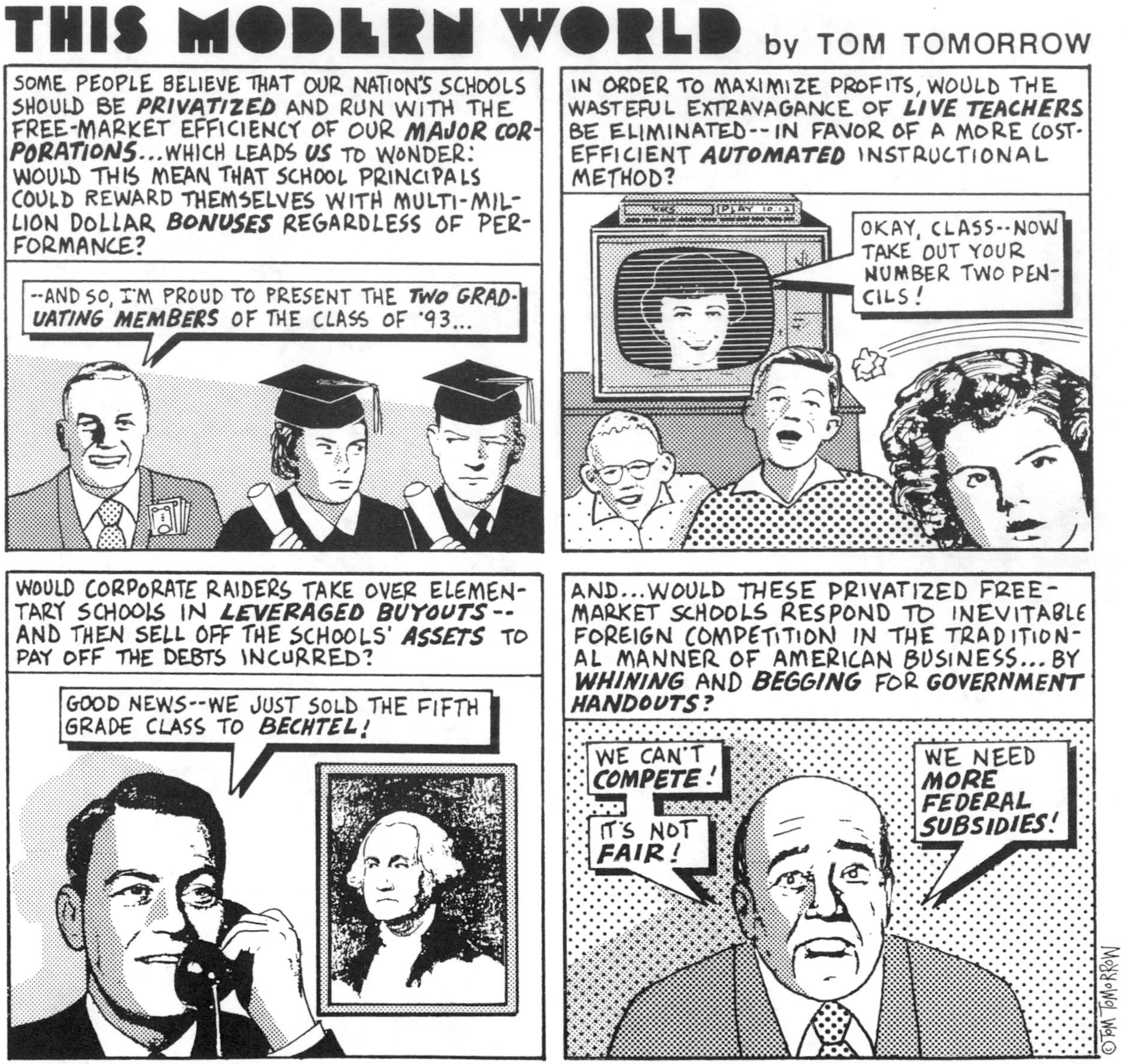
THIS MODERN WORLD by TOM TOMORROW
SOME PEOPLE BELIEVE THAT OUR NATION'S SCHOOLS SHOULD BE PRIVATIZED AND RUN WITH THE FREE-MARKET EFFICIENCY OF OUR MAJOR CORPORATIONS... WHICH LEADS US TO WONDER: WOULD THIS MEAN THAT SCHOOL PRINCIPALS COULD REWARD THEMSELVES WITH MULTI-MILLION DOLLAR BONUSES REGARDLESS OF PERFORMANCE?
--AND SO, I'M PROUD TO PRESENT THE TWO GRADUATING MEMBERS OF THE CLASS OF '93...
IN ORDER TO MAXIMIZE PROFITS, WOULD THE WASTEFUL EXTRAVAGANCE OF LIVE TEACHERS BE ELIMINATED--IN FAVOR OF A MORE COST-EFFICIENT AUTOMATED INSTRUCTIONAL METHOD?
OKAY, CLASS--NOW TAKE OUT YOUR NUMBER TWO PENCILS!
WOULD CORPORATE RAIDERS TAKE OVER ELEMENTARY SCHOOLS IN LEVERAGED BUYOUTS--AND THEN SELL OFF THE SCHOOLS' ASSETS TO PAY OFF THE DEBTS INCURRED?
GOOD NEWS--WE JUST SOLD THE FIFTH GRADE CLASS TO BECHTEL!
AND... WOULD THESE PRIVATIZED FREE-MARKET SCHOOLS RESPOND TO INEVITABLE FOREIGN COMPETITION IN THE TRADITIONAL MANNER OF AMERICAN BUSINESS... BY WHINING AND BEGGING FOR GOVERNMENT HANDOUTS?
WE CAN'T COMPETE!
IT'S NOT FAIR!
WE NEED MORE FEDERAL SUBSIDIES!
©TOM TOMORROW

THIS MODERN WORLD by TOM TOMORROW

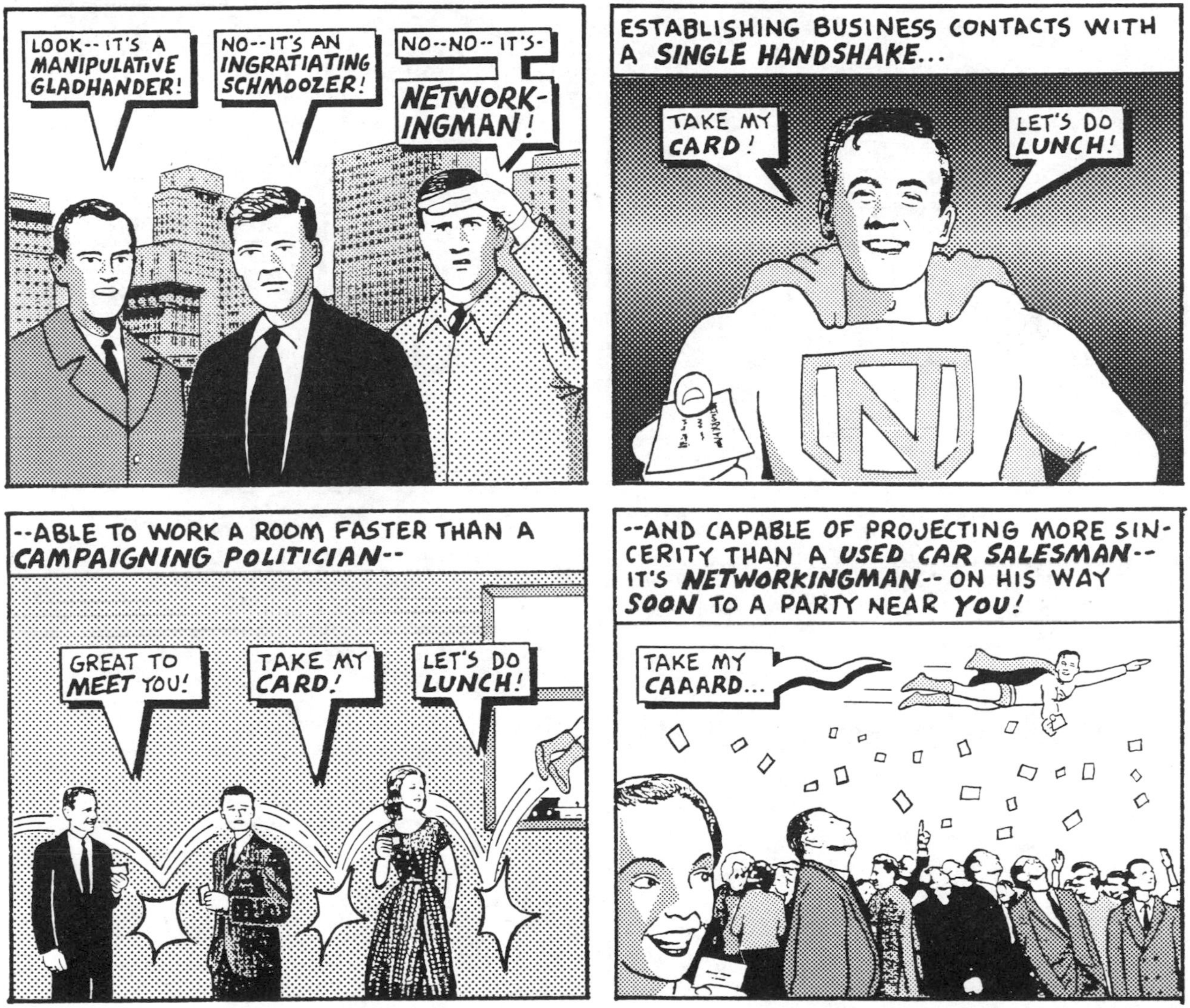
LOOK-- IT'S A MANIPULATIVE GLADHANDER!
NO--IT'S AN INGRATIATING SCHMOOZER!
NO--NO-- IT'S- NETWORK-INGMAN!
ESTABLISHING BUSINESS CONTACTS WITH A SINGLE HANDSHAKE...
TAKE MY CARD!
LET'S DO LUNCH!
--ABLE TO WORK A ROOM FASTER THAN A CAMPAIGNING POLITICIAN--
GREAT TO MEET YOU!
TAKE MY CARD!
LET'S DO LUNCH!
--AND CAPABLE OF PROJECTING MORE SINCERITY THAN A USED CAR SALESMAN-- IT'S NETWORKINGMAN-- ON HIS WAY SOON TO A PARTY NEAR YOU!
TAKE MY CAAARD...

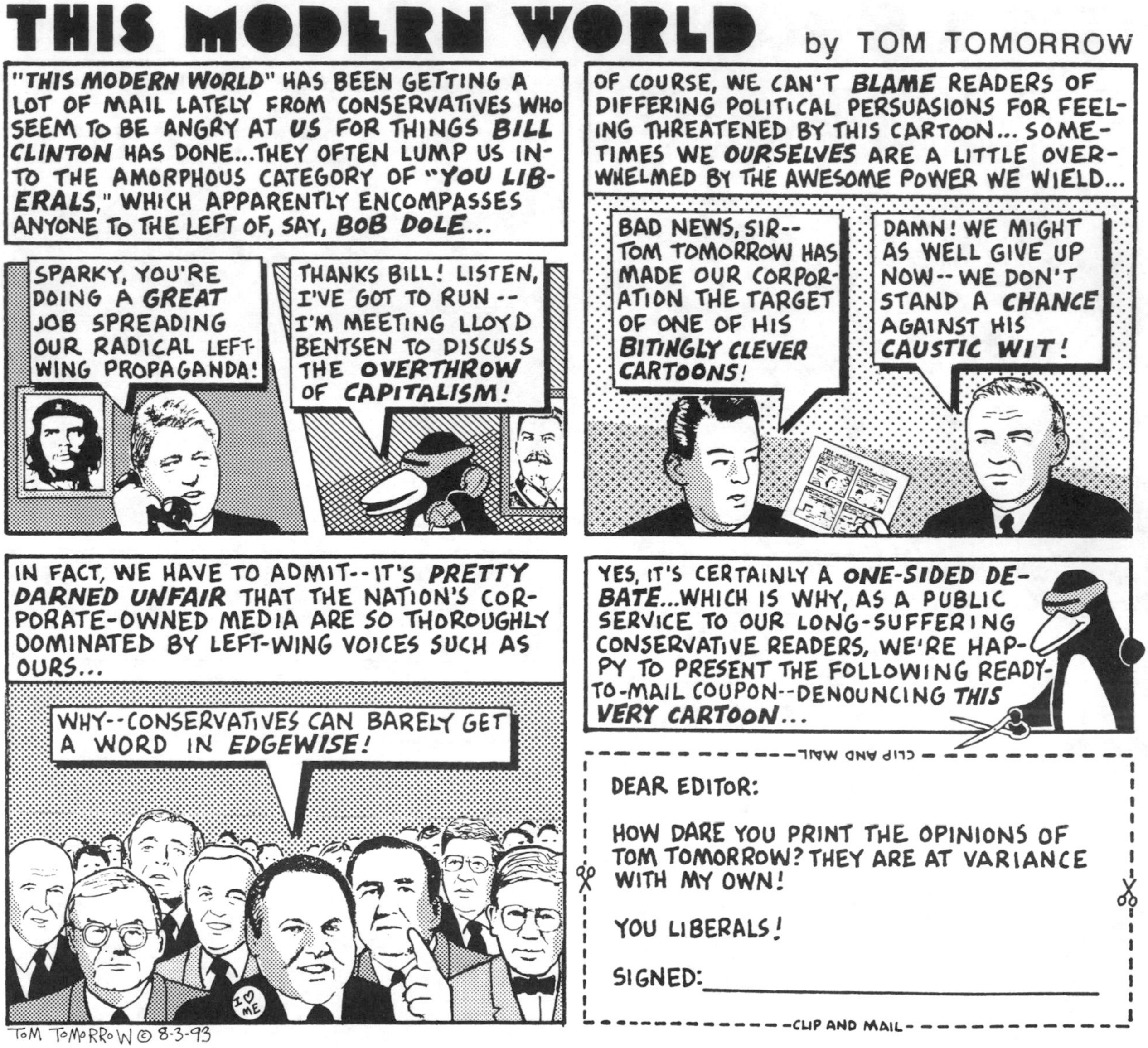
THIS MODERN WORLD by TOM TOMORROW
"THIS MODERN WORLD" HAS BEEN GETTING A LOT OF MAIL LATELY FROM CONSERVATIVES WHO SEEM TO BE ANGRY AT US FOR THINGS BILL CLINTON HAS DONE...THEY OFTEN LUMP US INTO THE AMORPHOUS CATEGORY OF "YOU LIBERALS," WHICH APPARENTLY ENCOMPASSES ANYONE TO THE LEFT OF, SAY, BOB DOLE...
SPARKY, YOU'RE DOING A GREAT JOB SPREADING OUR RADICAL LEFT-WING PROPAGANDA!
THANKS BILL! LISTEN, I'VE GOT TO RUN -- I'M MEETING LLOYD BENTSEN TO DISCUSS THE OVERTHROW OF CAPITALISM!
OF COURSE, WE CAN'T BLAME READERS OF DIFFERING POLITICAL PERSUASIONS FOR FEELING THREATENED BY THIS CARTOON... SOMETIMES WE OURSELVES ARE A LITTLE OVERWHELMED BY THE AWESOME POWER WE WIELD...
BAD NEWS, SIR-- TOM TOMORROW HAS MADE OUR CORPORATION THE TARGET OF ONE OF HIS BITINGLY CLEVER CARTOONS!
DAMN! WE MIGHT AS WELL GIVE UP NOW-- WE DON'T STAND A CHANCE AGAINST HIS CAUSTIC WIT!
IN FACT, WE HAVE TO ADMIT--IT'S PRETTY DARNED UNFAIR THAT THE NATION'S CORPORATE-OWNED MEDIA ARE SO THOROUGHLY DOMINATED BY LEFT-WING VOICES SUCH AS OURS...
WHY--CONSERVATIVES CAN BARELY GET A WORD IN EDGEWISE!
I ♡ ME
YES, IT'S CERTAINLY A ONE-SIDED DEBATE...WHICH IS WHY, AS A PUBLIC SERVICE TO OUR LONG-SUFFERING CONSERVATIVE READERS, WE'RE HAPPY TO PRESENT THE FOLLOWING READY-TO-MAIL COUPON--DENOUNCING THIS VERY CARTOON...
CLIP AND MAIL
DEAR EDITOR:
HOW DARE YOU PRINT THE OPINIONS OF TOM TOMORROW? THEY ARE AT VARIANCE WITH MY OWN!
YOU LIBERALS!
SIGNED:
CLIP AND MAIL
TOM TOMORROW © 8-3-93

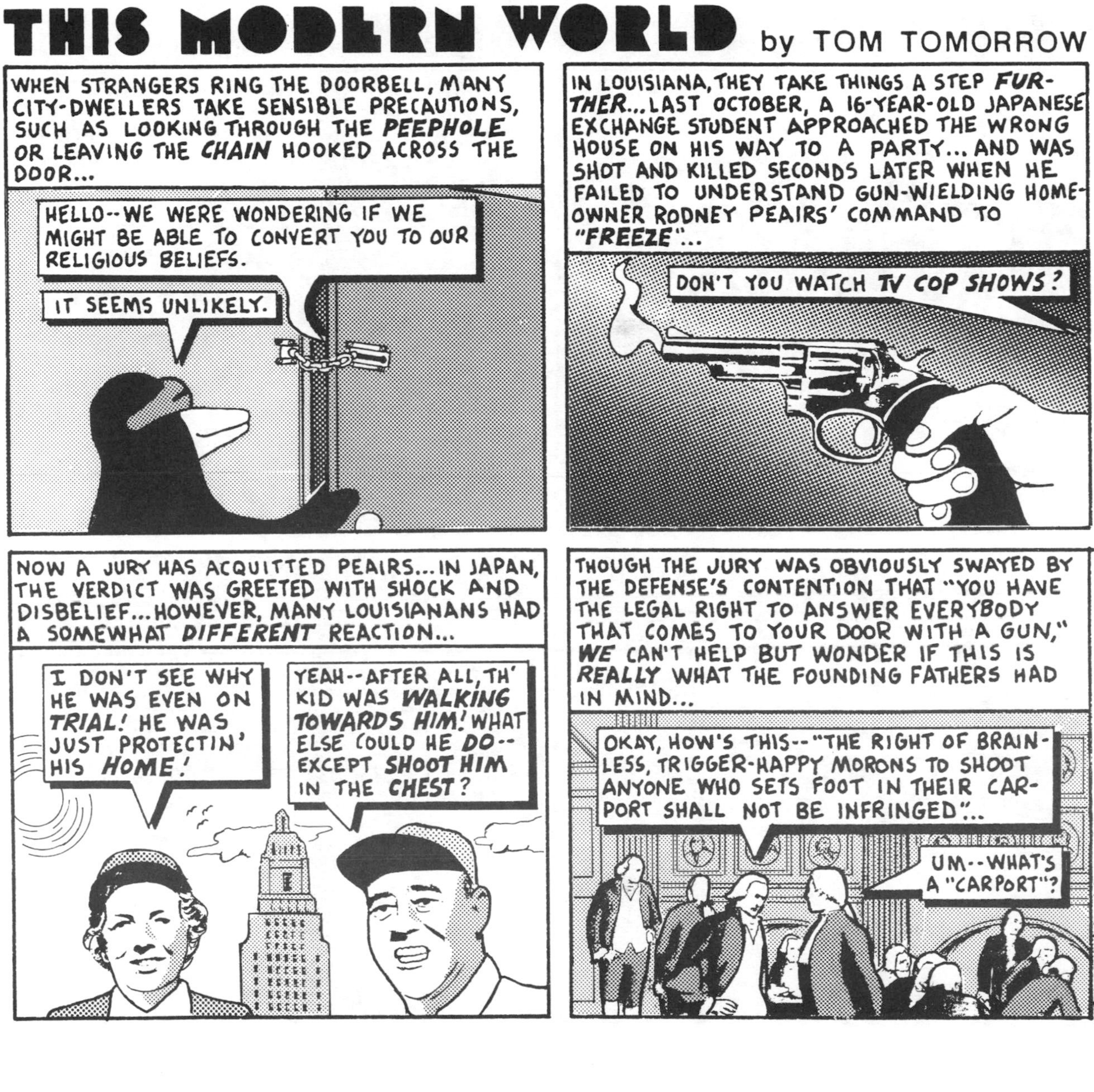
THIS MODERN WORLD by TOM TOMORROW
WHEN STRANGERS RING THE DOORBELL, MANY CITY-DWELLERS TAKE SENSIBLE PRECAUTIONS, SUCH AS LOOKING THROUGH THE PEEPHOLE OR LEAVING THE CHAIN HOOKED ACROSS THE DOOR...
HELLO--WE WERE WONDERING IF WE MIGHT BE ABLE TO CONVERT YOU TO OUR RELIGIOUS BELIEFS.
IT SEEMS UNLIKELY.
IN LOUISIANA, THEY TAKE THINGS A STEP FURTHER... LAST OCTOBER, A 16-YEAR-OLD JAPANESE EXCHANGE STUDENT APPROACHED THE WRONG HOUSE ON HIS WAY TO A PARTY... AND WAS SHOT AND KILLED SECONDS LATER WHEN HE FAILED TO UNDERSTAND GUN-WIELDING HOME-OWNER RODNEY PEAIRS' COMMAND TO "FREEZE"...
DON'T YOU WATCH TV COP SHOWS?
NOW A JURY HAS ACQUITTED PEAIRS... IN JAPAN, THE VERDICT WAS GREETED WITH SHOCK AND DISBELIEF... HOWEVER, MANY LOUISIANANS HAD A SOMEWHAT DIFFERENT REACTION...
I DON'T SEE WHY HE WAS EVEN ON TRIAL! HE WAS JUST PROTECTIN' HIS HOME!
YEAH--AFTER ALL, TH' KID WAS WALKING TOWARDS HIM! WHAT ELSE COULD HE DO--EXCEPT SHOOT HIM IN THE CHEST?
THOUGH THE JURY WAS OBVIOUSLY SWAYED BY THE DEFENSE'S CONTENTION THAT "YOU HAVE THE LEGAL RIGHT TO ANSWER EVERYBODY THAT COMES TO YOUR DOOR WITH A GUN," WE CAN'T HELP BUT WONDER IF THIS IS REALLY WHAT THE FOUNDING FATHERS HAD IN MIND...
OKAY, HOW'S THIS--"THE RIGHT OF BRAINLESS, TRIGGER-HAPPY MORONS TO SHOOT ANYONE WHO SETS FOOT IN THEIR CARPORT SHALL NOT BE INFRINGED"...
UM--WHAT'S A "CARPORT"?
TOM TOMORROW© 6-1-93

THIS MODERN WORLD by TOM TOMORROW

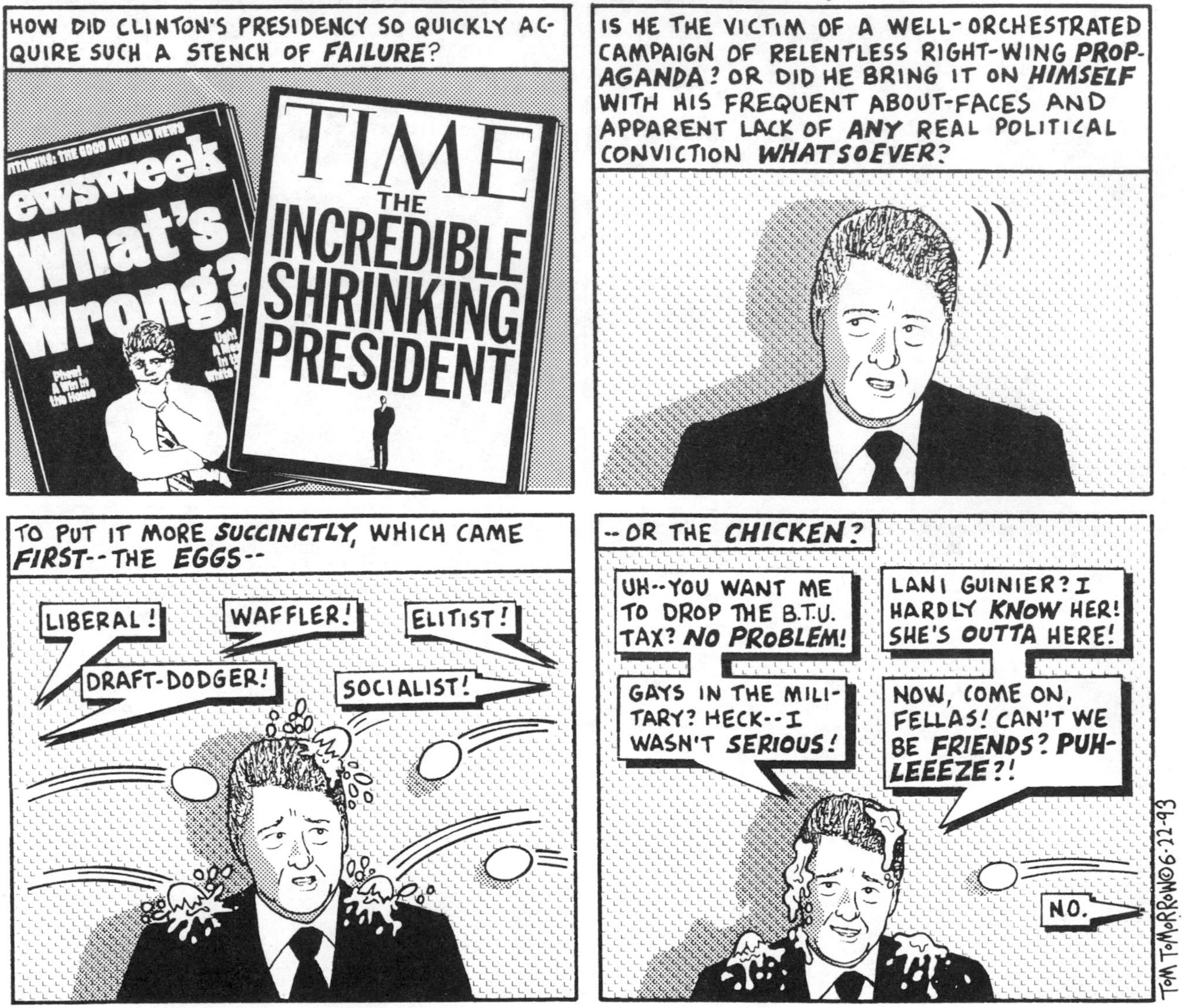

HOW DID CLINTON'S PRESIDENCY SO QUICKLY ACQUIRE SUCH A STENCH OF *FAILURE*?
ewsweek
What's Wrong?
TIME
THE INCREDIBLE SHRINKING PRESIDENT
IS HE THE VICTIM OF A WELL-ORCHESTRATED CAMPAIGN OF RELENTLESS RIGHT-WING *PROPAGANDA*? OR DID HE BRING IT ON *HIMSELF* WITH HIS FREQUENT ABOUT-FACES AND APPARENT LACK OF *ANY* REAL POLITICAL CONVICTION *WHATSOEVER*?
TO PUT IT MORE *SUCCINCTLY*, WHICH CAME *FIRST*--THE *EGGS*--
LIBERAL!
WAFFLER!
ELITIST!
DRAFT-DODGER!
SOCIALIST!
--OR THE *CHICKEN*?
UH--YOU WANT ME TO DROP THE B.T.U. TAX? *NO PROBLEM*!
LANI GUINIER? I HARDLY *KNOW* HER! SHE'S *OUTTA* HERE!
GAYS IN THE MILITARY? HECK--I WASN'T *SERIOUS*!
NOW, COME ON, FELLAS! CAN'T WE BE *FRIENDS*? *PUHLEEEZE*?!
NO.
TOM TOMORROW©6-22-93

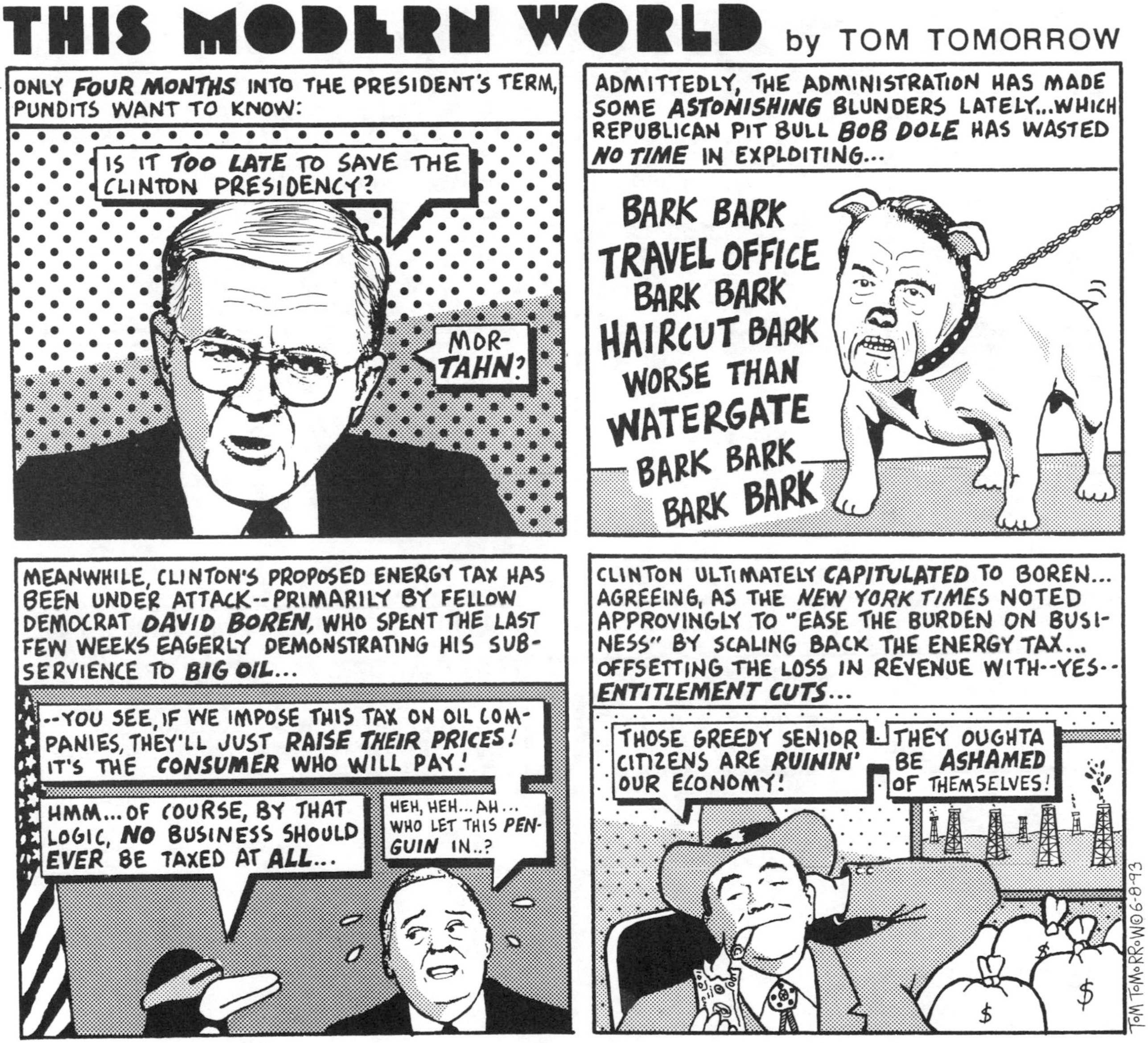
THIS MODERN WORLD by TOM TOMORROW
ONLY FOUR MONTHS INTO THE PRESIDENT'S TERM, PUNDITS WANT TO KNOW:
IS IT TOO LATE TO SAVE THE CLINTON PRESIDENCY?
MOR-TAHN?
ADMITTEDLY, THE ADMINISTRATION HAS MADE SOME ASTONISHING BLUNDERS LATELY...WHICH REPUBLICAN PIT BULL BOB DOLE HAS WASTED NO TIME IN EXPLOITING...
BARK BARK TRAVEL OFFICE BARK BARK HAIRCUT BARK WORSE THAN WATERGATE BARK BARK BARK BARK
MEANWHILE, CLINTON'S PROPOSED ENERGY TAX HAS BEEN UNDER ATTACK--PRIMARILY BY FELLOW DEMOCRAT DAVID BOREN, WHO SPENT THE LAST FEW WEEKS EAGERLY DEMONSTRATING HIS SUBSERVIENCE TO BIG OIL...
--YOU SEE, IF WE IMPOSE THIS TAX ON OIL COMPANIES, THEY'LL JUST RAISE THEIR PRICES! IT'S THE CONSUMER WHO WILL PAY!
HMM... OF COURSE, BY THAT LOGIC, NO BUSINESS SHOULD EVER BE TAXED AT ALL...
HEH, HEH... AH... WHO LET THIS PENGUIN IN..?
CLINTON ULTIMATELY CAPITULATED TO BOREN... AGREEING, AS THE NEW YORK TIMES NOTED APPROVINGLY TO "EASE THE BURDEN ON BUSINESS" BY SCALING BACK THE ENERGY TAX... OFFSETTING THE LOSS IN REVENUE WITH--YES--ENTITLEMENT CUTS...
THOSE GREEDY SENIOR CITIZENS ARE RUININ' OUR ECONOMY!
THEY OUGHTA BE ASHAMED OF THEMSELVES!
TOM TOMORROW©6-8-93

THIS MODERN WORLD by TOM TOMORROW

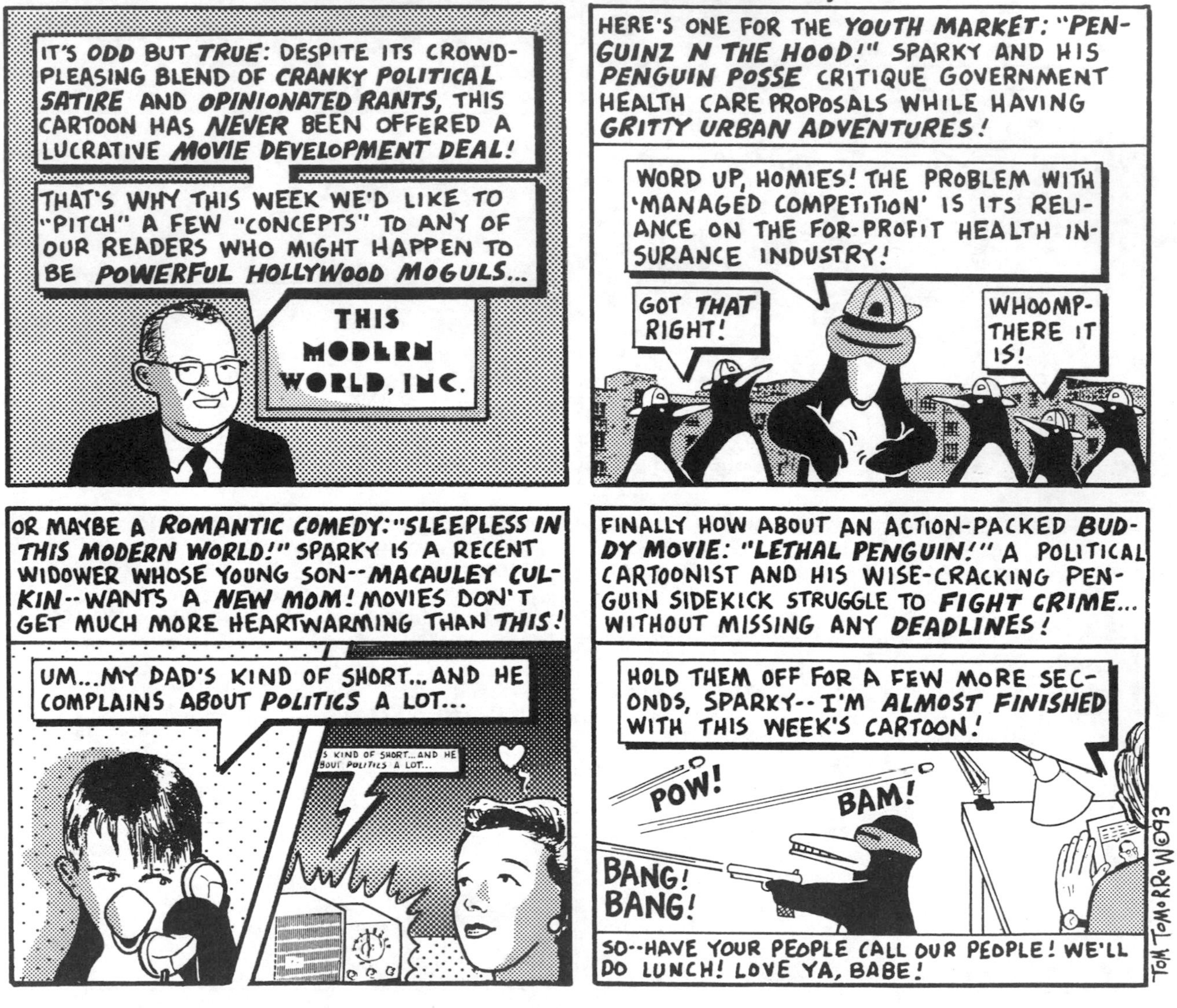
IT'S ODD BUT TRUE: DESPITE ITS CROWD-PLEASING BLEND OF CRANKY POLITICAL SATIRE AND OPINIONATED RANTS, THIS CARTOON HAS NEVER BEEN OFFERED A LUCRATIVE MOVIE DEVELOPMENT DEAL!
THAT'S WHY THIS WEEK WE'D LIKE TO "PITCH" A FEW "CONCEPTS" TO ANY OF OUR READERS WHO MIGHT HAPPEN TO BE POWERFUL HOLLYWOOD MOGULS...
THIS MODERN WORLD, INC.
HERE'S ONE FOR THE YOUTH MARKET: "PENGUINZ N THE HOOD!" SPARKY AND HIS PENGUIN POSSE CRITIQUE GOVERNMENT HEALTH CARE PROPOSALS WHILE HAVING GRITTY URBAN ADVENTURES!
WORD UP, HOMIES! THE PROBLEM WITH 'MANAGED COMPETITION' IS ITS RELIANCE ON THE FOR-PROFIT HEALTH INSURANCE INDUSTRY!
GOT THAT RIGHT!
WHOOMP-THERE IT IS!
OR MAYBE A ROMANTIC COMEDY: "SLEEPLESS IN THIS MODERN WORLD!" SPARKY IS A RECENT WIDOWER WHOSE YOUNG SON--MACAULEY CULKIN--WANTS A NEW MOM! MOVIES DON'T GET MUCH MORE HEARTWARMING THAN THIS!
UM...MY DAD'S KIND OF SHORT...AND HE COMPLAINS ABOUT POLITICS A LOT...
S KIND OF SHORT...AND HE BOUT POLITICS A LOT...
FINALLY HOW ABOUT AN ACTION-PACKED BUDDY MOVIE: "LETHAL PENGUIN!" A POLITICAL CARTOONIST AND HIS WISE-CRACKING PENGUIN SIDEKICK STRUGGLE TO FIGHT CRIME... WITHOUT MISSING ANY DEADLINES!
HOLD THEM OFF FOR A FEW MORE SECONDS, SPARKY--I'M ALMOST FINISHED WITH THIS WEEK'S CARTOON!
POW!
BAM!
BANG! BANG!
SO--HAVE YOUR PEOPLE CALL OUR PEOPLE! WE'LL DO LUNCH! LOVE YA, BABE!
TOM TOMORROW ©93

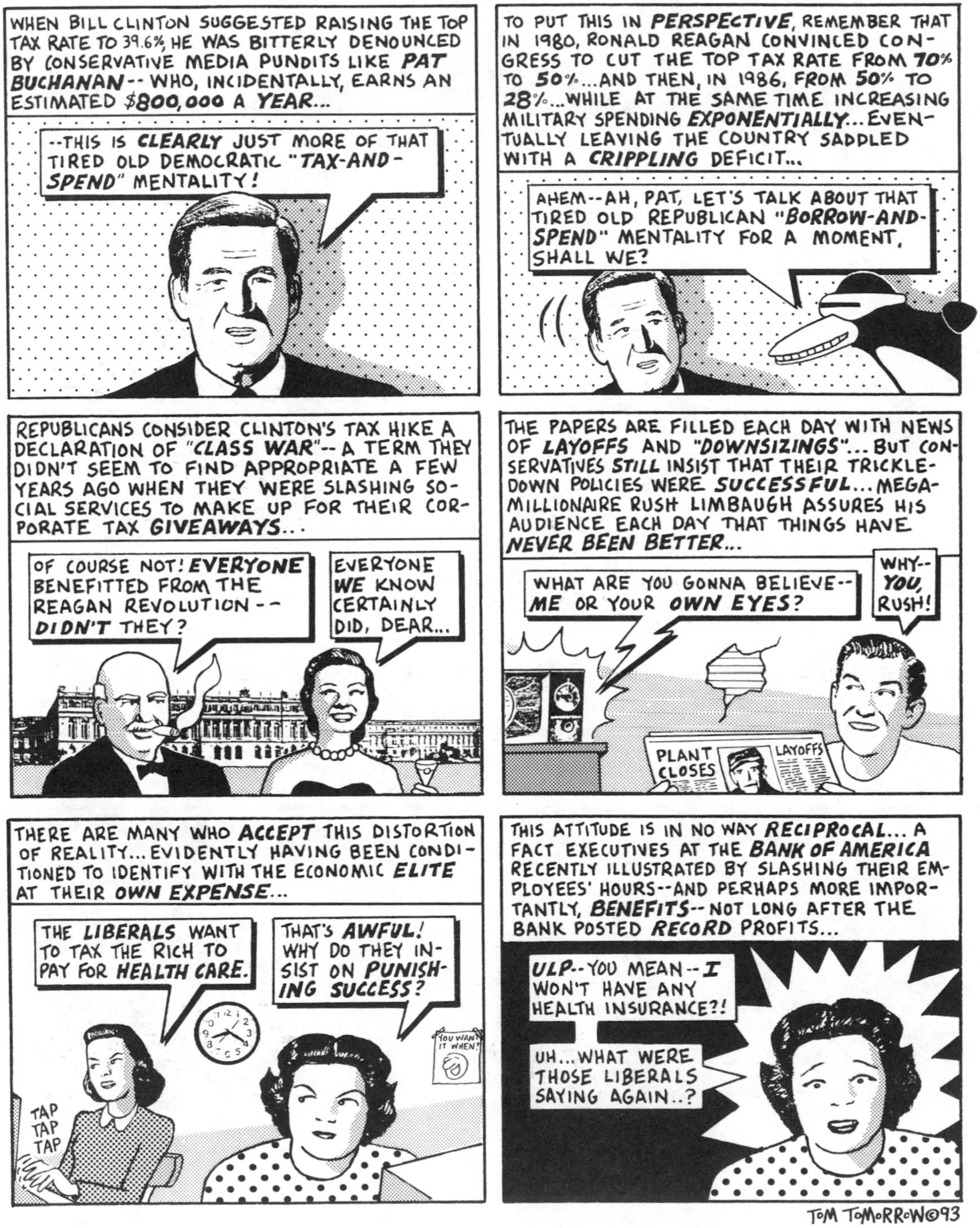
WHEN BILL CLINTON SUGGESTED RAISING THE TOP TAX RATE TO 39.6%, HE WAS BITTERLY DENOUNCED BY CONSERVATIVE MEDIA PUNDITS LIKE PAT BUCHANAN -- WHO, INCIDENTALLY, EARNS AN ESTIMATED $800,000 A YEAR...
--THIS IS CLEARLY JUST MORE OF THAT TIRED OLD DEMOCRATIC "TAX-AND-SPEND" MENTALITY!
TO PUT THIS IN PERSPECTIVE, REMEMBER THAT IN 1980, RONALD REAGAN CONVINCED CONGRESS TO CUT THE TOP TAX RATE FROM 70% TO 50%...AND THEN, IN 1986, FROM 50% TO 28%...WHILE AT THE SAME TIME INCREASING MILITARY SPENDING EXPONENTIALLY...EVENTUALLY LEAVING THE COUNTRY SADDLED WITH A CRIPPLING DEFICIT...
AHEM--AH, PAT, LET'S TALK ABOUT THAT TIRED OLD REPUBLICAN "BORROW-AND-SPEND" MENTALITY FOR A MOMENT, SHALL WE?
REPUBLICANS CONSIDER CLINTON'S TAX HIKE A DECLARATION OF "CLASS WAR"-- A TERM THEY DIDN'T SEEM TO FIND APPROPRIATE A FEW YEARS AGO WHEN THEY WERE SLASHING SOCIAL SERVICES TO MAKE UP FOR THEIR CORPORATE TAX GIVEAWAYS...
OF COURSE NOT! EVERYONE BENEFITTED FROM THE REAGAN REVOLUTION -- DIDN'T THEY?
EVERYONE WE KNOW CERTAINLY DID, DEAR...
THE PAPERS ARE FILLED EACH DAY WITH NEWS OF LAYOFFS AND "DOWNSIZINGS"... BUT CONSERVATIVES STILL INSIST THAT THEIR TRICKLE-DOWN POLICIES WERE SUCCESSFUL... MEGA-MILLIONAIRE RUSH LIMBAUGH ASSURES HIS AUDIENCE EACH DAY THAT THINGS HAVE NEVER BEEN BETTER...
WHAT ARE YOU GONNA BELIEVE-- ME OR YOUR OWN EYES?
WHY-- YOU, RUSH!
PLANT CLOSES
LAYOFFS
THERE ARE MANY WHO ACCEPT THIS DISTORTION OF REALITY... EVIDENTLY HAVING BEEN CONDITIONED TO IDENTIFY WITH THE ECONOMIC ELITE AT THEIR OWN EXPENSE...
THE LIBERALS WANT TO TAX THE RICH TO PAY FOR HEALTH CARE.
THAT'S AWFUL! WHY DO THEY INSIST ON PUNISHING SUCCESS?
YOU WANT IT WHEN?!
TAP TAP TAP
THIS ATTITUDE IS IN NO WAY RECIPROCAL... A FACT EXECUTIVES AT THE BANK OF AMERICA RECENTLY ILLUSTRATED BY SLASHING THEIR EMPLOYEES' HOURS--AND PERHAPS MORE IMPORTANTLY, BENEFITS-- NOT LONG AFTER THE BANK POSTED RECORD PROFITS...
ULP-- YOU MEAN-- I WON'T HAVE ANY HEALTH INSURANCE?!
UH...WHAT WERE THOSE LIBERALS SAYING AGAIN..?
TOM TOMORROW©93

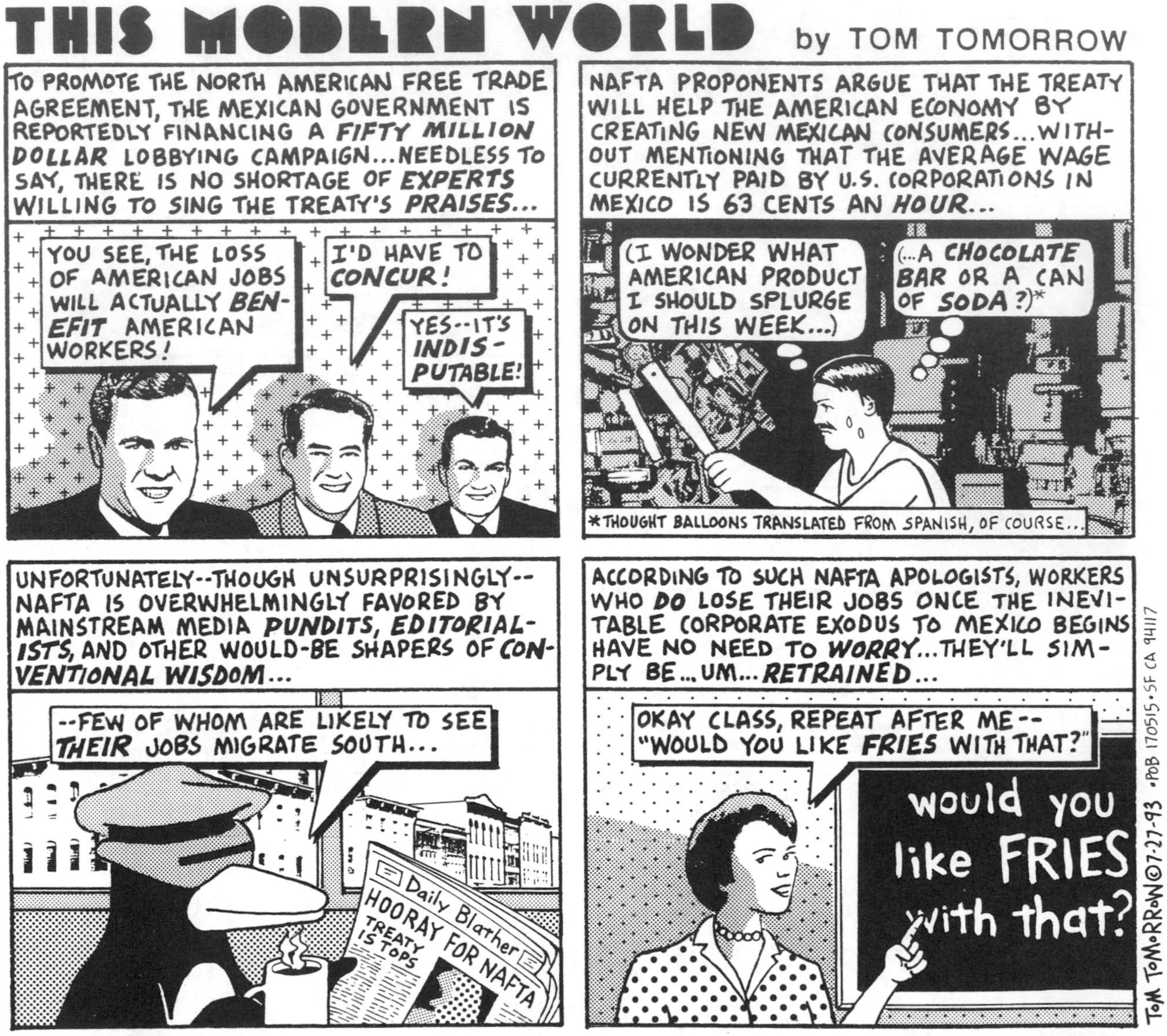
THIS MODERN WORLD by TOM TOMORROW
TO PROMOTE THE NORTH AMERICAN FREE TRADE AGREEMENT, THE MEXICAN GOVERNMENT IS REPORTEDLY FINANCING A FIFTY MILLION DOLLAR LOBBYING CAMPAIGN...NEEDLESS TO SAY, THERE IS NO SHORTAGE OF EXPERTS WILLING TO SING THE TREATY'S PRAISES...
YOU SEE, THE LOSS OF AMERICAN JOBS WILL ACTUALLY BENEFIT AMERICAN WORKERS!
I'D HAVE TO CONCUR!
YES--IT'S INDISPUTABLE!
NAFTA PROPONENTS ARGUE THAT THE TREATY WILL HELP THE AMERICAN ECONOMY BY CREATING NEW MEXICAN CONSUMERS...WITHOUT MENTIONING THAT THE AVERAGE WAGE CURRENTLY PAID BY U.S. CORPORATIONS IN MEXICO IS 63 CENTS AN HOUR...
(I WONDER WHAT AMERICAN PRODUCT I SHOULD SPLURGE ON THIS WEEK...)
(...A CHOCOLATE BAR OR A CAN OF SODA?)*
*THOUGHT BALLOONS TRANSLATED FROM SPANISH, OF COURSE...
UNFORTUNATELY--THOUGH UNSURPRISINGLY--NAFTA IS OVERWHELMINGLY FAVORED BY MAINSTREAM MEDIA PUNDITS, EDITORIALISTS, AND OTHER WOULD-BE SHAPERS OF CONVENTIONAL WISDOM...
--FEW OF WHOM ARE LIKELY TO SEE THEIR JOBS MIGRATE SOUTH...
Daily Blather
HOORAY FOR NAFTA
TREATY IS TOPS
ACCORDING TO SUCH NAFTA APOLOGISTS, WORKERS WHO DO LOSE THEIR JOBS ONCE THE INEVITABLE CORPORATE EXODUS TO MEXICO BEGINS HAVE NO NEED TO WORRY...THEY'LL SIMPLY BE...UM...RETRAINED...
OKAY CLASS, REPEAT AFTER ME--"WOULD YOU LIKE FRIES WITH THAT?"
would you like FRIES with that?
TOM TOMORROW©7-27-93 •POB 170515•SF CA 94117

THIS MODERN WORLD by TOM TOMORROW

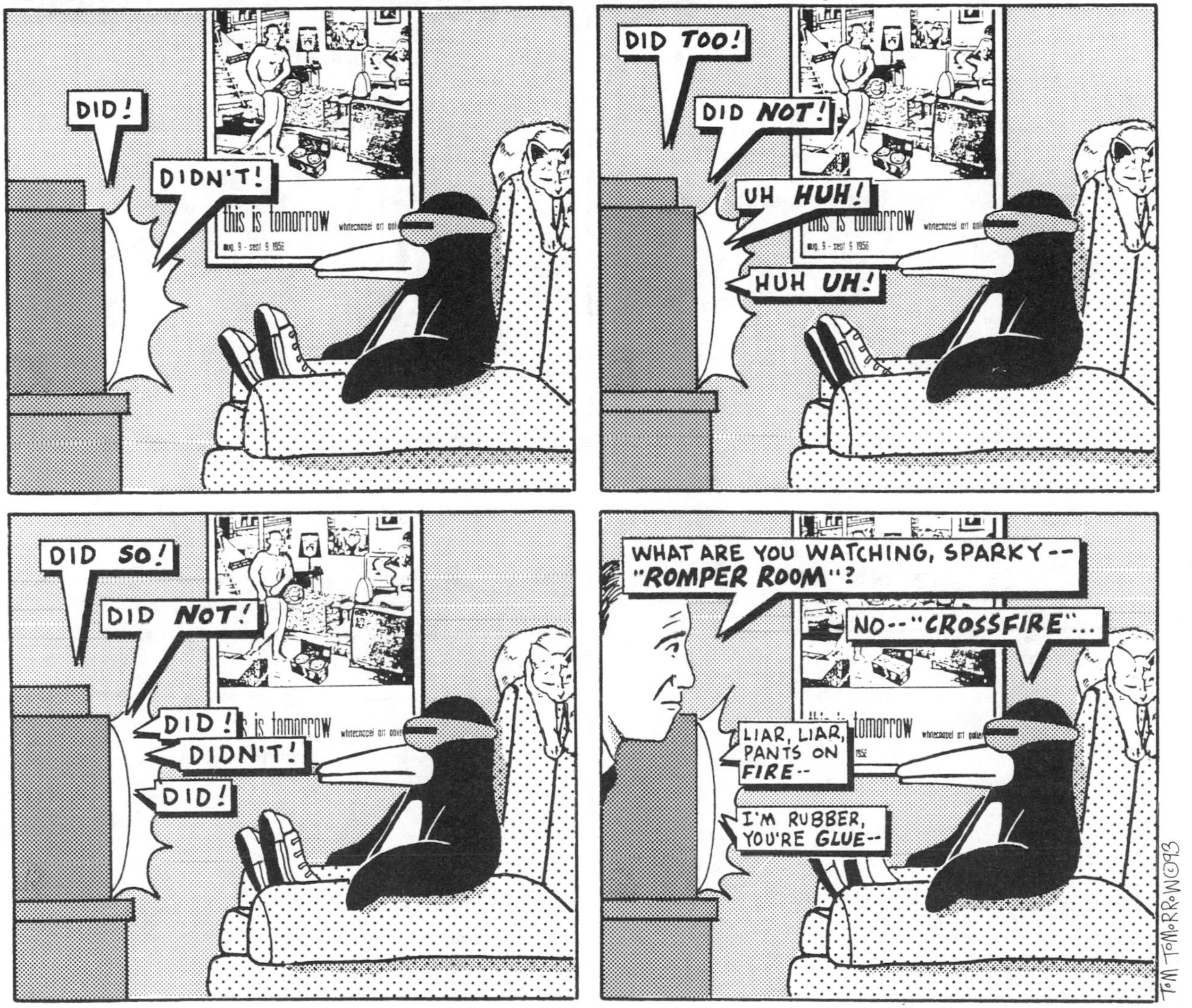
DID!
DIDN'T!
this is tomorrow
DID TOO!
DID NOT!
UH HUH!
HUH UH!
DID SO!
DID NOT!
DID!
DIDN'T!
DID!
WHAT ARE YOU WATCHING, SPARKY-- "ROMPER ROOM"?
NO--"CROSSFIRE"...
LIAR, LIAR, PANTS ON FIRE--
I'M RUBBER, YOU'RE GLUE--
TOM TOMORROW©93

THIS MODERN WORLD by TOM TOMORROW

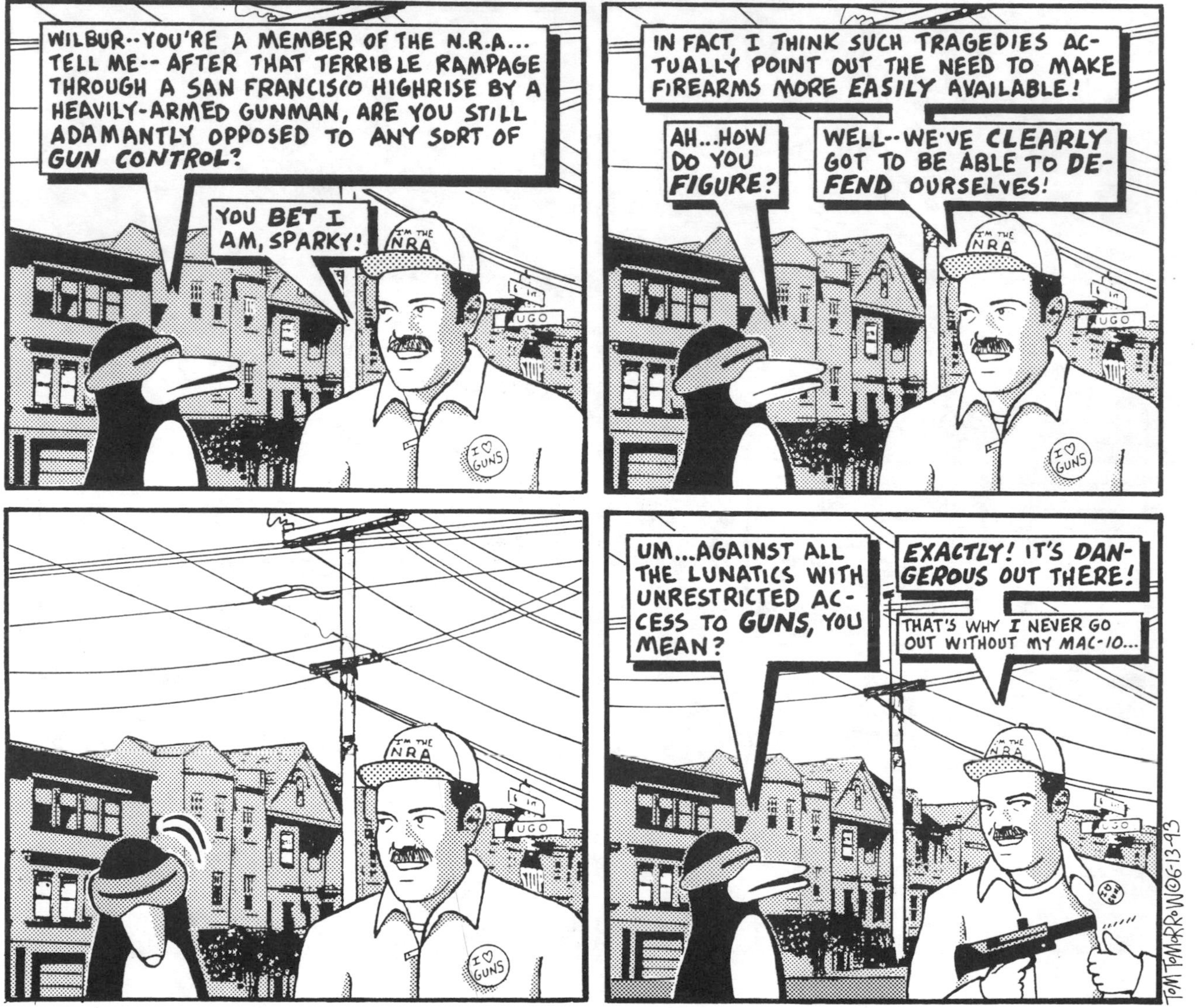
WILBUR--YOU'RE A MEMBER OF THE N.R.A.... TELL ME--AFTER THAT TERRIBLE RAMPAGE THROUGH A SAN FRANCISCO HIGHRISE BY A HEAVILY-ARMED GUNMAN, ARE YOU STILL ADAMANTLY OPPOSED TO ANY SORT OF GUN CONTROL?
YOU BET I AM, SPARKY!
I'M THE NRA
I ♡ GUNS
IN FACT, I THINK SUCH TRAGEDIES ACTUALLY POINT OUT THE NEED TO MAKE FIREARMS MORE EASILY AVAILABLE!
AH...HOW DO YOU FIGURE?
WELL--WE'VE CLEARLY GOT TO BE ABLE TO DEFEND OURSELVES!
UM...AGAINST ALL THE LUNATICS WITH UNRESTRICTED ACCESS TO GUNS, YOU MEAN?
EXACTLY! IT'S DANGEROUS OUT THERE!
THAT'S WHY I NEVER GO OUT WITHOUT MY MAC-10...
TOM TOMORROW©6-13-93

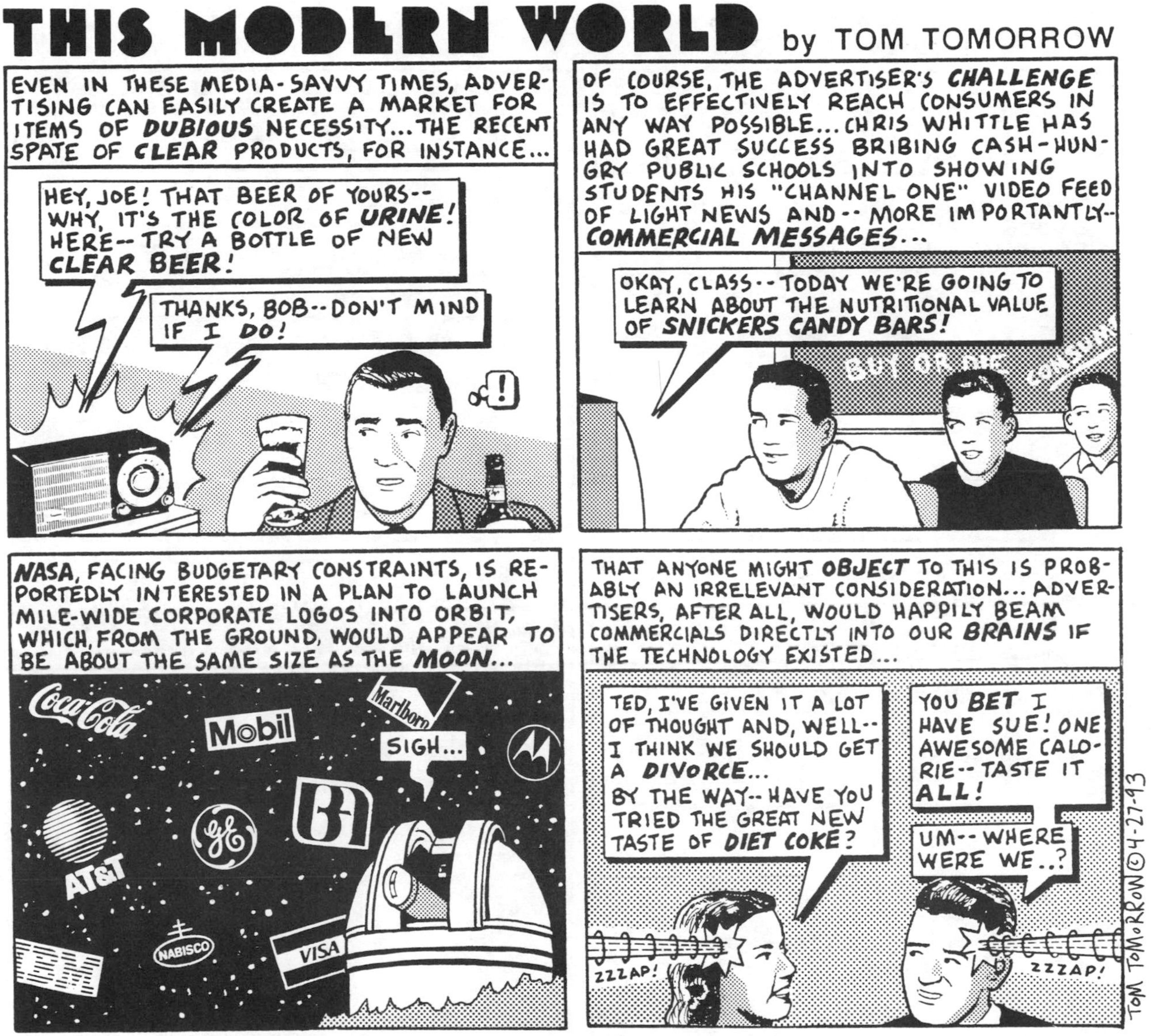
THIS MODERN WORLD by TOM TOMORROW
EVEN IN THESE MEDIA-SAVVY TIMES, ADVERTISING CAN EASILY CREATE A MARKET FOR ITEMS OF DUBIOUS NECESSITY... THE RECENT SPATE OF CLEAR PRODUCTS, FOR INSTANCE...
HEY, JOE! THAT BEER OF YOURS-- WHY, IT'S THE COLOR OF URINE! HERE-- TRY A BOTTLE OF NEW CLEAR BEER!
THANKS, BOB--DON'T MIND IF I DO!
OF COURSE, THE ADVERTISER'S CHALLENGE IS TO EFFECTIVELY REACH CONSUMERS IN ANY WAY POSSIBLE... CHRIS WHITTLE HAS HAD GREAT SUCCESS BRIBING CASH-HUNGRY PUBLIC SCHOOLS INTO SHOWING STUDENTS HIS "CHANNEL ONE" VIDEO FEED OF LIGHT NEWS AND-- MORE IMPORTANTLY-- COMMERCIAL MESSAGES...
OKAY, CLASS--TODAY WE'RE GOING TO LEARN ABOUT THE NUTRITIONAL VALUE OF SNICKERS CANDY BARS!
BUY OR DIE
NASA, FACING BUDGETARY CONSTRAINTS, IS REPORTEDLY INTERESTED IN A PLAN TO LAUNCH MILE-WIDE CORPORATE LOGOS INTO ORBIT, WHICH, FROM THE GROUND, WOULD APPEAR TO BE ABOUT THE SAME SIZE AS THE MOON...
Coca-Cola
Mobil
Marlboro
SIGH...
AT&T
NABISCO
VISA
IBM
THAT ANYONE MIGHT OBJECT TO THIS IS PROBABLY AN IRRELEVANT CONSIDERATION... ADVERTISERS, AFTER ALL, WOULD HAPPILY BEAM COMMERCIALS DIRECTLY INTO OUR BRAINS IF THE TECHNOLOGY EXISTED...
TED, I'VE GIVEN IT A LOT OF THOUGHT AND, WELL-- I THINK WE SHOULD GET A DIVORCE... BY THE WAY-- HAVE YOU TRIED THE GREAT NEW TASTE OF DIET COKE?
YOU BET I HAVE SUE! ONE AWESOME CALORIE-- TASTE IT ALL!
UM-- WHERE WERE WE..?
ZZZAP!
ZZZAP!
TOM TOMORROW © 4-27-93

THIS MODERN WORLD by TOM TOMORROW

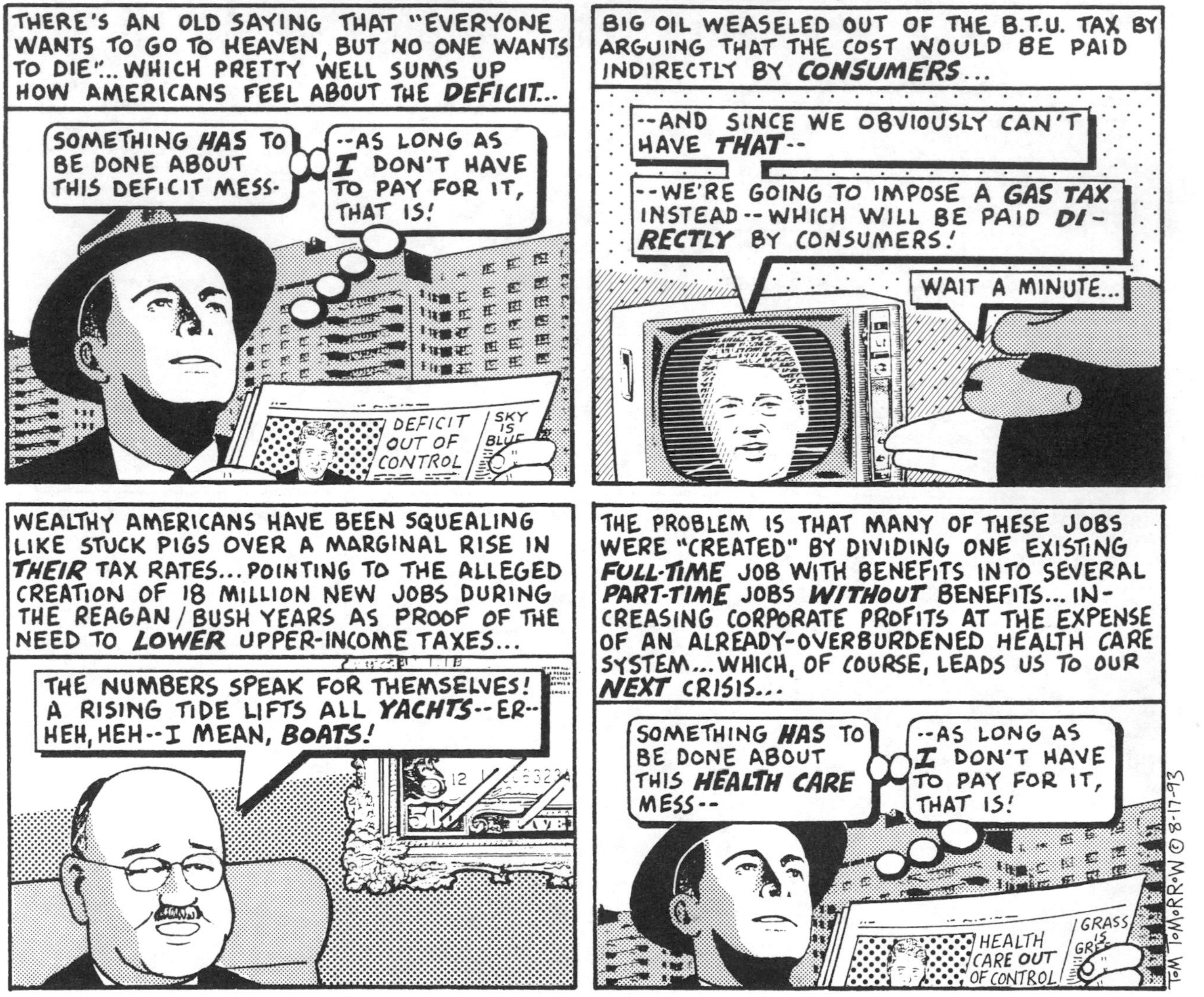

THERE'S AN OLD SAYING THAT "EVERYONE WANTS TO GO TO HEAVEN, BUT NO ONE WANTS TO DIE"... WHICH PRETTY WELL SUMS UP HOW AMERICANS FEEL ABOUT THE *DEFICIT*...
SOMETHING *HAS* TO BE DONE ABOUT THIS DEFICIT MESS-
--AS LONG AS *I* DON'T HAVE TO PAY FOR IT, THAT IS!
DEFICIT OUT OF CONTROL
SKY IS
BIG OIL WEASELED OUT OF THE B.T.U. TAX BY ARGUING THAT THE COST WOULD BE PAID INDIRECTLY BY *CONSUMERS*...
--AND SINCE WE OBVIOUSLY CAN'T HAVE *THAT*--
--WE'RE GOING TO IMPOSE A *GAS TAX* INSTEAD--WHICH WILL BE PAID *DIRECTLY* BY CONSUMERS!
WAIT A MINUTE...
WEALTHY AMERICANS HAVE BEEN SQUEALING LIKE STUCK PIGS OVER A MARGINAL RISE IN *THEIR* TAX RATES... POINTING TO THE ALLEGED CREATION OF 18 MILLION NEW JOBS DURING THE REAGAN / BUSH YEARS AS PROOF OF THE NEED TO *LOWER* UPPER-INCOME TAXES...
THE NUMBERS SPEAK FOR THEMSELVES! A RISING TIDE LIFTS ALL *YACHTS*--ER--HEH, HEH--I MEAN, *BOATS*!
THE PROBLEM IS THAT MANY OF THESE JOBS WERE "CREATED" BY DIVIDING ONE EXISTING *FULL-TIME* JOB WITH BENEFITS INTO SEVERAL *PART-TIME* JOBS *WITHOUT* BENEFITS... INCREASING CORPORATE PROFITS AT THE EXPENSE OF AN ALREADY-OVERBURDENED HEALTH CARE SYSTEM... WHICH, OF COURSE, LEADS US TO OUR *NEXT* CRISIS...
SOMETHING *HAS* TO BE DONE ABOUT THIS *HEALTH CARE* MESS--
--AS LONG AS *I* DON'T HAVE TO PAY FOR IT, THAT IS!
HEALTH CARE OUT OF CONTROL
GRASS IS
TOM TOMORROW © 8-17-93

THIS MODERN WORLD by TOM TOMORROW

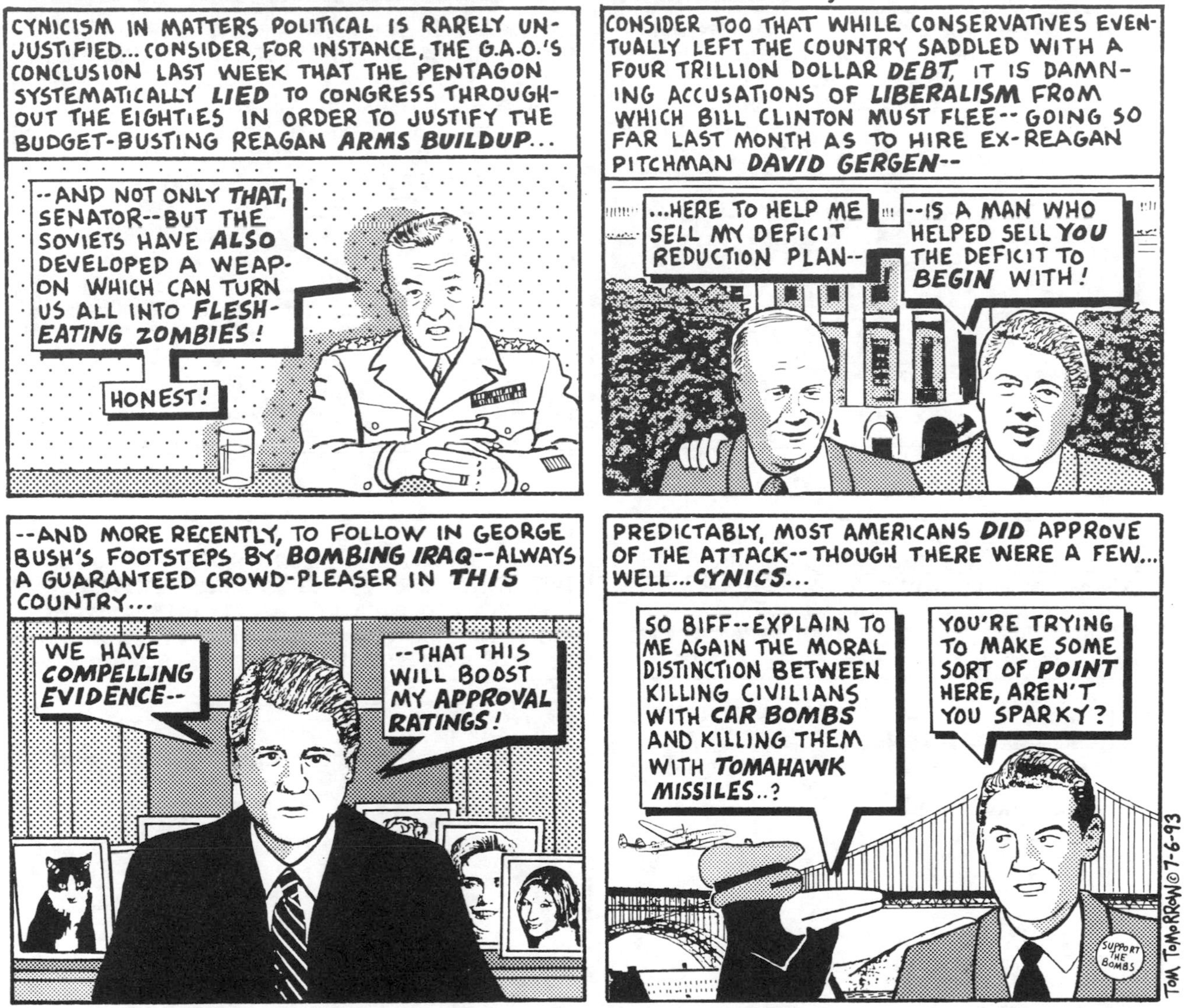
CYNICISM IN MATTERS POLITICAL IS RARELY UNJUSTIFIED... CONSIDER, FOR INSTANCE, THE G.A.O.'S CONCLUSION LAST WEEK THAT THE PENTAGON SYSTEMATICALLY *LIED* TO CONGRESS THROUGHOUT THE EIGHTIES IN ORDER TO JUSTIFY THE BUDGET-BUSTING REAGAN *ARMS BUILDUP*...
--AND NOT ONLY *THAT*, SENATOR--BUT THE SOVIETS HAVE *ALSO* DEVELOPED A WEAPON WHICH CAN TURN US ALL INTO *FLESH-EATING ZOMBIES!*
HONEST!
CONSIDER TOO THAT WHILE CONSERVATIVES EVENTUALLY LEFT THE COUNTRY SADDLED WITH A FOUR TRILLION DOLLAR *DEBT*, IT IS DAMNING ACCUSATIONS OF *LIBERALISM* FROM WHICH BILL CLINTON MUST FLEE-- GOING SO FAR LAST MONTH AS TO HIRE EX-REAGAN PITCHMAN *DAVID GERGEN*--
...HERE TO HELP ME SELL MY DEFICIT REDUCTION PLAN--
--IS A MAN WHO HELPED SELL *YOU* THE DEFICIT TO *BEGIN* WITH!
--AND MORE RECENTLY, TO FOLLOW IN GEORGE BUSH'S FOOTSTEPS BY *BOMBING IRAQ*--ALWAYS A GUARANTEED CROWD-PLEASER IN *THIS* COUNTRY...
WE HAVE *COMPELLING EVIDENCE*--
--THAT THIS WILL BOOST MY *APPROVAL RATINGS!*
PREDICTABLY, MOST AMERICANS *DID* APPROVE OF THE ATTACK-- THOUGH THERE WERE A FEW... WELL... *CYNICS*...
SO BIFF--EXPLAIN TO ME AGAIN THE MORAL DISTINCTION BETWEEN KILLING CIVILIANS WITH *CAR BOMBS* AND KILLING THEM WITH *TOMAHAWK MISSILES*..?
YOU'RE TRYING TO MAKE SOME SORT OF *POINT* HERE, AREN'T YOU SPARKY?
SUPPORT THE BOMBS
TOM TOMORROW © 7-6-93

THIS MODERN WORLD by TOM TOMORROW

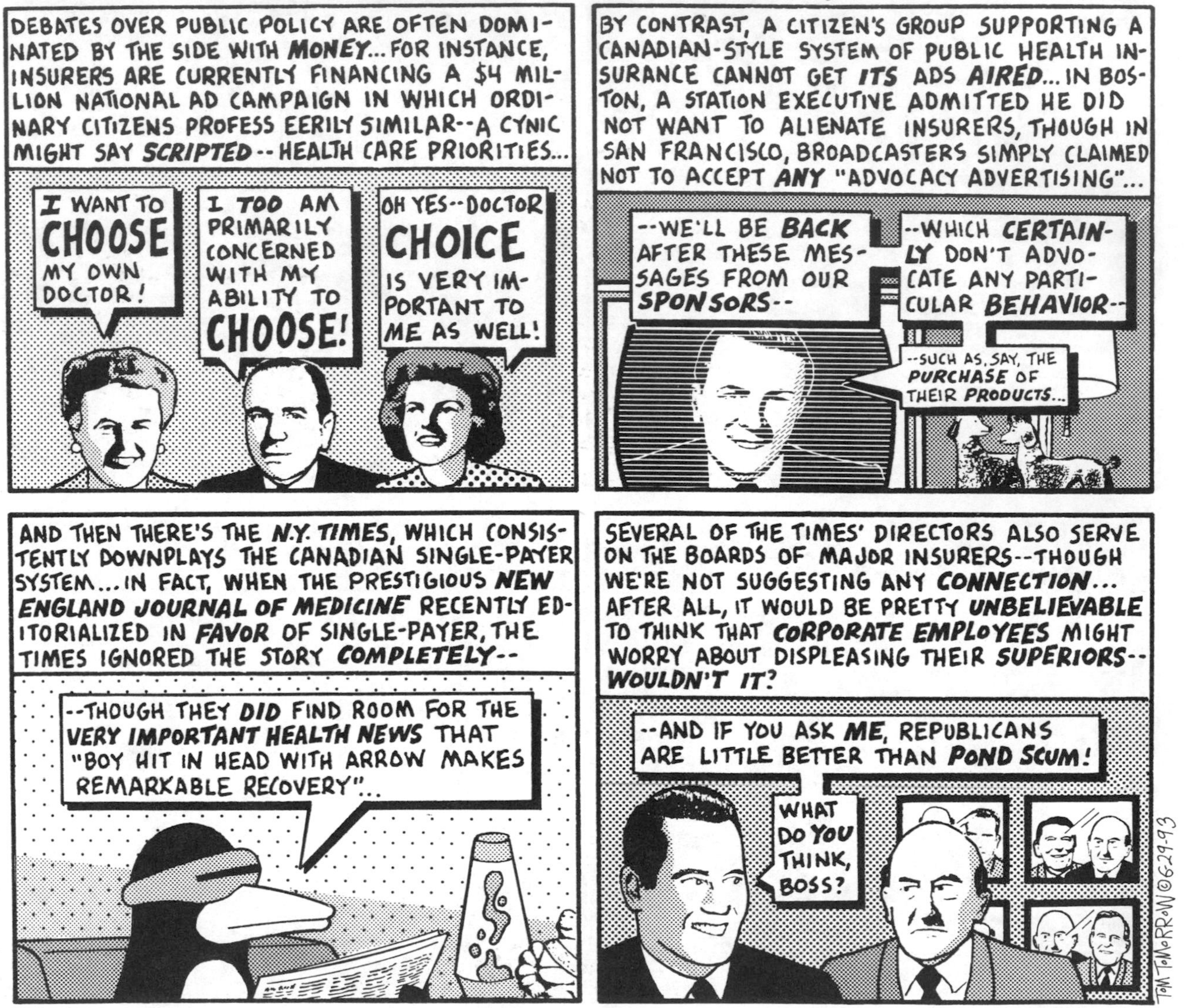
DEBATES OVER PUBLIC POLICY ARE OFTEN DOMINATED BY THE SIDE WITH MONEY... FOR INSTANCE, INSURERS ARE CURRENTLY FINANCING A $4 MILLION NATIONAL AD CAMPAIGN IN WHICH ORDINARY CITIZENS PROFESS EERILY SIMILAR--A CYNIC MIGHT SAY SCRIPTED--HEALTH CARE PRIORITIES...
I WANT TO CHOOSE MY OWN DOCTOR!
I TOO AM PRIMARILY CONCERNED WITH MY ABILITY TO CHOOSE!
OH YES--DOCTOR CHOICE IS VERY IMPORTANT TO ME AS WELL!
BY CONTRAST, A CITIZEN'S GROUP SUPPORTING A CANADIAN-STYLE SYSTEM OF PUBLIC HEALTH INSURANCE CANNOT GET ITS ADS AIRED... IN BOSTON, A STATION EXECUTIVE ADMITTED HE DID NOT WANT TO ALIENATE INSURERS, THOUGH IN SAN FRANCISCO, BROADCASTERS SIMPLY CLAIMED NOT TO ACCEPT ANY "ADVOCACY ADVERTISING"...
--WE'LL BE BACK AFTER THESE MESSAGES FROM OUR SPONSORS--
--WHICH CERTAINLY DON'T ADVOCATE ANY PARTICULAR BEHAVIOR--
--SUCH AS, SAY, THE PURCHASE OF THEIR PRODUCTS...
AND THEN THERE'S THE N.Y. TIMES, WHICH CONSISTENTLY DOWNPLAYS THE CANADIAN SINGLE-PAYER SYSTEM... IN FACT, WHEN THE PRESTIGIOUS NEW ENGLAND JOURNAL OF MEDICINE RECENTLY EDITORIALIZED IN FAVOR OF SINGLE-PAYER, THE TIMES IGNORED THE STORY COMPLETELY--
--THOUGH THEY DID FIND ROOM FOR THE VERY IMPORTANT HEALTH NEWS THAT "BOY HIT IN HEAD WITH ARROW MAKES REMARKABLE RECOVERY"...
SEVERAL OF THE TIMES' DIRECTORS ALSO SERVE ON THE BOARDS OF MAJOR INSURERS--THOUGH WE'RE NOT SUGGESTING ANY CONNECTION... AFTER ALL, IT WOULD BE PRETTY UNBELIEVABLE TO THINK THAT CORPORATE EMPLOYEES MIGHT WORRY ABOUT DISPLEASING THEIR SUPERIORS--WOULDN'T IT?
--AND IF YOU ASK ME, REPUBLICANS ARE LITTLE BETTER THAN POND SCUM!
WHAT DO YOU THINK, BOSS?
TOM TOMORROW ©6-29-93

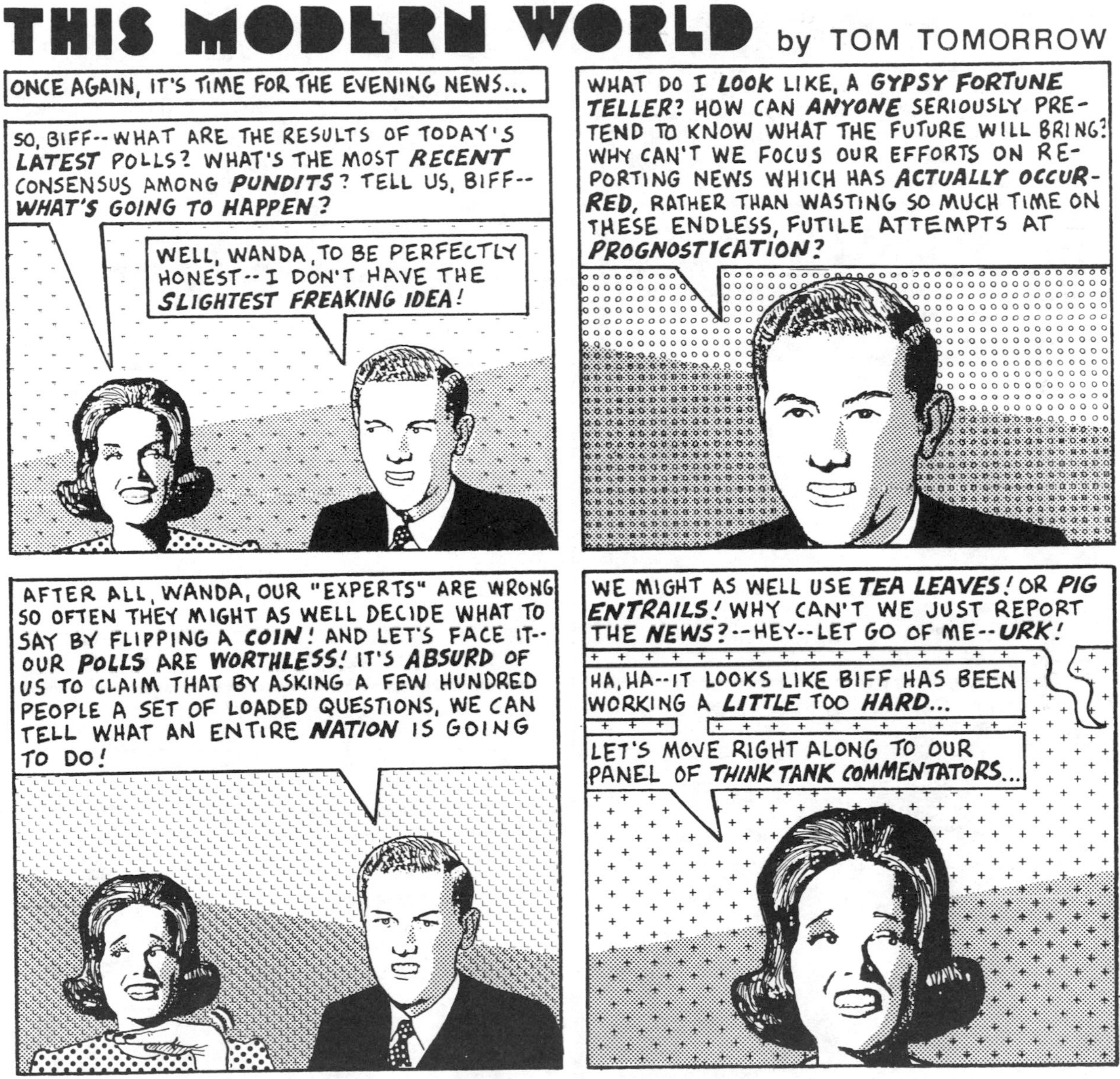
THIS MODERN WORLD by TOM TOMORROW
ONCE AGAIN, IT'S TIME FOR THE EVENING NEWS...
SO, BIFF--WHAT ARE THE RESULTS OF TODAY'S LATEST POLLS? WHAT'S THE MOST RECENT CONSENSUS AMONG PUNDITS? TELL US, BIFF--WHAT'S GOING TO HAPPEN?
WELL, WANDA, TO BE PERFECTLY HONEST--I DON'T HAVE THE SLIGHTEST FREAKING IDEA!
WHAT DO I LOOK LIKE, A GYPSY FORTUNE TELLER? HOW CAN ANYONE SERIOUSLY PRETEND TO KNOW WHAT THE FUTURE WILL BRING? WHY CAN'T WE FOCUS OUR EFFORTS ON REPORTING NEWS WHICH HAS ACTUALLY OCCURRED, RATHER THAN WASTING SO MUCH TIME ON THESE ENDLESS, FUTILE ATTEMPTS AT PROGNOSTICATION?
AFTER ALL, WANDA, OUR "EXPERTS" ARE WRONG SO OFTEN THEY MIGHT AS WELL DECIDE WHAT TO SAY BY FLIPPING A COIN! AND LET'S FACE IT--OUR POLLS ARE WORTHLESS! IT'S ABSURD OF US TO CLAIM THAT BY ASKING A FEW HUNDRED PEOPLE A SET OF LOADED QUESTIONS, WE CAN TELL WHAT AN ENTIRE NATION IS GOING TO DO!
WE MIGHT AS WELL USE TEA LEAVES! OR PIG ENTRAILS! WHY CAN'T WE JUST REPORT THE NEWS?--HEY--LET GO OF ME--URK!
HA, HA--IT LOOKS LIKE BIFF HAS BEEN WORKING A LITTLE TOO HARD...
LET'S MOVE RIGHT ALONG TO OUR PANEL OF THINK TANK COMMENTATORS...
TOM TOMORROW©11-2-93

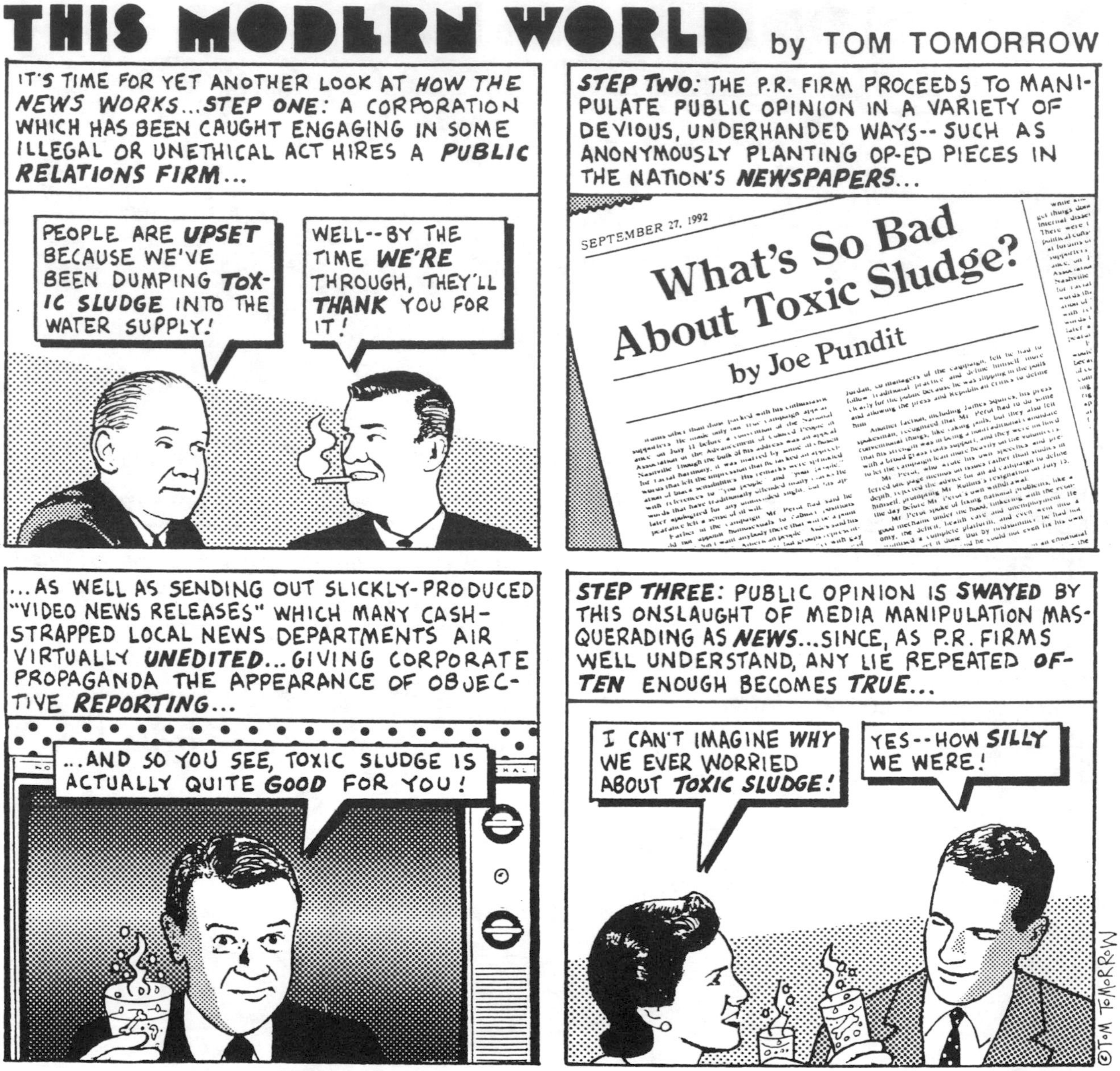
THIS MODERN WORLD by TOM TOMORROW
IT'S TIME FOR YET ANOTHER LOOK AT HOW THE NEWS WORKS... STEP ONE: A CORPORATION WHICH HAS BEEN CAUGHT ENGAGING IN SOME ILLEGAL OR UNETHICAL ACT HIRES A PUBLIC RELATIONS FIRM...
PEOPLE ARE UPSET BECAUSE WE'VE BEEN DUMPING TOXIC SLUDGE INTO THE WATER SUPPLY!
WELL--BY THE TIME WE'RE THROUGH, THEY'LL THANK YOU FOR IT!
STEP TWO: THE P.R. FIRM PROCEEDS TO MANIPULATE PUBLIC OPINION IN A VARIETY OF DEVIOUS, UNDERHANDED WAYS-- SUCH AS ANONYMOUSLY PLANTING OP-ED PIECES IN THE NATION'S NEWSPAPERS...
SEPTEMBER 27, 1992
What's So Bad About Toxic Sludge?
by Joe Pundit
...AS WELL AS SENDING OUT SLICKLY-PRODUCED "VIDEO NEWS RELEASES" WHICH MANY CASH-STRAPPED LOCAL NEWS DEPARTMENTS AIR VIRTUALLY UNEDITED... GIVING CORPORATE PROPAGANDA THE APPEARANCE OF OBJECTIVE REPORTING...
...AND SO YOU SEE, TOXIC SLUDGE IS ACTUALLY QUITE GOOD FOR YOU!
STEP THREE: PUBLIC OPINION IS SWAYED BY THIS ONSLAUGHT OF MEDIA MANIPULATION MASQUERADING AS NEWS... SINCE, AS P.R. FIRMS WELL UNDERSTAND, ANY LIE REPEATED OFTEN ENOUGH BECOMES TRUE...
I CAN'T IMAGINE WHY WE EVER WORRIED ABOUT TOXIC SLUDGE!
YES--HOW SILLY WE WERE!
©TOM TOMORROW

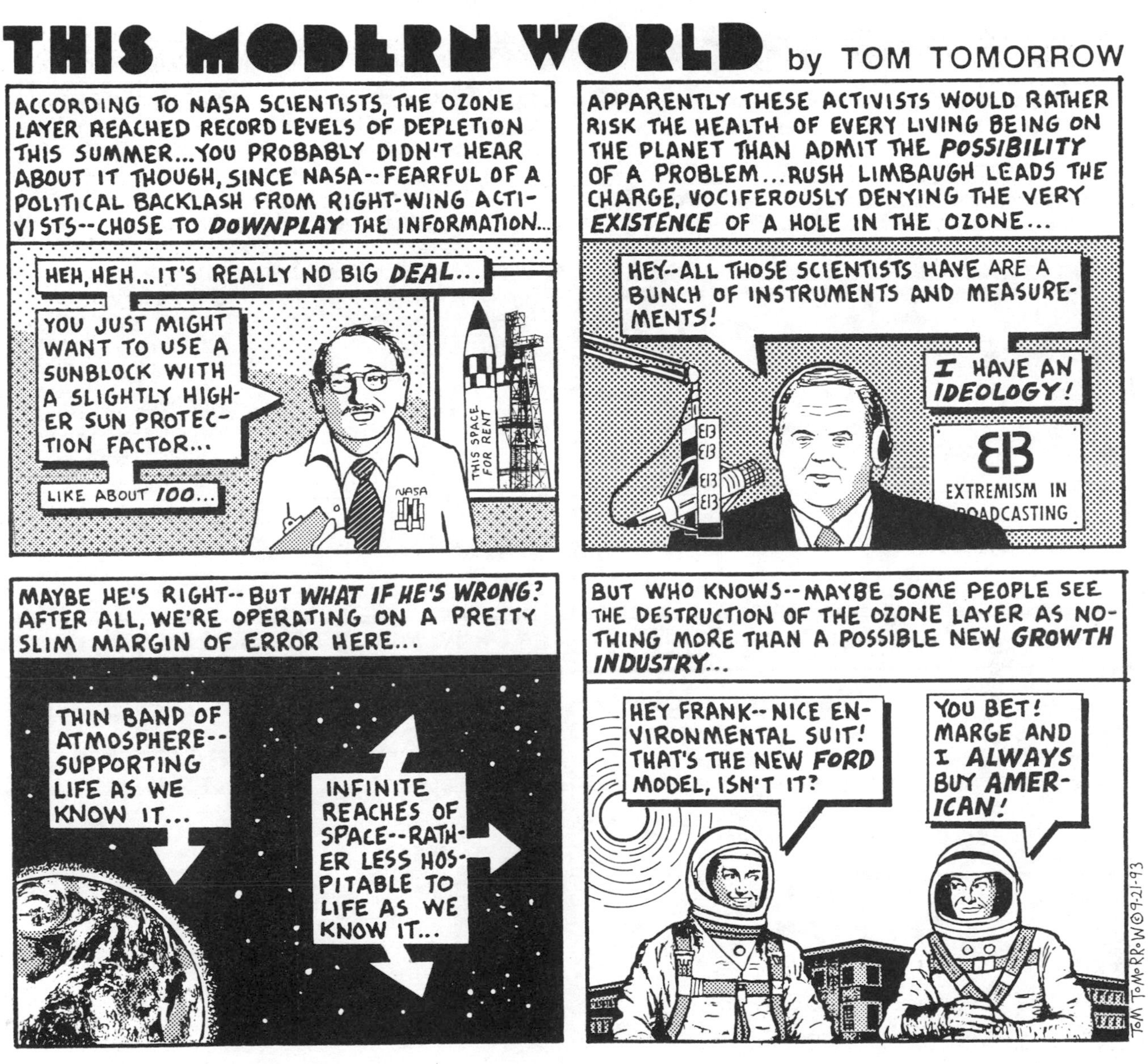
THIS MODERN WORLD by TOM TOMORROW
ACCORDING TO NASA SCIENTISTS, THE OZONE LAYER REACHED RECORD LEVELS OF DEPLETION THIS SUMMER...YOU PROBABLY DIDN'T HEAR ABOUT IT THOUGH, SINCE NASA--FEARFUL OF A POLITICAL BACKLASH FROM RIGHT-WING ACTIVISTS--CHOSE TO DOWNPLAY THE INFORMATION...
HEH, HEH...IT'S REALLY NO BIG DEAL...
YOU JUST MIGHT WANT TO USE A SUNBLOCK WITH A SLIGHTLY HIGHER SUN PROTECTION FACTOR...
LIKE ABOUT 100...
THIS SPACE FOR RENT
NASA
APPARENTLY THESE ACTIVISTS WOULD RATHER RISK THE HEALTH OF EVERY LIVING BEING ON THE PLANET THAN ADMIT THE POSSIBILITY OF A PROBLEM...RUSH LIMBAUGH LEADS THE CHARGE, VOCIFEROUSLY DENYING THE VERY EXISTENCE OF A HOLE IN THE OZONE...
HEY--ALL THOSE SCIENTISTS HAVE ARE A BUNCH OF INSTRUMENTS AND MEASUREMENTS!
I HAVE AN IDEOLOGY!
EIB
EXTREMISM IN BROADCASTING
MAYBE HE'S RIGHT--BUT WHAT IF HE'S WRONG? AFTER ALL, WE'RE OPERATING ON A PRETTY SLIM MARGIN OF ERROR HERE...
THIN BAND OF ATMOSPHERE--SUPPORTING LIFE AS WE KNOW IT...
INFINITE REACHES OF SPACE--RATHER LESS HOSPITABLE TO LIFE AS WE KNOW IT...
BUT WHO KNOWS--MAYBE SOME PEOPLE SEE THE DESTRUCTION OF THE OZONE LAYER AS NOTHING MORE THAN A POSSIBLE NEW GROWTH INDUSTRY...
HEY FRANK--NICE ENVIRONMENTAL SUIT! THAT'S THE NEW FORD MODEL, ISN'T IT?
YOU BET! MARGE AND I ALWAYS BUY AMERICAN!
TOM TOMORROW©9-21-93

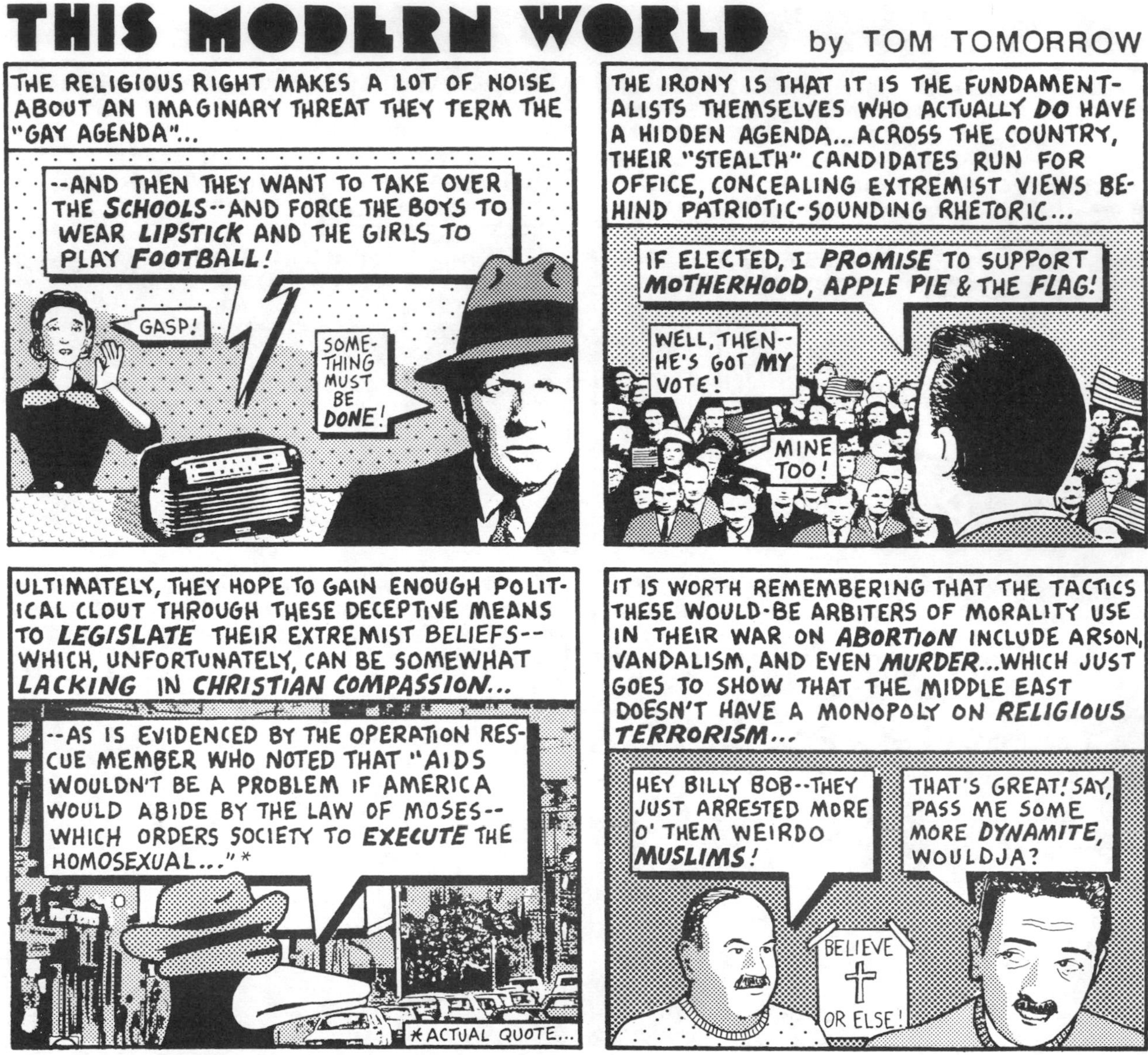
THIS MODERN WORLD
by TOM TOMORROW
THE RELIGIOUS RIGHT MAKES A LOT OF NOISE ABOUT AN IMAGINARY THREAT THEY TERM THE "GAY AGENDA"...
--AND THEN THEY WANT TO TAKE OVER THE SCHOOLS--AND FORCE THE BOYS TO WEAR LIPSTICK AND THE GIRLS TO PLAY FOOTBALL!
GASP!
SOMETHING MUST BE DONE!
THE IRONY IS THAT IT IS THE FUNDAMENTALISTS THEMSELVES WHO ACTUALLY DO HAVE A HIDDEN AGENDA...ACROSS THE COUNTRY, THEIR "STEALTH" CANDIDATES RUN FOR OFFICE, CONCEALING EXTREMIST VIEWS BEHIND PATRIOTIC-SOUNDING RHETORIC...
IF ELECTED, I PROMISE TO SUPPORT MOTHERHOOD, APPLE PIE & THE FLAG!
WELL, THEN--HE'S GOT MY VOTE!
MINE TOO!
ULTIMATELY, THEY HOPE TO GAIN ENOUGH POLITICAL CLOUT THROUGH THESE DECEPTIVE MEANS TO LEGISLATE THEIR EXTREMIST BELIEFS--WHICH, UNFORTUNATELY, CAN BE SOMEWHAT LACKING IN CHRISTIAN COMPASSION...
--AS IS EVIDENCED BY THE OPERATION RESCUE MEMBER WHO NOTED THAT "AIDS WOULDN'T BE A PROBLEM IF AMERICA WOULD ABIDE BY THE LAW OF MOSES--WHICH ORDERS SOCIETY TO EXECUTE THE HOMOSEXUAL..."*
*ACTUAL QUOTE...
IT IS WORTH REMEMBERING THAT THE TACTICS THESE WOULD-BE ARBITERS OF MORALITY USE IN THEIR WAR ON ABORTION INCLUDE ARSON, VANDALISM, AND EVEN MURDER...WHICH JUST GOES TO SHOW THAT THE MIDDLE EAST DOESN'T HAVE A MONOPOLY ON RELIGIOUS TERRORISM...
HEY BILLY BOB--THEY JUST ARRESTED MORE O' THEM WEIRDO MUSLIMS!
THAT'S GREAT! SAY, PASS ME SOME MORE DYNAMITE, WOULDJA?
BELIEVE
OR ELSE!
TOM TOMORROW© 9-7-93

THIS MODERN WORLD by TOM TOMORROW

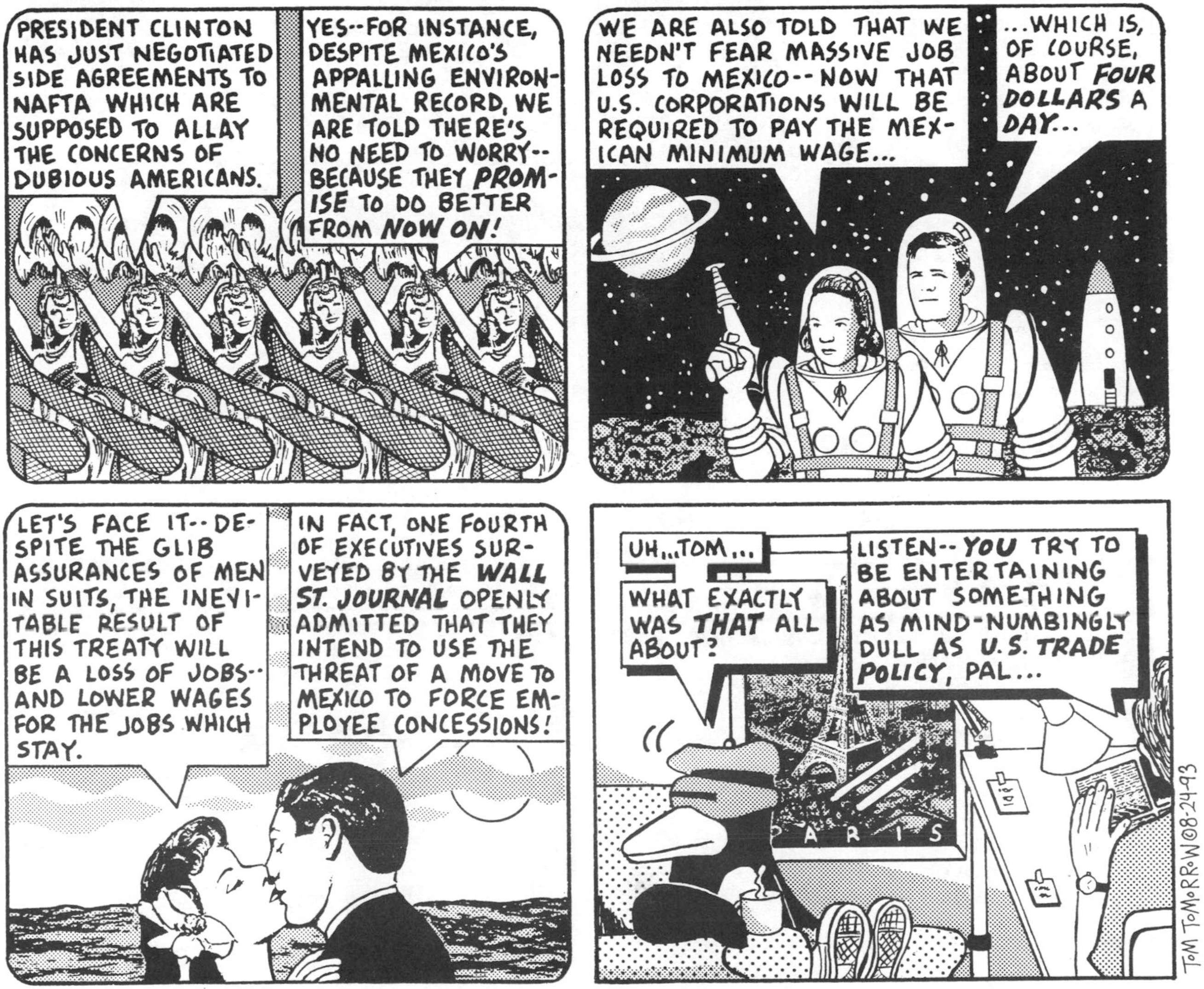
PRESIDENT CLINTON HAS JUST NEGOTIATED SIDE AGREEMENTS TO NAFTA WHICH ARE SUPPOSED TO ALLAY THE CONCERNS OF DUBIOUS AMERICANS.
YES--FOR INSTANCE, DESPITE MEXICO'S APPALLING ENVIRONMENTAL RECORD, WE ARE TOLD THERE'S NO NEED TO WORRY--BECAUSE THEY *PROMISE* TO DO BETTER FROM *NOW ON!*
WE ARE ALSO TOLD THAT WE NEEDN'T FEAR MASSIVE JOB LOSS TO MEXICO--NOW THAT U.S. CORPORATIONS WILL BE REQUIRED TO PAY THE MEXICAN MINIMUM WAGE...
...WHICH IS, OF COURSE, ABOUT *FOUR DOLLARS* A *DAY*...
LET'S FACE IT--DESPITE THE GLIB ASSURANCES OF MEN IN SUITS, THE INEVITABLE RESULT OF THIS TREATY WILL BE A LOSS OF JOBS--AND LOWER WAGES FOR THE JOBS WHICH STAY.
IN FACT, ONE FOURTH OF EXECUTIVES SURVEYED BY THE *WALL ST. JOURNAL* OPENLY ADMITTED THAT THEY INTEND TO USE THE THREAT OF A MOVE TO MEXICO TO FORCE EMPLOYEE CONCESSIONS!
UH...TOM...
WHAT EXACTLY WAS *THAT* ALL ABOUT?
LISTEN--*YOU* TRY TO BE ENTERTAINING ABOUT SOMETHING AS MIND-NUMBINGLY DULL AS *U.S. TRADE POLICY*, PAL...
PARIS
TOM TOMORROW©08-24-93

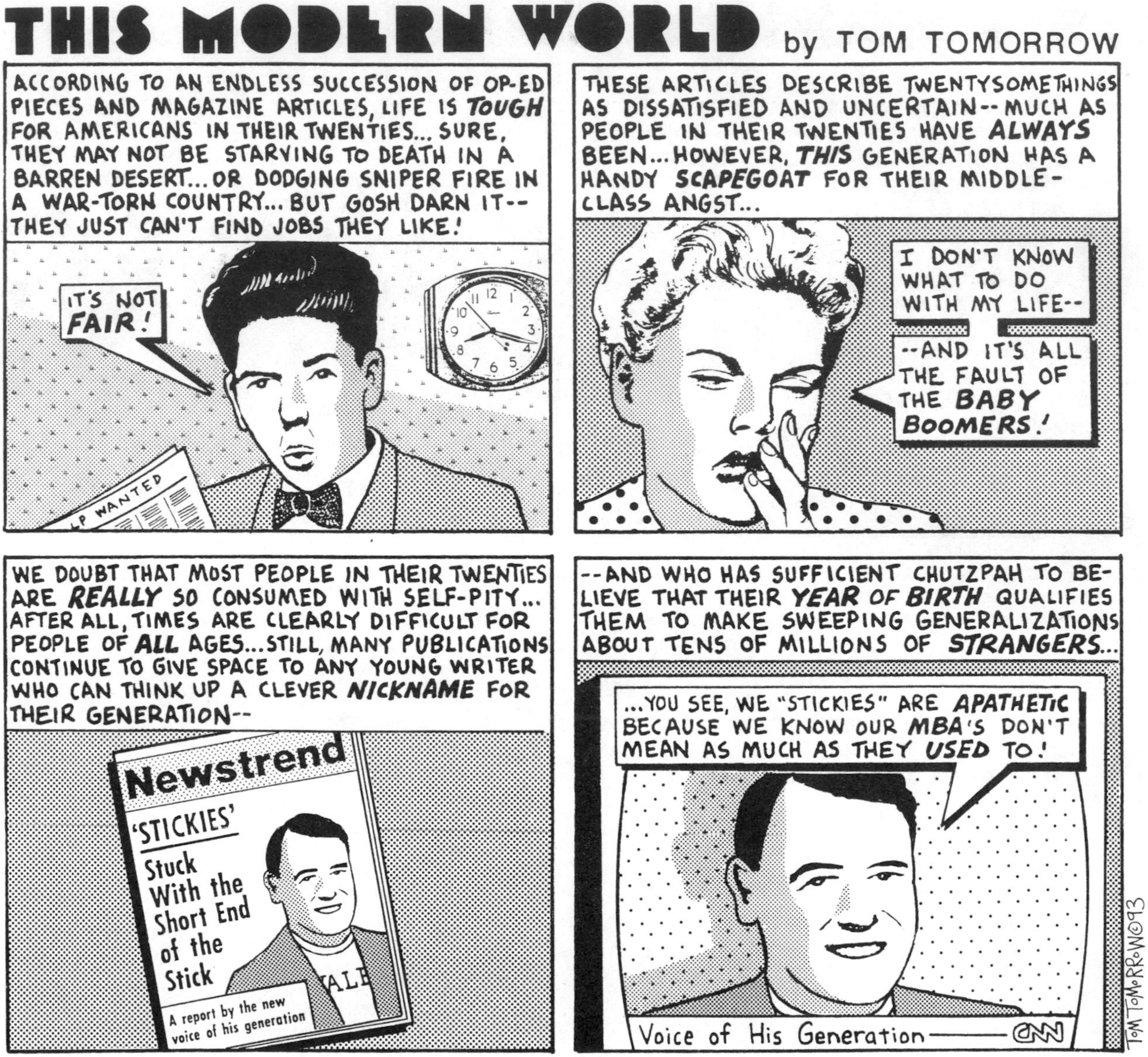
THIS MODERN WORLD by TOM TOMORROW
ACCORDING TO AN ENDLESS SUCCESSION OF OP-ED PIECES AND MAGAZINE ARTICLES, LIFE IS TOUGH FOR AMERICANS IN THEIR TWENTIES... SURE, THEY MAY NOT BE STARVING TO DEATH IN A BARREN DESERT... OR DODGING SNIPER FIRE IN A WAR-TORN COUNTRY... BUT GOSH DARN IT-- THEY JUST CAN'T FIND JOBS THEY LIKE!
IT'S NOT FAIR!
HELP WANTED
THESE ARTICLES DESCRIBE TWENTYSOMETHINGS AS DISSATISFIED AND UNCERTAIN-- MUCH AS PEOPLE IN THEIR TWENTIES HAVE ALWAYS BEEN... HOWEVER, THIS GENERATION HAS A HANDY SCAPEGOAT FOR THEIR MIDDLE-CLASS ANGST...
I DON'T KNOW WHAT TO DO WITH MY LIFE--
--AND IT'S ALL THE FAULT OF THE BABY BOOMERS!
WE DOUBT THAT MOST PEOPLE IN THEIR TWENTIES ARE REALLY SO CONSUMED WITH SELF-PITY... AFTER ALL, TIMES ARE CLEARLY DIFFICULT FOR PEOPLE OF ALL AGES... STILL, MANY PUBLICATIONS CONTINUE TO GIVE SPACE TO ANY YOUNG WRITER WHO CAN THINK UP A CLEVER NICKNAME FOR THEIR GENERATION--
Newstrend
'STICKIES'
Stuck With the Short End of the Stick
YALE
A report by the new voice of his generation
--AND WHO HAS SUFFICIENT CHUTZPAH TO BELIEVE THAT THEIR YEAR OF BIRTH QUALIFIES THEM TO MAKE SWEEPING GENERALIZATIONS ABOUT TENS OF MILLIONS OF STRANGERS...
...YOU SEE, WE "STICKIES" ARE APATHETIC BECAUSE WE KNOW OUR MBA'S DON'T MEAN AS MUCH AS THEY USED TO!
Voice of His Generation —— CNN
TOM TOMORROW©93

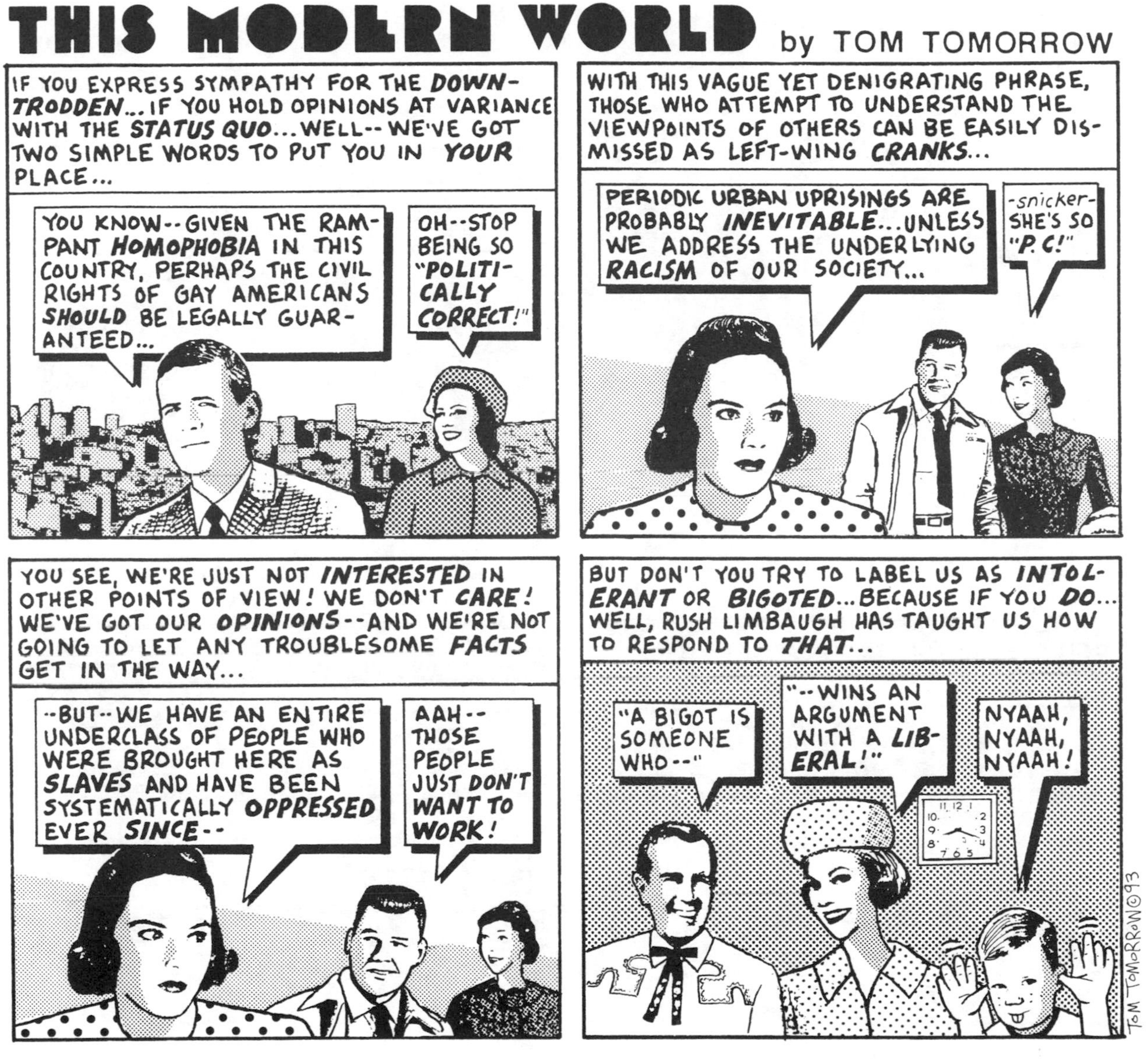
THIS MODERN WORLD by TOM TOMORROW
IF YOU EXPRESS SYMPATHY FOR THE DOWN-TRODDEN... IF YOU HOLD OPINIONS AT VARIANCE WITH THE STATUS QUO... WELL-- WE'VE GOT TWO SIMPLE WORDS TO PUT YOU IN YOUR PLACE...
YOU KNOW--GIVEN THE RAMPANT HOMOPHOBIA IN THIS COUNTRY, PERHAPS THE CIVIL RIGHTS OF GAY AMERICANS SHOULD BE LEGALLY GUARANTEED...
OH--STOP BEING SO "POLITICALLY CORRECT!"
WITH THIS VAGUE YET DENIGRATING PHRASE, THOSE WHO ATTEMPT TO UNDERSTAND THE VIEWPOINTS OF OTHERS CAN BE EASILY DISMISSED AS LEFT-WING CRANKS...
PERIODIC URBAN UPRISINGS ARE PROBABLY INEVITABLE...UNLESS WE ADDRESS THE UNDERLYING RACISM OF OUR SOCIETY...
-snicker- SHE'S SO "P.C!"
YOU SEE, WE'RE JUST NOT INTERESTED IN OTHER POINTS OF VIEW! WE DON'T CARE! WE'VE GOT OUR OPINIONS--AND WE'RE NOT GOING TO LET ANY TROUBLESOME FACTS GET IN THE WAY...
--BUT--WE HAVE AN ENTIRE UNDERCLASS OF PEOPLE WHO WERE BROUGHT HERE AS SLAVES AND HAVE BEEN SYSTEMATICALLY OPPRESSED EVER SINCE--
AAH--THOSE PEOPLE JUST DON'T WANT TO WORK!
BUT DON'T YOU TRY TO LABEL US AS INTOLERANT OR BIGOTED...BECAUSE IF YOU DO... WELL, RUSH LIMBAUGH HAS TAUGHT US HOW TO RESPOND TO THAT...
"A BIGOT IS SOMEONE WHO--"
"--WINS AN ARGUMENT WITH A LIBERAL!"
NYAAH, NYAAH, NYAAH!
TOM TOMORROW©93

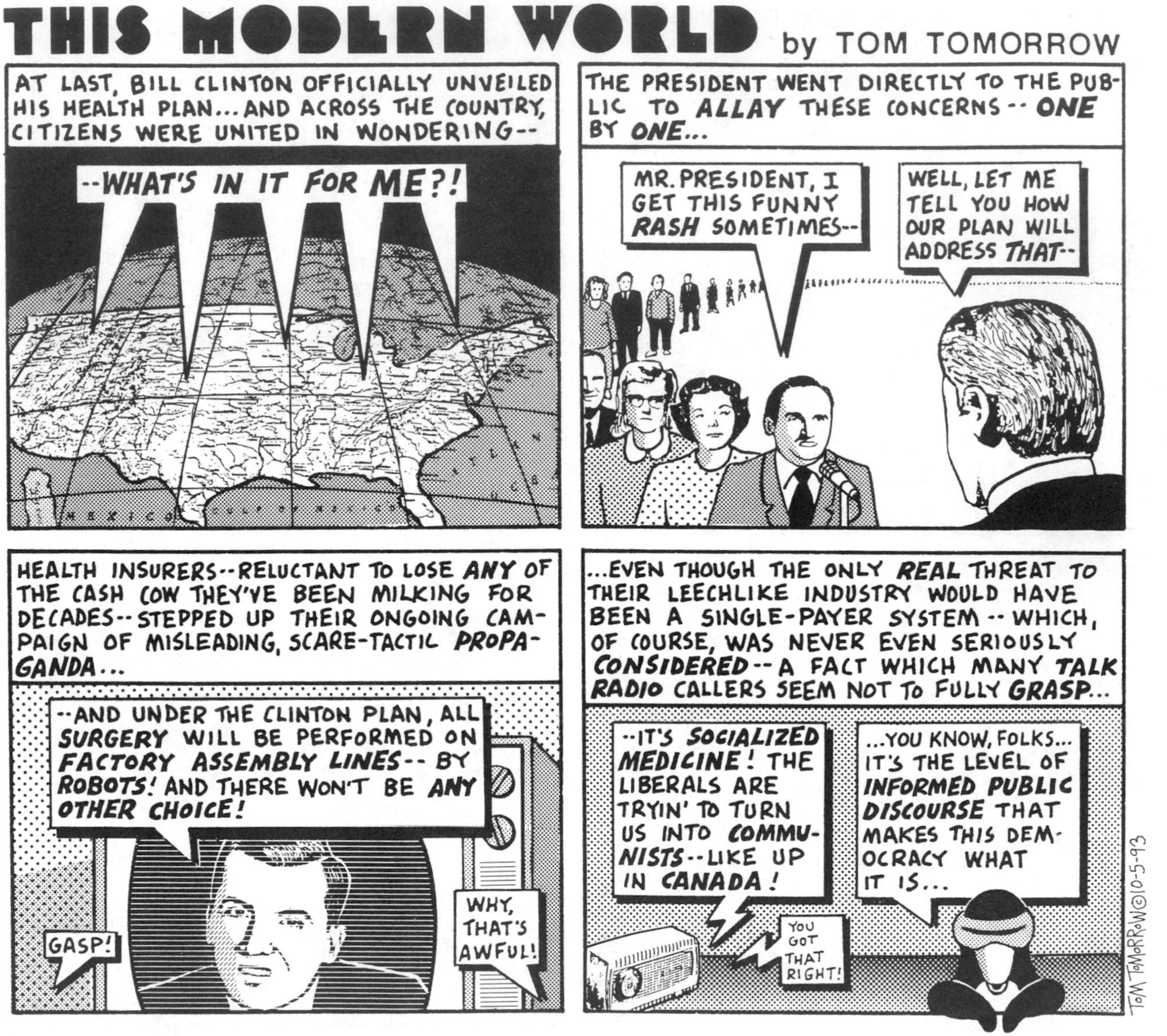
THIS MODERN WORLD by TOM TOMORROW
AT LAST, BILL CLINTON OFFICIALLY UNVEILED HIS HEALTH PLAN... AND ACROSS THE COUNTRY, CITIZENS WERE UNITED IN WONDERING--
--WHAT'S IN IT FOR ME?!
THE PRESIDENT WENT DIRECTLY TO THE PUBLIC TO ALLAY THESE CONCERNS -- ONE BY ONE...
MR. PRESIDENT, I GET THIS FUNNY RASH SOMETIMES--
WELL, LET ME TELL YOU HOW OUR PLAN WILL ADDRESS THAT--
HEALTH INSURERS--RELUCTANT TO LOSE ANY OF THE CASH COW THEY'VE BEEN MILKING FOR DECADES--STEPPED UP THEIR ONGOING CAMPAIGN OF MISLEADING, SCARE-TACTIC PROPAGANDA...
--AND UNDER THE CLINTON PLAN, ALL SURGERY WILL BE PERFORMED ON FACTORY ASSEMBLY LINES-- BY ROBOTS! AND THERE WON'T BE ANY OTHER CHOICE!
GASP!
WHY, THAT'S AWFUL!
...EVEN THOUGH THE ONLY REAL THREAT TO THEIR LEECHLIKE INDUSTRY WOULD HAVE BEEN A SINGLE-PAYER SYSTEM -- WHICH, OF COURSE, WAS NEVER EVEN SERIOUSLY CONSIDERED -- A FACT WHICH MANY TALK RADIO CALLERS SEEM NOT TO FULLY GRASP...
--IT'S SOCIALIZED MEDICINE! THE LIBERALS ARE TRYIN' TO TURN US INTO COMMUNISTS--LIKE UP IN CANADA!
YOU GOT THAT RIGHT!
...YOU KNOW, FOLKS... IT'S THE LEVEL OF INFORMED PUBLIC DISCOURSE THAT MAKES THIS DEMOCRACY WHAT IT IS...
TOM TOMORROW©10-5-93

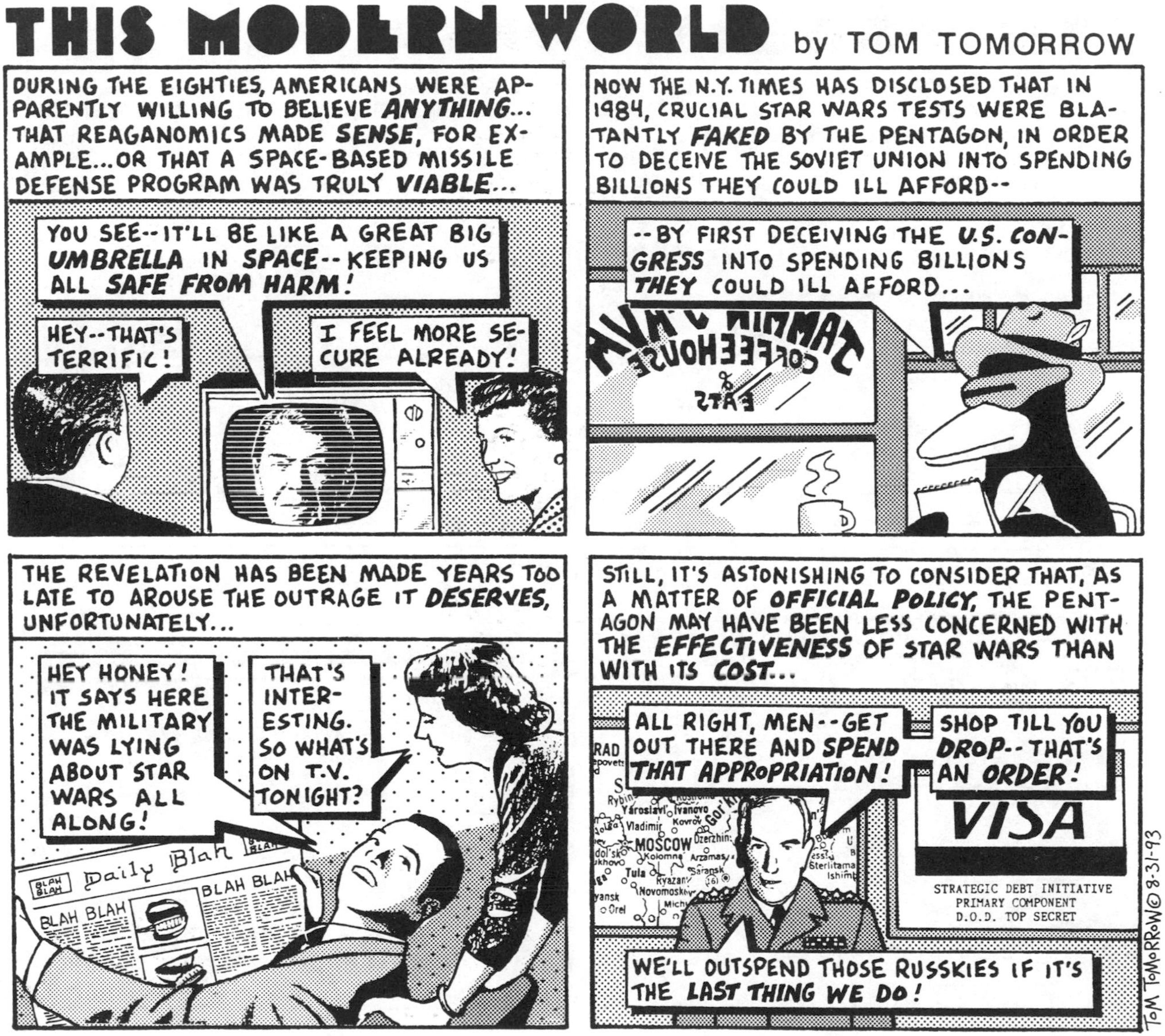
THIS MODERN WORLD by TOM TOMORROW
DURING THE EIGHTIES, AMERICANS WERE APPARENTLY WILLING TO BELIEVE ANYTHING... THAT REAGANOMICS MADE SENSE, FOR EXAMPLE...OR THAT A SPACE-BASED MISSILE DEFENSE PROGRAM WAS TRULY VIABLE...
YOU SEE--IT'LL BE LIKE A GREAT BIG UMBRELLA IN SPACE--KEEPING US ALL SAFE FROM HARM!
HEY--THAT'S TERRIFIC!
I FEEL MORE SECURE ALREADY!
NOW THE N.Y. TIMES HAS DISCLOSED THAT IN 1984, CRUCIAL STAR WARS TESTS WERE BLATANTLY FAKED BY THE PENTAGON, IN ORDER TO DECEIVE THE SOVIET UNION INTO SPENDING BILLIONS THEY COULD ILL AFFORD--
--BY FIRST DECEIVING THE U.S. CONGRESS INTO SPENDING BILLIONS THEY COULD ILL AFFORD...
THE REVELATION HAS BEEN MADE YEARS TOO LATE TO AROUSE THE OUTRAGE IT DESERVES, UNFORTUNATELY...
HEY HONEY! IT SAYS HERE THE MILITARY WAS LYING ABOUT STAR WARS ALL ALONG!
THAT'S INTERESTING. SO WHAT'S ON T.V. TONIGHT?
Daily Blah
BLAH BLAH
BLAH BLAH
STILL, IT'S ASTONISHING TO CONSIDER THAT, AS A MATTER OF OFFICIAL POLICY, THE PENTAGON MAY HAVE BEEN LESS CONCERNED WITH THE EFFECTIVENESS OF STAR WARS THAN WITH ITS COST...
ALL RIGHT, MEN--GET OUT THERE AND SPEND THAT APPROPRIATION!
SHOP TILL YOU DROP--THAT'S AN ORDER!
MOSCOW
VISA
STRATEGIC DEBT INITIATIVE
PRIMARY COMPONENT
D.O.D. TOP SECRET
WE'LL OUTSPEND THOSE RUSSKIES IF IT'S THE LAST THING WE DO!
TOM TOMORROW © 8-31-93

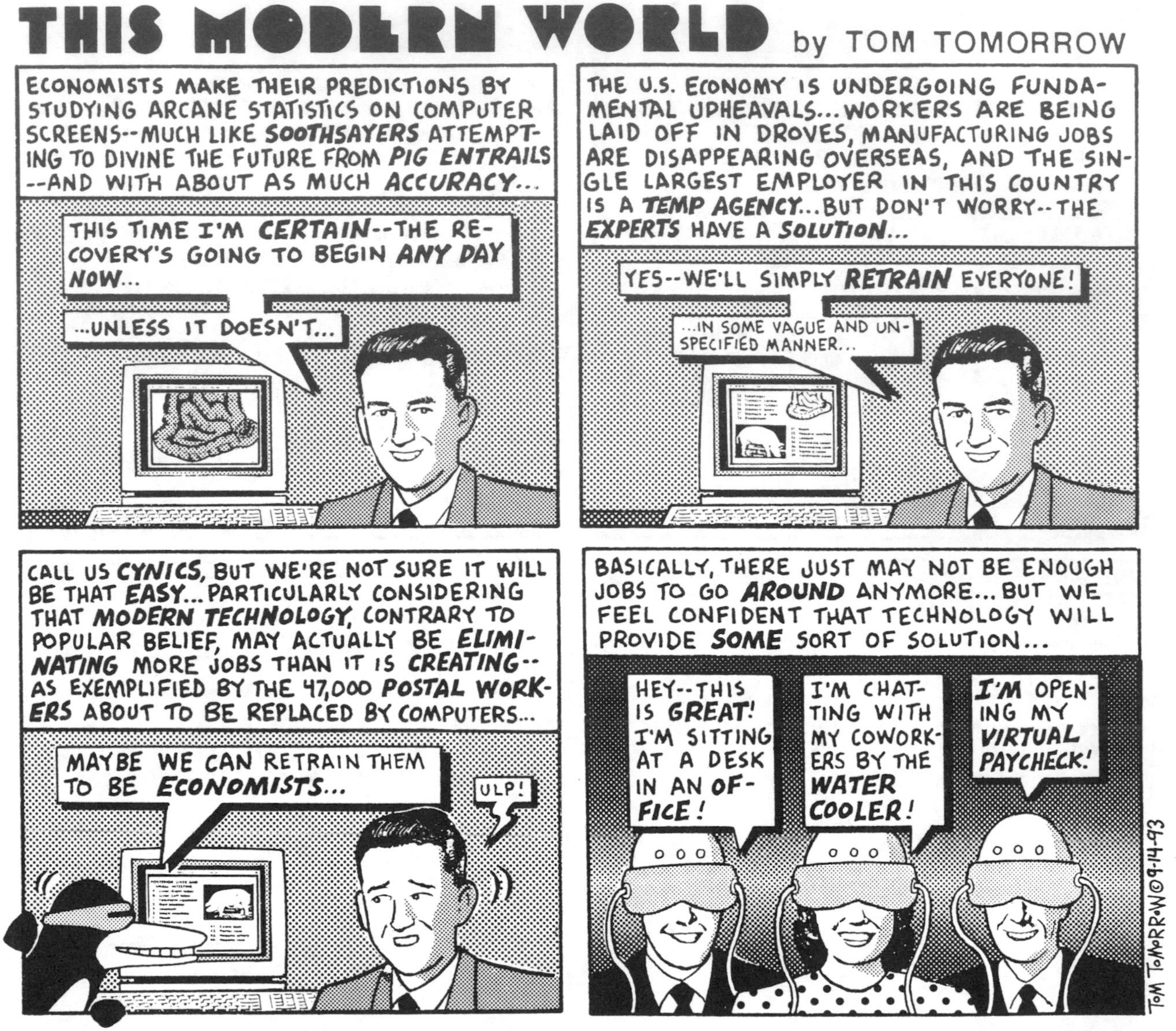
THIS MODERN WORLD by TOM TOMORROW
ECONOMISTS MAKE THEIR PREDICTIONS BY STUDYING ARCANE STATISTICS ON COMPUTER SCREENS--MUCH LIKE SOOTHSAYERS ATTEMPTING TO DIVINE THE FUTURE FROM PIG ENTRAILS --AND WITH ABOUT AS MUCH ACCURACY...
THIS TIME I'M CERTAIN--THE RECOVERY'S GOING TO BEGIN ANY DAY NOW...
...UNLESS IT DOESN'T...
THE U.S. ECONOMY IS UNDERGOING FUNDAMENTAL UPHEAVALS...WORKERS ARE BEING LAID OFF IN DROVES, MANUFACTURING JOBS ARE DISAPPEARING OVERSEAS, AND THE SINGLE LARGEST EMPLOYER IN THIS COUNTRY IS A TEMP AGENCY...BUT DON'T WORRY--THE EXPERTS HAVE A SOLUTION...
YES--WE'LL SIMPLY RETRAIN EVERYONE!
...IN SOME VAGUE AND UNSPECIFIED MANNER...
CALL US CYNICS, BUT WE'RE NOT SURE IT WILL BE THAT EASY...PARTICULARLY CONSIDERING THAT MODERN TECHNOLOGY, CONTRARY TO POPULAR BELIEF, MAY ACTUALLY BE ELIMINATING MORE JOBS THAN IT IS CREATING--AS EXEMPLIFIED BY THE 47,000 POSTAL WORKERS ABOUT TO BE REPLACED BY COMPUTERS...
MAYBE WE CAN RETRAIN THEM TO BE ECONOMISTS...
ULP!
BASICALLY, THERE JUST MAY NOT BE ENOUGH JOBS TO GO AROUND ANYMORE...BUT WE FEEL CONFIDENT THAT TECHNOLOGY WILL PROVIDE SOME SORT OF SOLUTION...
HEY--THIS IS GREAT! I'M SITTING AT A DESK IN AN OFFICE!
I'M CHATTING WITH MY COWORKERS BY THE WATER COOLER!
I'M OPENING MY VIRTUAL PAYCHECK!
TOM TOMORROW©9-14-93

THIS MODERN WORLD by TOM TOMORROW

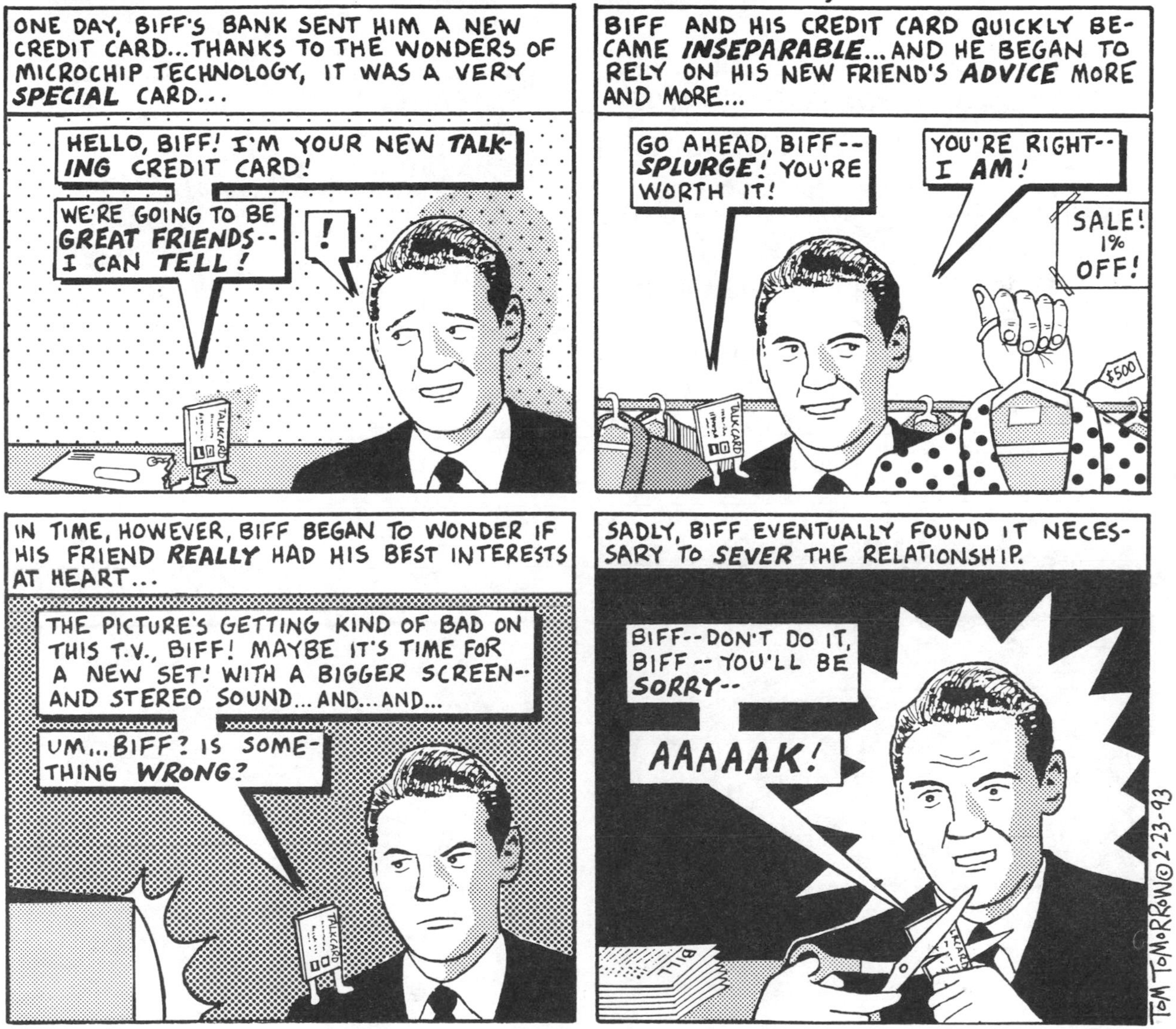

ONE DAY, BIFF'S BANK SENT HIM A NEW CREDIT CARD...THANKS TO THE WONDERS OF MICROCHIP TECHNOLOGY, IT WAS A VERY SPECIAL CARD...
HELLO, BIFF! I'M YOUR NEW TALKING CREDIT CARD!
WE'RE GOING TO BE GREAT FRIENDS-- I CAN TELL!
!
TALKCARD
BIFF AND HIS CREDIT CARD QUICKLY BECAME INSEPARABLE...AND HE BEGAN TO RELY ON HIS NEW FRIEND'S ADVICE MORE AND MORE...
GO AHEAD, BIFF-- SPLURGE! YOU'RE WORTH IT!
YOU'RE RIGHT-- I AM!
SALE! 1% OFF!
$500
TALKCARD
IN TIME, HOWEVER, BIFF BEGAN TO WONDER IF HIS FRIEND REALLY HAD HIS BEST INTERESTS AT HEART...
THE PICTURE'S GETTING KIND OF BAD ON THIS T.V., BIFF! MAYBE IT'S TIME FOR A NEW SET! WITH A BIGGER SCREEN-- AND STEREO SOUND...AND...AND...
UM...BIFF? IS SOMETHING WRONG?
TALKCARD
SADLY, BIFF EVENTUALLY FOUND IT NECESSARY TO SEVER THE RELATIONSHIP.
BIFF--DON'T DO IT, BIFF--YOU'LL BE SORRY--
AAAAAK!
BILL
TOM TOMORROW©2-23-93

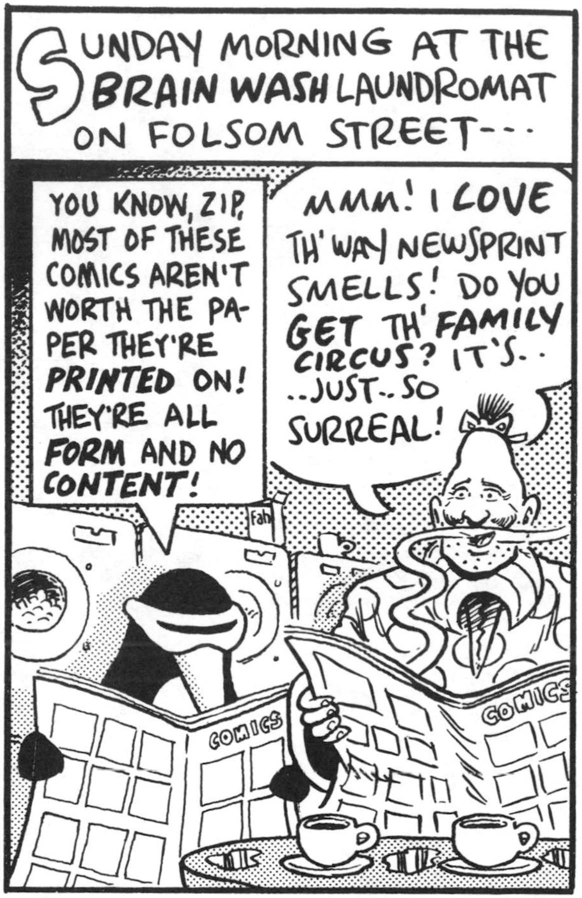
SUNDAY MORNING AT THE BRAIN WASH LAUNDROMAT ON FOLSOM STREET---
YOU KNOW, ZIP, MOST OF THESE COMICS AREN'T WORTH THE PAPER THEY'RE PRINTED ON! THEY'RE ALL FORM AND NO CONTENT!
MMM! I LOVE TH' WAY NEWSPRINT SMELLS! DO YOU GET TH' FAMILY CIRCUS? IT'S.. ..JUST.. SO SURREAL!
COMICS
COMICS

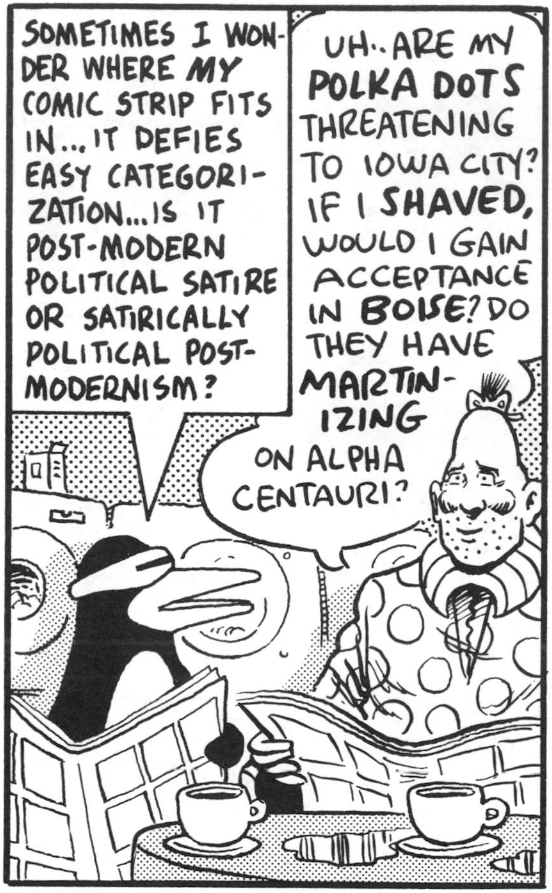
SOMETIMES I WONDER WHERE MY COMIC STRIP FITS IN... IT DEFIES EASY CATEGORIZATION... IS IT POST-MODERN POLITICAL SATIRE OR SATIRICALLY POLITICAL POST-MODERNISM?
UH.. ARE MY POLKA DOTS THREATENING TO IOWA CITY? IF I SHAVED, WOULD I GAIN ACCEPTANCE IN BOISE? DO THEY HAVE MARTIN-IZING ON ALPHA CENTAURI?

THE STRIP IS ALSO VERBOSE IN THE *EXTREME*... EDITORS COMPLAIN, BUT I HAVE FAITH IN THE READERS... AFTER ALL, THAT'S WHY THEY'RE CALLED *"READERS,"* ISN'T IT? BECAUSE THEY *READ?* AMERICA'S NOT COMPLETELY POST-LITERATE... *YET*... WHAT DO THEY WANT FROM ME? MEANINGLESS *SIGHT GAGS?* INFANTILE JOKES ABOUT BODY ODOR? I HAVE BETTER THINGS TO MUTTER MUTTER MUMBLE...

I *LOVE* WORDS! I LOVE TH' WORD *"WORD"!* WORD, WHIRRED... WORLD, WEIRD... *WEIRD!!* IS IT "I" BEFORE "E", OR IS IT MEMOREX? & WHY DO THEY CALL THESE THINGS *BALLOONS?* ARE THEY FILLED WITH HOT AIR? AM I A WORD PROCESSOR OR A FOOD PROCESSOR? IS ANYBODY READING THIS IN HAYWARD, OR AM I YAWN...

OF COURSE, A MEANINGLESS SIGHT GAG *CAN* HELP SOFTEN A HARSH AND FRIGHTENING MESSAGE... LIKE THE FACT THAT THE NATION'S BANKING SYSTEM IS ON THE VERGE OF *COLLAPSE*... MMPH!

HMM... A PLEASANT *LEMONY TARTNESS*... BUT COULD USE A TAD MORE POLYSORBATE 80!

©TOM TOMORROW / ©BILL GRIFFITH

97

THIS MODERN WORLD by TOM TOMORROW

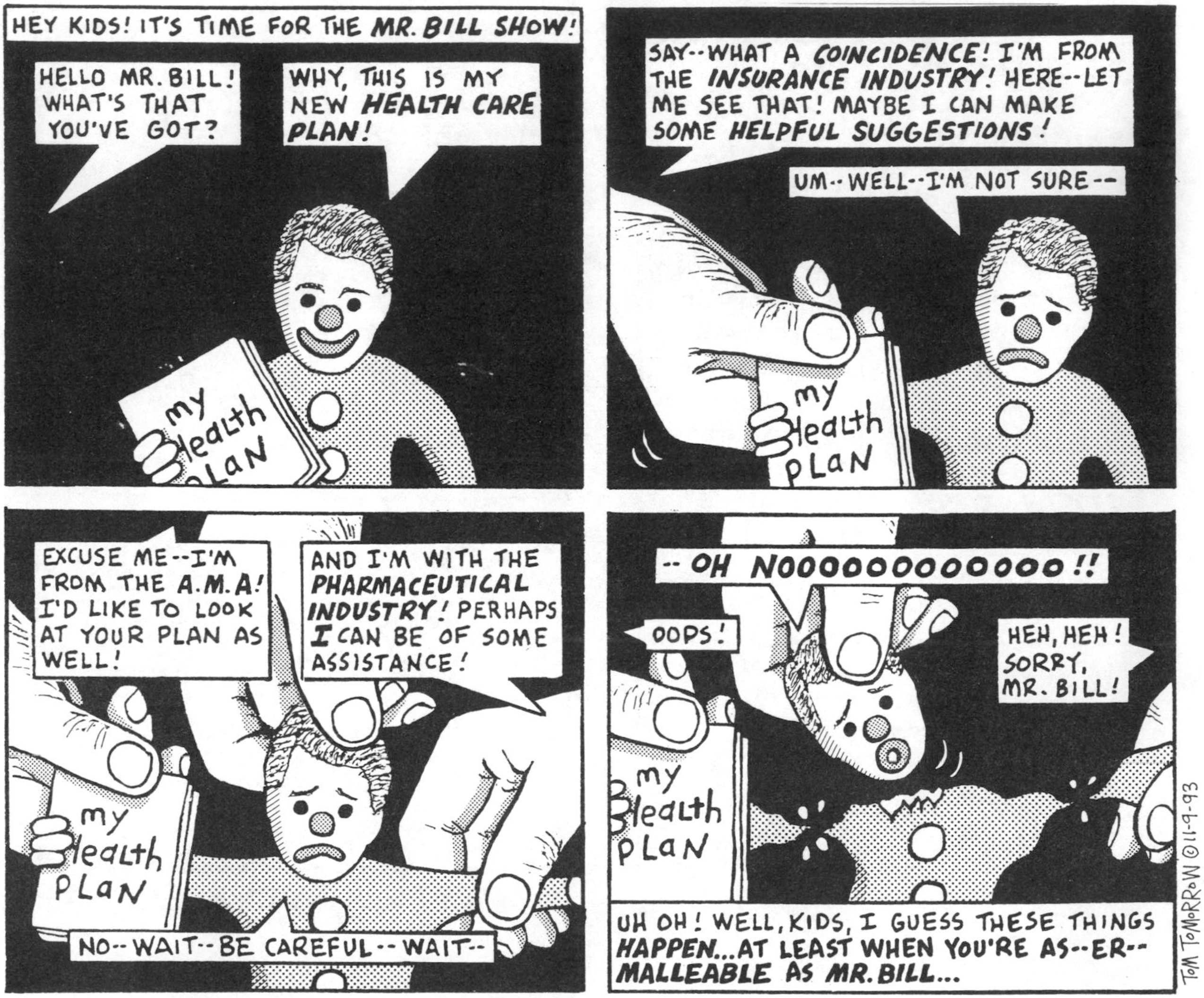
HEY KIDS! IT'S TIME FOR THE MR. BILL SHOW!
HELLO MR. BILL! WHAT'S THAT YOU'VE GOT?
WHY, THIS IS MY NEW HEALTH CARE PLAN!
my Health PLAN
SAY--WHAT A COINCIDENCE! I'M FROM THE INSURANCE INDUSTRY! HERE--LET ME SEE THAT! MAYBE I CAN MAKE SOME HELPFUL SUGGESTIONS!
UM--WELL--I'M NOT SURE--
my Health PLAN
EXCUSE ME--I'M FROM THE A.M.A! I'D LIKE TO LOOK AT YOUR PLAN AS WELL!
AND I'M WITH THE PHARMACEUTICAL INDUSTRY! PERHAPS I CAN BE OF SOME ASSISTANCE!
my Health PLAN
NO--WAIT--BE CAREFUL--WAIT--
--OH NOOOOOOOOOOOO!!
OOPS!
HEH, HEH! SORRY, MR. BILL!
my Health PLAN
UH OH! WELL, KIDS, I GUESS THESE THINGS HAPPEN...AT LEAST WHEN YOU'RE AS--ER--MALLEABLE AS MR. BILL...
TOM TOMORROW ©11-9-93

THIS MODERN WORLD by TOM TOMORROW

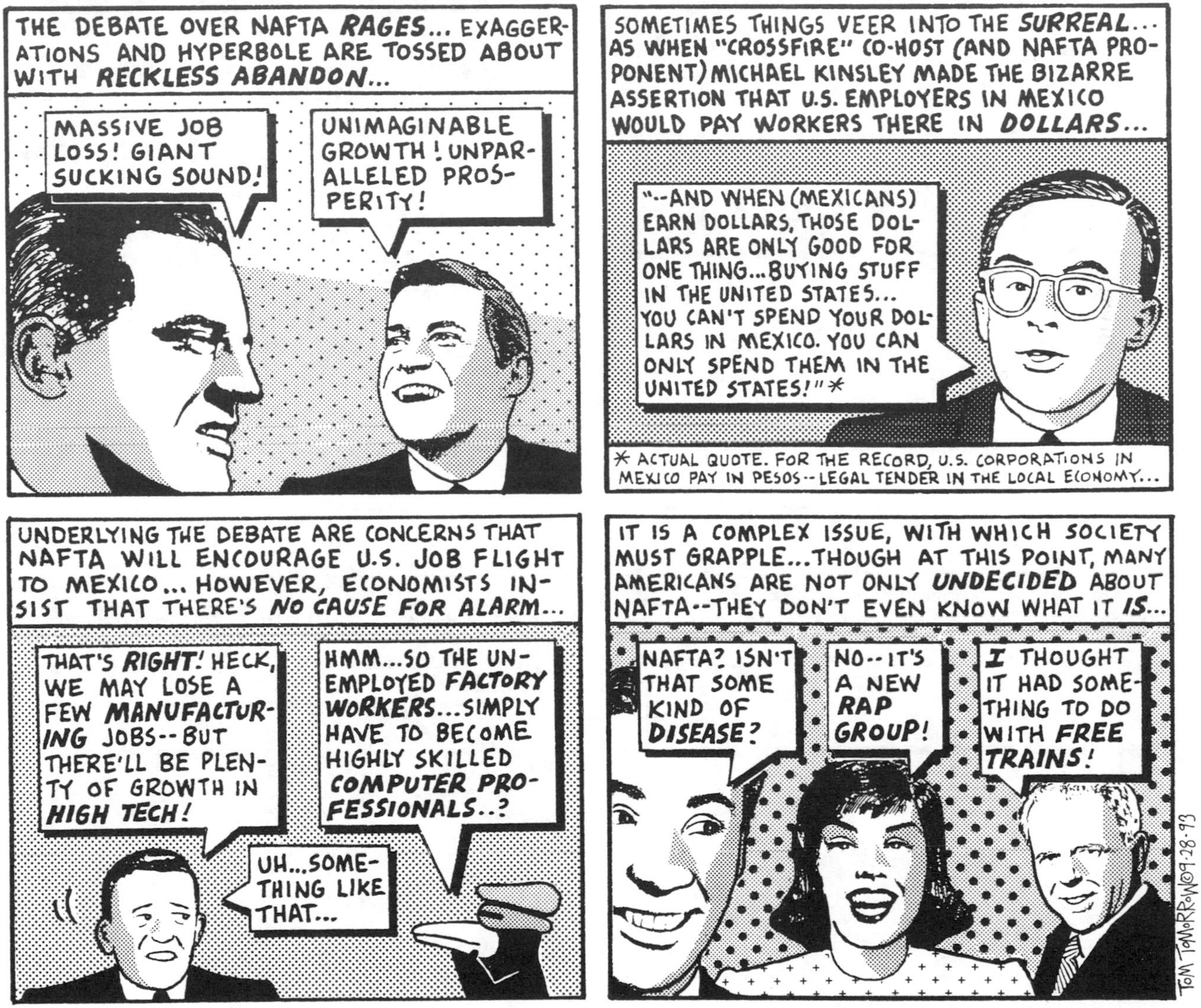
THE DEBATE OVER NAFTA RAGES... EXAGGERATIONS AND HYPERBOLE ARE TOSSED ABOUT WITH RECKLESS ABANDON...
MASSIVE JOB LOSS! GIANT SUCKING SOUND!
UNIMAGINABLE GROWTH! UNPARALLELED PROSPERITY!
SOMETIMES THINGS VEER INTO THE SURREAL... AS WHEN "CROSSFIRE" CO-HOST (AND NAFTA PROPONENT) MICHAEL KINSLEY MADE THE BIZARRE ASSERTION THAT U.S. EMPLOYERS IN MEXICO WOULD PAY WORKERS THERE IN DOLLARS...
"--AND WHEN (MEXICANS) EARN DOLLARS, THOSE DOLLARS ARE ONLY GOOD FOR ONE THING...BUYING STUFF IN THE UNITED STATES... YOU CAN'T SPEND YOUR DOLLARS IN MEXICO. YOU CAN ONLY SPEND THEM IN THE UNITED STATES!"*
* ACTUAL QUOTE. FOR THE RECORD, U.S. CORPORATIONS IN MEXICO PAY IN PESOS--LEGAL TENDER IN THE LOCAL ECONOMY...
UNDERLYING THE DEBATE ARE CONCERNS THAT NAFTA WILL ENCOURAGE U.S. JOB FLIGHT TO MEXICO... HOWEVER, ECONOMISTS INSIST THAT THERE'S NO CAUSE FOR ALARM...
THAT'S RIGHT! HECK, WE MAY LOSE A FEW MANUFACTURING JOBS--BUT THERE'LL BE PLENTY OF GROWTH IN HIGH TECH!
HMM...SO THE UNEMPLOYED FACTORY WORKERS...SIMPLY HAVE TO BECOME HIGHLY SKILLED COMPUTER PROFESSIONALS..?
UH...SOMETHING LIKE THAT...
IT IS A COMPLEX ISSUE, WITH WHICH SOCIETY MUST GRAPPLE...THOUGH AT THIS POINT, MANY AMERICANS ARE NOT ONLY UNDECIDED ABOUT NAFTA--THEY DON'T EVEN KNOW WHAT IT IS...
NAFTA? ISN'T THAT SOME KIND OF DISEASE?
NO--IT'S A NEW RAP GROUP!
I THOUGHT IT HAD SOMETHING TO DO WITH FREE TRAINS!
TOM TOMORROW©9-28-93

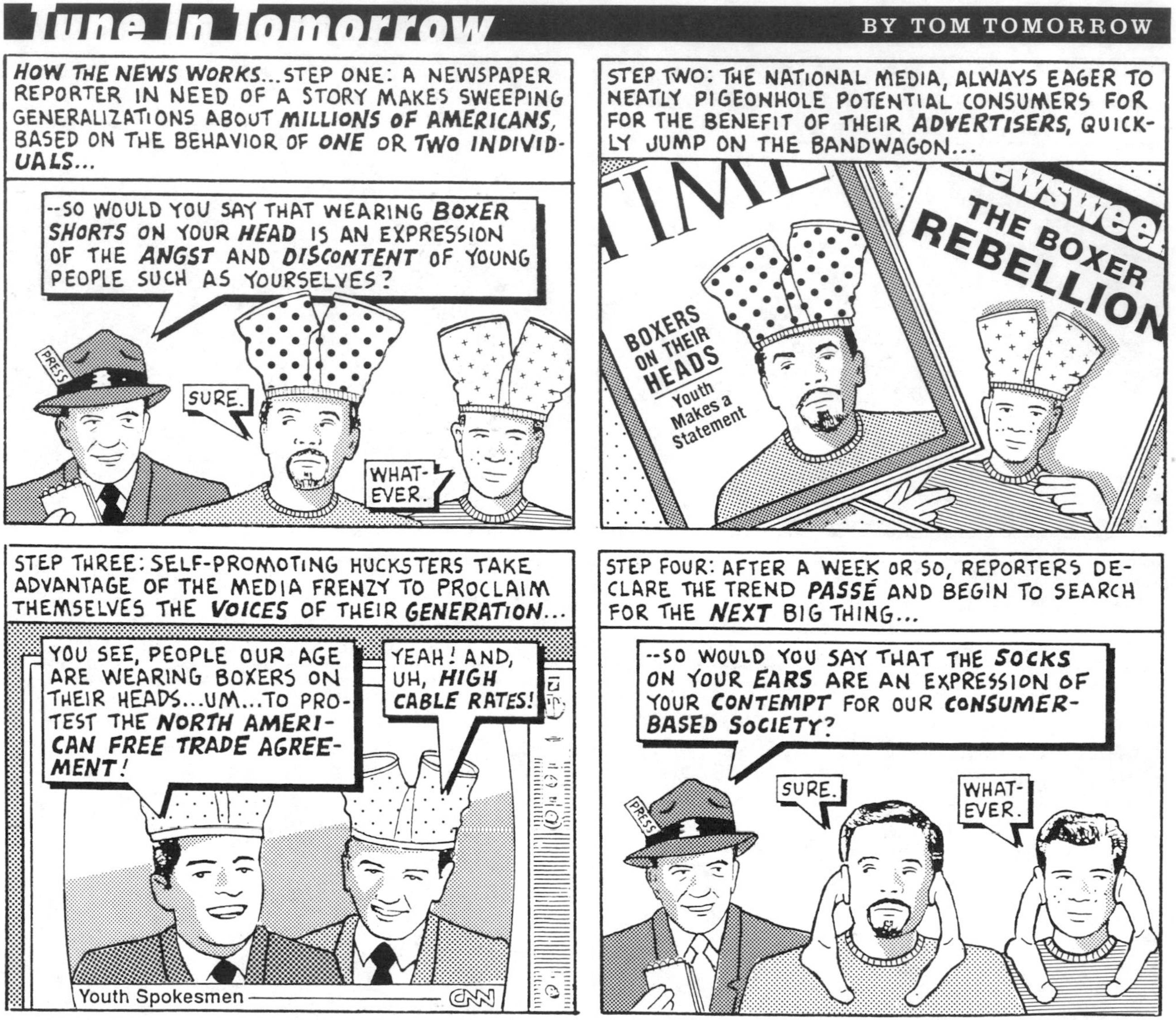
Tune In Tomorrow
BY TOM TOMORROW
HOW THE NEWS WORKS...STEP ONE: A NEWSPAPER REPORTER IN NEED OF A STORY MAKES SWEEPING GENERALIZATIONS ABOUT MILLIONS OF AMERICANS, BASED ON THE BEHAVIOR OF ONE OR TWO INDIVIDUALS...
--SO WOULD YOU SAY THAT WEARING BOXER SHORTS ON YOUR HEAD IS AN EXPRESSION OF THE ANGST AND DISCONTENT OF YOUNG PEOPLE SUCH AS YOURSELVES?
PRESS
SURE.
WHAT-EVER.
STEP TWO: THE NATIONAL MEDIA, ALWAYS EAGER TO NEATLY PIGEONHOLE POTENTIAL CONSUMERS FOR FOR THE BENEFIT OF THEIR ADVERTISERS, QUICKLY JUMP ON THE BANDWAGON...
TIME
BOXERS ON THEIR HEADS
Youth Makes a Statement
Newsweek
THE BOXER REBELLION
STEP THREE: SELF-PROMOTING HUCKSTERS TAKE ADVANTAGE OF THE MEDIA FRENZY TO PROCLAIM THEMSELVES THE VOICES OF THEIR GENERATION...
YOU SEE, PEOPLE OUR AGE ARE WEARING BOXERS ON THEIR HEADS...UM...TO PROTEST THE NORTH AMERICAN FREE TRADE AGREEMENT!
YEAH! AND, UH, HIGH CABLE RATES!
Youth Spokesmen
CNN
STEP FOUR: AFTER A WEEK OR SO, REPORTERS DECLARE THE TREND PASSÉ AND BEGIN TO SEARCH FOR THE NEXT BIG THING...
--SO WOULD YOU SAY THAT THE SOCKS ON YOUR EARS ARE AN EXPRESSION OF YOUR CONTEMPT FOR OUR CONSUMER-BASED SOCIETY?
PRESS
SURE.
WHAT-EVER.

Tune In Tomorrow

BY TOM TOMORROW

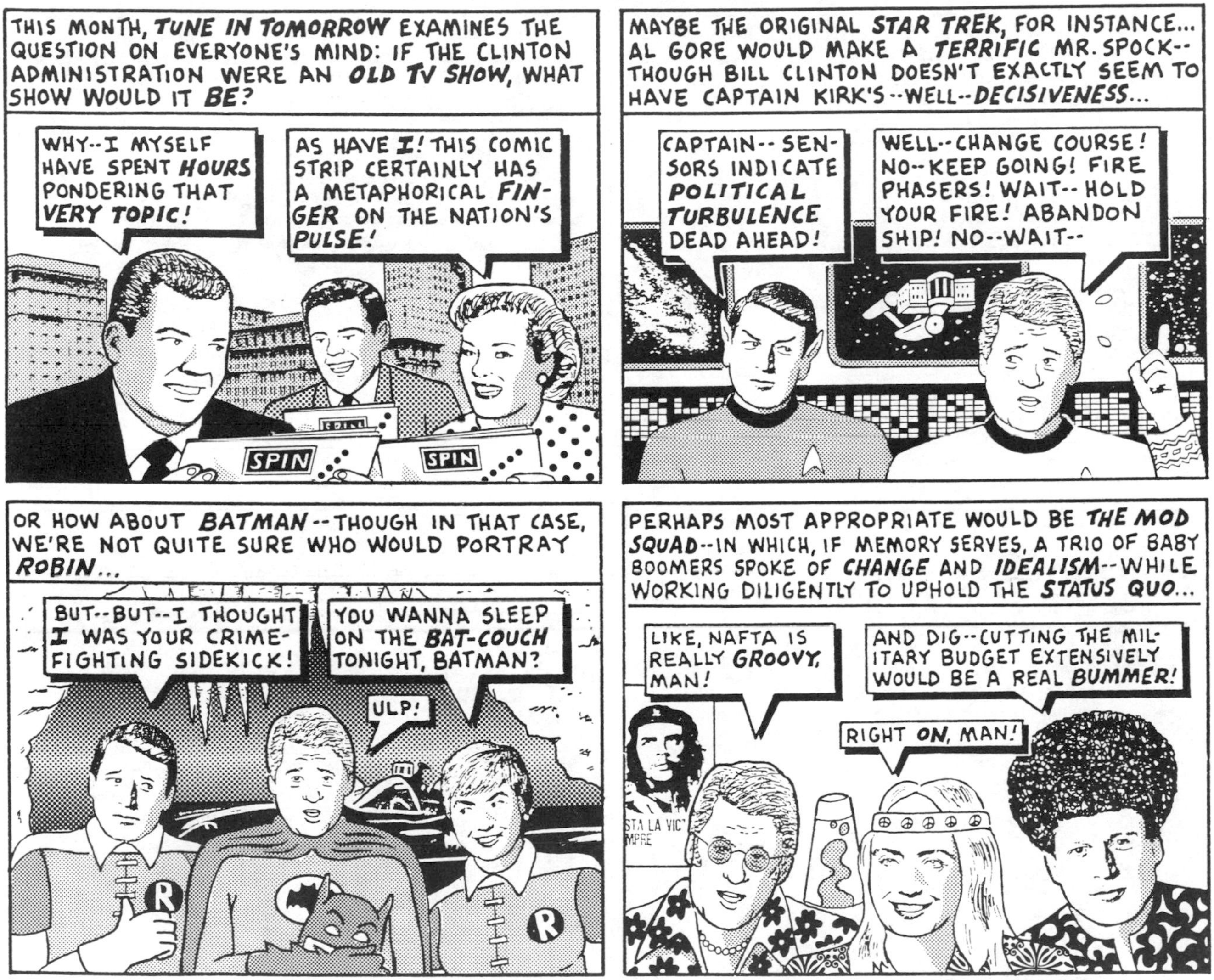
THIS MONTH, TUNE IN TOMORROW EXAMINES THE QUESTION ON EVERYONE'S MIND: IF THE CLINTON ADMINISTRATION WERE AN OLD TV SHOW, WHAT SHOW WOULD IT BE?
WHY--I MYSELF HAVE SPENT HOURS PONDERING THAT VERY TOPIC!
AS HAVE I! THIS COMIC STRIP CERTAINLY HAS A METAPHORICAL FINGER ON THE NATION'S PULSE!
SPIN
SPIN
MAYBE THE ORIGINAL STAR TREK, FOR INSTANCE... AL GORE WOULD MAKE A TERRIFIC MR. SPOCK--THOUGH BILL CLINTON DOESN'T EXACTLY SEEM TO HAVE CAPTAIN KIRK'S--WELL--DECISIVENESS...
CAPTAIN--SENSORS INDICATE POLITICAL TURBULENCE DEAD AHEAD!
WELL--CHANGE COURSE! NO--KEEP GOING! FIRE PHASERS! WAIT--HOLD YOUR FIRE! ABANDON SHIP! NO--WAIT--
OR HOW ABOUT BATMAN--THOUGH IN THAT CASE, WE'RE NOT QUITE SURE WHO WOULD PORTRAY ROBIN...
BUT--BUT--I THOUGHT I WAS YOUR CRIME-FIGHTING SIDEKICK!
YOU WANNA SLEEP ON THE BAT-COUCH TONIGHT, BATMAN?
ULP!
PERHAPS MOST APPROPRIATE WOULD BE THE MOD SQUAD--IN WHICH, IF MEMORY SERVES, A TRIO OF BABY BOOMERS SPOKE OF CHANGE AND IDEALISM--WHILE WORKING DILIGENTLY TO UPHOLD THE STATUS QUO...
LIKE, NAFTA IS REALLY GROOVY, MAN!
AND DIG--CUTTING THE MILITARY BUDGET EXTENSIVELY WOULD BE A REAL BUMMER!
RIGHT ON, MAN!

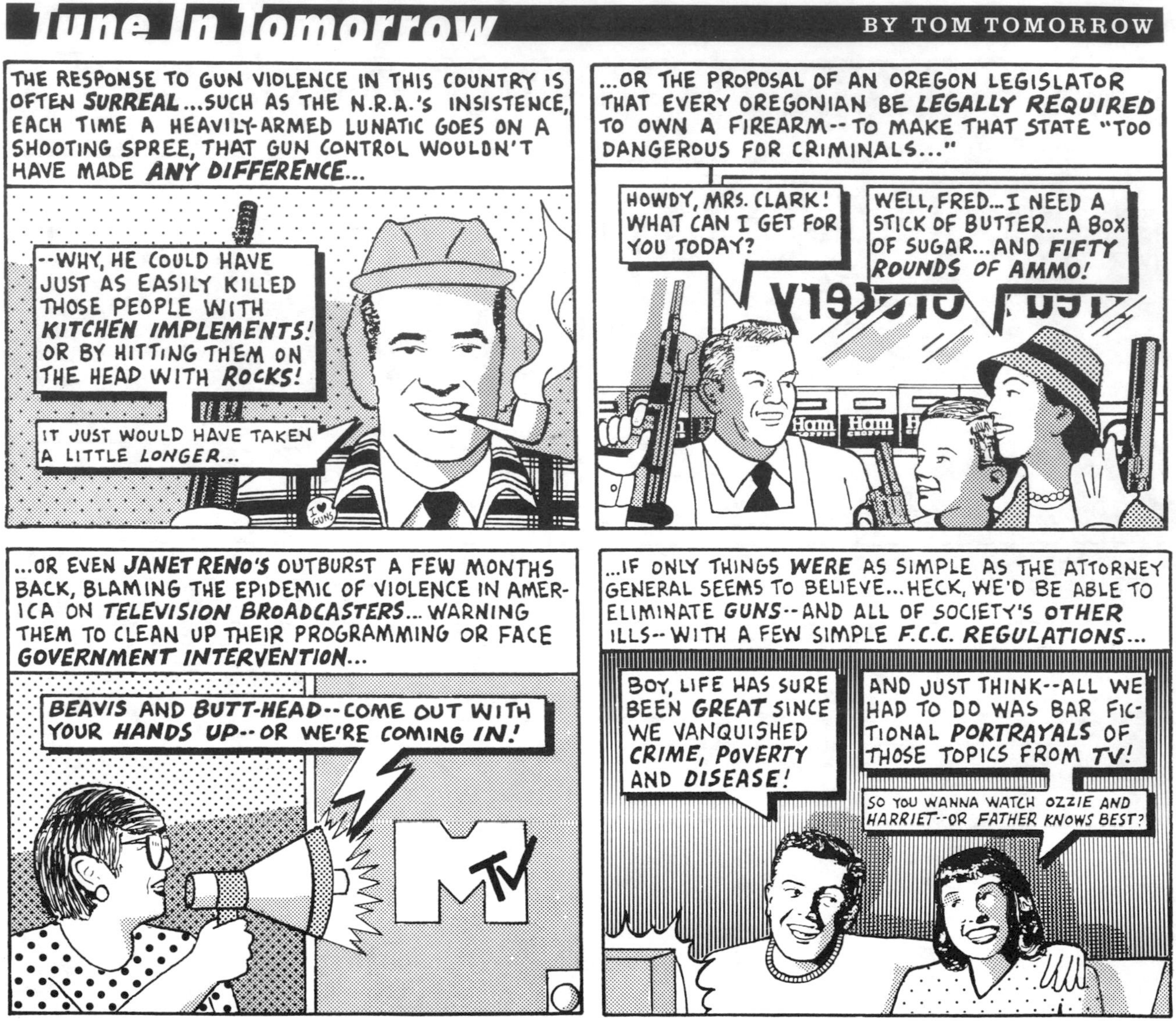
Tune In Tomorrow
BY TOM TOMORROW
THE RESPONSE TO GUN VIOLENCE IN THIS COUNTRY IS OFTEN SURREAL ...SUCH AS THE N.R.A.'S INSISTENCE, EACH TIME A HEAVILY-ARMED LUNATIC GOES ON A SHOOTING SPREE, THAT GUN CONTROL WOULDN'T HAVE MADE ANY DIFFERENCE...
--WHY, HE COULD HAVE JUST AS EASILY KILLED THOSE PEOPLE WITH KITCHEN IMPLEMENTS! OR BY HITTING THEM ON THE HEAD WITH ROCKS!
IT JUST WOULD HAVE TAKEN A LITTLE LONGER...
I ♥ GUNS
...OR THE PROPOSAL OF AN OREGON LEGISLATOR THAT EVERY OREGONIAN BE LEGALLY REQUIRED TO OWN A FIREARM--TO MAKE THAT STATE "TOO DANGEROUS FOR CRIMINALS..."
HOWDY, MRS. CLARK! WHAT CAN I GET FOR YOU TODAY?
WELL, FRED...I NEED A STICK OF BUTTER...A BOX OF SUGAR...AND FIFTY ROUNDS OF AMMO!
Ham
Ham
...OR EVEN JANET RENO'S OUTBURST A FEW MONTHS BACK, BLAMING THE EPIDEMIC OF VIOLENCE IN AMERICA ON TELEVISION BROADCASTERS... WARNING THEM TO CLEAN UP THEIR PROGRAMMING OR FACE GOVERNMENT INTERVENTION...
BEAVIS AND BUTT-HEAD--COME OUT WITH YOUR HANDS UP--OR WE'RE COMING IN!
MTV
...IF ONLY THINGS WERE AS SIMPLE AS THE ATTORNEY GENERAL SEEMS TO BELIEVE...HECK, WE'D BE ABLE TO ELIMINATE GUNS--AND ALL OF SOCIETY'S OTHER ILLS--WITH A FEW SIMPLE F.C.C. REGULATIONS...
BOY, LIFE HAS SURE BEEN GREAT SINCE WE VANQUISHED CRIME, POVERTY AND DISEASE!
AND JUST THINK--ALL WE HAD TO DO WAS BAR FICTIONAL PORTRAYALS OF THOSE TOPICS FROM TV!
SO YOU WANNA WATCH OZZIE AND HARRIET--OR FATHER KNOWS BEST?

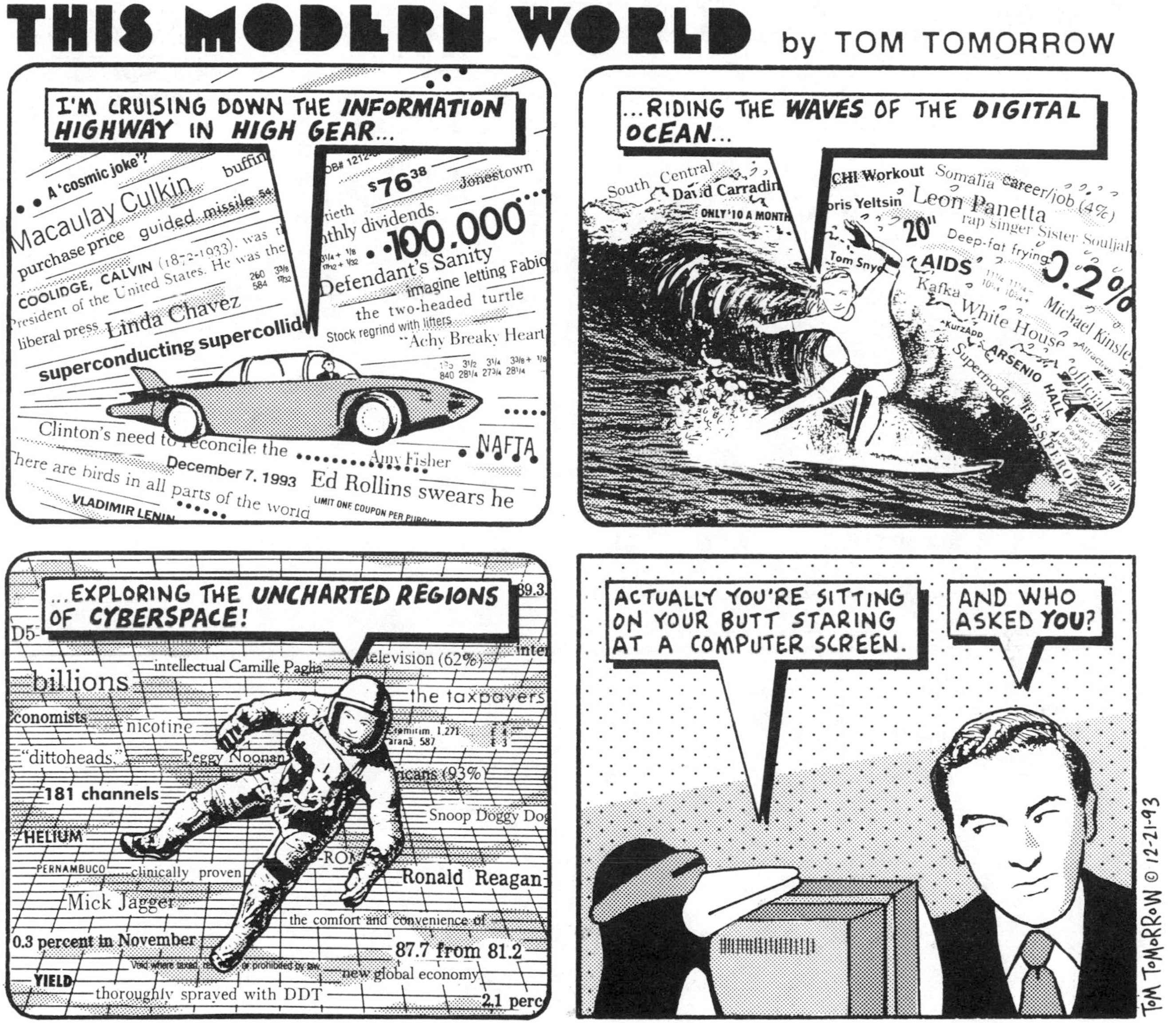
THIS MODERN WORLD by TOM TOMORROW
I'M CRUISING DOWN THE INFORMATION HIGHWAY IN HIGH GEAR...
...RIDING THE WAVES OF THE DIGITAL OCEAN...
...EXPLORING THE UNCHARTED REGIONS OF CYBERSPACE!
ACTUALLY YOU'RE SITTING ON YOUR BUTT STARING AT A COMPUTER SCREEN.
AND WHO ASKED YOU?
TOM TOMORROW © 12-21-93

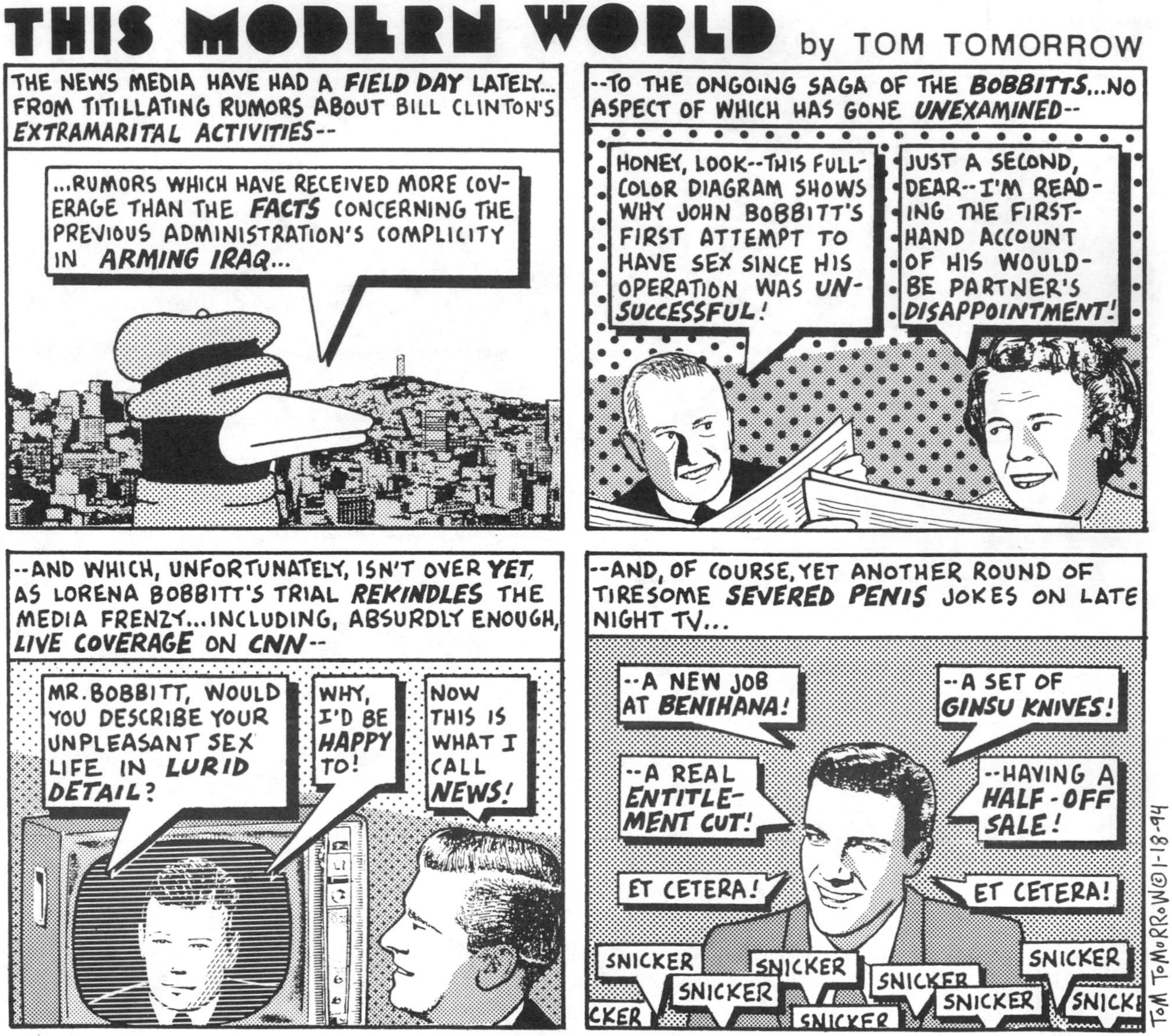
THIS MODERN WORLD by TOM TOMORROW
THE NEWS MEDIA HAVE HAD A FIELD DAY LATELY... FROM TITILLATING RUMORS ABOUT BILL CLINTON'S EXTRAMARITAL ACTIVITIES--
...RUMORS WHICH HAVE RECEIVED MORE COVERAGE THAN THE FACTS CONCERNING THE PREVIOUS ADMINISTRATION'S COMPLICITY IN ARMING IRAQ...
--TO THE ONGOING SAGA OF THE BOBBITTS...NO ASPECT OF WHICH HAS GONE UNEXAMINED--
HONEY, LOOK--THIS FULL-COLOR DIAGRAM SHOWS WHY JOHN BOBBITT'S FIRST ATTEMPT TO HAVE SEX SINCE HIS OPERATION WAS UNSUCCESSFUL!
JUST A SECOND, DEAR--I'M READING THE FIRST-HAND ACCOUNT OF HIS WOULD-BE PARTNER'S DISAPPOINTMENT!
--AND WHICH, UNFORTUNATELY, ISN'T OVER YET, AS LORENA BOBBITT'S TRIAL REKINDLES THE MEDIA FRENZY...INCLUDING, ABSURDLY ENOUGH, LIVE COVERAGE ON CNN--
MR. BOBBITT, WOULD YOU DESCRIBE YOUR UNPLEASANT SEX LIFE IN LURID DETAIL?
WHY, I'D BE HAPPY TO!
NOW THIS IS WHAT I CALL NEWS!
--AND, OF COURSE, YET ANOTHER ROUND OF TIRESOME SEVERED PENIS JOKES ON LATE NIGHT TV...
--A NEW JOB AT BENIHANA!
--A SET OF GINSU KNIVES!
--A REAL ENTITLEMENT CUT!
--HAVING A HALF-OFF SALE!
ET CETERA!
ET CETERA!
SNICKER
SNICKER
SNICKER
SNICKER
SNICKER
SNICKER
TOM TOMORROW©1-18-94

THIS MODERN WORLD by TOM TOMORROW

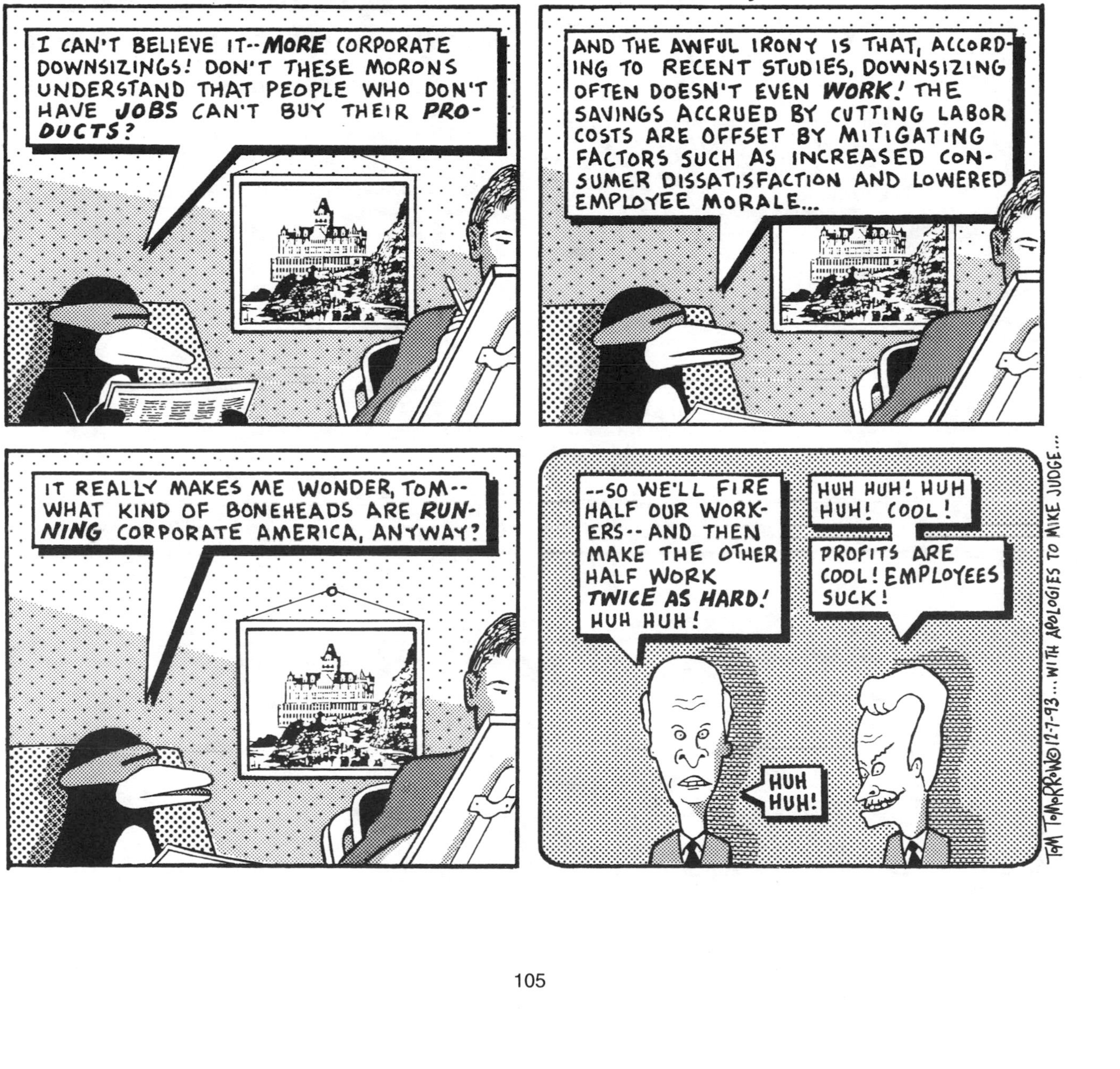
I CAN'T BELIEVE IT--MORE CORPORATE DOWNSIZINGS! DON'T THESE MORONS UNDERSTAND THAT PEOPLE WHO DON'T HAVE JOBS CAN'T BUY THEIR PRODUCTS?
AND THE AWFUL IRONY IS THAT, ACCORDING TO RECENT STUDIES, DOWNSIZING OFTEN DOESN'T EVEN WORK! THE SAVINGS ACCRUED BY CUTTING LABOR COSTS ARE OFFSET BY MITIGATING FACTORS SUCH AS INCREASED CONSUMER DISSATISFACTION AND LOWERED EMPLOYEE MORALE...
IT REALLY MAKES ME WONDER, TOM--WHAT KIND OF BONEHEADS ARE RUNNING CORPORATE AMERICA, ANYWAY?
--SO WE'LL FIRE HALF OUR WORKERS--AND THEN MAKE THE OTHER HALF WORK TWICE AS HARD! HUH HUH!
HUH HUH! HUH HUH! COOL!
PROFITS ARE COOL! EMPLOYEES SUCK!
HUH HUH!
TOM TOMORROW©12-7-93...WITH APOLOGIES TO MIKE JUDGE...

THIS MODERN WORLD by TOM TOMORROW

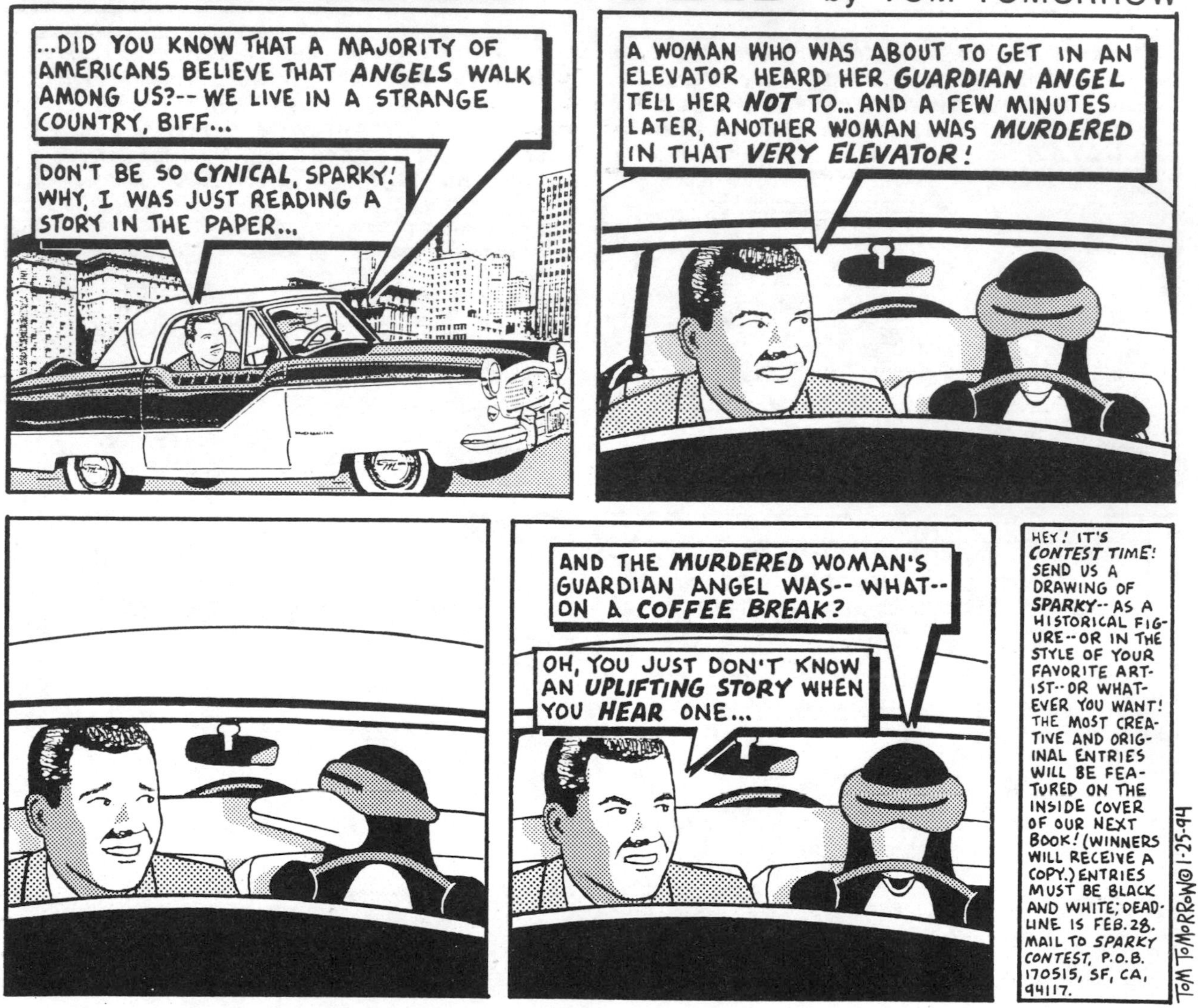
...DID YOU KNOW THAT A MAJORITY OF AMERICANS BELIEVE THAT ANGELS WALK AMONG US?-- WE LIVE IN A STRANGE COUNTRY, BIFF...
DON'T BE SO CYNICAL, SPARKY! WHY, I WAS JUST READING A STORY IN THE PAPER...
A WOMAN WHO WAS ABOUT TO GET IN AN ELEVATOR HEARD HER GUARDIAN ANGEL TELL HER NOT TO... AND A FEW MINUTES LATER, ANOTHER WOMAN WAS MURDERED IN THAT VERY ELEVATOR!
AND THE MURDERED WOMAN'S GUARDIAN ANGEL WAS-- WHAT-- ON A COFFEE BREAK?
OH, YOU JUST DON'T KNOW AN UPLIFTING STORY WHEN YOU HEAR ONE...
HEY! IT'S CONTEST TIME! SEND US A DRAWING OF SPARKY-- AS A HISTORICAL FIGURE--OR IN THE STYLE OF YOUR FAVORITE ARTIST--OR WHATEVER YOU WANT! THE MOST CREATIVE AND ORIGINAL ENTRIES WILL BE FEATURED ON THE INSIDE COVER OF OUR NEXT BOOK! (WINNERS WILL RECEIVE A COPY.) ENTRIES MUST BE BLACK AND WHITE; DEADLINE IS FEB. 28. MAIL TO SPARKY CONTEST, P.O.B. 170515, SF, CA, 94117.
TOM TOMORROW©1-25-94

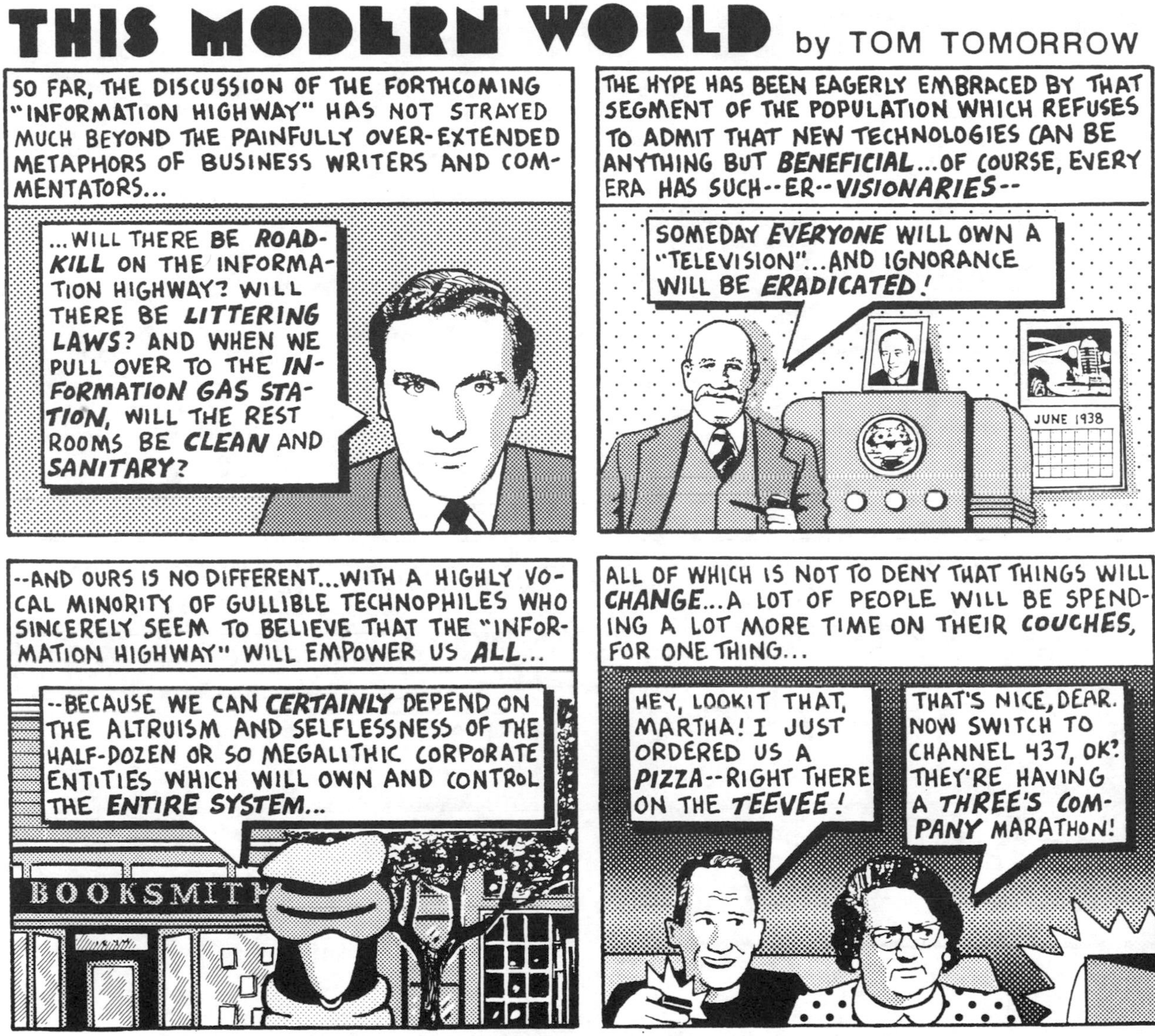
THIS MODERN WORLD by TOM TOMORROW
SO FAR, THE DISCUSSION OF THE FORTHCOMING "INFORMATION HIGHWAY" HAS NOT STRAYED MUCH BEYOND THE PAINFULLY OVER-EXTENDED METAPHORS OF BUSINESS WRITERS AND COMMENTATORS...
...WILL THERE BE ROAD-KILL ON THE INFORMATION HIGHWAY? WILL THERE BE LITTERING LAWS? AND WHEN WE PULL OVER TO THE INFORMATION GAS STATION, WILL THE REST ROOMS BE CLEAN AND SANITARY?
THE HYPE HAS BEEN EAGERLY EMBRACED BY THAT SEGMENT OF THE POPULATION WHICH REFUSES TO ADMIT THAT NEW TECHNOLOGIES CAN BE ANYTHING BUT BENEFICIAL...OF COURSE, EVERY ERA HAS SUCH--ER--VISIONARIES--
SOMEDAY EVERYONE WILL OWN A "TELEVISION"...AND IGNORANCE WILL BE ERADICATED!
JUNE 1938
--AND OURS IS NO DIFFERENT...WITH A HIGHLY VOCAL MINORITY OF GULLIBLE TECHNOPHILES WHO SINCERELY SEEM TO BELIEVE THAT THE "INFORMATION HIGHWAY" WILL EMPOWER US ALL...
--BECAUSE WE CAN CERTAINLY DEPEND ON THE ALTRUISM AND SELFLESSNESS OF THE HALF-DOZEN OR SO MEGALITHIC CORPORATE ENTITIES WHICH WILL OWN AND CONTROL THE ENTIRE SYSTEM...
BOOKSMITH
ALL OF WHICH IS NOT TO DENY THAT THINGS WILL CHANGE...A LOT OF PEOPLE WILL BE SPENDING A LOT MORE TIME ON THEIR COUCHES, FOR ONE THING...
HEY, LOOKIT THAT, MARTHA! I JUST ORDERED US A PIZZA--RIGHT THERE ON THE TEEVEE!
THAT'S NICE, DEAR. NOW SWITCH TO CHANNEL 437, OK? THEY'RE HAVING A THREE'S COMPANY MARATHON!
TOM TOMORROW © 11-16-93

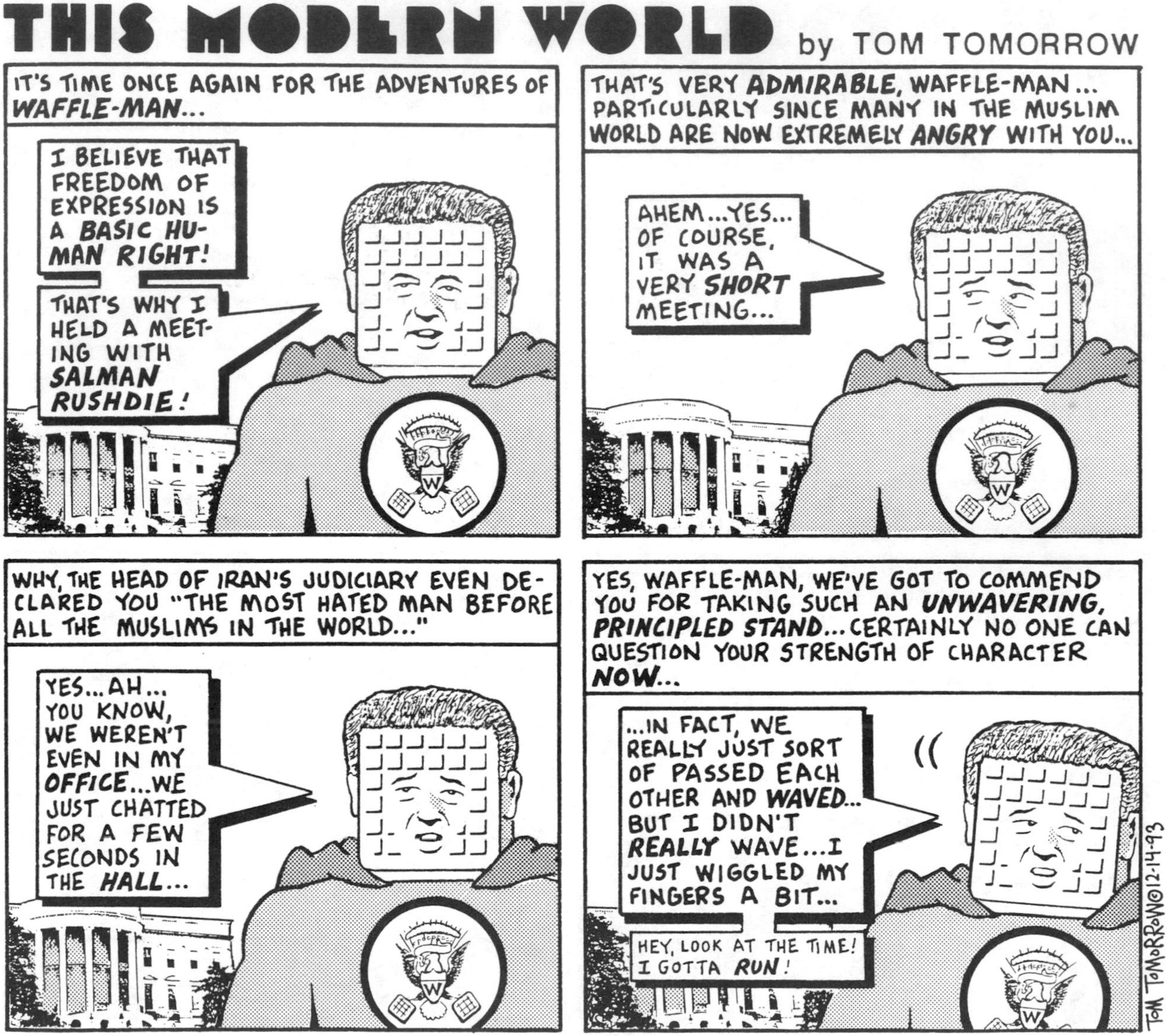
THIS MODERN WORLD by TOM TOMORROW
IT'S TIME ONCE AGAIN FOR THE ADVENTURES OF WAFFLE-MAN...
I BELIEVE THAT FREEDOM OF EXPRESSION IS A BASIC HUMAN RIGHT!
THAT'S WHY I HELD A MEETING WITH SALMAN RUSHDIE!
THAT'S VERY ADMIRABLE, WAFFLE-MAN... PARTICULARLY SINCE MANY IN THE MUSLIM WORLD ARE NOW EXTREMELY ANGRY WITH YOU...
AHEM...YES... OF COURSE, IT WAS A VERY SHORT MEETING...
WHY, THE HEAD OF IRAN'S JUDICIARY EVEN DECLARED YOU "THE MOST HATED MAN BEFORE ALL THE MUSLIMS IN THE WORLD..."
YES...AH... YOU KNOW, WE WEREN'T EVEN IN MY OFFICE...WE JUST CHATTED FOR A FEW SECONDS IN THE HALL...
YES, WAFFLE-MAN, WE'VE GOT TO COMMEND YOU FOR TAKING SUCH AN UNWAVERING, PRINCIPLED STAND...CERTAINLY NO ONE CAN QUESTION YOUR STRENGTH OF CHARACTER NOW...
...IN FACT, WE REALLY JUST SORT OF PASSED EACH OTHER AND WAVED... BUT I DIDN'T REALLY WAVE...I JUST WIGGLED MY FINGERS A BIT...
HEY, LOOK AT THE TIME! I GOTTA RUN!
TOM TOMORROW©12-14-93

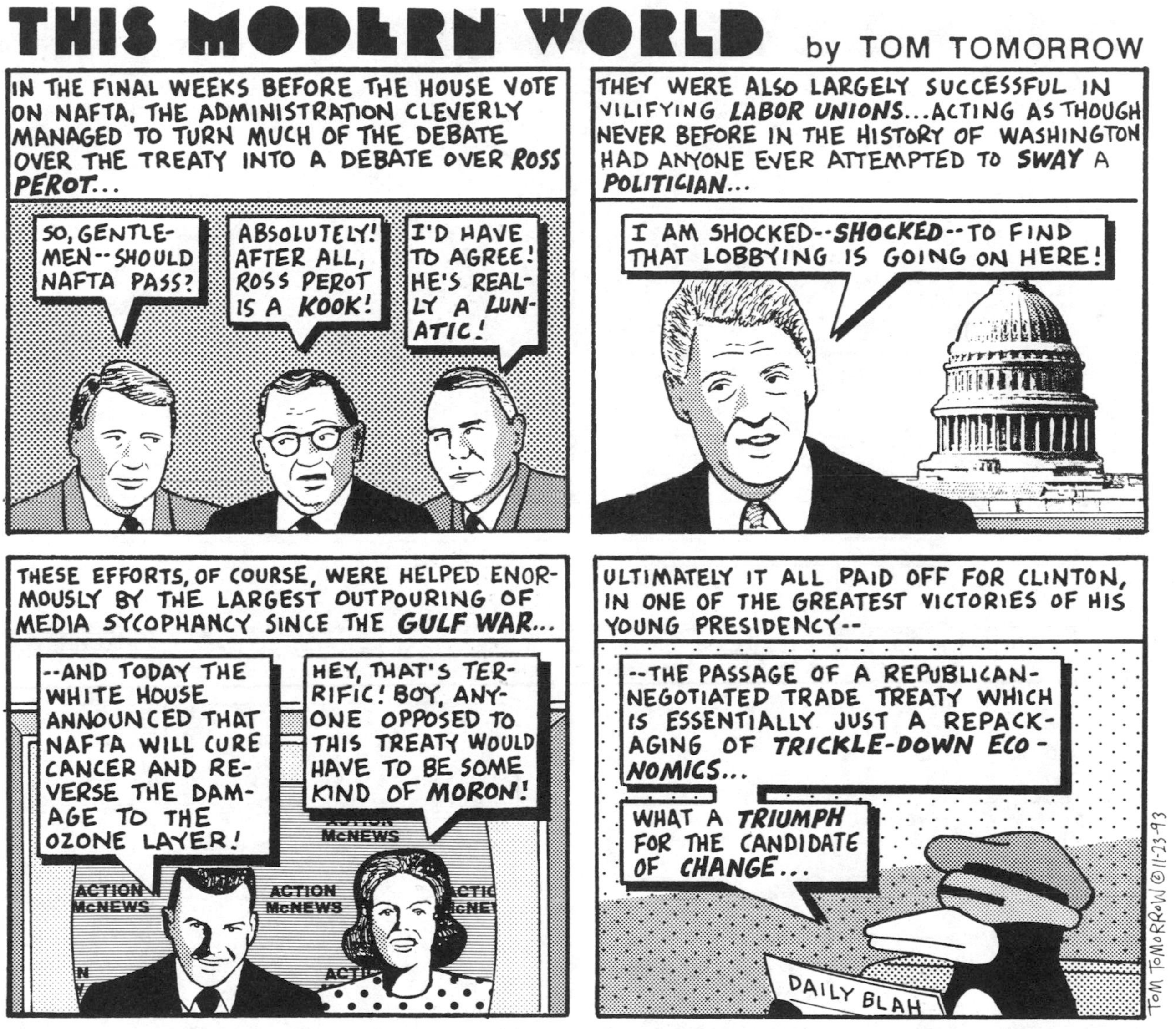
THIS MODERN WORLD
by TOM TOMORROW
IN THE FINAL WEEKS BEFORE THE HOUSE VOTE ON NAFTA, THE ADMINISTRATION CLEVERLY MANAGED TO TURN MUCH OF THE DEBATE OVER THE TREATY INTO A DEBATE OVER ROSS PEROT...
SO, GENTLEMEN--SHOULD NAFTA PASS?
ABSOLUTELY! AFTER ALL, ROSS PEROT IS A KOOK!
I'D HAVE TO AGREE! HE'S REALLY A LUNATIC!
THEY WERE ALSO LARGELY SUCCESSFUL IN VILIFYING LABOR UNIONS...ACTING AS THOUGH NEVER BEFORE IN THE HISTORY OF WASHINGTON HAD ANYONE EVER ATTEMPTED TO SWAY A POLITICIAN...
I AM SHOCKED--SHOCKED--TO FIND THAT LOBBYING IS GOING ON HERE!
THESE EFFORTS, OF COURSE, WERE HELPED ENORMOUSLY BY THE LARGEST OUTPOURING OF MEDIA SYCOPHANCY SINCE THE GULF WAR...
--AND TODAY THE WHITE HOUSE ANNOUNCED THAT NAFTA WILL CURE CANCER AND REVERSE THE DAMAGE TO THE OZONE LAYER!
HEY, THAT'S TERRIFIC! BOY, ANYONE OPPOSED TO THIS TREATY WOULD HAVE TO BE SOME KIND OF MORON!
ACTION McNEWS
ULTIMATELY IT ALL PAID OFF FOR CLINTON, IN ONE OF THE GREATEST VICTORIES OF HIS YOUNG PRESIDENCY--
--THE PASSAGE OF A REPUBLICAN-NEGOTIATED TRADE TREATY WHICH IS ESSENTIALLY JUST A REPACKAGING OF TRICKLE-DOWN ECONOMICS...
WHAT A TRIUMPH FOR THE CANDIDATE OF CHANGE...
DAILY BLAH
TOM TOMORROW ©11-23-93

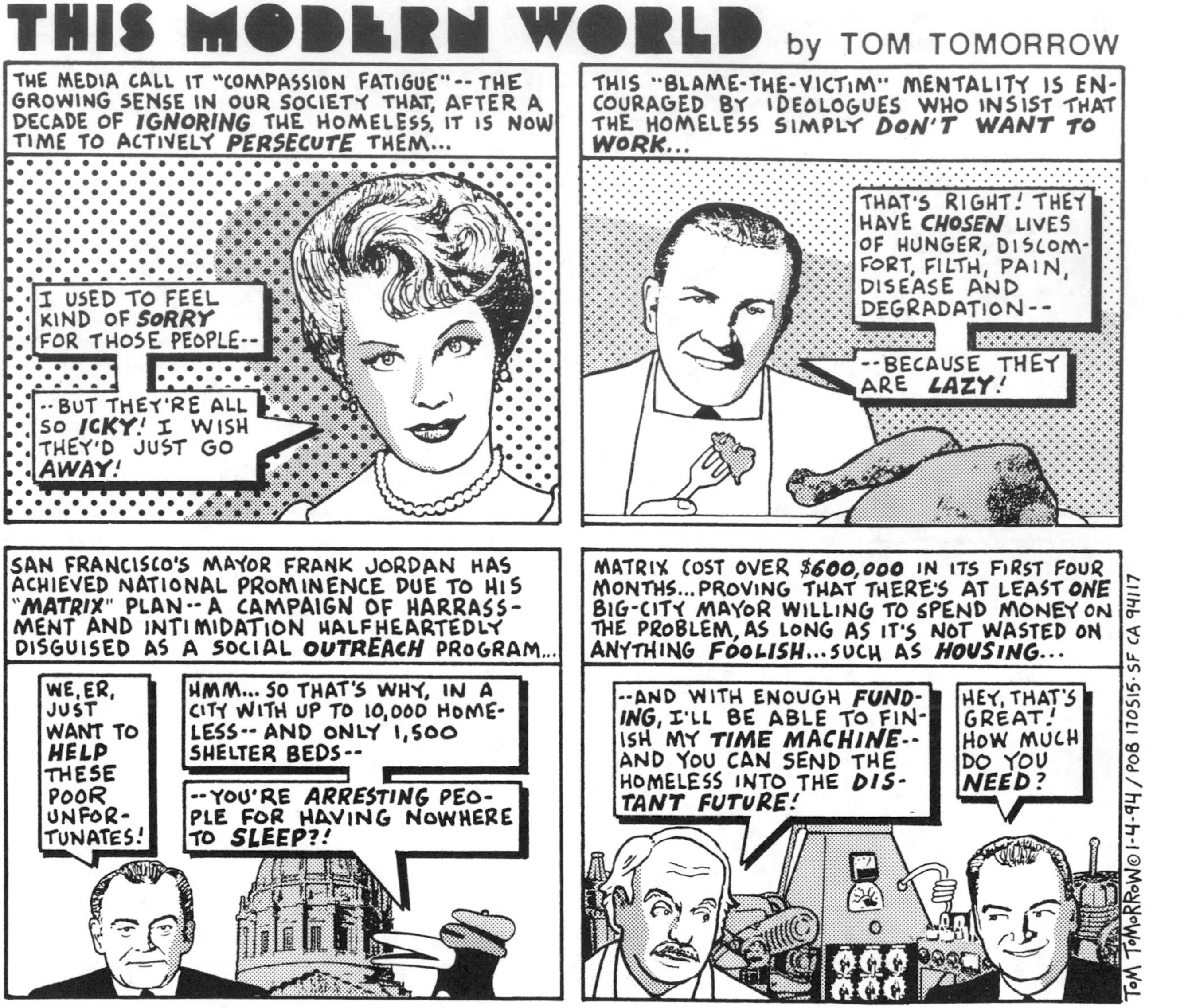
THIS MODERN WORLD by TOM TOMORROW
THE MEDIA CALL IT "COMPASSION FATIGUE" -- THE GROWING SENSE IN OUR SOCIETY THAT, AFTER A DECADE OF IGNORING THE HOMELESS, IT IS NOW TIME TO ACTIVELY PERSECUTE THEM...
I USED TO FEEL KIND OF SORRY FOR THOSE PEOPLE--
--BUT THEY'RE ALL SO ICKY! I WISH THEY'D JUST GO AWAY!
THIS "BLAME-THE-VICTIM" MENTALITY IS ENCOURAGED BY IDEOLOGUES WHO INSIST THAT THE HOMELESS SIMPLY DON'T WANT TO WORK...
THAT'S RIGHT! THEY HAVE CHOSEN LIVES OF HUNGER, DISCOMFORT, FILTH, PAIN, DISEASE AND DEGRADATION--
--BECAUSE THEY ARE LAZY!
SAN FRANCISCO'S MAYOR FRANK JORDAN HAS ACHIEVED NATIONAL PROMINENCE DUE TO HIS "MATRIX" PLAN--A CAMPAIGN OF HARRASSMENT AND INTIMIDATION HALFHEARTEDLY DISGUISED AS A SOCIAL OUTREACH PROGRAM...
WE, ER, JUST WANT TO HELP THESE POOR UNFORTUNATES!
HMM... SO THAT'S WHY, IN A CITY WITH UP TO 10,000 HOMELESS--AND ONLY 1,500 SHELTER BEDS--
--YOU'RE ARRESTING PEOPLE FOR HAVING NOWHERE TO SLEEP?!
MATRIX COST OVER $600,000 IN ITS FIRST FOUR MONTHS... PROVING THAT THERE'S AT LEAST ONE BIG-CITY MAYOR WILLING TO SPEND MONEY ON THE PROBLEM, AS LONG AS IT'S NOT WASTED ON ANYTHING FOOLISH... SUCH AS HOUSING...
--AND WITH ENOUGH FUNDING, I'LL BE ABLE TO FINISH MY TIME MACHINE--AND YOU CAN SEND THE HOMELESS INTO THE DISTANT FUTURE!
HEY, THAT'S GREAT! HOW MUCH DO YOU NEED?
TOM TOMORROW © 1-4-94 / POB 170515 · SF CA 94117

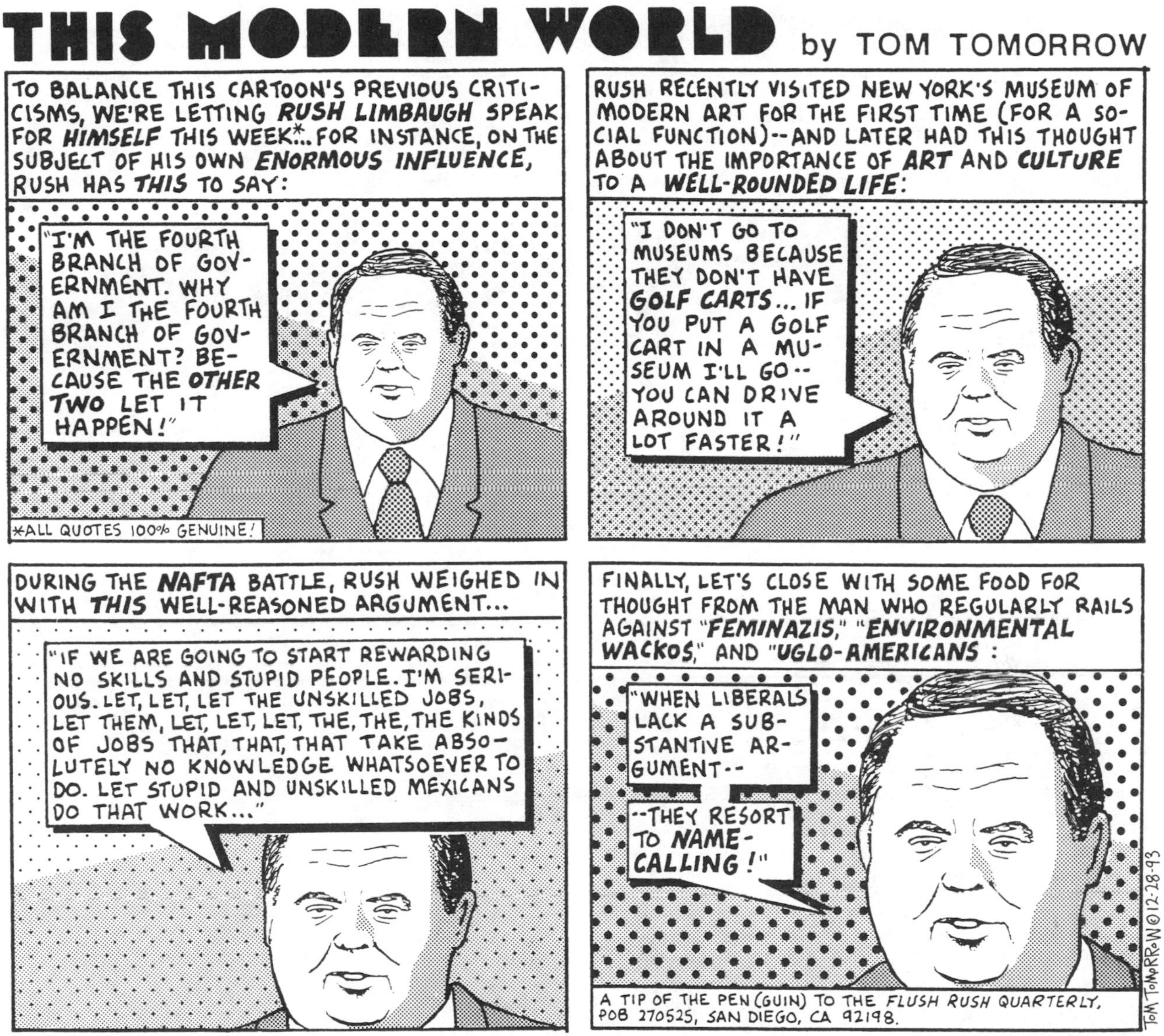
THIS MODERN WORLD by TOM TOMORROW
TO BALANCE THIS CARTOON'S PREVIOUS CRITICISMS, WE'RE LETTING RUSH LIMBAUGH SPEAK FOR HIMSELF THIS WEEK*... FOR INSTANCE, ON THE SUBJECT OF HIS OWN ENORMOUS INFLUENCE, RUSH HAS THIS TO SAY:
"I'M THE FOURTH BRANCH OF GOVERNMENT. WHY AM I THE FOURTH BRANCH OF GOVERNMENT? BECAUSE THE OTHER TWO LET IT HAPPEN!"
*ALL QUOTES 100% GENUINE!
RUSH RECENTLY VISITED NEW YORK'S MUSEUM OF MODERN ART FOR THE FIRST TIME (FOR A SOCIAL FUNCTION)--AND LATER HAD THIS THOUGHT ABOUT THE IMPORTANCE OF ART AND CULTURE TO A WELL-ROUNDED LIFE:
"I DON'T GO TO MUSEUMS BECAUSE THEY DON'T HAVE GOLF CARTS... IF YOU PUT A GOLF CART IN A MUSEUM I'LL GO-- YOU CAN DRIVE AROUND IT A LOT FASTER!"
DURING THE NAFTA BATTLE, RUSH WEIGHED IN WITH THIS WELL-REASONED ARGUMENT...
"IF WE ARE GOING TO START REWARDING NO SKILLS AND STUPID PEOPLE. I'M SERIOUS. LET, LET, LET THE UNSKILLED JOBS, LET THEM, LET, LET, LET, THE, THE, THE KINDS OF JOBS THAT, THAT, THAT TAKE ABSOLUTELY NO KNOWLEDGE WHATSOEVER TO DO. LET STUPID AND UNSKILLED MEXICANS DO THAT WORK..."
FINALLY, LET'S CLOSE WITH SOME FOOD FOR THOUGHT FROM THE MAN WHO REGULARLY RAILS AGAINST "FEMINAZIS," "ENVIRONMENTAL WACKOS," AND "UGLO-AMERICANS":
"WHEN LIBERALS LACK A SUBSTANTIVE ARGUMENT--
--THEY RESORT TO NAME-CALLING!"
A TIP OF THE PEN(GUIN) TO THE FLUSH RUSH QUARTERLY, POB 270525, SAN DIEGO, CA 92198.
TOM TOMORROW©12-28-93

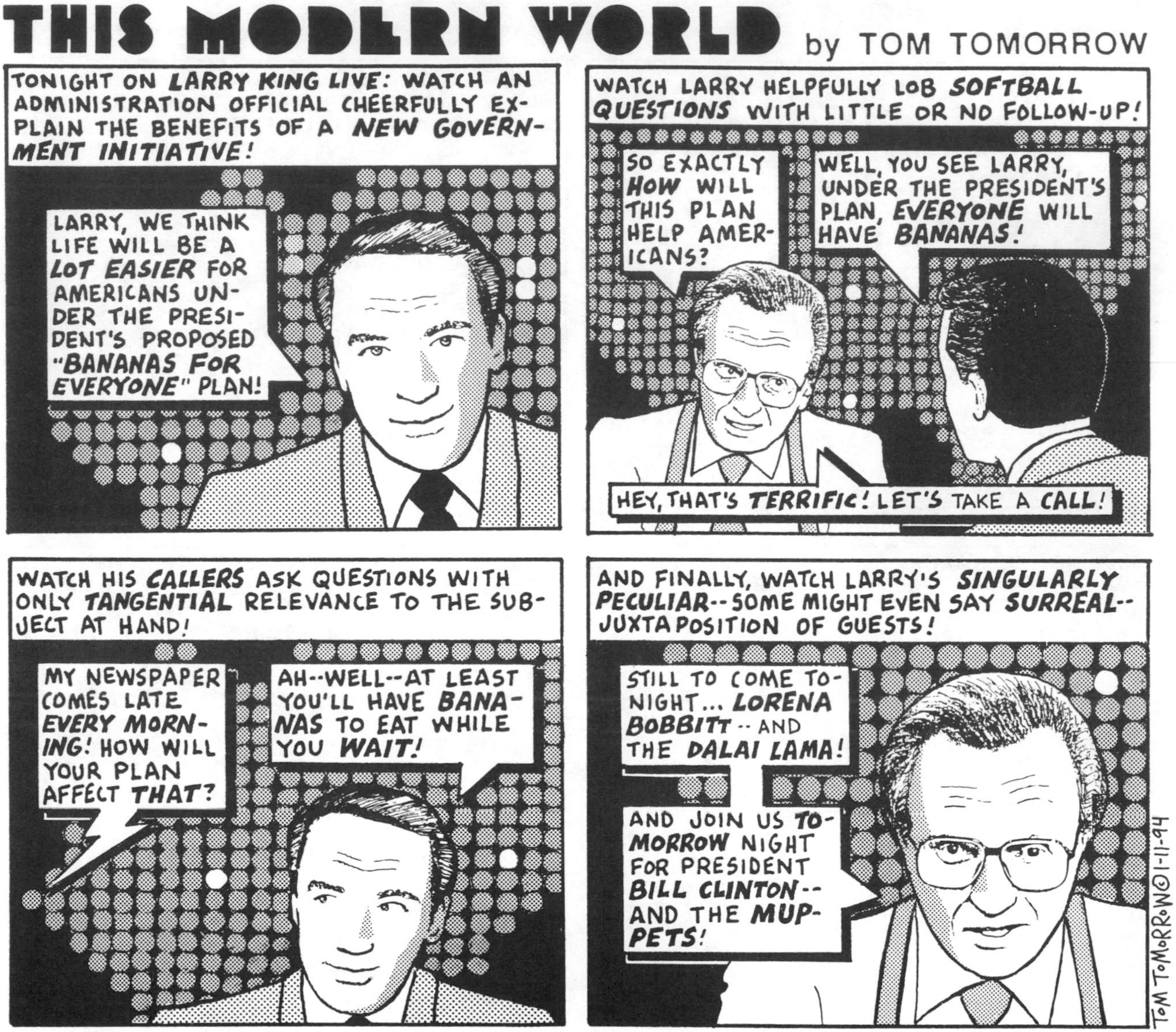
THIS MODERN WORLD by TOM TOMORROW
TONIGHT ON LARRY KING LIVE: WATCH AN ADMINISTRATION OFFICIAL CHEERFULLY EXPLAIN THE BENEFITS OF A NEW GOVERNMENT INITIATIVE!
LARRY, WE THINK LIFE WILL BE A LOT EASIER FOR AMERICANS UNDER THE PRESIDENT'S PROPOSED "BANANAS FOR EVERYONE" PLAN!
WATCH LARRY HELPFULLY LOB SOFTBALL QUESTIONS WITH LITTLE OR NO FOLLOW-UP!
SO EXACTLY HOW WILL THIS PLAN HELP AMERICANS?
WELL, YOU SEE LARRY, UNDER THE PRESIDENT'S PLAN, EVERYONE WILL HAVE BANANAS!
HEY, THAT'S TERRIFIC! LET'S TAKE A CALL!
WATCH HIS CALLERS ASK QUESTIONS WITH ONLY TANGENTIAL RELEVANCE TO THE SUBJECT AT HAND!
MY NEWSPAPER COMES LATE EVERY MORNING! HOW WILL YOUR PLAN AFFECT THAT?
AH--WELL--AT LEAST YOU'LL HAVE BANANAS TO EAT WHILE YOU WAIT!
AND FINALLY, WATCH LARRY'S SINGULARLY PECULIAR--SOME MIGHT EVEN SAY SURREAL--JUXTAPOSITION OF GUESTS!
STILL TO COME TONIGHT... LORENA BOBBITT -- AND THE DALAI LAMA!
AND JOIN US TOMORROW NIGHT FOR PRESIDENT BILL CLINTON -- AND THE MUPPETS!
TOM TOMORROW©1-11-94

THIS MODERN WORLD by TOM TOMORROW

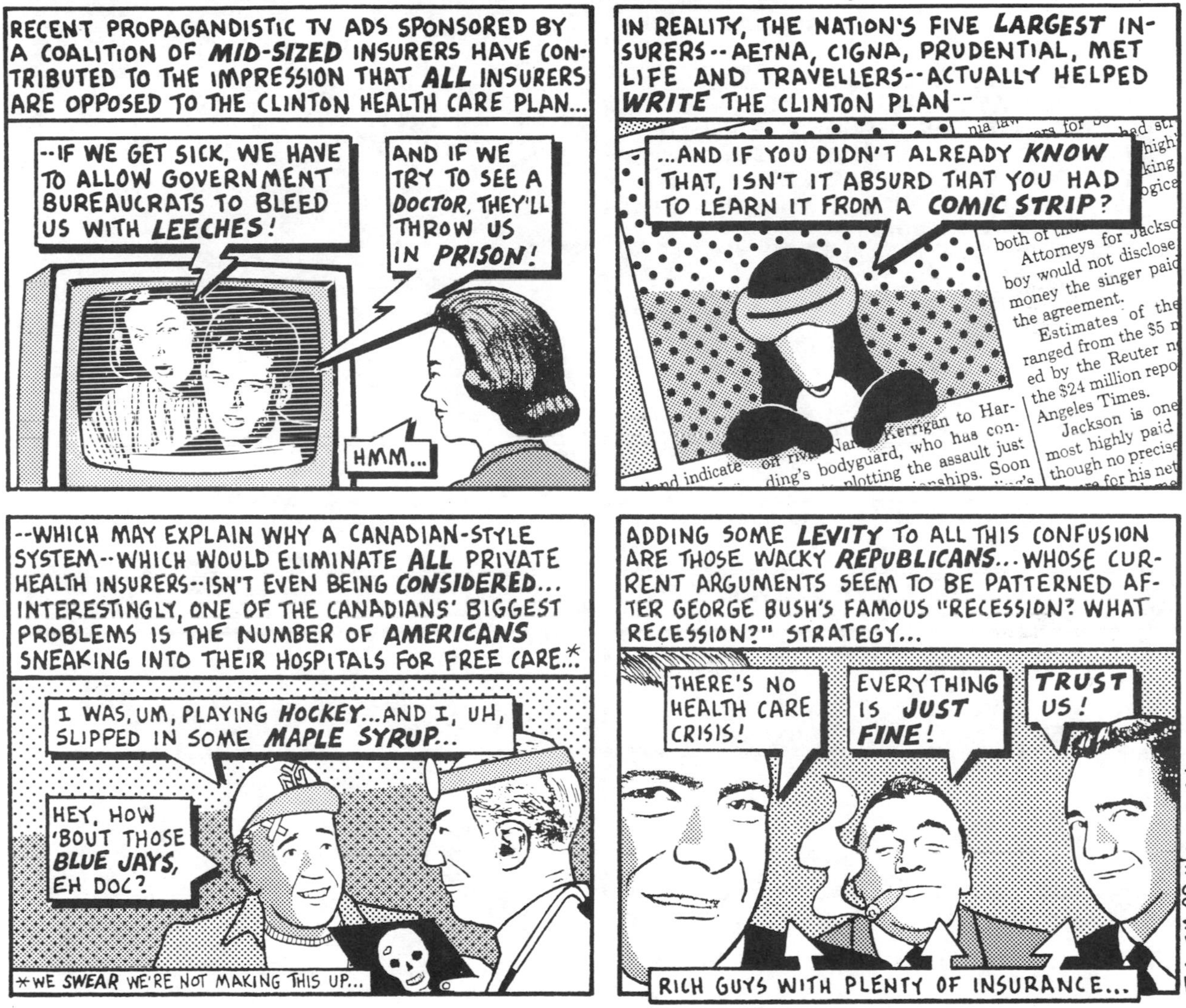
RECENT PROPAGANDISTIC TV ADS SPONSORED BY A COALITION OF MID-SIZED INSURERS HAVE CONTRIBUTED TO THE IMPRESSION THAT ALL INSURERS ARE OPPOSED TO THE CLINTON HEALTH CARE PLAN...
--IF WE GET SICK, WE HAVE TO ALLOW GOVERNMENT BUREAUCRATS TO BLEED US WITH LEECHES!
AND IF WE TRY TO SEE A DOCTOR, THEY'LL THROW US IN PRISON!
HMM...
IN REALITY, THE NATION'S FIVE LARGEST INSURERS--AETNA, CIGNA, PRUDENTIAL, MET LIFE AND TRAVELLERS--ACTUALLY HELPED WRITE THE CLINTON PLAN--
...AND IF YOU DIDN'T ALREADY KNOW THAT, ISN'T IT ABSURD THAT YOU HAD TO LEARN IT FROM A COMIC STRIP?
--WHICH MAY EXPLAIN WHY A CANADIAN-STYLE SYSTEM--WHICH WOULD ELIMINATE ALL PRIVATE HEALTH INSURERS--ISN'T EVEN BEING CONSIDERED... INTERESTINGLY, ONE OF THE CANADIANS' BIGGEST PROBLEMS IS THE NUMBER OF AMERICANS SNEAKING INTO THEIR HOSPITALS FOR FREE CARE...*
I WAS, UM, PLAYING HOCKEY...AND I, UH, SLIPPED IN SOME MAPLE SYRUP...
HEY, HOW 'BOUT THOSE BLUE JAYS, EH DOC?
*WE SWEAR WE'RE NOT MAKING THIS UP...
ADDING SOME LEVITY TO ALL THIS CONFUSION ARE THOSE WACKY REPUBLICANS... WHOSE CURRENT ARGUMENTS SEEM TO BE PATTERNED AFTER GEORGE BUSH'S FAMOUS "RECESSION? WHAT RECESSION?" STRATEGY...
THERE'S NO HEALTH CARE CRISIS!
EVERYTHING IS JUST FINE!
TRUST US!
RICH GUYS WITH PLENTY OF INSURANCE...
TOM TOMORROW © 2-8-94

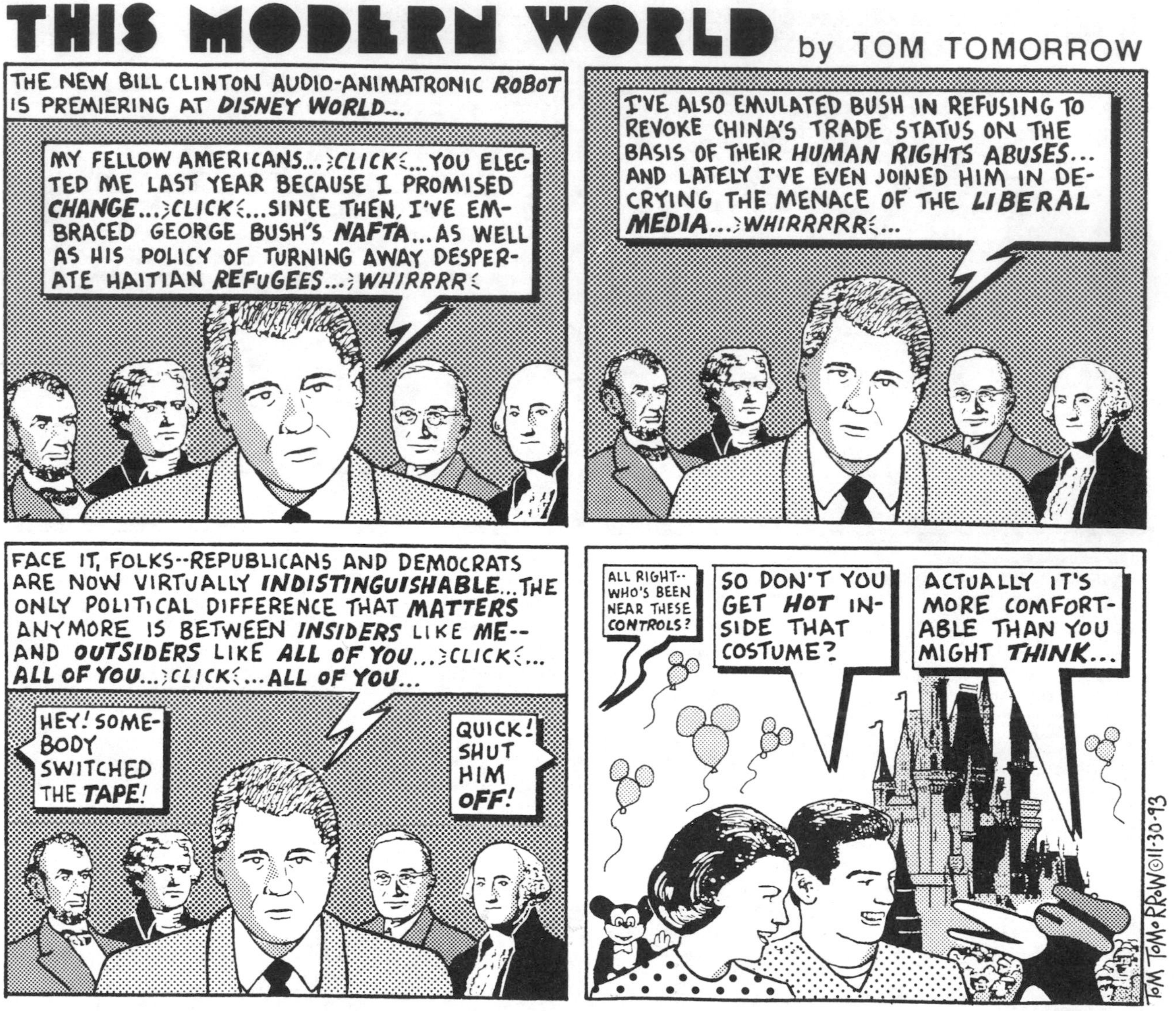
THIS MODERN WORLD by TOM TOMORROW
THE NEW BILL CLINTON AUDIO-ANIMATRONIC ROBOT IS PREMIERING AT DISNEY WORLD...
MY FELLOW AMERICANS... ›CLICK‹ ...YOU ELECTED ME LAST YEAR BECAUSE I PROMISED CHANGE... ›CLICK‹ ...SINCE THEN, I'VE EMBRACED GEORGE BUSH'S NAFTA... AS WELL AS HIS POLICY OF TURNING AWAY DESPERATE HAITIAN REFUGEES... ›WHIRRRR‹
I'VE ALSO EMULATED BUSH IN REFUSING TO REVOKE CHINA'S TRADE STATUS ON THE BASIS OF THEIR HUMAN RIGHTS ABUSES... AND LATELY I'VE EVEN JOINED HIM IN DECRYING THE MENACE OF THE LIBERAL MEDIA... ›WHIRRRRRR‹...
FACE IT, FOLKS--REPUBLICANS AND DEMOCRATS ARE NOW VIRTUALLY INDISTINGUISHABLE... THE ONLY POLITICAL DIFFERENCE THAT MATTERS ANYMORE IS BETWEEN INSIDERS LIKE ME-- AND OUTSIDERS LIKE ALL OF YOU... ›CLICK‹... ALL OF YOU... ›CLICK‹ ...ALL OF YOU...
HEY! SOMEBODY SWITCHED THE TAPE!
QUICK! SHUT HIM OFF!
ALL RIGHT-- WHO'S BEEN NEAR THESE CONTROLS?
SO DON'T YOU GET HOT INSIDE THAT COSTUME?
ACTUALLY IT'S MORE COMFORTABLE THAN YOU MIGHT THINK...
TOM TOMORROW©11-30-93

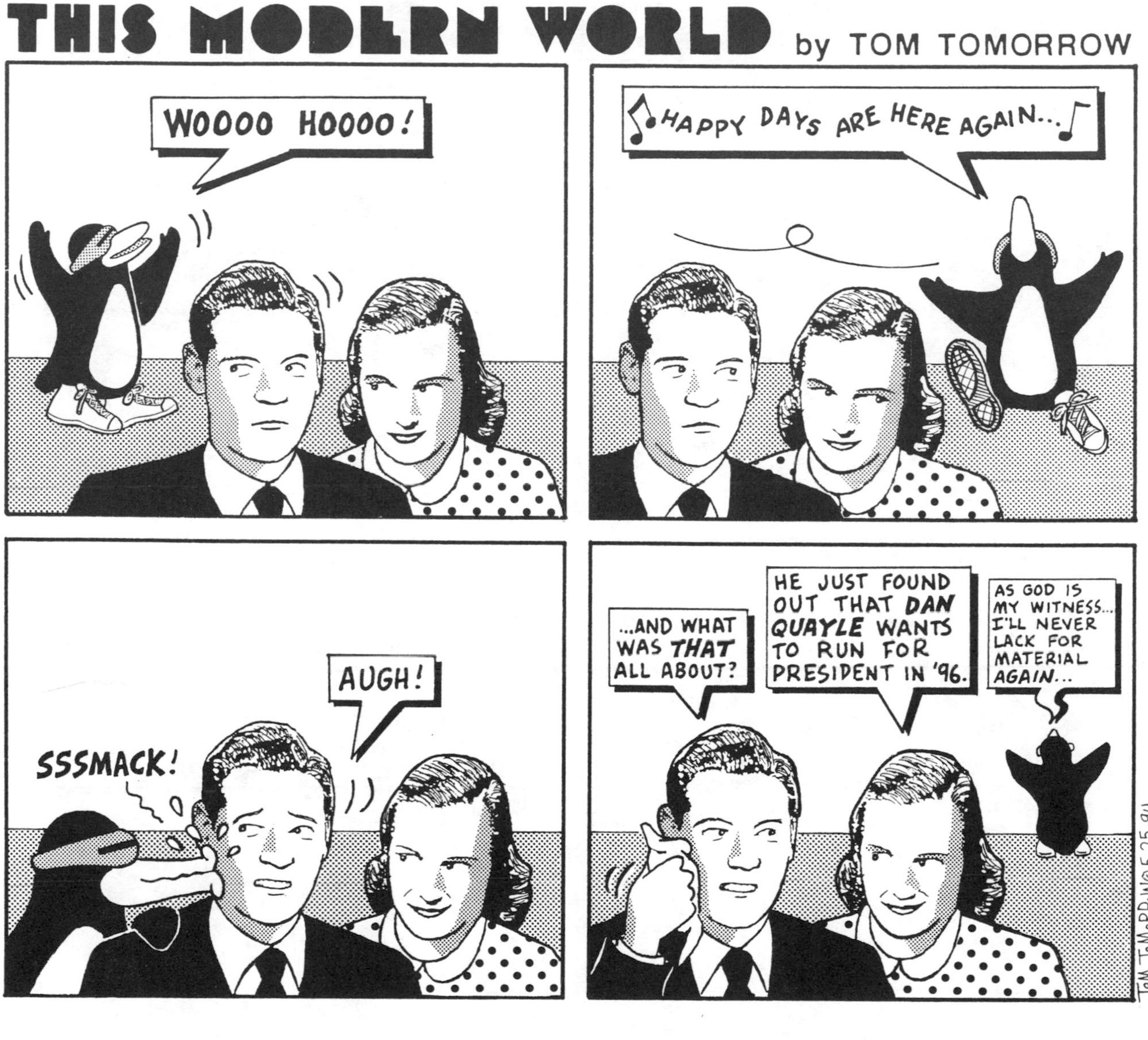
THIS MODERN WORLD by TOM TOMORROW
WOOOO HOOOO!
HAPPY DAYS ARE HERE AGAIN...
SSSMACK!
AUGH!
...AND WHAT WAS THAT ALL ABOUT?
HE JUST FOUND OUT THAT DAN QUAYLE WANTS TO RUN FOR PRESIDENT IN '96.
AS GOD IS MY WITNESS... I'LL NEVER LACK FOR MATERIAL AGAIN...
TOM TOMORROW©5-25-94

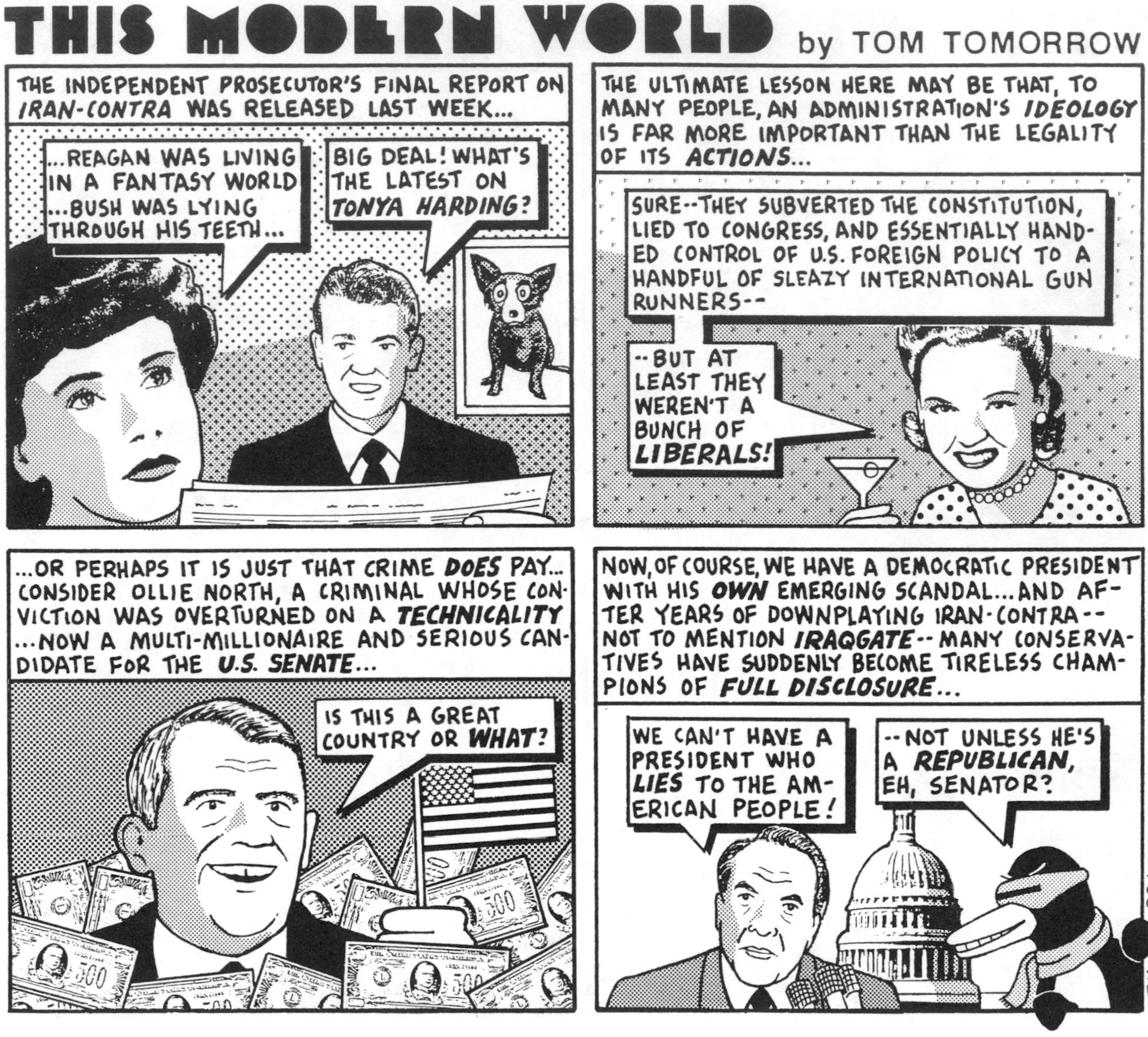
THIS MODERN WORLD by TOM TOMORROW
THE INDEPENDENT PROSECUTOR'S FINAL REPORT ON IRAN-CONTRA WAS RELEASED LAST WEEK...
...REAGAN WAS LIVING IN A FANTASY WORLD ...BUSH WAS LYING THROUGH HIS TEETH...
BIG DEAL! WHAT'S THE LATEST ON TONYA HARDING?
THE ULTIMATE LESSON HERE MAY BE THAT, TO MANY PEOPLE, AN ADMINISTRATION'S IDEOLOGY IS FAR MORE IMPORTANT THAN THE LEGALITY OF ITS ACTIONS...
SURE--THEY SUBVERTED THE CONSTITUTION, LIED TO CONGRESS, AND ESSENTIALLY HANDED CONTROL OF U.S. FOREIGN POLICY TO A HANDFUL OF SLEAZY INTERNATIONAL GUN RUNNERS--
--BUT AT LEAST THEY WEREN'T A BUNCH OF LIBERALS!
...OR PERHAPS IT IS JUST THAT CRIME DOES PAY... CONSIDER OLLIE NORTH, A CRIMINAL WHOSE CONVICTION WAS OVERTURNED ON A TECHNICALITY ...NOW A MULTI-MILLIONAIRE AND SERIOUS CANDIDATE FOR THE U.S. SENATE...
IS THIS A GREAT COUNTRY OR WHAT?
NOW, OF COURSE, WE HAVE A DEMOCRATIC PRESIDENT WITH HIS OWN EMERGING SCANDAL...AND AFTER YEARS OF DOWNPLAYING IRAN-CONTRA--NOT TO MENTION IRAQGATE--MANY CONSERVATIVES HAVE SUDDENLY BECOME TIRELESS CHAMPIONS OF FULL DISCLOSURE...
WE CAN'T HAVE A PRESIDENT WHO LIES TO THE AMERICAN PEOPLE!
--NOT UNLESS HE'S A REPUBLICAN, EH, SENATOR?
TOM TOMORROW©2-1-94

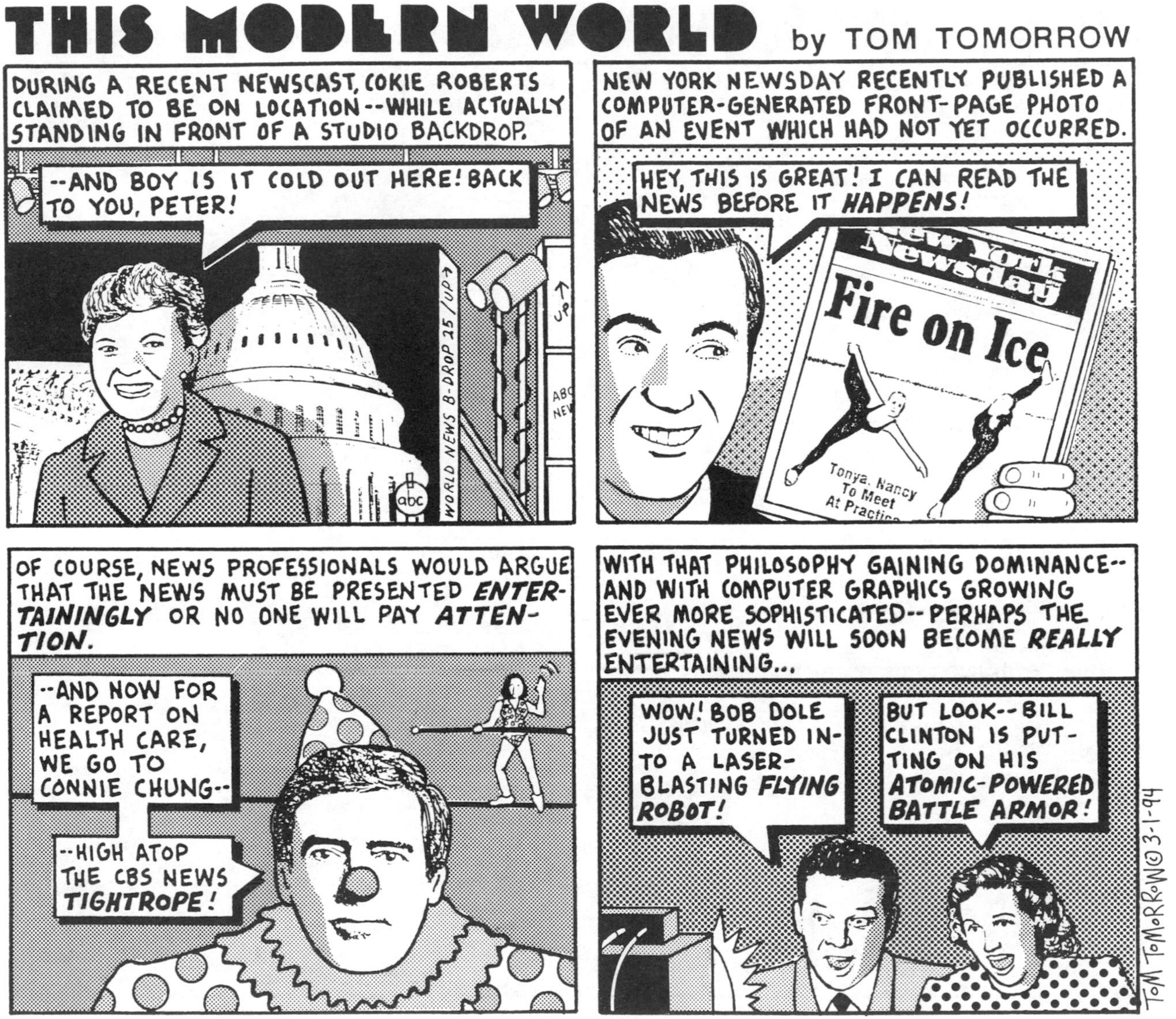
THIS MODERN WORLD by TOM TOMORROW
DURING A RECENT NEWSCAST, COKIE ROBERTS CLAIMED TO BE ON LOCATION--WHILE ACTUALLY STANDING IN FRONT OF A STUDIO BACKDROP.
--AND BOY IS IT COLD OUT HERE! BACK TO YOU, PETER!
WORLD NEWS B-DROP 25 / UP
abc
NEW YORK NEWSDAY RECENTLY PUBLISHED A COMPUTER-GENERATED FRONT-PAGE PHOTO OF AN EVENT WHICH HAD NOT YET OCCURRED.
HEY, THIS IS GREAT! I CAN READ THE NEWS BEFORE IT *HAPPENS*!
New York Newsday
Fire on Ice
Tonya, Nancy To Meet At Practice
OF COURSE, NEWS PROFESSIONALS WOULD ARGUE THAT THE NEWS MUST BE PRESENTED *ENTERTAININGLY* OR NO ONE WILL PAY *ATTENTION*.
--AND NOW FOR A REPORT ON HEALTH CARE, WE GO TO CONNIE CHUNG--
--HIGH ATOP THE CBS NEWS *TIGHTROPE*!
WITH THAT PHILOSOPHY GAINING DOMINANCE--AND WITH COMPUTER GRAPHICS GROWING EVER MORE SOPHISTICATED--PERHAPS THE EVENING NEWS WILL SOON BECOME *REALLY* ENTERTAINING...
WOW! BOB DOLE JUST TURNED INTO A LASER-BLASTING *FLYING ROBOT*!
BUT LOOK--BILL CLINTON IS PUTTING ON HIS *ATOMIC-POWERED BATTLE ARMOR*!
TOM TOMORROW © 3-1-94

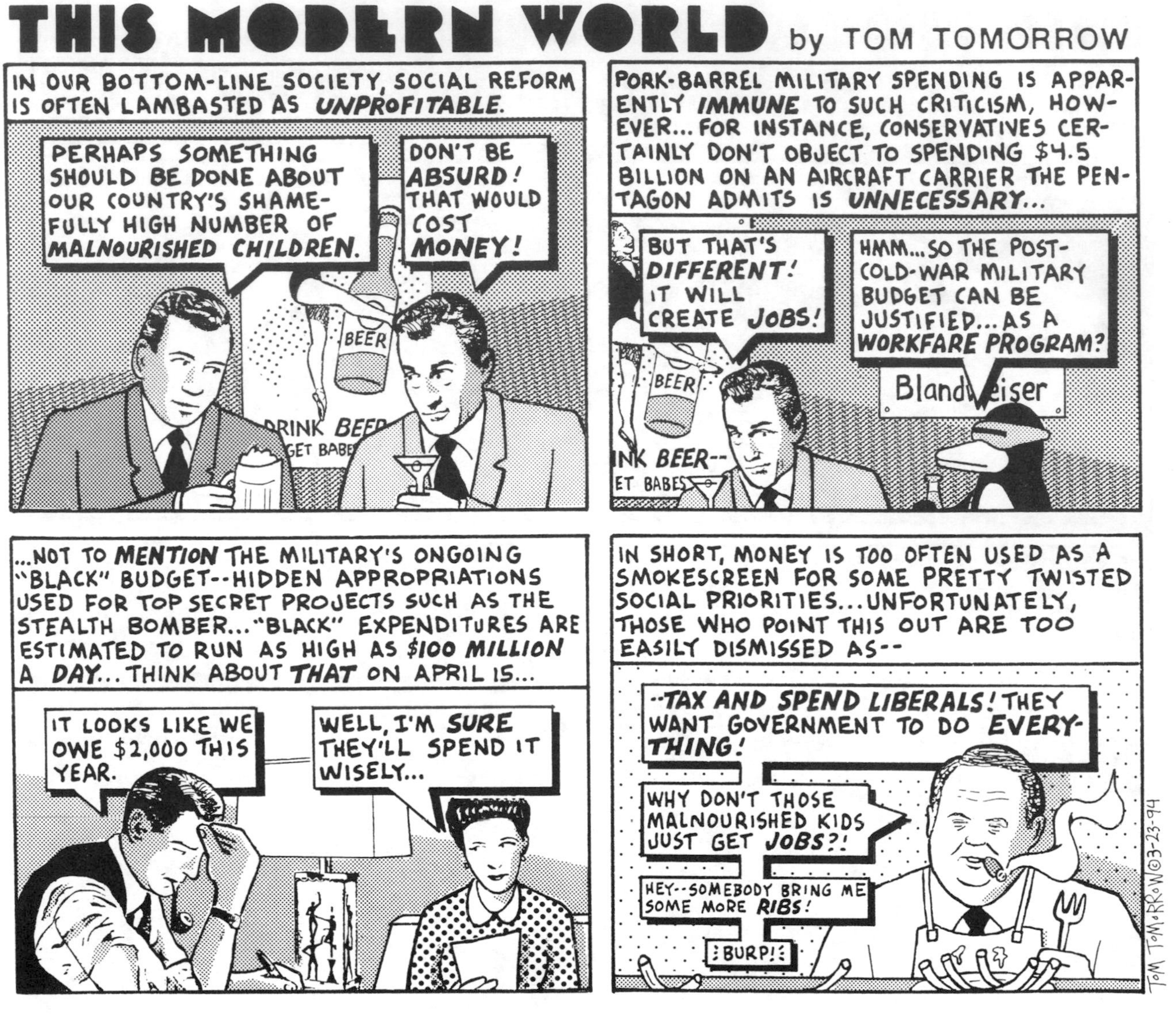
THIS MODERN WORLD by TOM TOMORROW
IN OUR BOTTOM-LINE SOCIETY, SOCIAL REFORM IS OFTEN LAMBASTED AS UNPROFITABLE.
PERHAPS SOMETHING SHOULD BE DONE ABOUT OUR COUNTRY'S SHAMEFULLY HIGH NUMBER OF MALNOURISHED CHILDREN.
DON'T BE ABSURD! THAT WOULD COST MONEY!
BEER
DRINK BEER
GET BABE
PORK-BARREL MILITARY SPENDING IS APPARENTLY IMMUNE TO SUCH CRITICISM, HOWEVER... FOR INSTANCE, CONSERVATIVES CERTAINLY DON'T OBJECT TO SPENDING $4.5 BILLION ON AN AIRCRAFT CARRIER THE PENTAGON ADMITS IS UNNECESSARY...
BUT THAT'S DIFFERENT! IT WILL CREATE JOBS!
HMM... SO THE POST-COLD-WAR MILITARY BUDGET CAN BE JUSTIFIED... AS A WORKFARE PROGRAM?
BEER
BlandWeiser
INK BEER--
ET BABES
...NOT TO MENTION THE MILITARY'S ONGOING "BLACK" BUDGET--HIDDEN APPROPRIATIONS USED FOR TOP SECRET PROJECTS SUCH AS THE STEALTH BOMBER... "BLACK" EXPENDITURES ARE ESTIMATED TO RUN AS HIGH AS $100 MILLION A DAY... THINK ABOUT THAT ON APRIL 15...
IT LOOKS LIKE WE OWE $2,000 THIS YEAR.
WELL, I'M SURE THEY'LL SPEND IT WISELY...
IN SHORT, MONEY IS TOO OFTEN USED AS A SMOKESCREEN FOR SOME PRETTY TWISTED SOCIAL PRIORITIES... UNFORTUNATELY, THOSE WHO POINT THIS OUT ARE TOO EASILY DISMISSED AS--
--TAX AND SPEND LIBERALS! THEY WANT GOVERNMENT TO DO EVERYTHING!
WHY DON'T THOSE MALNOURISHED KIDS JUST GET JOBS?!
HEY--SOMEBODY BRING ME SOME MORE RIBS!
BURP!
TOM TOMORROW©3-23-94

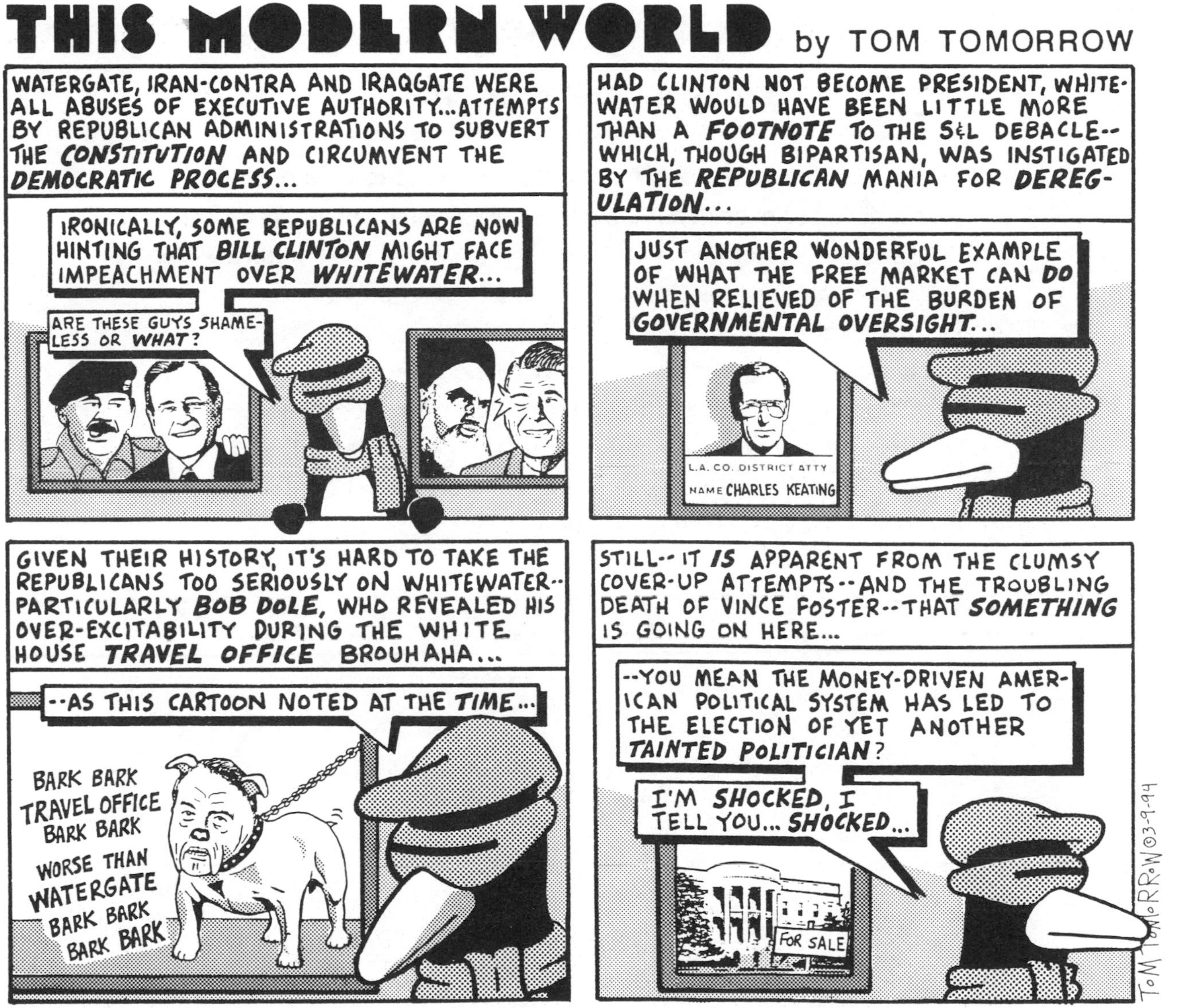
THIS MODERN WORLD by TOM TOMORROW
WATERGATE, IRAN-CONTRA AND IRAQGATE WERE ALL ABUSES OF EXECUTIVE AUTHORITY...ATTEMPTS BY REPUBLICAN ADMINISTRATIONS TO SUBVERT THE CONSTITUTION AND CIRCUMVENT THE DEMOCRATIC PROCESS...
IRONICALLY, SOME REPUBLICANS ARE NOW HINTING THAT BILL CLINTON MIGHT FACE IMPEACHMENT OVER WHITEWATER...
ARE THESE GUYS SHAMELESS OR WHAT?
HAD CLINTON NOT BECOME PRESIDENT, WHITEWATER WOULD HAVE BEEN LITTLE MORE THAN A FOOTNOTE TO THE S&L DEBACLE--WHICH, THOUGH BIPARTISAN, WAS INSTIGATED BY THE REPUBLICAN MANIA FOR DEREGULATION...
JUST ANOTHER WONDERFUL EXAMPLE OF WHAT THE FREE MARKET CAN DO WHEN RELIEVED OF THE BURDEN OF GOVERNMENTAL OVERSIGHT...
L.A. CO. DISTRICT ATTY
NAME CHARLES KEATING
GIVEN THEIR HISTORY, IT'S HARD TO TAKE THE REPUBLICANS TOO SERIOUSLY ON WHITEWATER--PARTICULARLY BOB DOLE, WHO REVEALED HIS OVER-EXCITABILITY DURING THE WHITE HOUSE TRAVEL OFFICE BROUHAHA...
--AS THIS CARTOON NOTED AT THE TIME...
BARK BARK TRAVEL OFFICE BARK BARK WORSE THAN WATERGATE BARK BARK BARK BARK
STILL--IT IS APPARENT FROM THE CLUMSY COVER-UP ATTEMPTS--AND THE TROUBLING DEATH OF VINCE FOSTER--THAT SOMETHING IS GOING ON HERE...
--YOU MEAN THE MONEY-DRIVEN AMERICAN POLITICAL SYSTEM HAS LED TO THE ELECTION OF YET ANOTHER TAINTED POLITICIAN?
I'M SHOCKED, I TELL YOU... SHOCKED...
FOR SALE
TOM TOMORROW ©3-9-94

ABOUT THE AUTHOR

For reasons known only to himself, Tom Tomorrow conducts his daily business under the rather unlikely pseudonym "Dan Perkins." His cartoons appear regularly in approximately eighty papers across the country, and have been featured in *Spin* magazine, the *Utne Reader*, the *Nation*, the *Village Voice*, *The New York Times*, the *Washington Post*, and many other publications. He has been a guest on such national radio programs as "Fresh Air" and "Talk of the Nation," and was once described as "the most important cartoonist in America" by some drunk guy at a party.

He can be reached at:
P.O.B. 170515
San Francisco, CA 94117

or by E-mail:
tomorrow@well.com